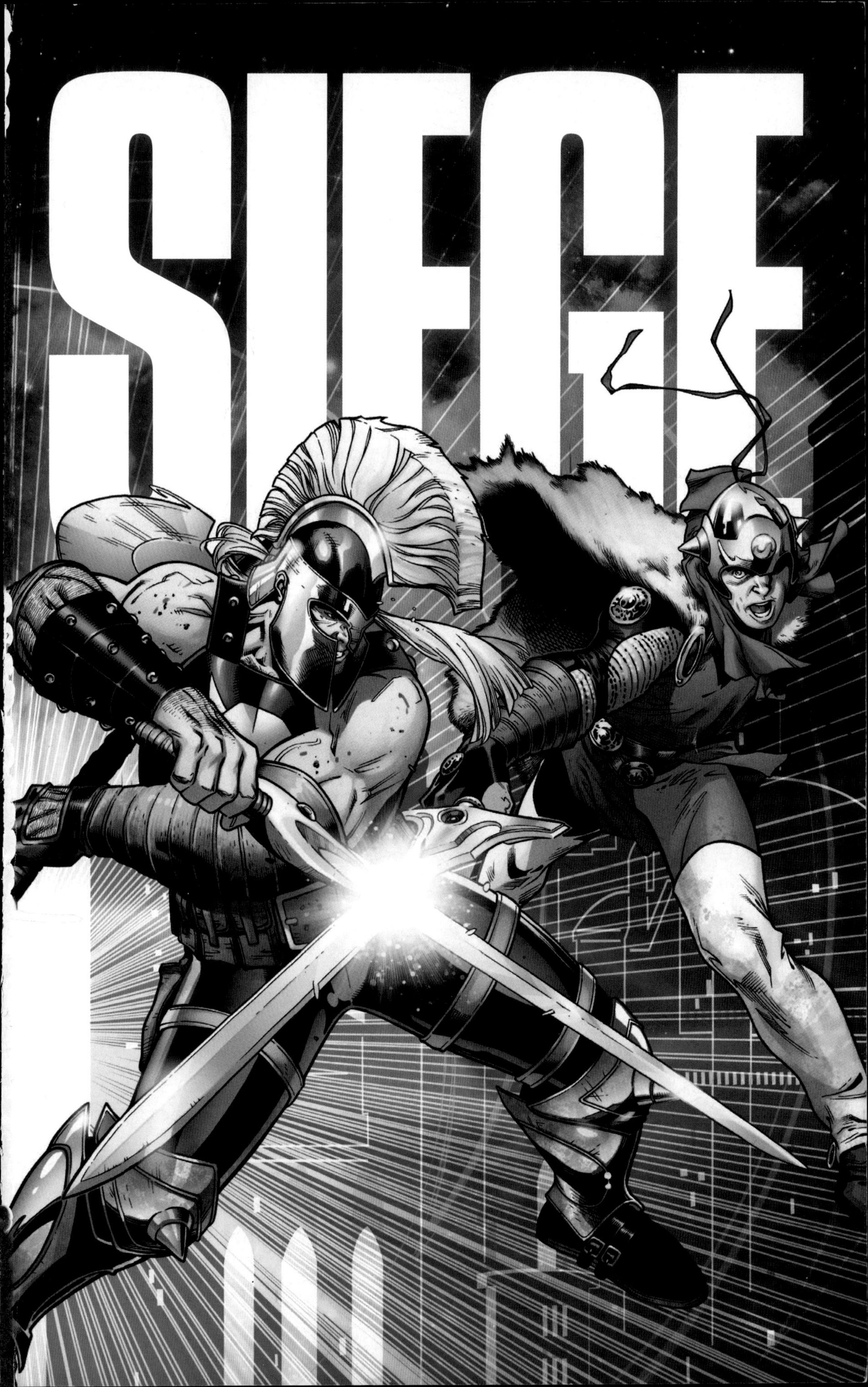
SIEGE

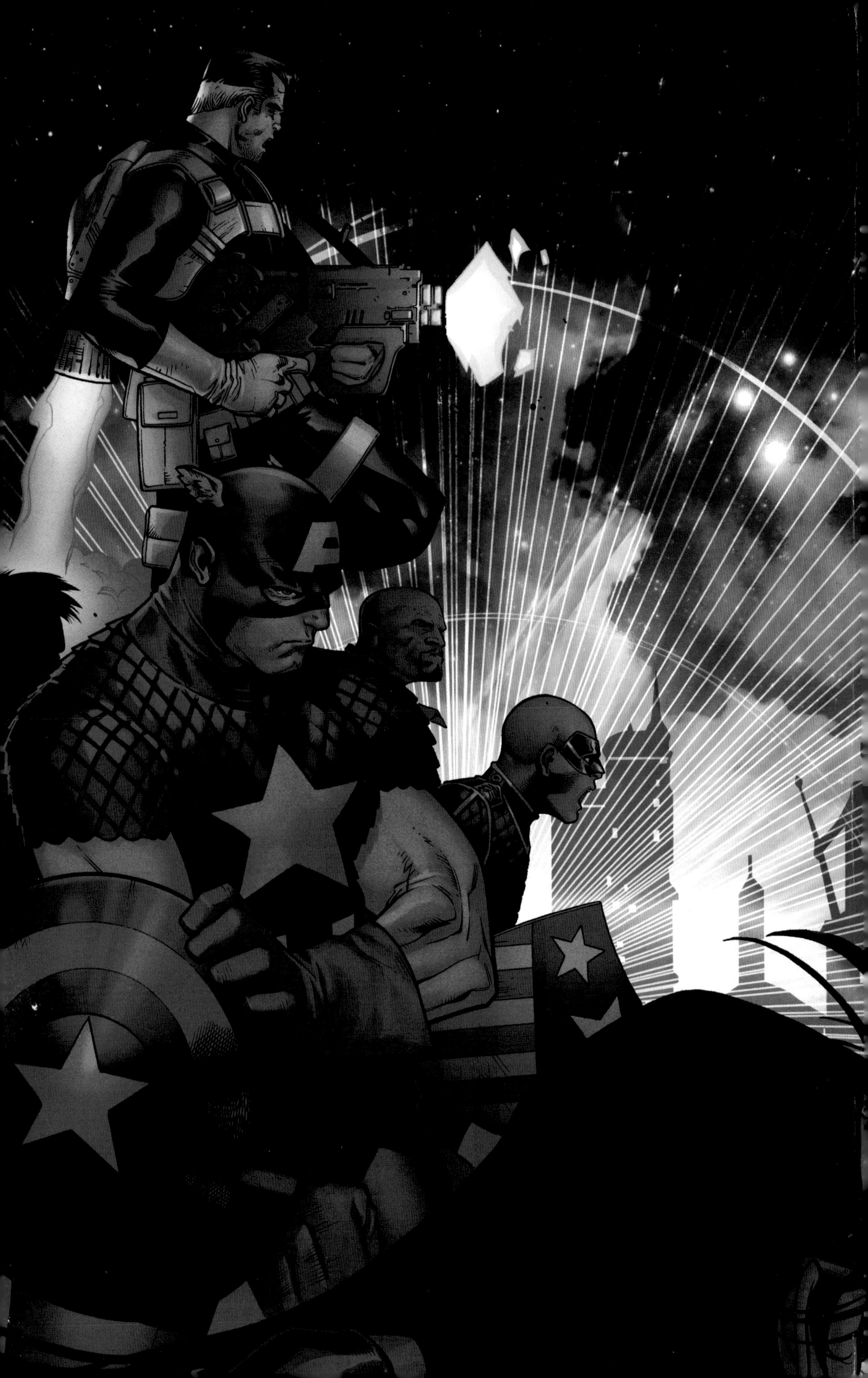

SIEGE

WRITER: **BRIAN MICHAEL BENDIS**

THE CABAL
PENCILER: **MICHAEL LARK** • INKER: **STEFANO GAUDIANO**
COLORIST: **MATT HOLLINGSWORTH** • LETTERER: **CHRIS ELIOPOULOS**
COVER ART: **DAVID FINCH & JASON KEITH**

PROLOGUE
ARTIST: **LUCIO PARRILLO** • LETTERER: **CHRIS ELIOPOULOS**

SIEGE #1-4
PENCILER: **OLIVIER COIPEL** • INKER: **MARK MORALES**
COLORIST: **LAURA MARTIN**
COVER ART: **OLIVIER COIPEL, MARK MORALES & LAURA MARTIN**

"THE WAY THINGS ARE..."
PENCILER: **JIM CHEUNG** • INKER: **MARK MORALES**
COLORIST: **JOHN RAUCH**
COVER ART: **JIM CHEUNG & LAURA MARTIN**

LETTERER: **CHRIS ELIOPOULOS**
WITH **CORY PETIT** *("THE WAY THINGS ARE...")*
ASSOCIATE EDITOR: **LAUREN SANKOVITCH** WITH **JEANINE SCHAEFER**
EDITOR: **TOM BREVOORT**

COLLECTION EDITOR: **JENNIFER GRÜNWALD** • ASSISTANT EDITOR: **ALEX STARBUCK**
ASSOCIATE EDITOR: **JOHN DENNING** • EDITOR, SPECIAL PROJECTS: **MARK D. BEAZLEY**
SENIOR EDITOR, SPECIAL PROJECTS: **JEFF YOUNGQUIST**
SENIOR VICE PRESIDENT OF SALES: **DAVID GABRIEL** • BOOK DESIGNER: **RODOLFO MURAGUCHI**

EDITOR IN CHIEF: **JOE QUESADA**
PUBLISHER: **DAN BUCKLEY**
EXECUTIVE PRODUCER: **ALAN FINE**

SIEGE. Contains material originally published in magazine form as SIEGE #1-4, SIEGE: THE CABAL and FREE COMIC BOOK DAY 2009 (AVENGERS). First printing 2010. ISBN# 978-0-7851-4810-4. Published by MARVEL WORLDWIDE, INC., a subsidiary of MARVEL ENTERTAINMENT, LLC. OFFICE OF PUBLICATION: 417 5th Avenue, New York, NY 10016. Copyright © 2009 and 2010 Marvel Characters, Inc. All rights reserved. $24.99 per copy in the U.S. and $27.99 in Canada (GST #R127032852); Canadian Agreement #40668537. All characters featured in this issue and the distinctive names and likenesses thereof, and all related indicia are trademarks of Marvel Characters, Inc. No similarity between any of the names, characters, persons, and/or institutions in this magazine with those of any living or dead person or institution is intended, and any such similarity which may exist is purely coincidental. **Printed in the U.S.A.** ALAN FINE, EVP - Office of the President, Marvel Worldwide, Inc. and EVP & CMO Marvel Characters B.V.; DAN BUCKLEY, Chief Executive Officer and Publisher - Print, Animation & Digital Media; JIM SOKOLOWSKI, Chief Operating Officer; DAVID GABRIEL, SVP of Publishing Sales & Circulation; DAVID BOGART, SVP of Business Affairs & Talent Management; MICHAEL PASCIULLO, VP Merchandising & Communications; JIM O'KEEFE, VP of Operations & Logistics; DAN CARR, Executive Director of Publishing Technology; JUSTIN F. GABRIE, Director of Publishing & Editorial Operations; SUSAN CRESPI, Editorial Operations Manager; ALEX MORALES, Publishing Operations Manager; STAN LEE, Chairman Emeritus. For information regarding advertising in Marvel Comics or on Marvel.com, please contact Ron Stern, VP of Business Development, at rstern@marvel.com. For Marvel subscription inquiries, please call 800-217-9158. **Manufactured between 5/24/10 and 6/23/10 by R.R. DONNELLEY, INC., SALEM, VA, USA.**

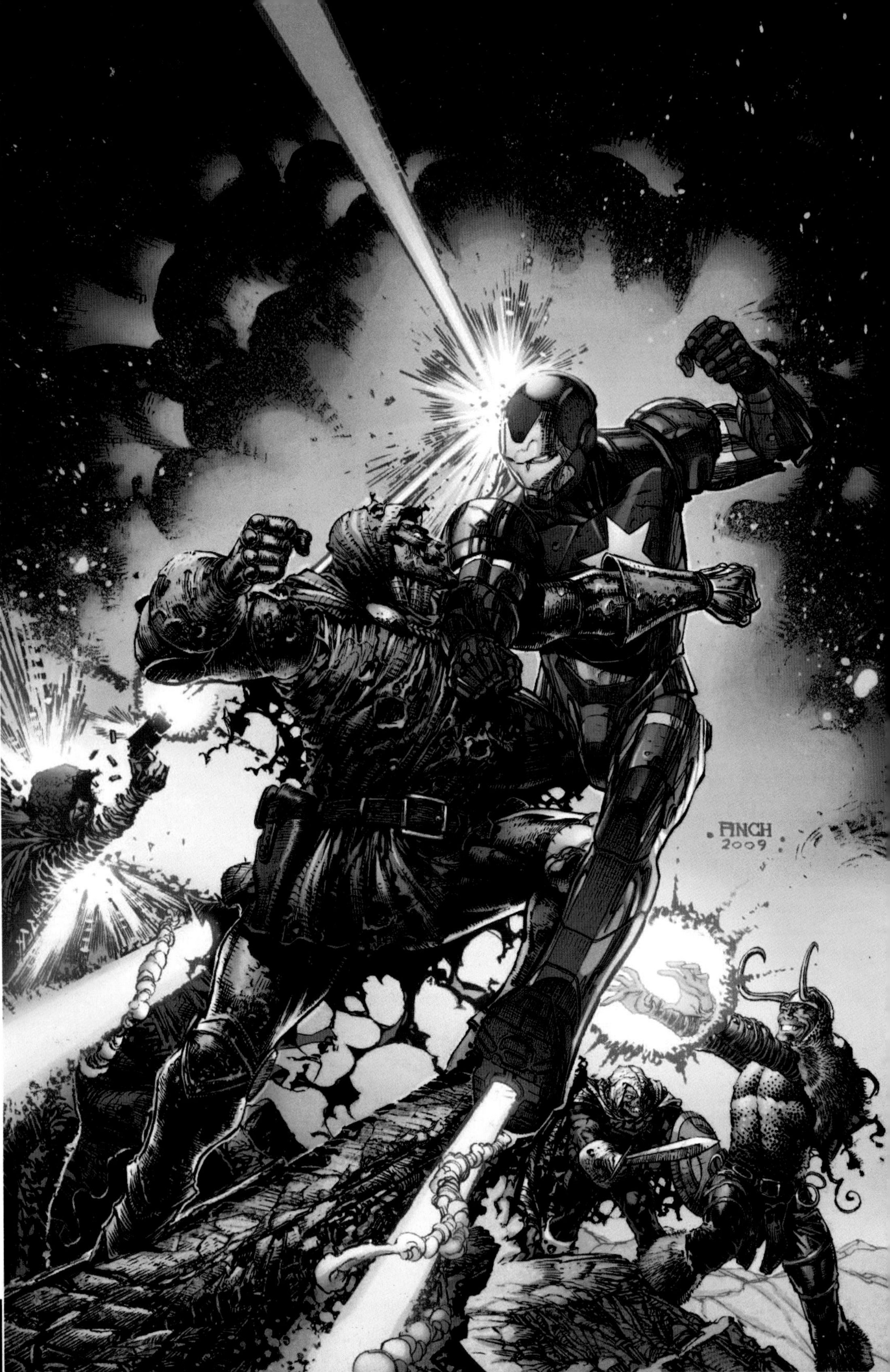
FINCH
2009

SIEGE
THE CABAL

NORMAN OSBORN IS THE NEW POLITICAL AND MEDIA DARLING AND DIRECTOR OF H.A.M.M.E.R., THE NATIONAL PEACEKEEPING TASK FORCE, WHICH INCLUDES HIS OWN TEAM OF AVENGERS.

NORMAN HAS UNVEILED HIS NEW IDENTITY AS THE IRON PATRIOT AND HAS MADE BOLD MOVES ACROSS THE UNITED STATES TO REMAKE THE COUNTRY'S STATUS QUO INTO HIS IMAGE OF JUSTICE AND FAIRNESS…AN IMAGE THAT DOES NOT INCLUDE MUTANT, MONSTER OR VIGILANTE.

IN THE SHADOWS, NORMAN HAS CALLED TOGETHER A CABAL OF THE MOST DANGEROUS BEINGS IN THE WORLD IN AN EFFORT TO MUTUALLY BENEFIT ONE ANOTHER: DR. DOOM, LOKI, THE HOOD, EMMA FROST, AND NAMOR. WITH NAMOR AND FROST HAVING NOW DISTANCED THEMSELVES FROM THE GROUP, THE CRACKS ARE STARTING TO SHOW…

THE MIGHTY THOR, GOD OF THUNDER, HAS RECENTLY RETURNED TO EARTH AND BROUGHT THE GOLDEN CITY OF ASGARD, ALONG WITH ALL THE GODS WHO CALLED IT HOME, WITH HIM. ASGARD FLOATS JUST FEET ABOVE THE FIELDS OF OKLAHOMA.

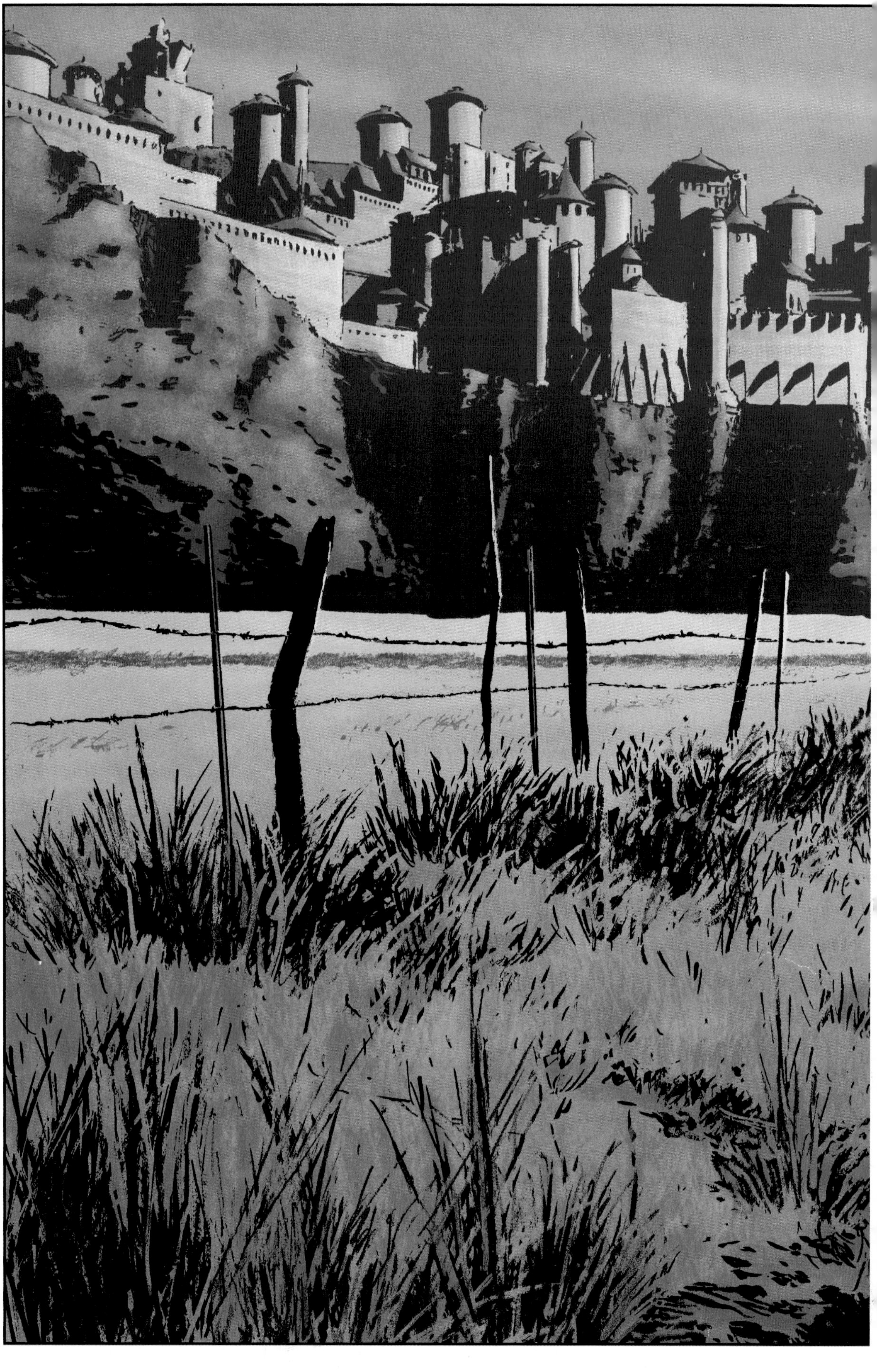

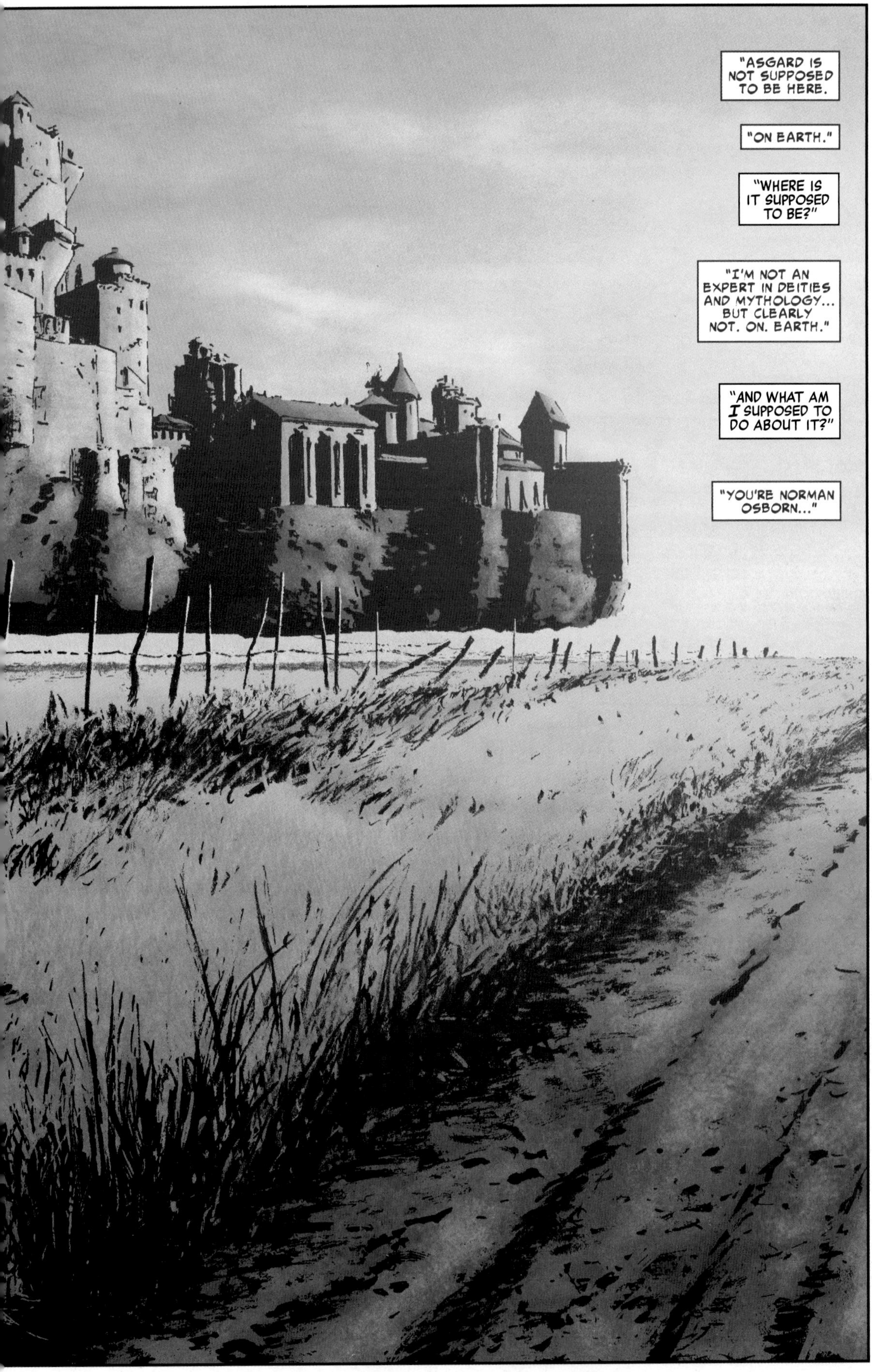
"ASGARD IS NOT SUPPOSED TO BE HERE.
"ON EARTH."
"WHERE IS IT SUPPOSED TO BE?"
"I'M NOT AN EXPERT IN DEITIES AND MYTHOLOGY... BUT CLEARLY NOT. ON. EARTH."
"AND WHAT AM I SUPPOSED TO DO ABOUT IT?"
"YOU'RE NORMAN OSBORN..."

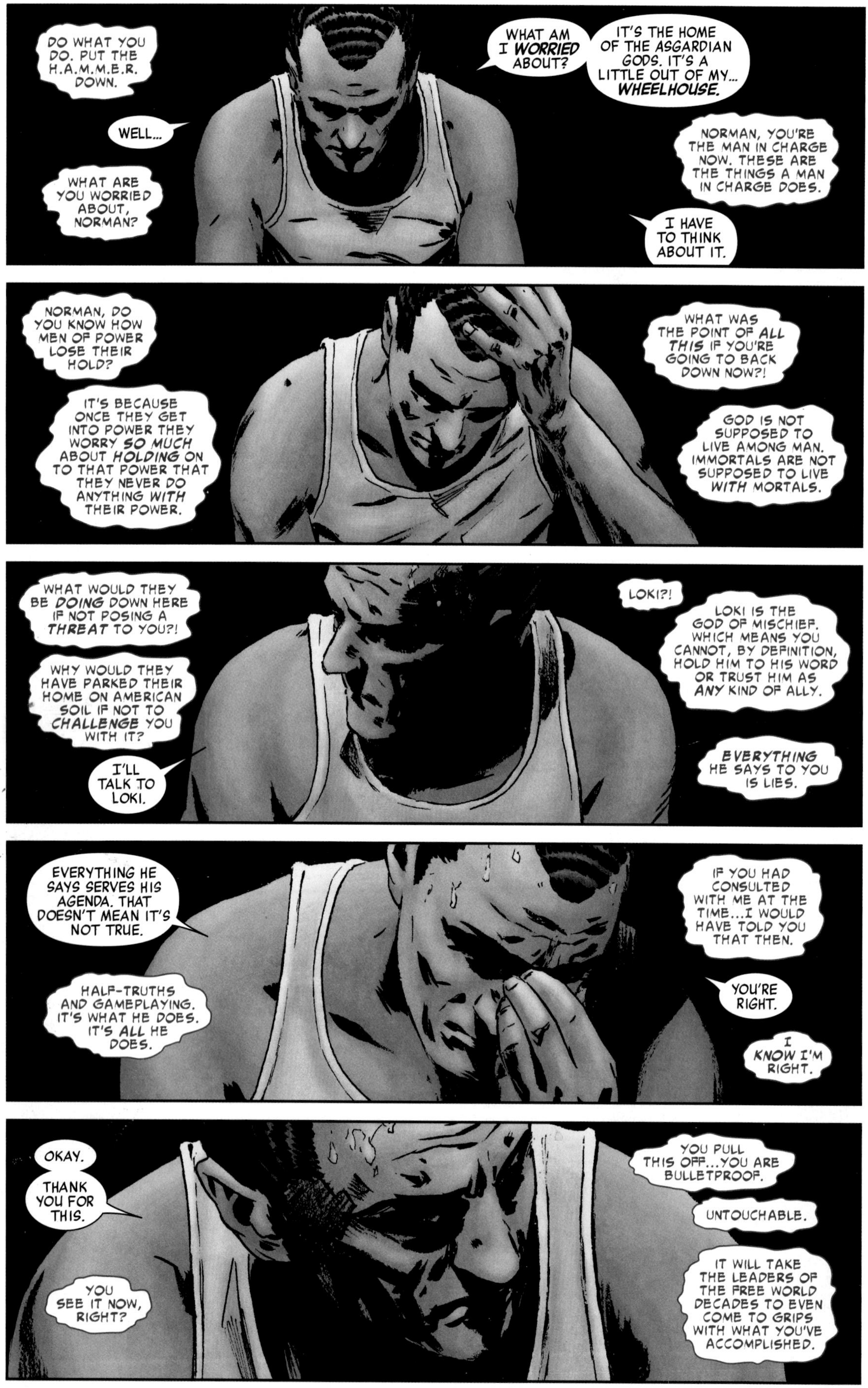

DO WHAT YOU DO. PUT THE H.A.M.M.E.R. DOWN.
WHAT AM I WORRIED ABOUT?
IT'S THE HOME OF THE ASGARDIAN GODS. IT'S A LITTLE OUT OF MY... WHEELHOUSE.
WELL...
NORMAN, YOU'RE THE MAN IN CHARGE NOW. THESE ARE THE THINGS A MAN IN CHARGE DOES.
WHAT ARE YOU WORRIED ABOUT, NORMAN?
I HAVE TO THINK ABOUT IT.
NORMAN, DO YOU KNOW HOW MEN OF POWER LOSE THEIR HOLD?
WHAT WAS THE POINT OF ALL THIS IF YOU'RE GOING TO BACK DOWN NOW?!
IT'S BECAUSE ONCE THEY GET INTO POWER THEY WORRY SO MUCH ABOUT HOLDING ON TO THAT POWER THAT THEY NEVER DO ANYTHING WITH THEIR POWER.
GOD IS NOT SUPPOSED TO LIVE AMONG MAN. IMMORTALS ARE NOT SUPPOSED TO LIVE WITH MORTALS.
WHAT WOULD THEY BE DOING DOWN HERE IF NOT POSING A THREAT TO YOU?!
LOKI?!
LOKI IS THE GOD OF MISCHIEF. WHICH MEANS YOU CANNOT, BY DEFINITION, HOLD HIM TO HIS WORD OR TRUST HIM AS ANY KIND OF ALLY.
WHY WOULD THEY HAVE PARKED THEIR HOME ON AMERICAN SOIL IF NOT TO CHALLENGE YOU WITH IT?
I'LL TALK TO LOKI.
EVERYTHING HE SAYS TO YOU IS LIES.
EVERYTHING HE SAYS SERVES HIS AGENDA. THAT DOESN'T MEAN IT'S NOT TRUE.
IF YOU HAD CONSULTED WITH ME AT THE TIME...I WOULD HAVE TOLD YOU THAT THEN.
HALF-TRUTHS AND GAMEPLAYING. IT'S WHAT HE DOES. IT'S ALL HE DOES.
YOU'RE RIGHT.
I KNOW I'M RIGHT.
OKAY.
YOU PULL THIS OFF...YOU ARE BULLETPROOF.
THANK YOU FOR THIS.
UNTOUCHABLE.
YOU SEE IT NOW, RIGHT?
IT WILL TAKE THE LEADERS OF THE FREE WORLD DECADES TO EVEN COME TO GRIPS WITH WHAT YOU'VE ACCOMPLISHED.

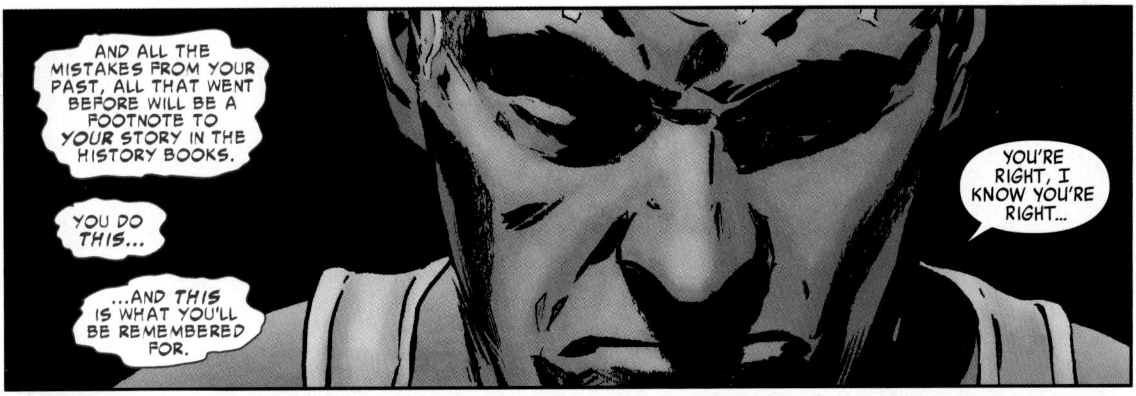
AND ALL THE MISTAKES FROM YOUR PAST, ALL THAT WENT BEFORE WILL BE A FOOTNOTE TO YOUR STORY IN THE HISTORY BOOKS.
YOU DO THIS...
...AND THIS IS WHAT YOU'LL BE REMEMBERED FOR.
YOU'RE RIGHT, I KNOW YOU'RE RIGHT...

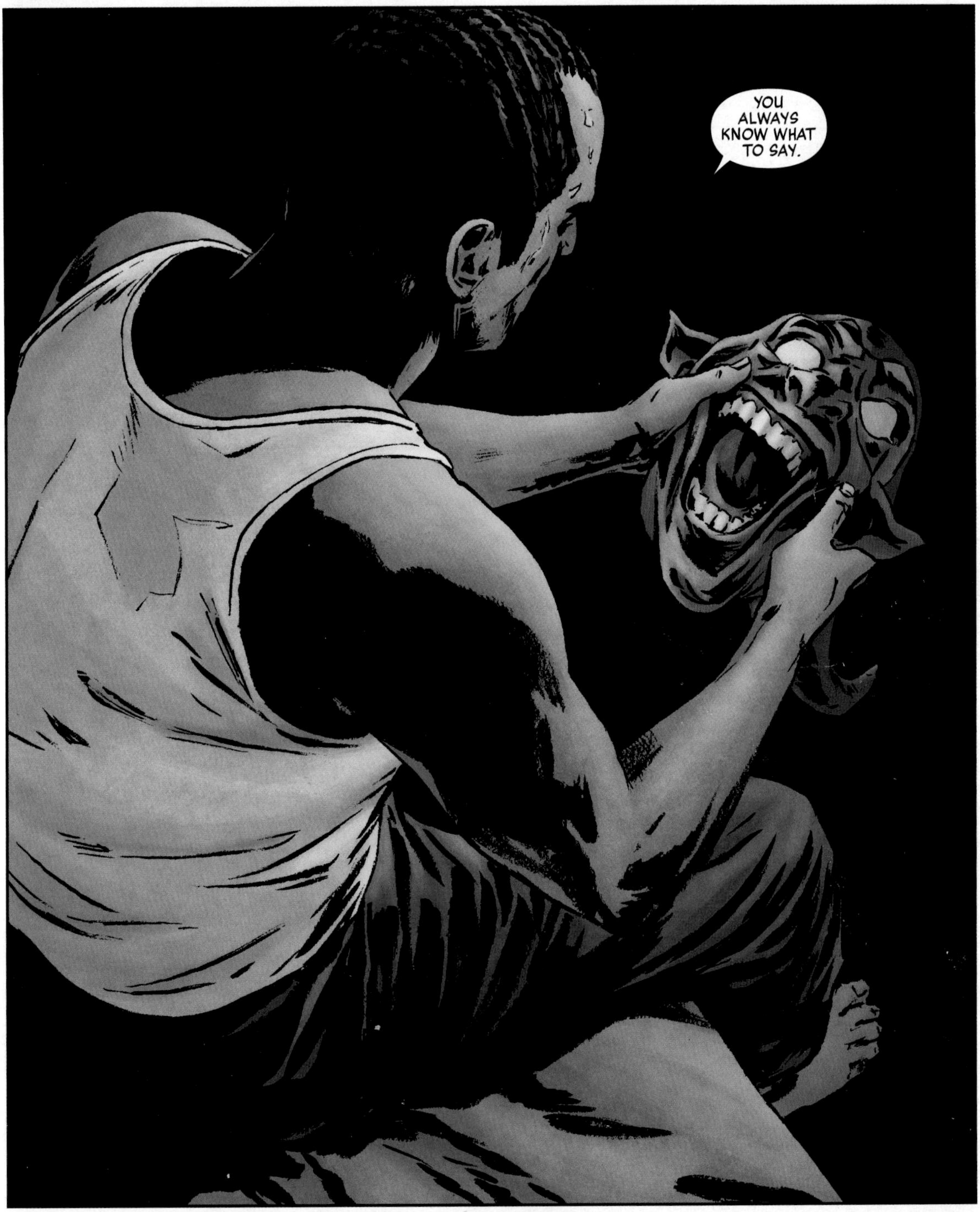
YOU ALWAYS KNOW WHAT TO SAY.

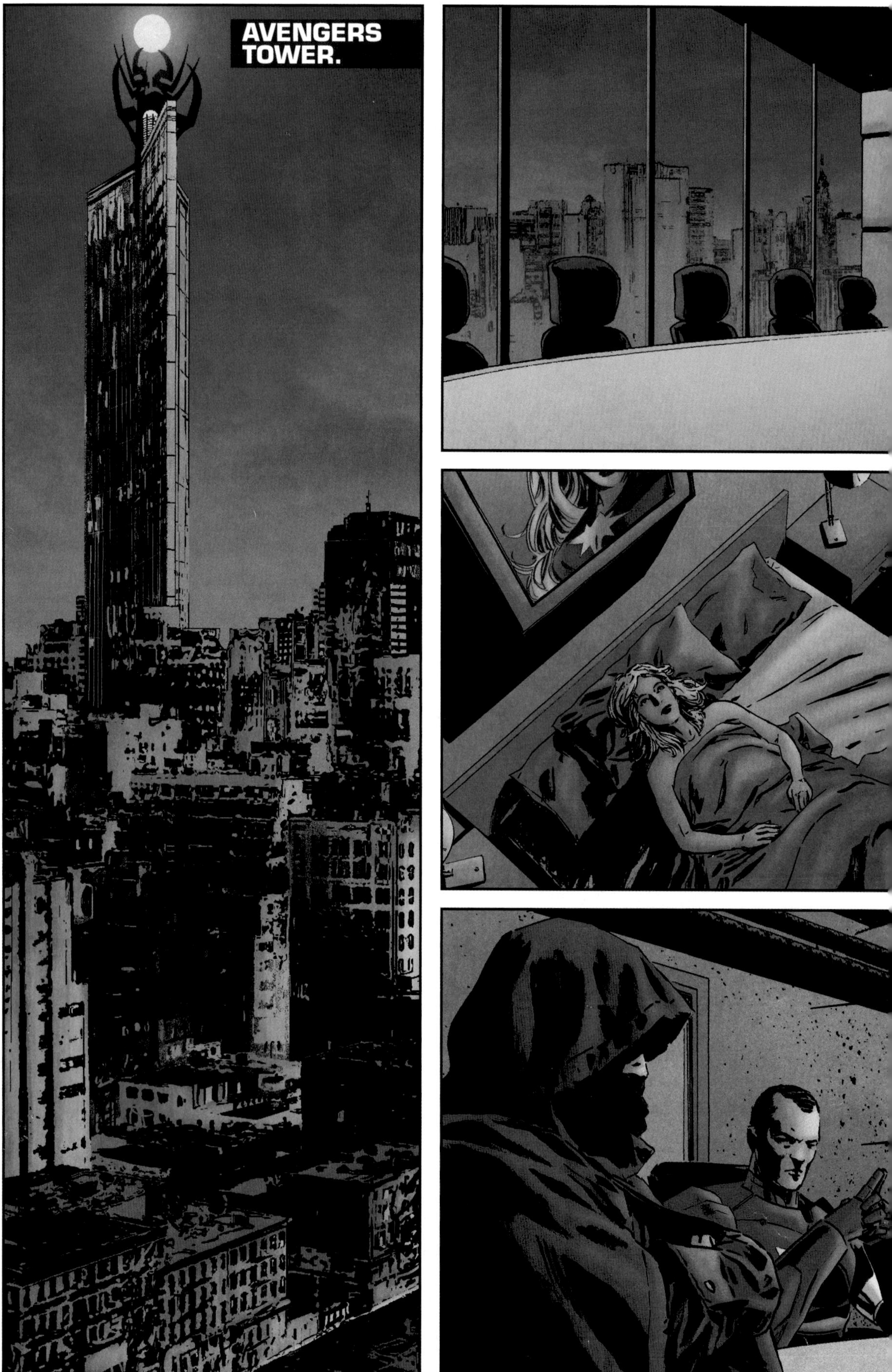
AVENGERS TOWER.

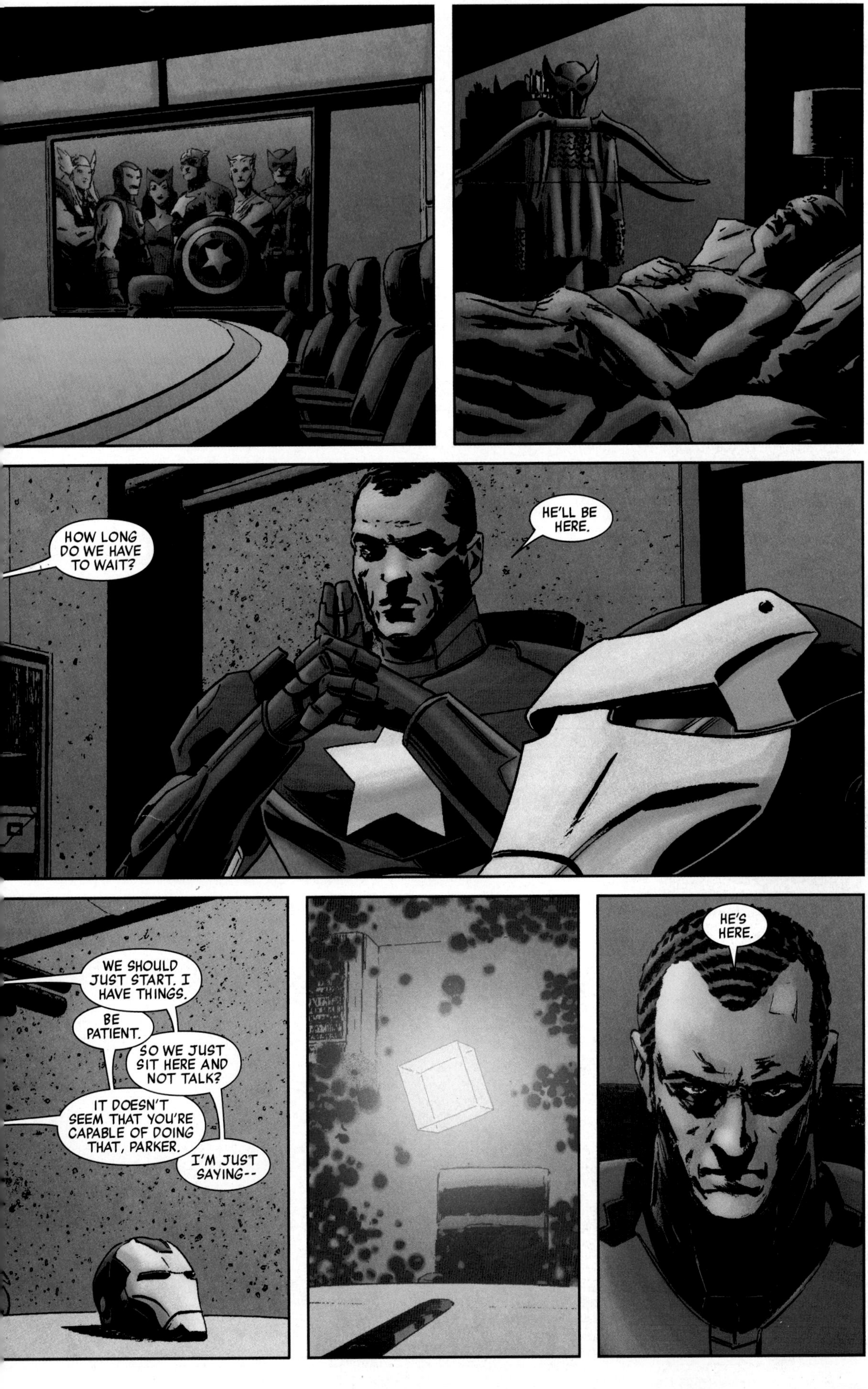
HOW LONG DO WE HAVE TO WAIT?
HE'LL BE HERE.
WE SHOULD JUST START. I HAVE THINGS.
BE PATIENT.
SO WE JUST SIT HERE AND NOT TALK?
IT DOESN'T SEEM THAT YOU'RE CAPABLE OF DOING THAT, PARKER.
I'M JUST SAYING--
HE'S HERE.

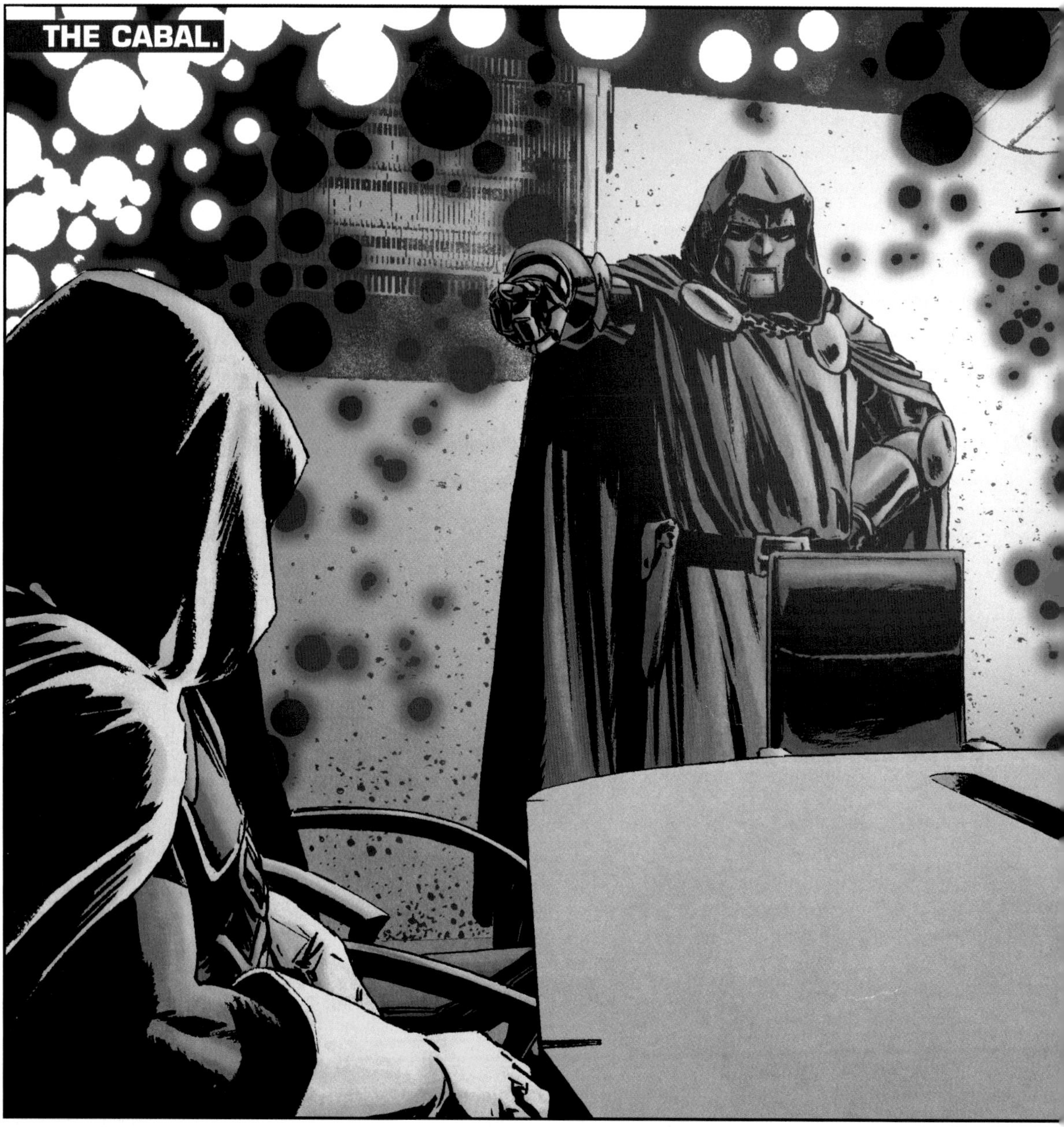
THE CABAL.

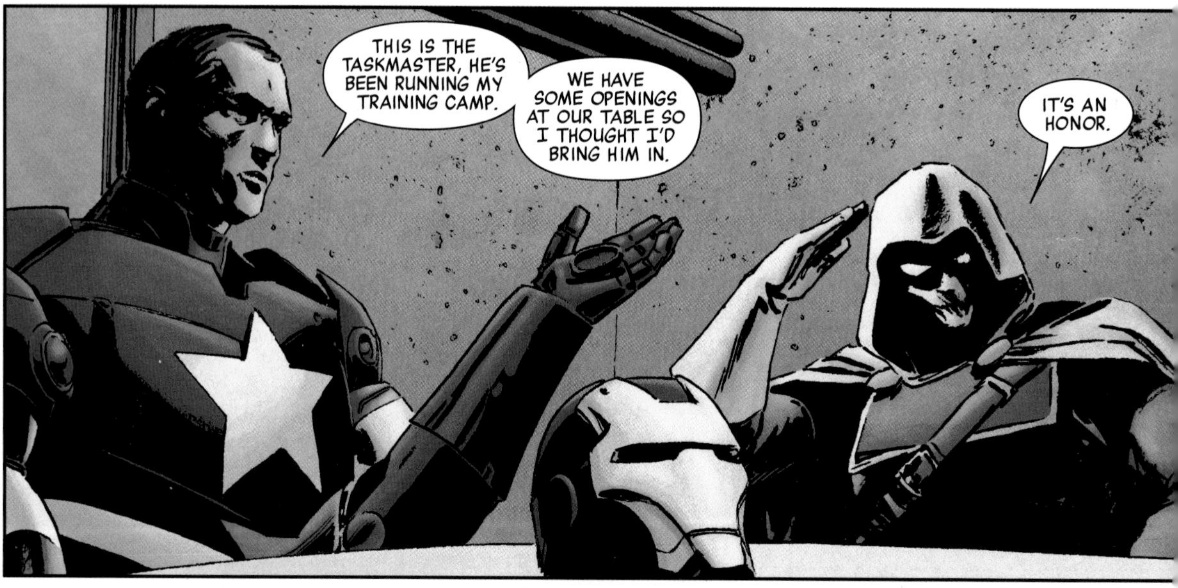
THIS IS THE TASKMASTER, HE'S BEEN RUNNING MY TRAINING CAMP.
WE HAVE SOME OPENINGS AT OUR TABLE SO I THOUGHT I'D BRING HIM IN.
IT'S AN HONOR.

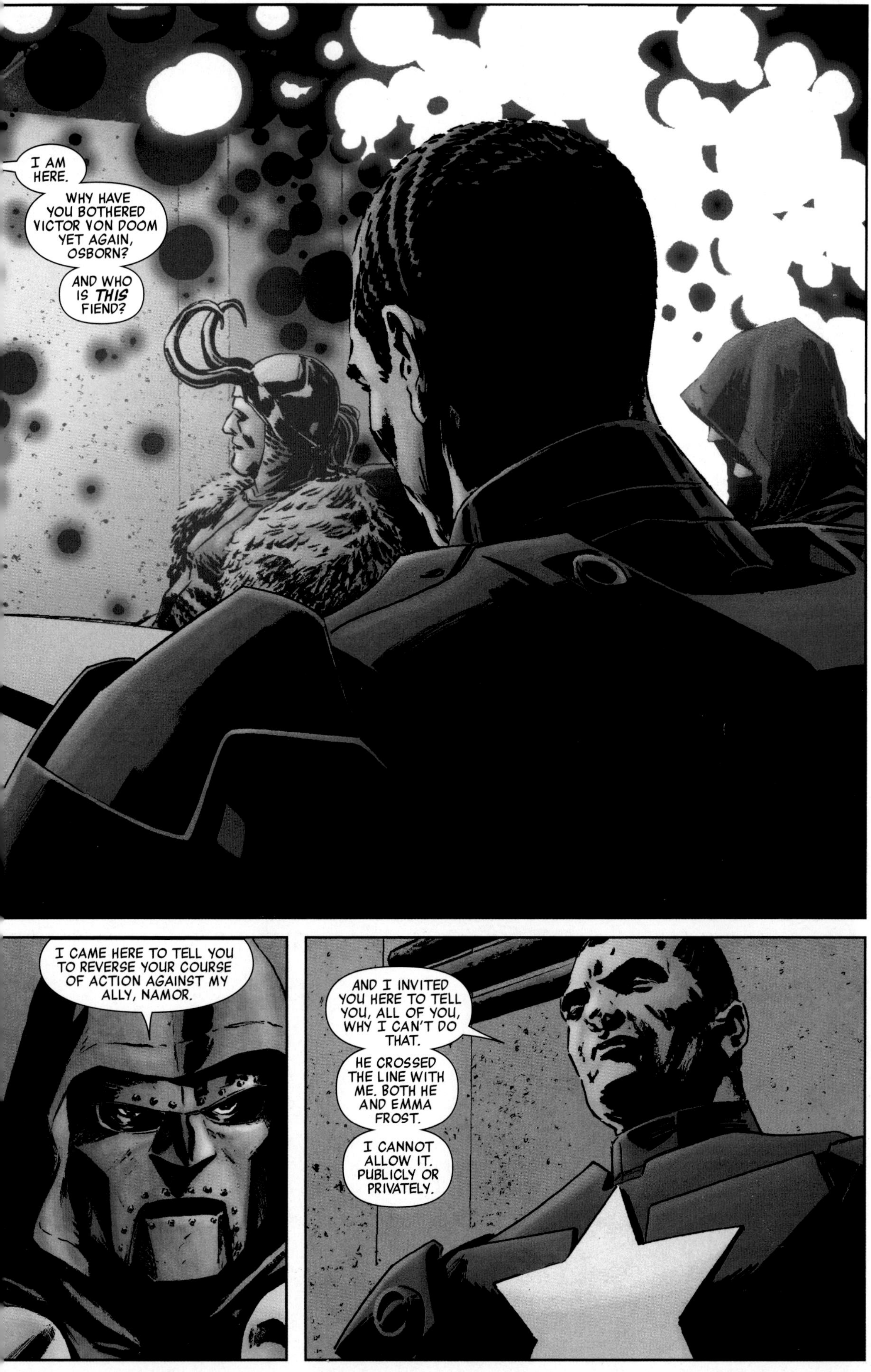
I AM HERE.
WHY HAVE YOU BOTHERED VICTOR VON DOOM YET AGAIN, OSBORN?
AND WHO IS *THIS* FIEND?
I CAME HERE TO TELL YOU TO REVERSE YOUR COURSE OF ACTION AGAINST MY ALLY, NAMOR.
AND I INVITED YOU HERE TO TELL YOU, ALL OF YOU, WHY I CAN'T DO THAT.
HE CROSSED THE LINE WITH ME. BOTH HE AND EMMA FROST.
I CANNOT ALLOW IT. PUBLICLY OR PRIVATELY.

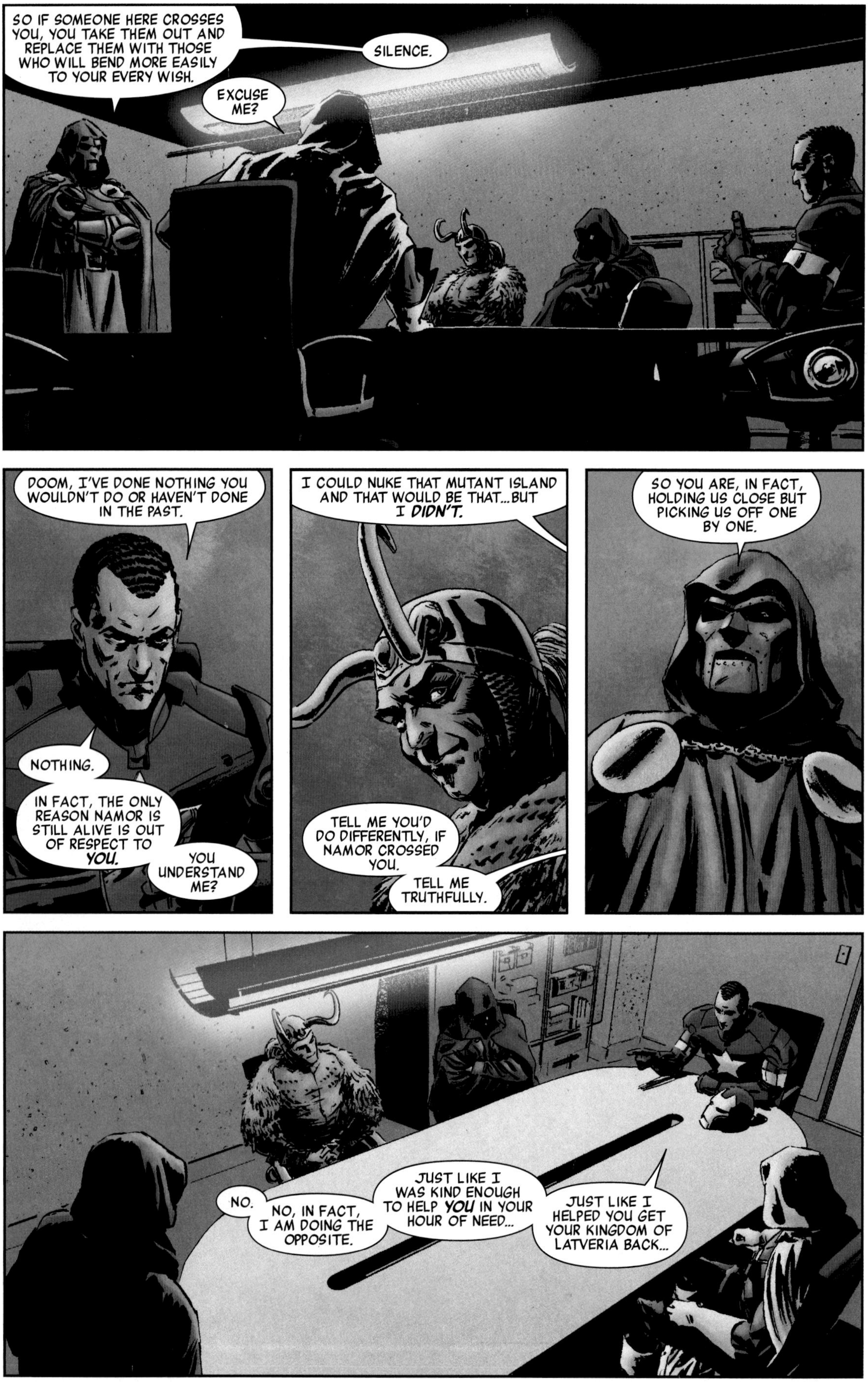
SO IF SOMEONE HERE CROSSES YOU, YOU TAKE THEM OUT AND REPLACE THEM WITH THOSE WHO WILL BEND MORE EASILY TO YOUR EVERY WISH.
SILENCE.
EXCUSE ME?
DOOM, I'VE DONE NOTHING YOU WOULDN'T DO OR HAVEN'T DONE IN THE PAST.
NOTHING.
IN FACT, THE ONLY REASON NAMOR IS STILL ALIVE IS OUT OF RESPECT TO *YOU.*
YOU UNDERSTAND ME?
I COULD NUKE THAT MUTANT ISLAND AND THAT WOULD BE THAT...BUT I *DIDN'T.*
TELL ME YOU'D DO DIFFERENTLY, IF NAMOR CROSSED YOU.
TELL ME TRUTHFULLY.
SO YOU ARE, IN FACT, HOLDING US CLOSE BUT PICKING US OFF ONE BY ONE.
NO.
NO, IN FACT, I AM DOING THE OPPOSITE.
JUST LIKE I WAS KIND ENOUGH TO HELP *YOU* IN YOUR HOUR OF NEED...
JUST LIKE I HELPED YOU GET YOUR KINGDOM OF LATVERIA BACK...

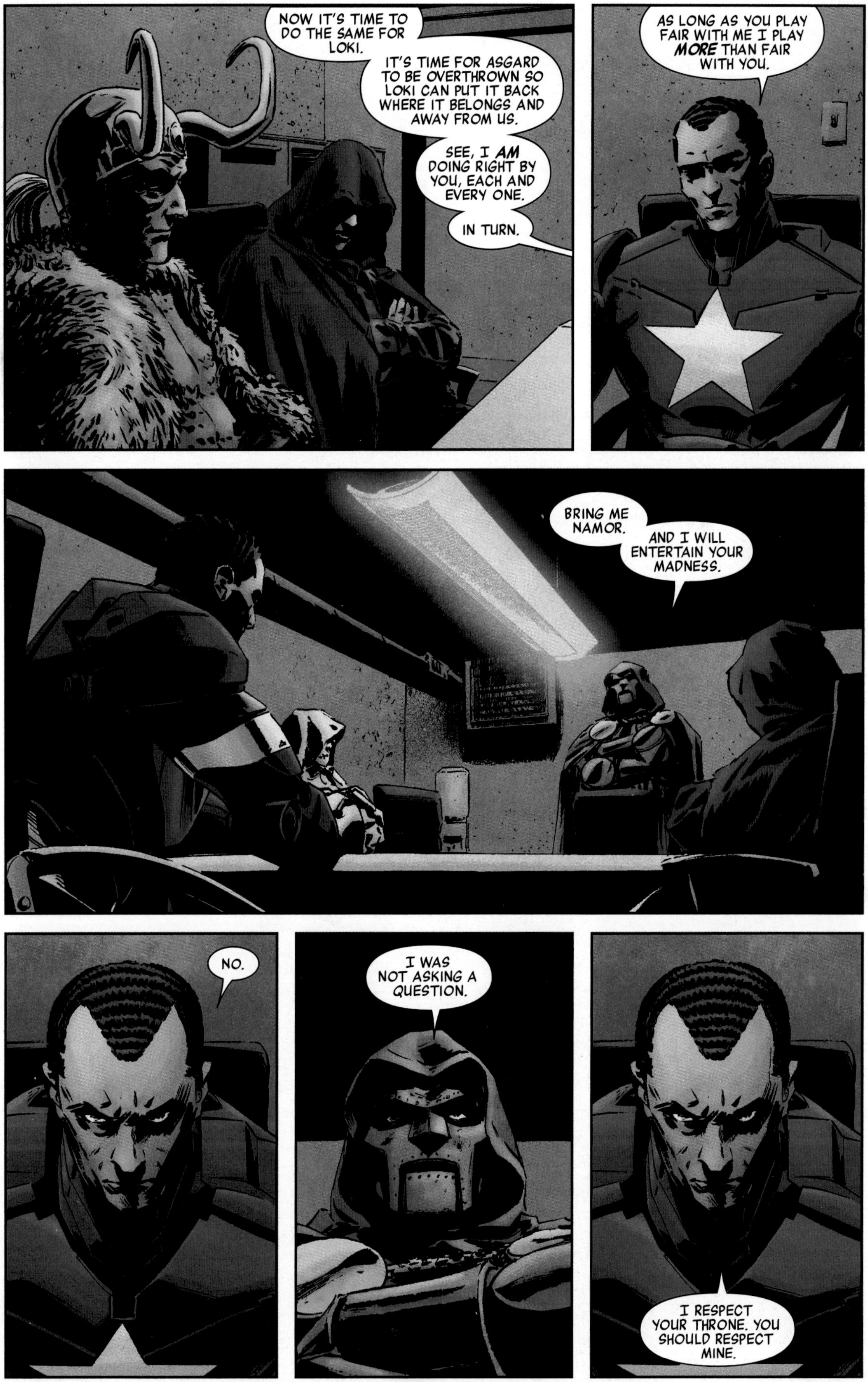
NOW IT'S TIME TO DO THE SAME FOR LOKI.
IT'S TIME FOR ASGARD TO BE OVERTHROWN SO LOKI CAN PUT IT BACK WHERE IT BELONGS AND AWAY FROM US.
SEE, I *AM* DOING RIGHT BY YOU, EACH AND EVERY ONE.
IN TURN.
AS LONG AS YOU PLAY FAIR WITH ME I PLAY *MORE* THAN FAIR WITH YOU.
BRING ME NAMOR.
AND I WILL ENTERTAIN YOUR MADNESS.
NO.
I WAS NOT ASKING A QUESTION.
I RESPECT YOUR THRONE. YOU SHOULD RESPECT MINE.

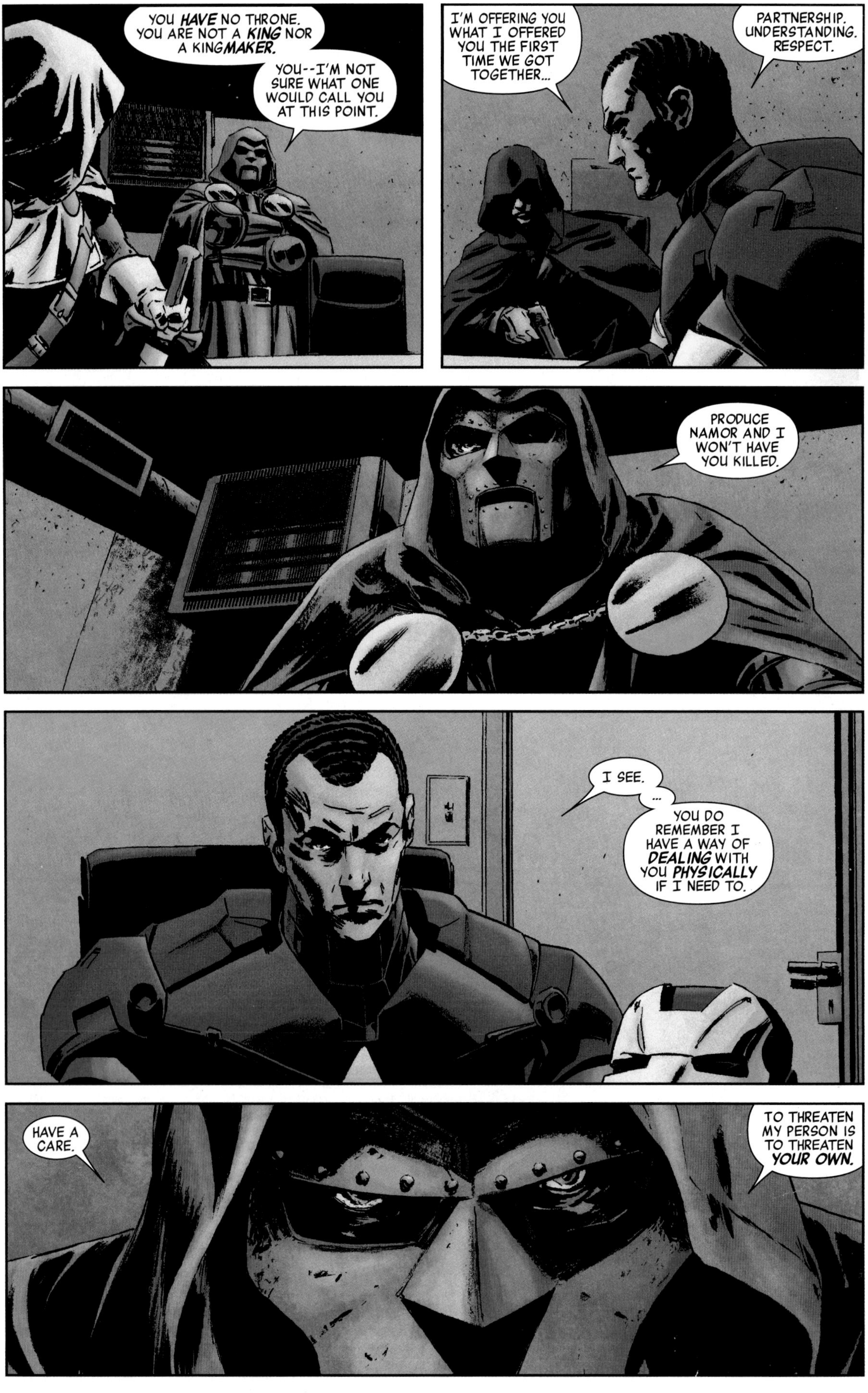
YOU HAVE NO THRONE. YOU ARE NOT A KING NOR A KINGMAKER.
YOU--I'M NOT SURE WHAT ONE WOULD CALL YOU AT THIS POINT.
I'M OFFERING YOU WHAT I OFFERED YOU THE FIRST TIME WE GOT TOGETHER...
PARTNERSHIP. UNDERSTANDING. RESPECT.
PRODUCE NAMOR AND I WON'T HAVE YOU KILLED.
I SEE.
...
YOU DO REMEMBER I HAVE A WAY OF DEALING WITH YOU PHYSICALLY IF I NEED TO.
HAVE A CARE.
TO THREATEN MY PERSON IS TO THREATEN YOUR OWN.

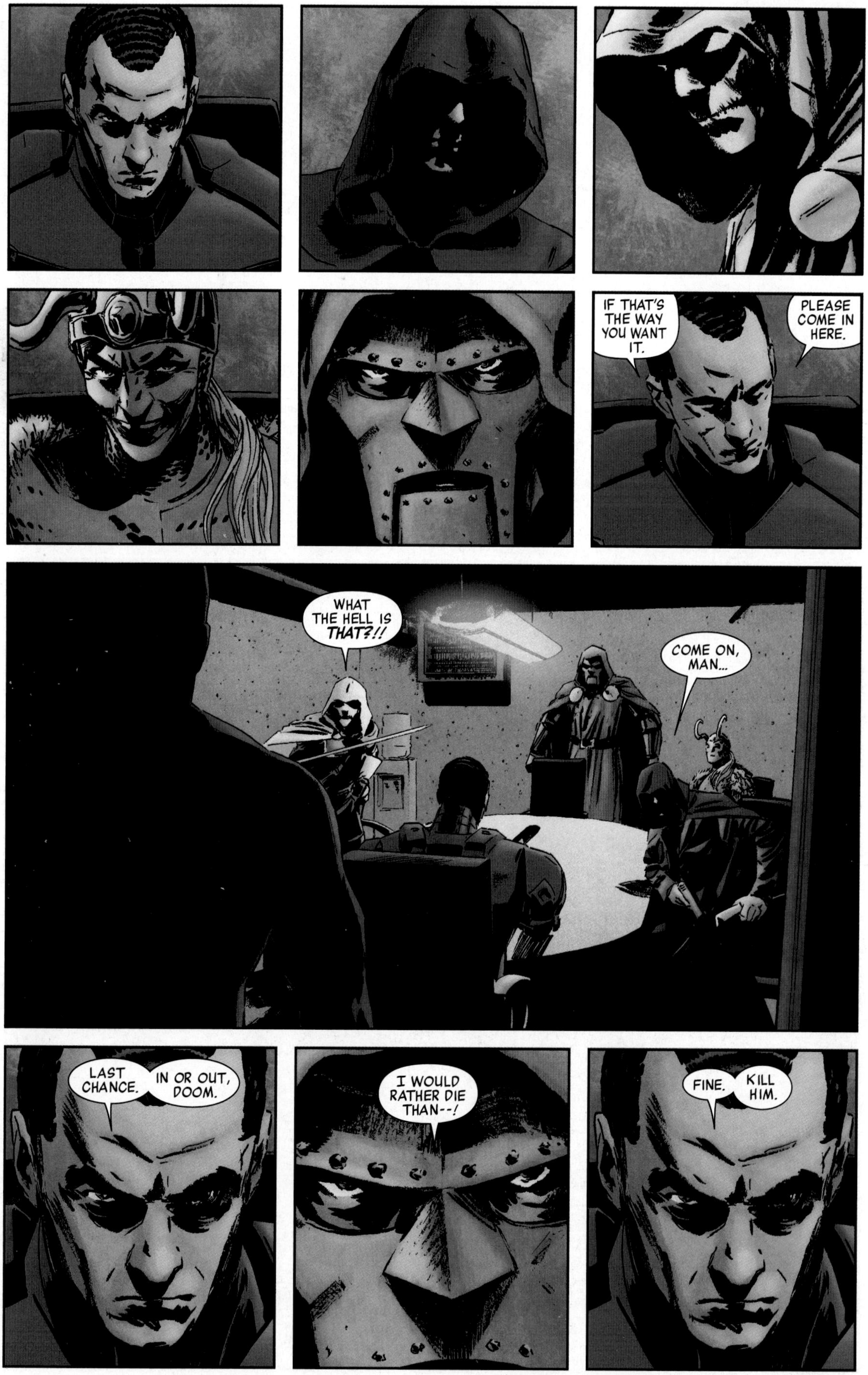
IF THAT'S THE WAY YOU WANT IT.
PLEASE COME IN HERE.
WHAT THE HELL IS *THAT?!!*
COME ON, MAN...
LAST CHANCE.
IN OR OUT, DOOM.
I WOULD RATHER DIE THAN--!
FINE.
KILL HIM.

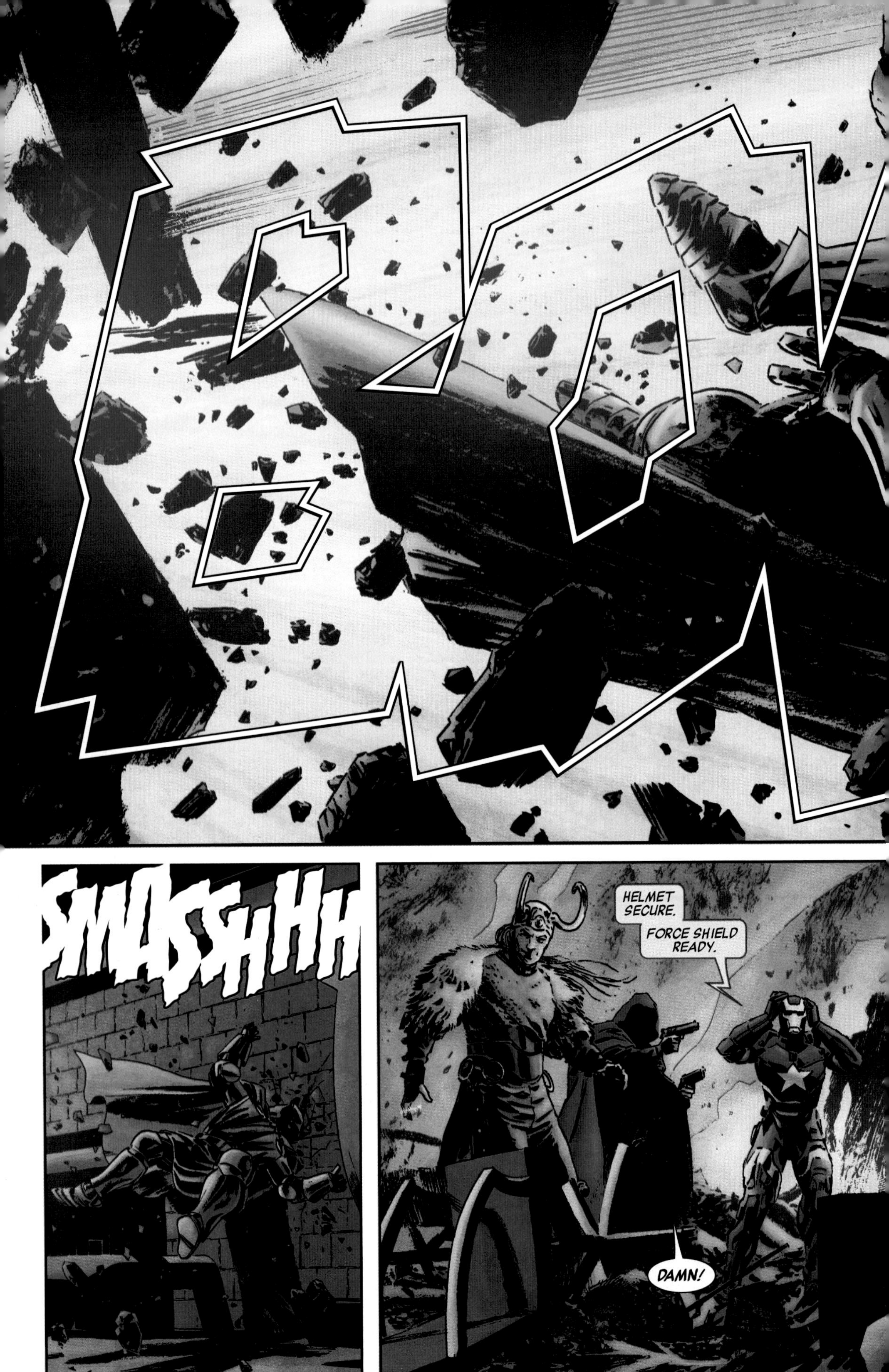
SMASSHHH
HELMET SECURE.
FORCE SHIELD READY.
DAMN!

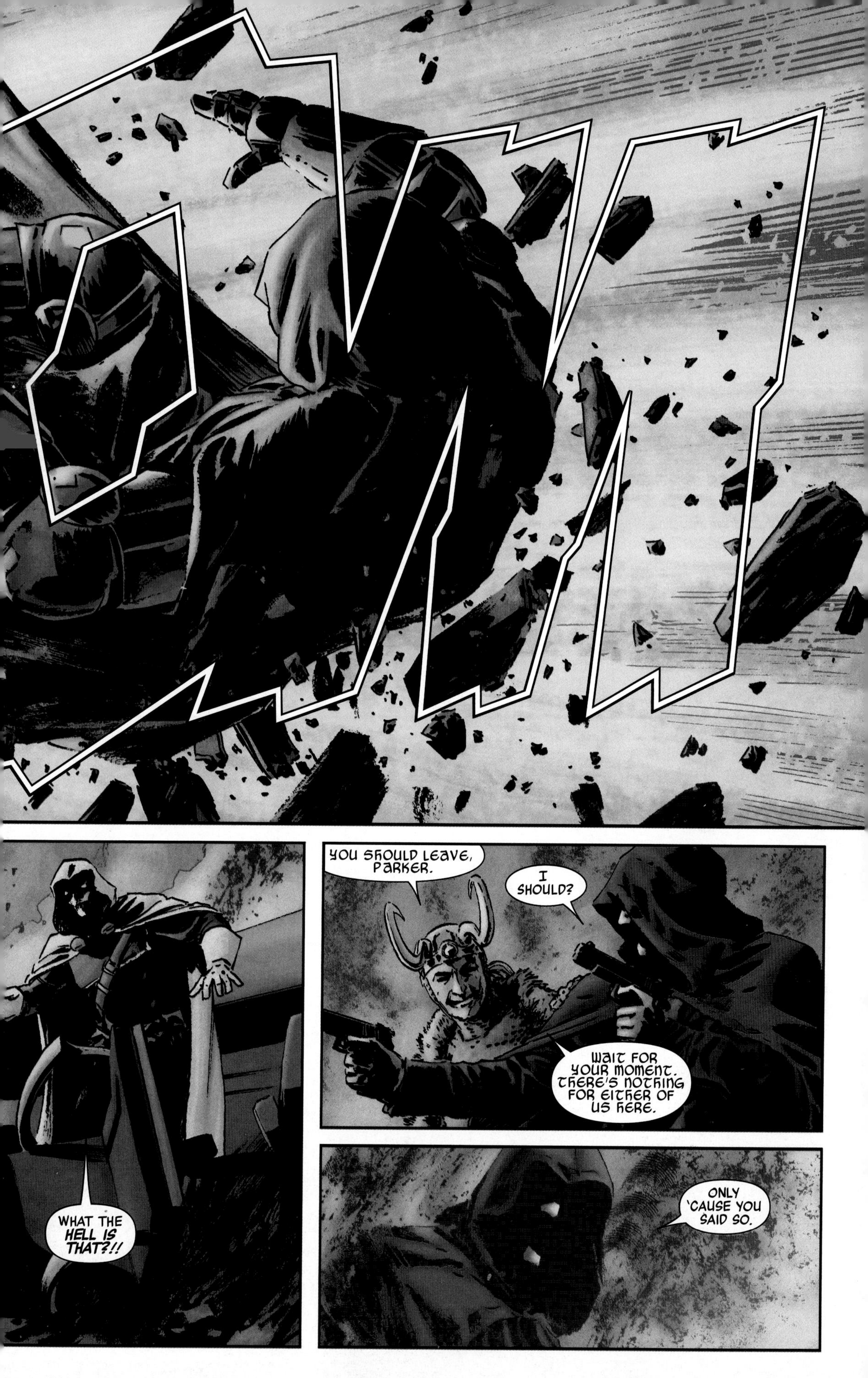

WHAT THE HELL IS THAT?!!
YOU SHOULD LEAVE, PARKER.
I SHOULD?
WAIT FOR YOUR MOMENT. THERE'S NOTHING FOR EITHER OF US HERE.
ONLY 'CAUSE YOU SAID SO.

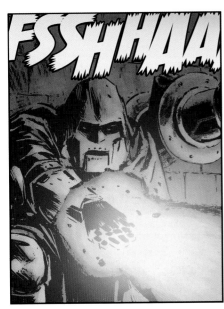

FSSHHAA

WWWMM

GYAAARRGGHH!!

HIT HIM AGAIN!

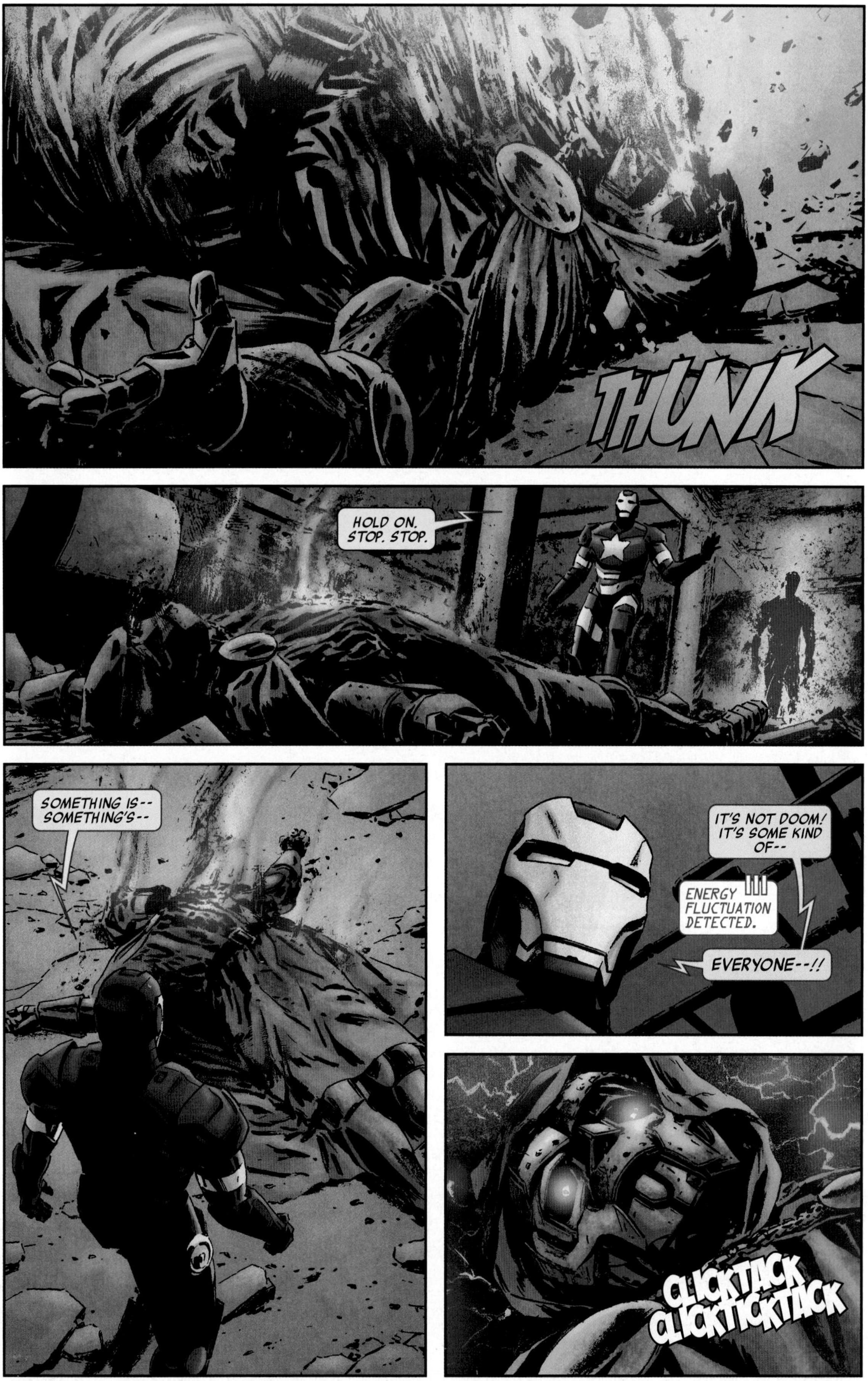
THUNK
HOLD ON. STOP. STOP.
SOMETHING IS-- SOMETHING'S--
IT'S NOT DOOM! IT'S SOME KIND OF--
ENERGY FLUCTUATION DETECTED.
EVERYONE--!!
CLICKTACK CLICKTICKTACK

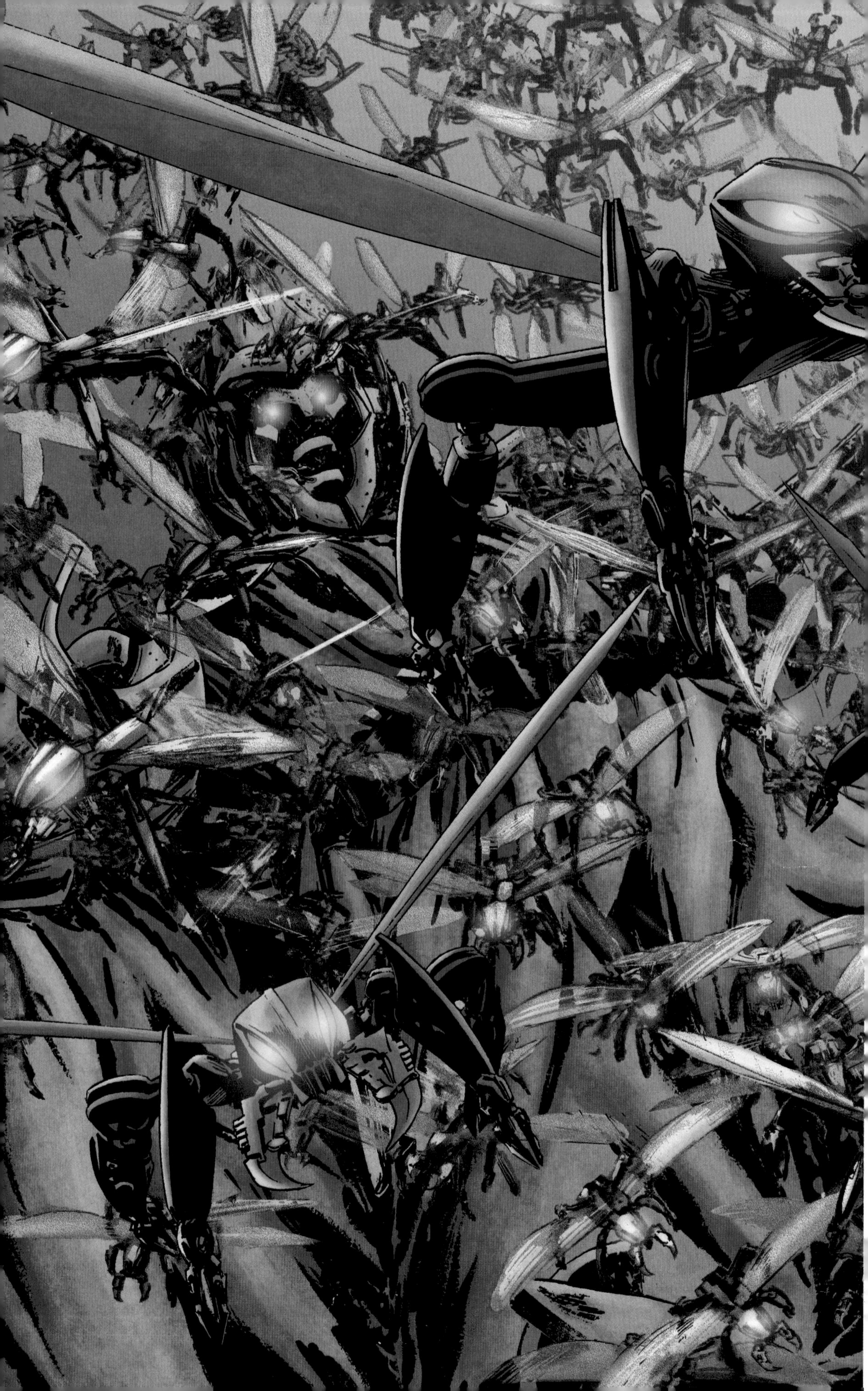

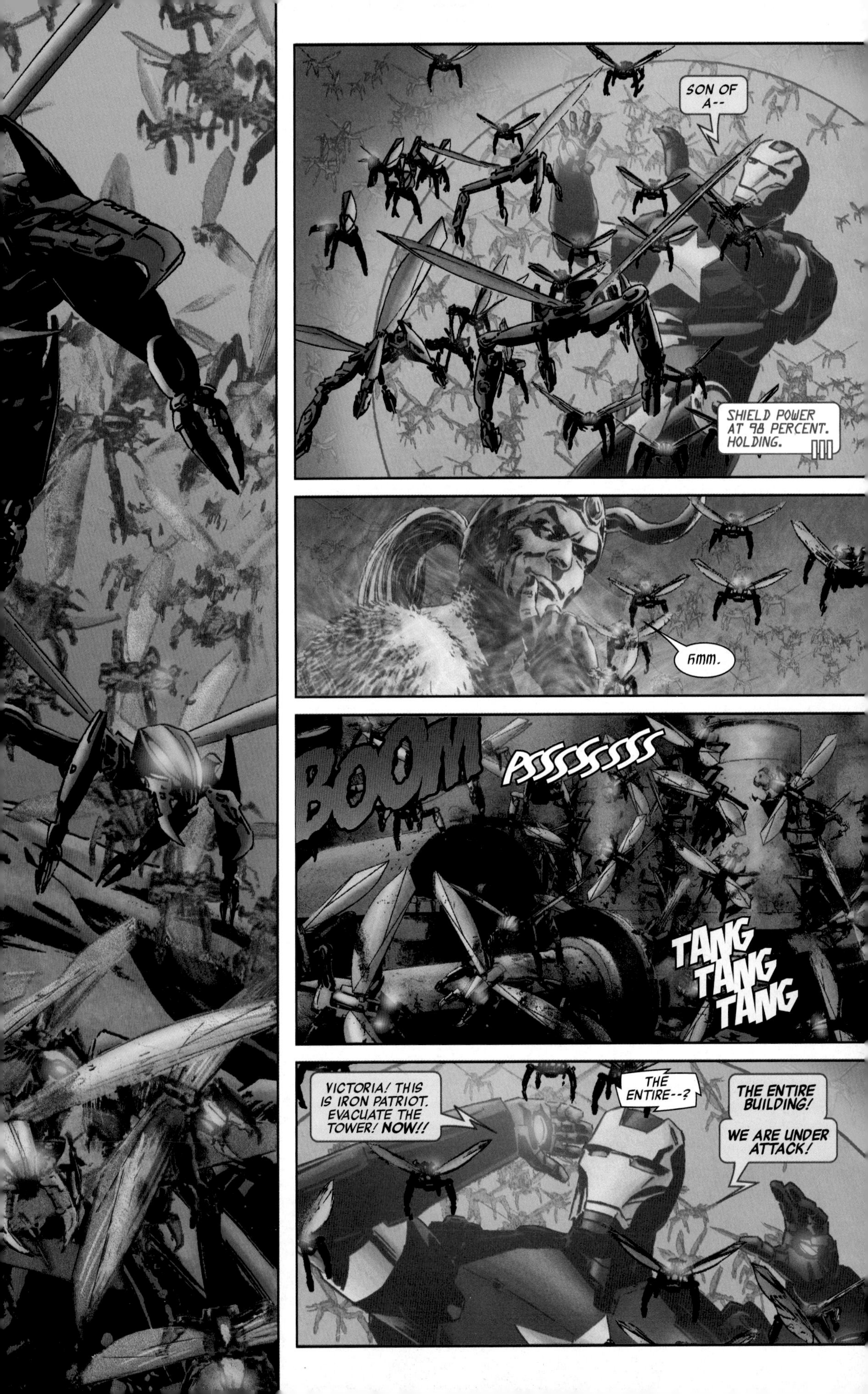
SON OF A--
SHIELD POWER AT 98 PERCENT. HOLDING.
HMM.
BOOM
PSSSSSS
TANG TANG TANG
VICTORIA! THIS IS IRON PATRIOT. EVACUATE THE TOWER! NOW!!
THE ENTIRE--?
THE ENTIRE BUILDING!
WE ARE UNDER ATTACK!

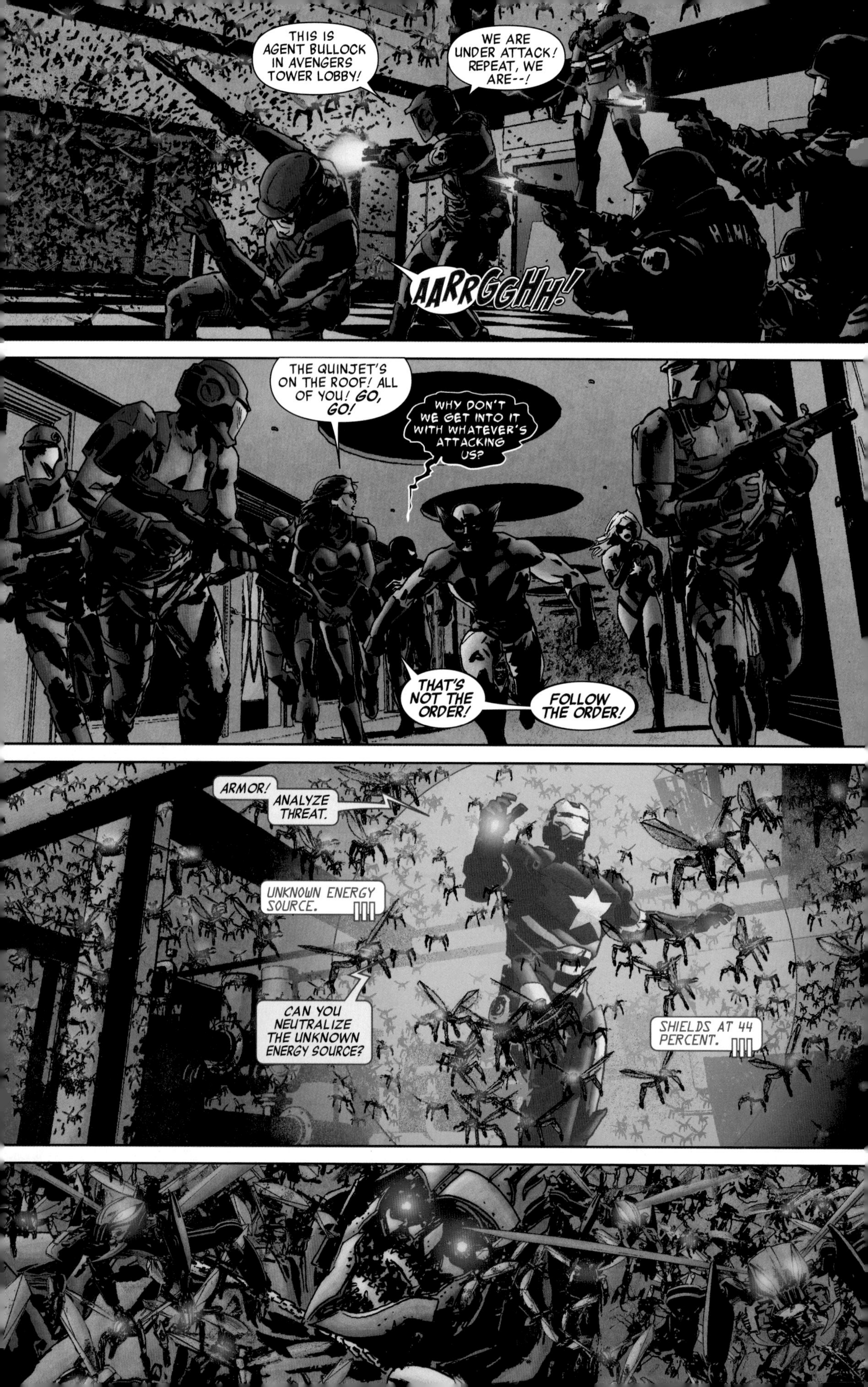
THIS IS AGENT BULLOCK IN AVENGERS TOWER LOBBY!
WE ARE UNDER ATTACK! REPEAT, WE ARE--!
AARRGGHH!
THE QUINJET'S ON THE ROOF! ALL OF YOU! GO, GO!
WHY DON'T WE GET INTO IT WITH WHATEVER'S ATTACKING US?
THAT'S NOT THE ORDER!
FOLLOW THE ORDER!
ARMOR!
ANALYZE THREAT.
UNKNOWN ENERGY SOURCE.
CAN YOU NEUTRALIZE THE UNKNOWN ENERGY SOURCE?
SHIELDS AT 44 PERCENT.

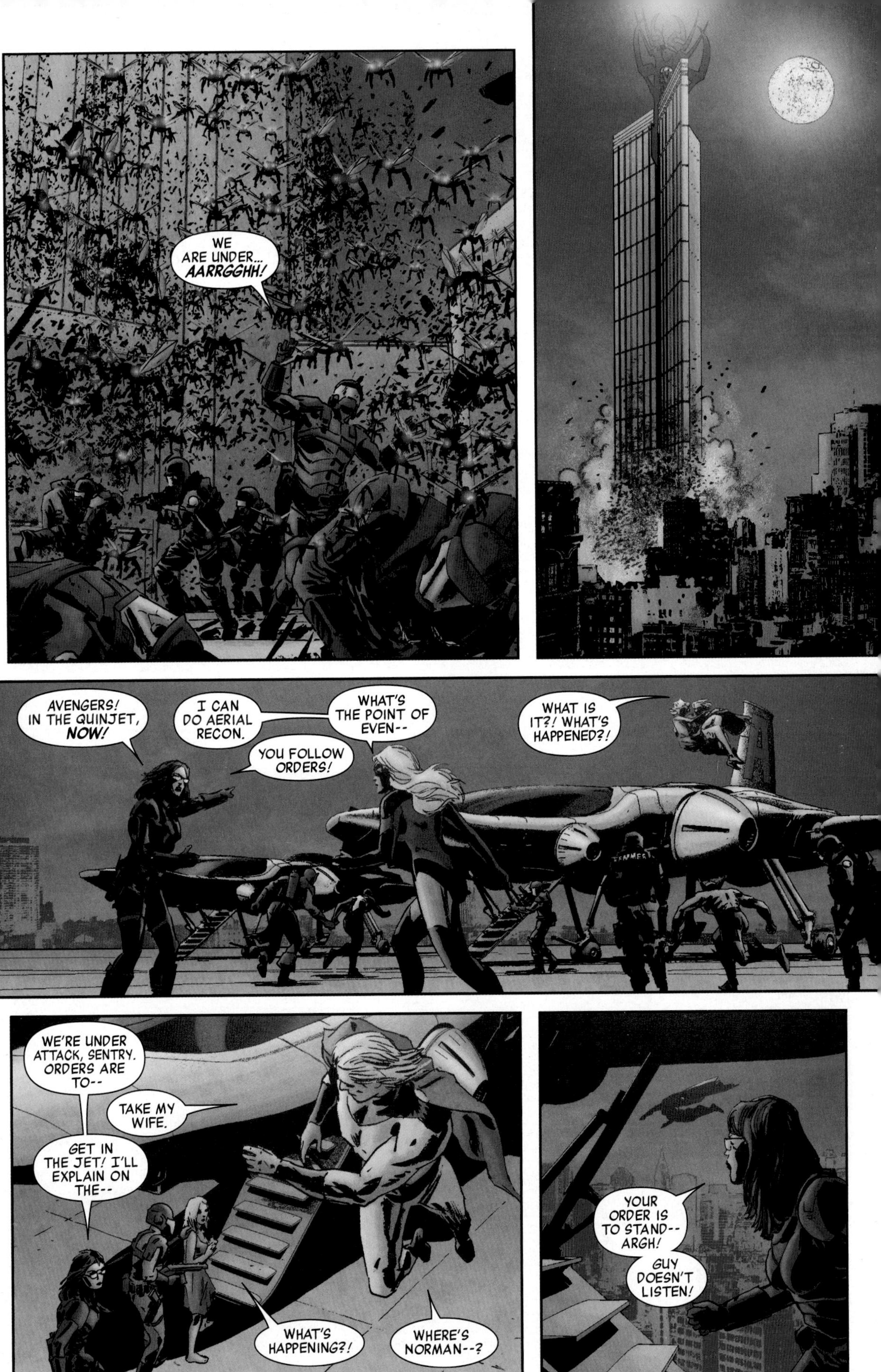

WE ARE UNDER... AARRGGHH!
AVENGERS! IN THE QUINJET, NOW!
I CAN DO AERIAL RECON.
YOU FOLLOW ORDERS!
WHAT'S THE POINT OF EVEN--
WHAT IS IT?! WHAT'S HAPPENED?!
WE'RE UNDER ATTACK, SENTRY. ORDERS ARE TO--
TAKE MY WIFE.
GET IN THE JET! I'LL EXPLAIN ON THE--
WHAT'S HAPPENING?!
WHERE'S NORMAN--?
YOUR ORDER IS TO STAND-- ARGH!
GUY DOESN'T LISTEN!

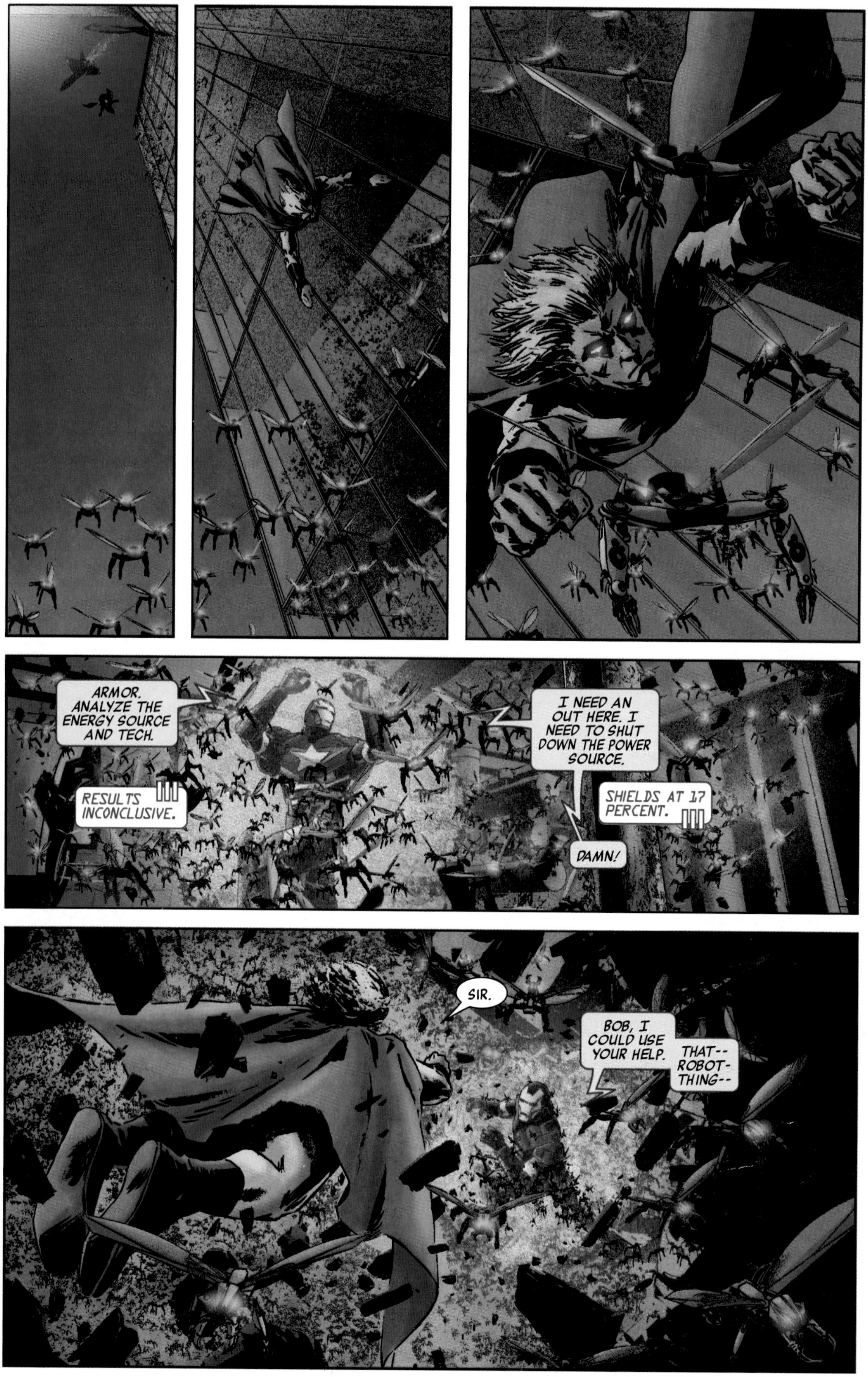
ARMOR. ANALYZE THE ENERGY SOURCE AND TECH.
RESULTS INCONCLUSIVE.
I NEED AN OUT HERE. I NEED TO SHUT DOWN THE POWER SOURCE.
SHIELDS AT 17 PERCENT.
DAMN!
SIR.
BOB, I COULD USE YOUR HELP.
THAT--ROBOT-THING--

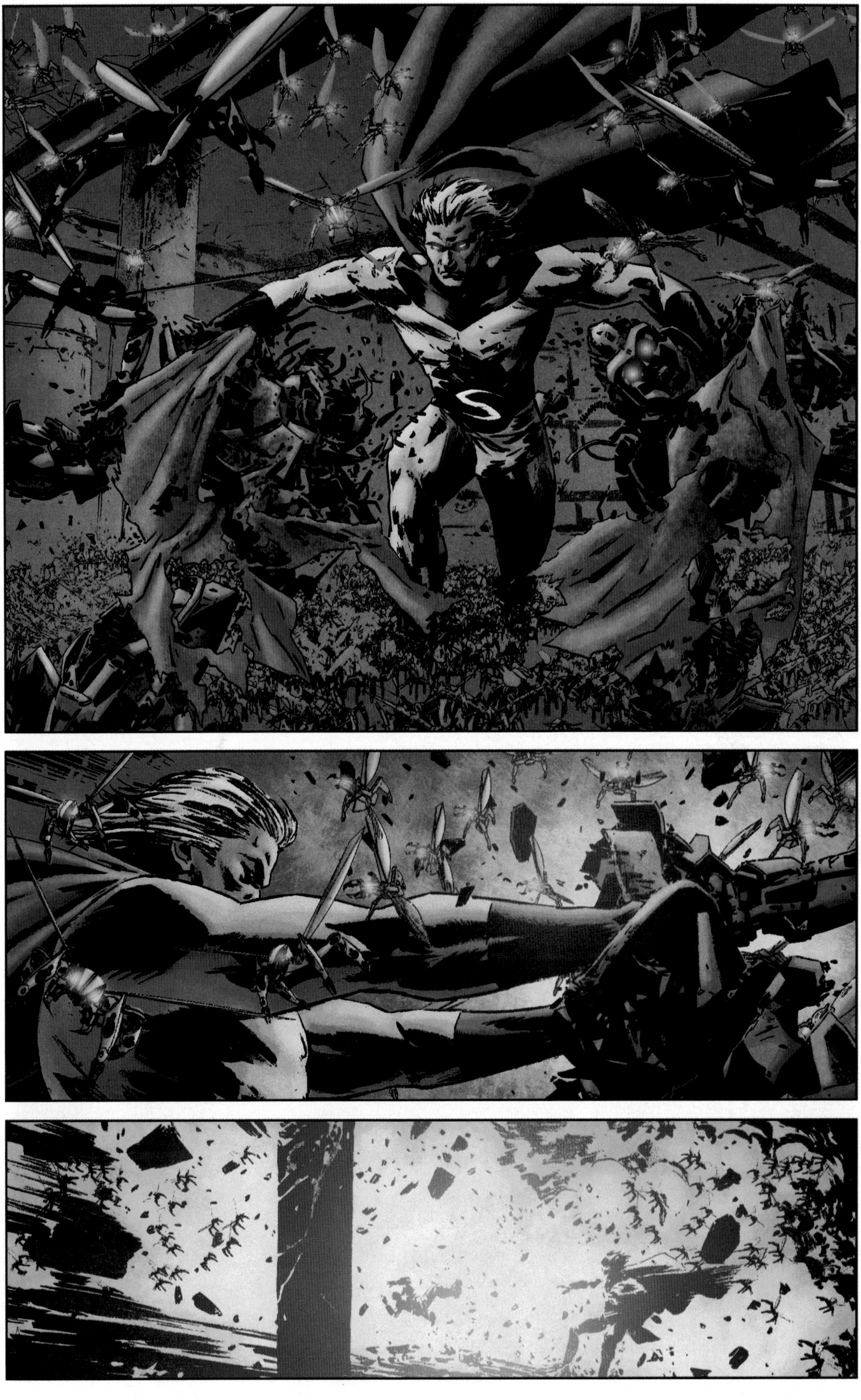

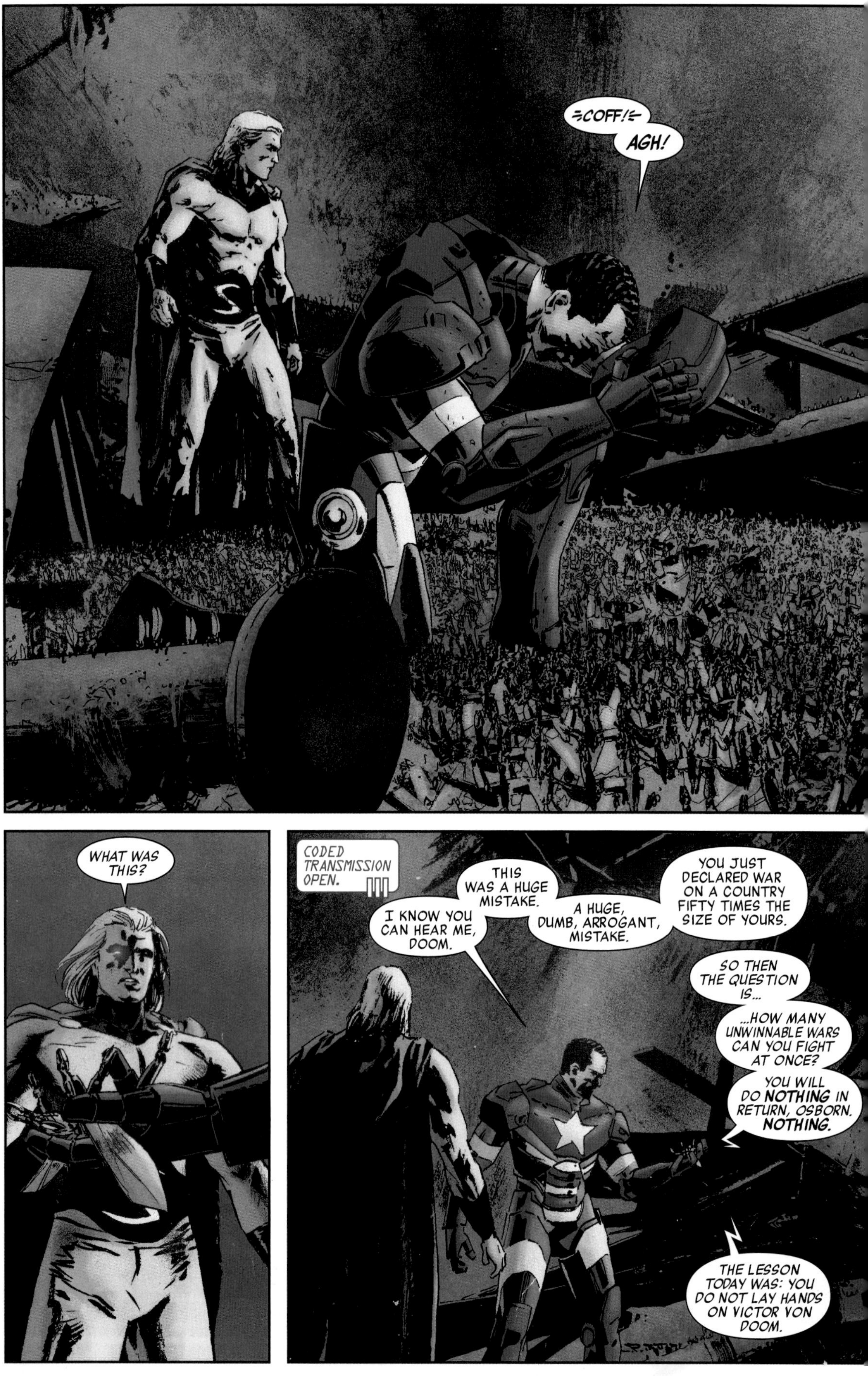

≈COFF!≈
AGH!
WHAT WAS THIS?
CODED TRANSMISSION OPEN.
I KNOW YOU CAN HEAR ME, DOOM.
THIS WAS A HUGE MISTAKE.
A HUGE, DUMB, ARROGANT, MISTAKE.
YOU JUST DECLARED WAR ON A COUNTRY FIFTY TIMES THE SIZE OF YOURS.
SO THEN THE QUESTION IS...
...HOW MANY UNWINNABLE WARS CAN YOU FIGHT AT ONCE?
YOU WILL DO **NOTHING** IN RETURN, OSBORN. **NOTHING.**
THE LESSON TODAY WAS: YOU DO NOT LAY HANDS ON VICTOR VON DOOM.

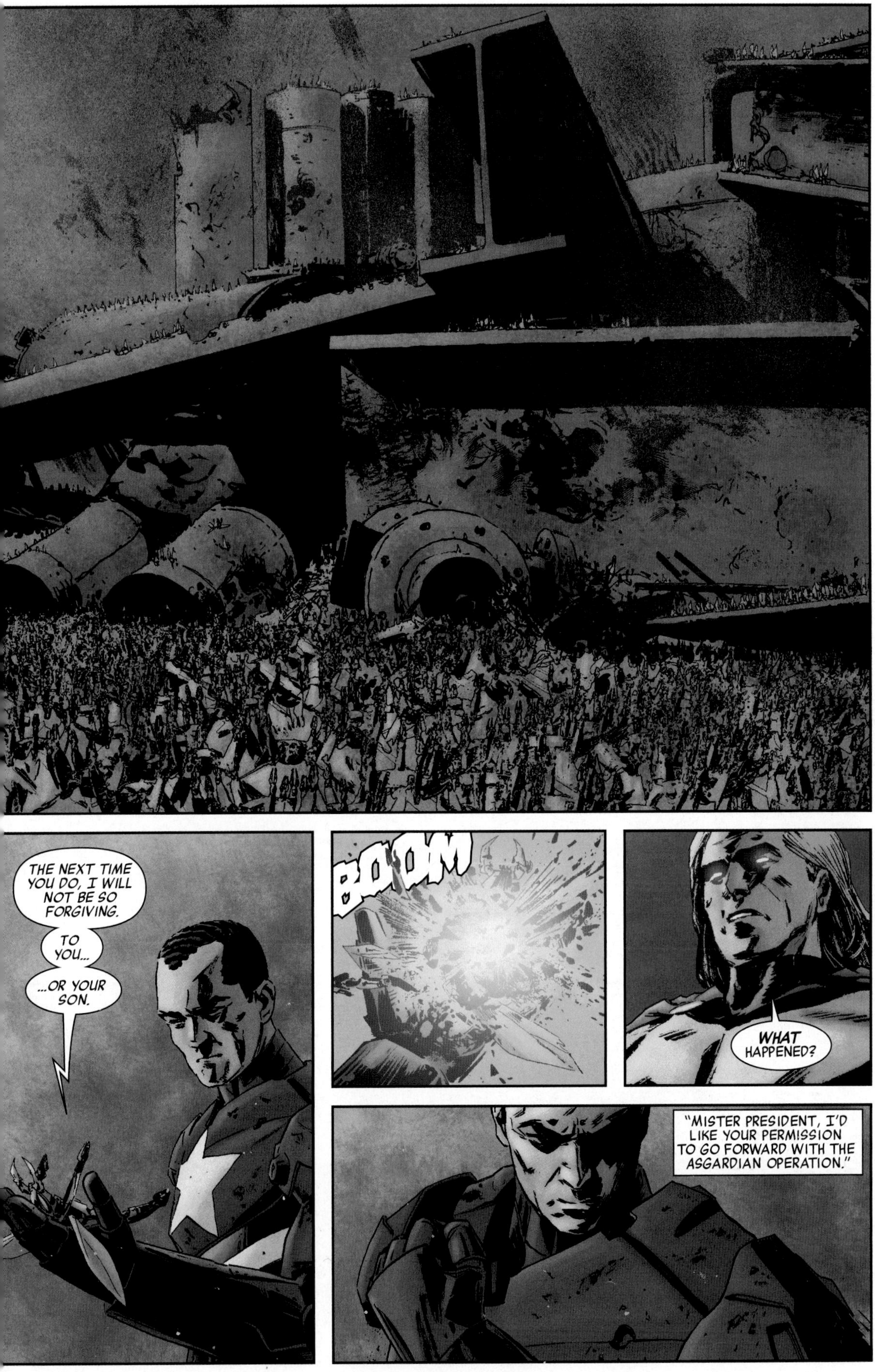
THE NEXT TIME YOU DO, I WILL NOT BE SO FORGIVING.
TO YOU...
...OR YOUR SON.
BOOM
WHAT HAPPENED?
"MISTER PRESIDENT, I'D LIKE YOUR PERMISSION TO GO FORWARD WITH THE ASGARDIAN OPERATION."

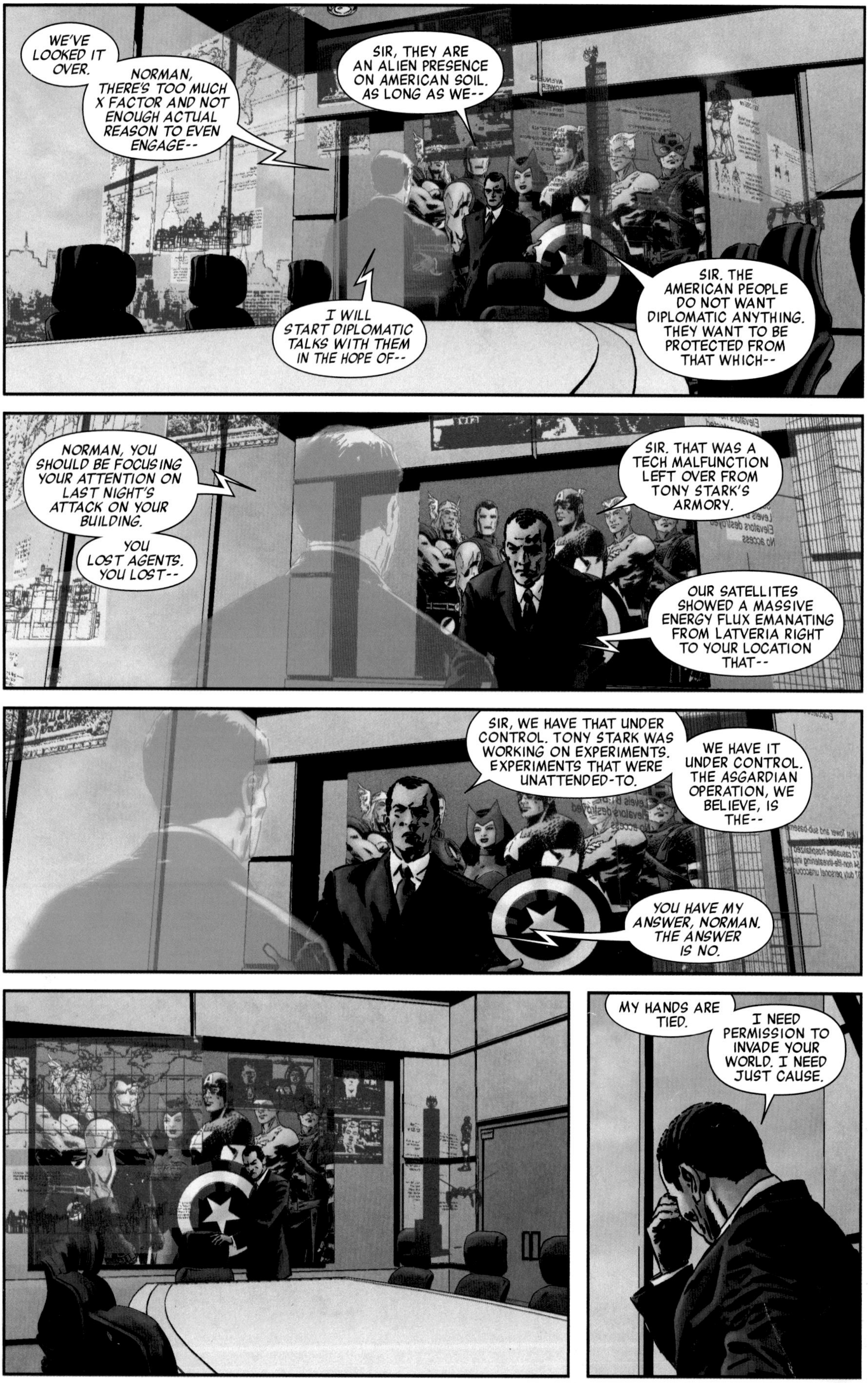
WE'VE LOOKED IT OVER.
NORMAN, THERE'S TOO MUCH X FACTOR AND NOT ENOUGH ACTUAL REASON TO EVEN ENGAGE--
SIR, THEY ARE AN ALIEN PRESENCE ON AMERICAN SOIL. AS LONG AS WE--
I WILL START DIPLOMATIC TALKS WITH THEM IN THE HOPE OF--
SIR. THE AMERICAN PEOPLE DO NOT WANT DIPLOMATIC ANYTHING. THEY WANT TO BE PROTECTED FROM THAT WHICH--
NORMAN, YOU SHOULD BE FOCUSING YOUR ATTENTION ON LAST NIGHT'S ATTACK ON YOUR BUILDING.
YOU LOST AGENTS. YOU LOST--
SIR. THAT WAS A TECH MALFUNCTION LEFT OVER FROM TONY STARK'S ARMORY.
OUR SATELLITES SHOWED A MASSIVE ENERGY FLUX EMANATING FROM LATVERIA RIGHT TO YOUR LOCATION THAT--
SIR, WE HAVE THAT UNDER CONTROL. TONY STARK WAS WORKING ON EXPERIMENTS. EXPERIMENTS THAT WERE UNATTENDED-TO.
WE HAVE IT UNDER CONTROL. THE ASGARDIAN OPERATION, WE BELIEVE, IS THE--
YOU HAVE MY ANSWER, NORMAN. THE ANSWER IS NO.
MY HANDS ARE TIED.
I NEED PERMISSION TO INVADE YOUR WORLD. I NEED JUST CAUSE.

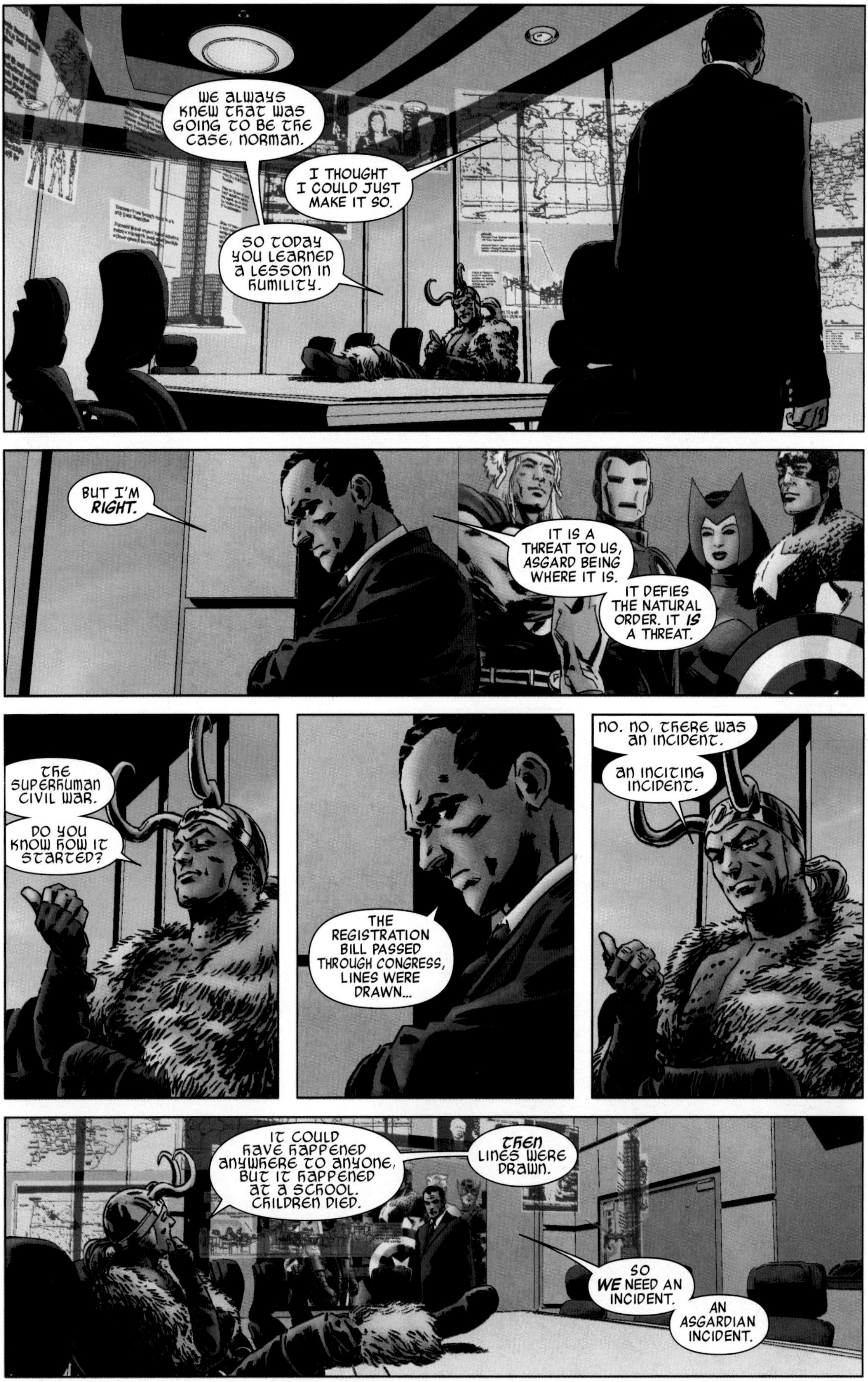
WE ALWAYS KNEW THAT WAS GOING TO BE THE CASE, NORMAN.
I THOUGHT I COULD JUST MAKE IT SO.
SO TODAY YOU LEARNED A LESSON IN HUMILITY.
BUT I'M RIGHT.
IT IS A THREAT TO US, ASGARD BEING WHERE IT IS.
IT DEFIES THE NATURAL ORDER. IT IS A THREAT.
THE SUPERHUMAN CIVIL WAR.
DO YOU KNOW HOW IT STARTED?
THE REGISTRATION BILL PASSED THROUGH CONGRESS, LINES WERE DRAWN...
NO. NO, THERE WAS AN INCIDENT.
AN INCITING INCIDENT.
IT COULD HAVE HAPPENED ANYWHERE TO ANYONE, BUT IT HAPPENED AT A SCHOOL. CHILDREN DIED.
THEN LINES WERE DRAWN.
SO WE NEED AN INCIDENT.
AN ASGARDIAN INCIDENT.

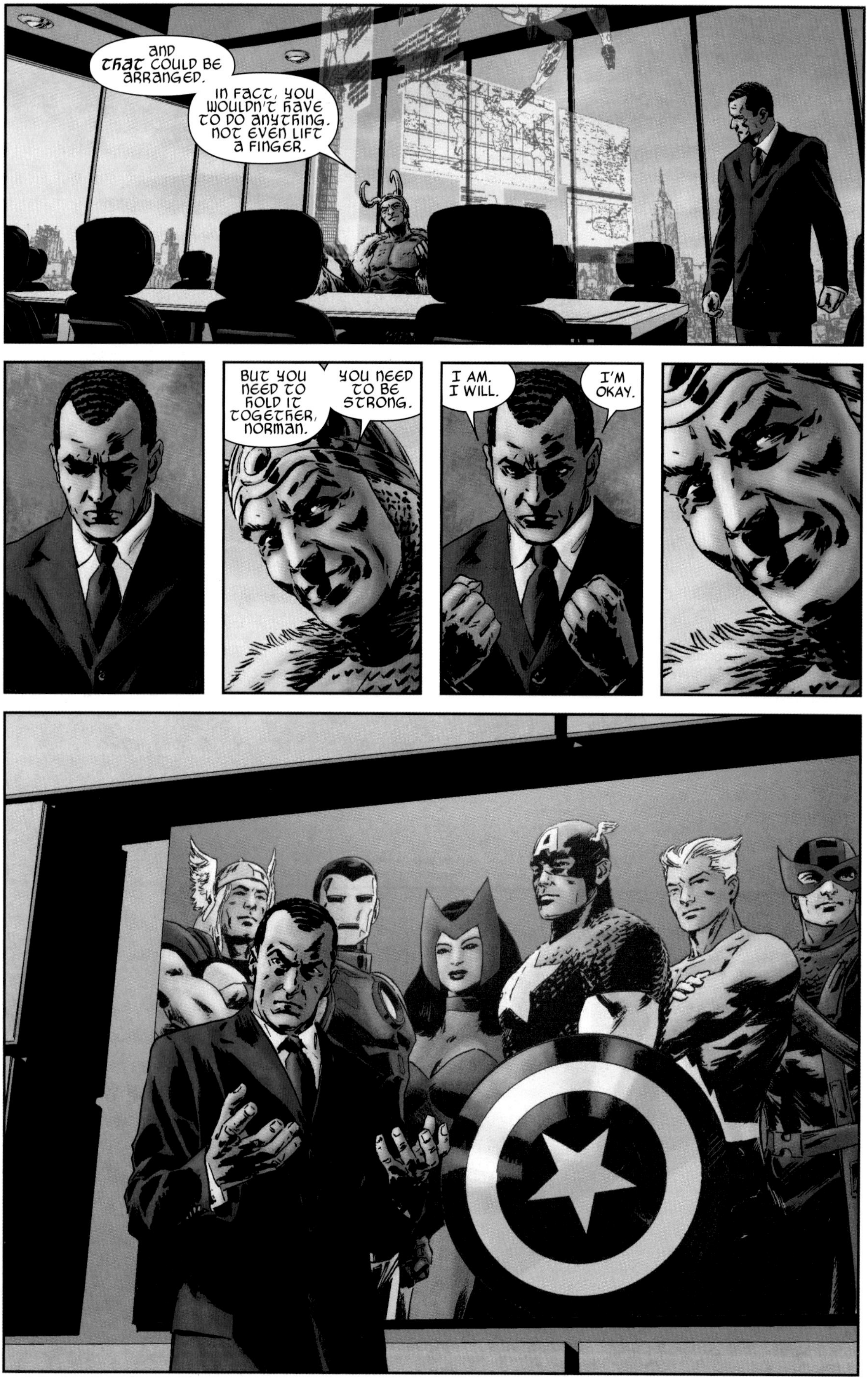
AND THAT COULD BE ARRANGED.
IN FACT, YOU WOULDN'T HAVE TO DO ANYTHING. NOT EVEN LIFT A FINGER.
BUT YOU NEED TO HOLD IT TOGETHER, NORMAN.
YOU NEED TO BE STRONG.
I AM. I WILL.
I'M OKAY.

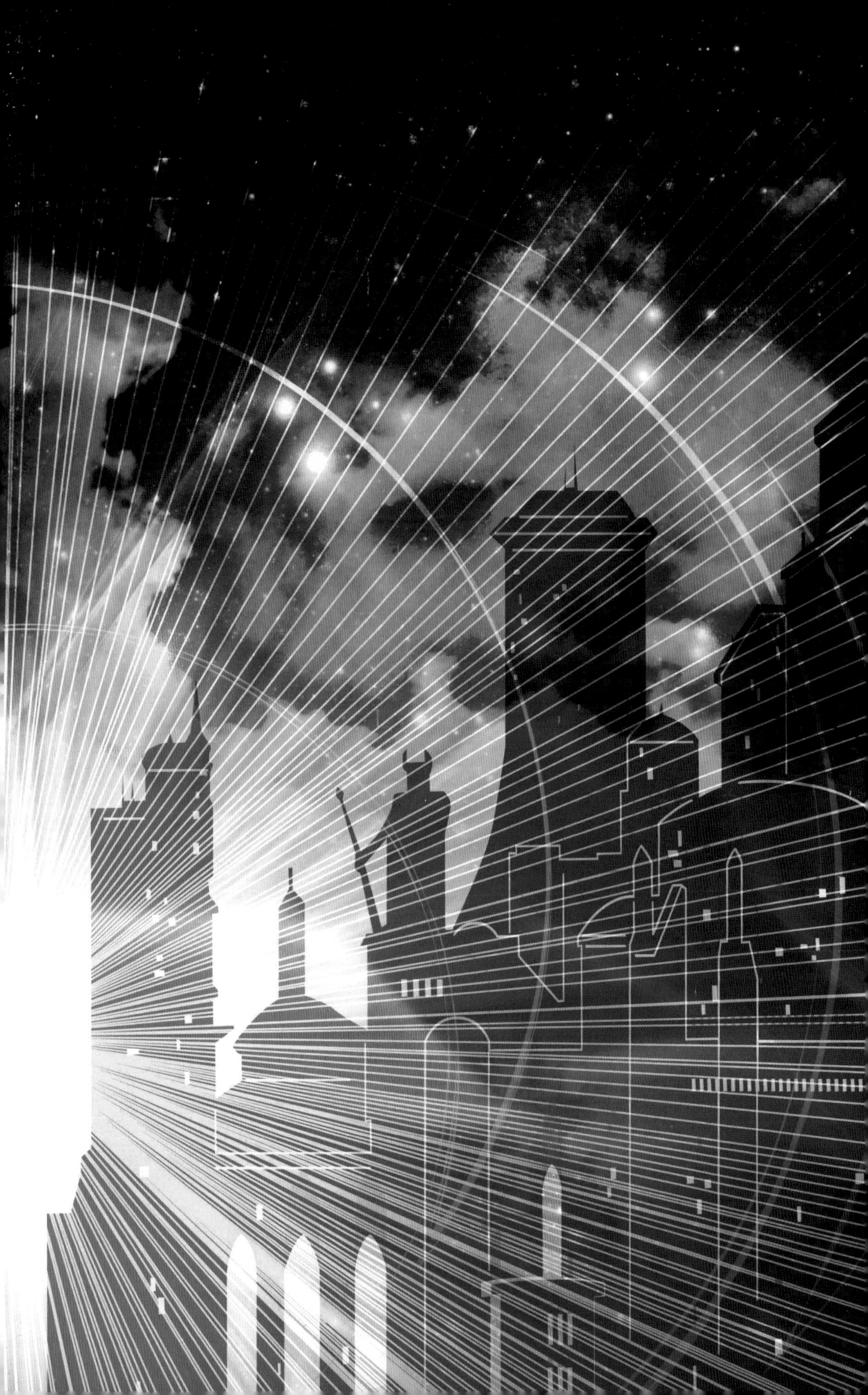

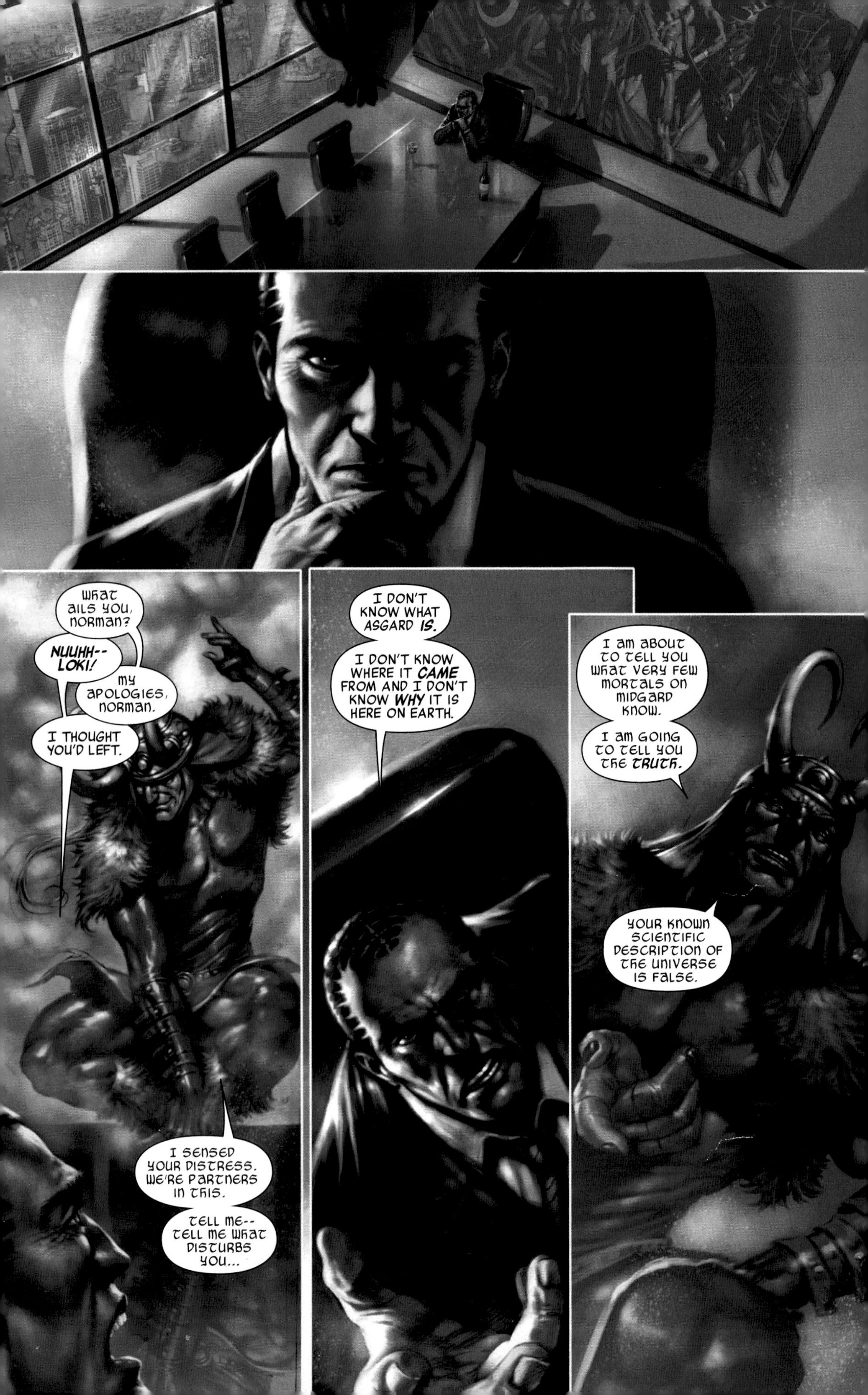
WHAT AILS YOU, NORMAN?
NUUHH-- LOKI!
MY APOLOGIES, NORMAN.
I THOUGHT YOU'D LEFT.
I SENSED YOUR DISTRESS. WE'RE PARTNERS IN THIS.
TELL ME-- TELL ME WHAT DISTURBS YOU...
I DON'T KNOW WHAT ASGARD IS.
I DON'T KNOW WHERE IT CAME FROM AND I DON'T KNOW WHY IT IS HERE ON EARTH.
I AM ABOUT TO TELL YOU WHAT VERY FEW MORTALS ON MIDGARD KNOW.
I AM GOING TO TELL YOU THE TRUTH.
YOUR KNOWN SCIENTIFIC DESCRIPTION OF THE UNIVERSE IS FALSE.

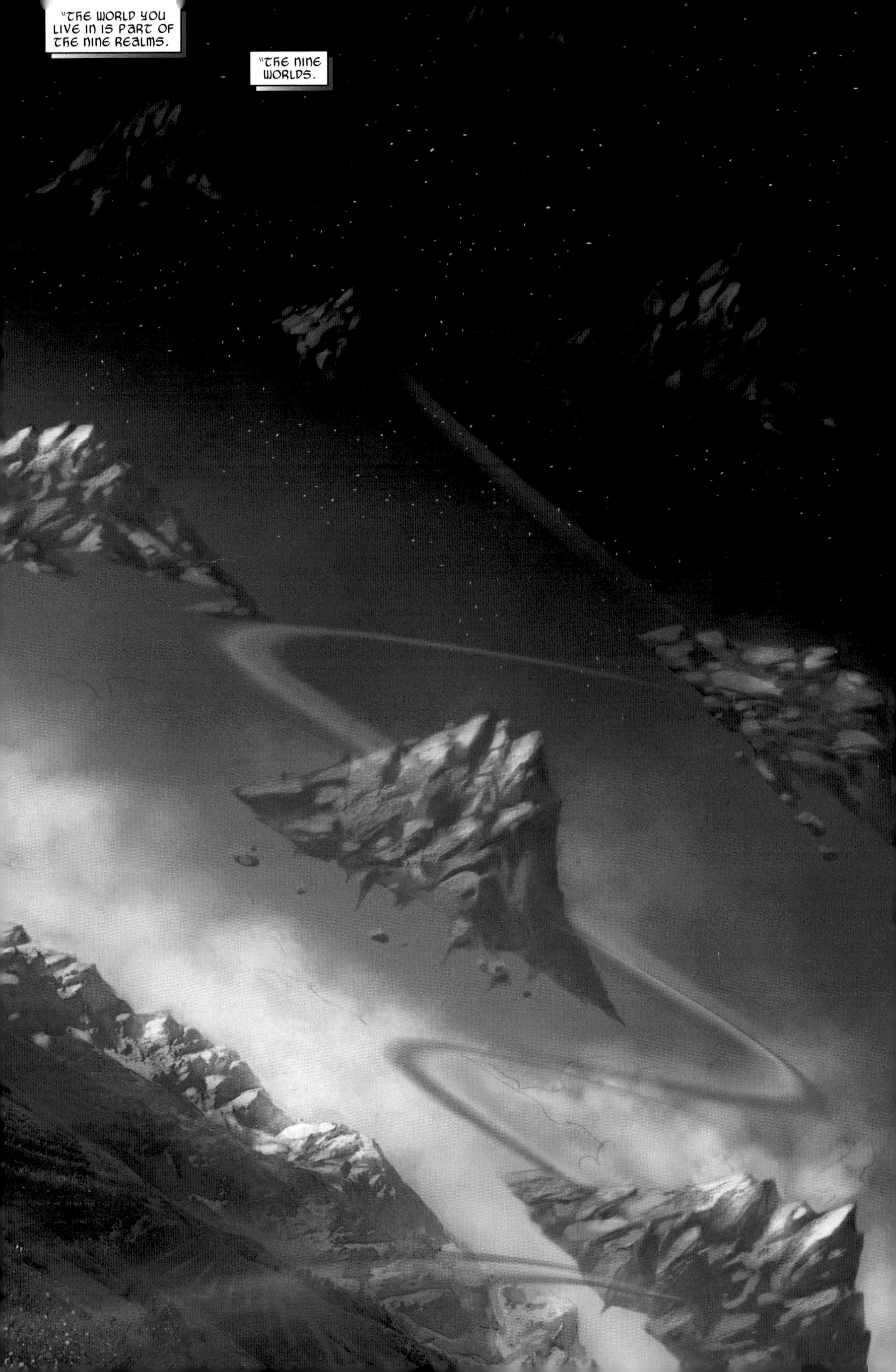
"THE WORLD YOU LIVE IN IS PART OF THE NINE REALMS.
"THE NINE WORLDS.

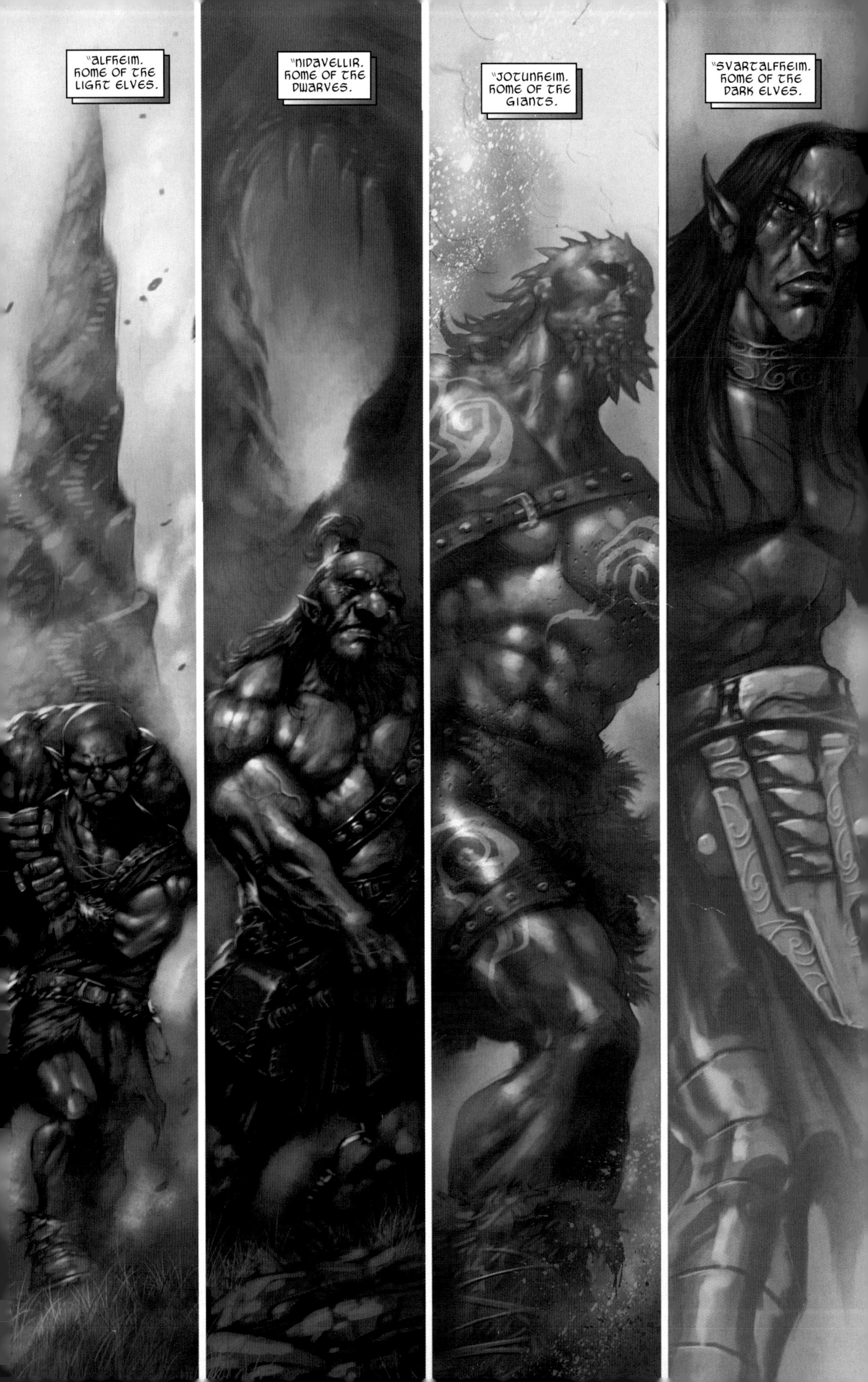
"ALFHEIM. HOME OF THE LIGHT ELVES.
"NIDAVELLIR. HOME OF THE DWARVES.
"JOTUNHEIM. HOME OF THE GIANTS.
"SVARTALFHEIM. HOME OF THE DARK ELVES.

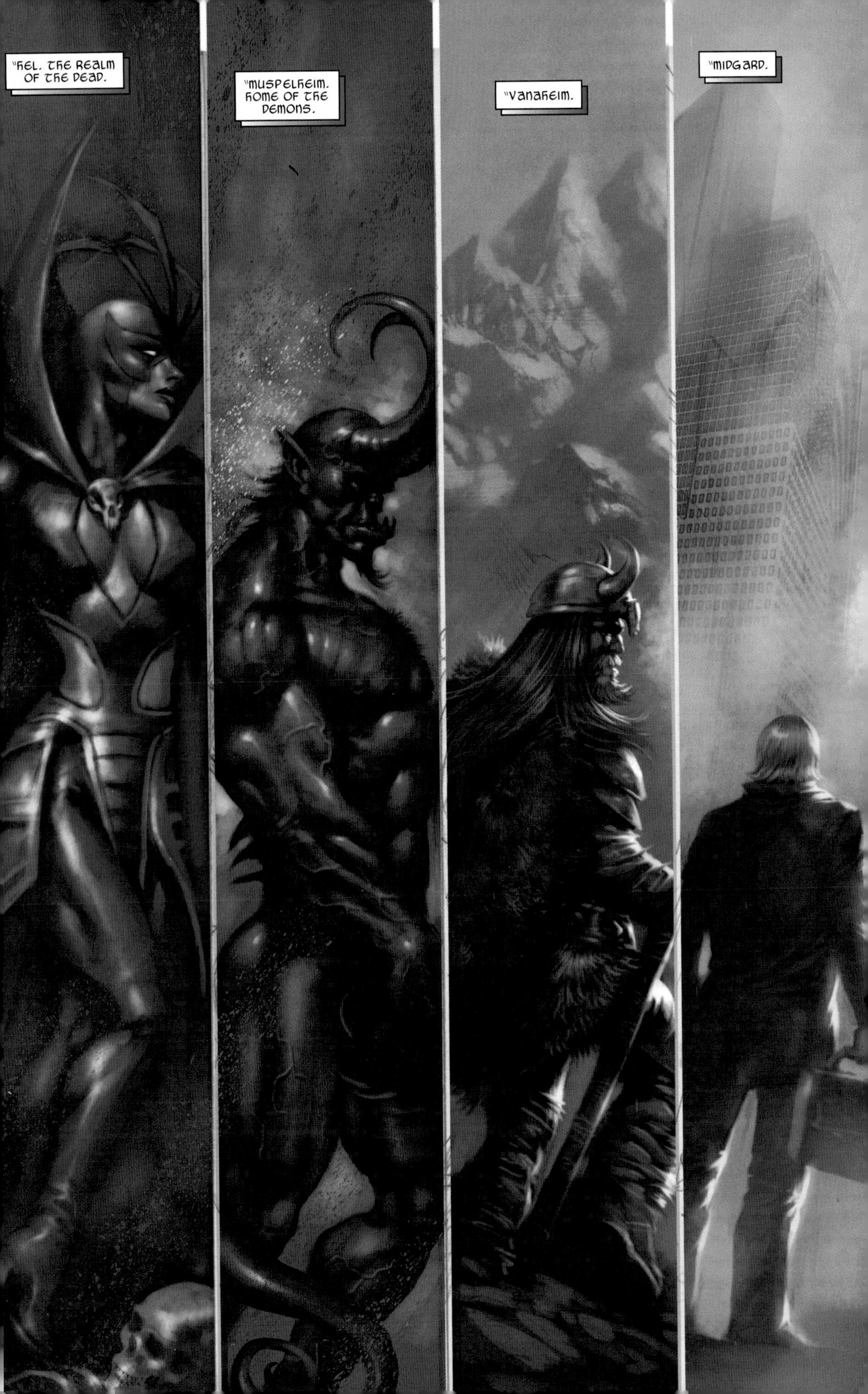
"HEL. THE REALM OF THE DEAD.
"MUSPELHEIM. HOME OF THE DEMONS.
"VANAHEIM.
"MIDGARD.

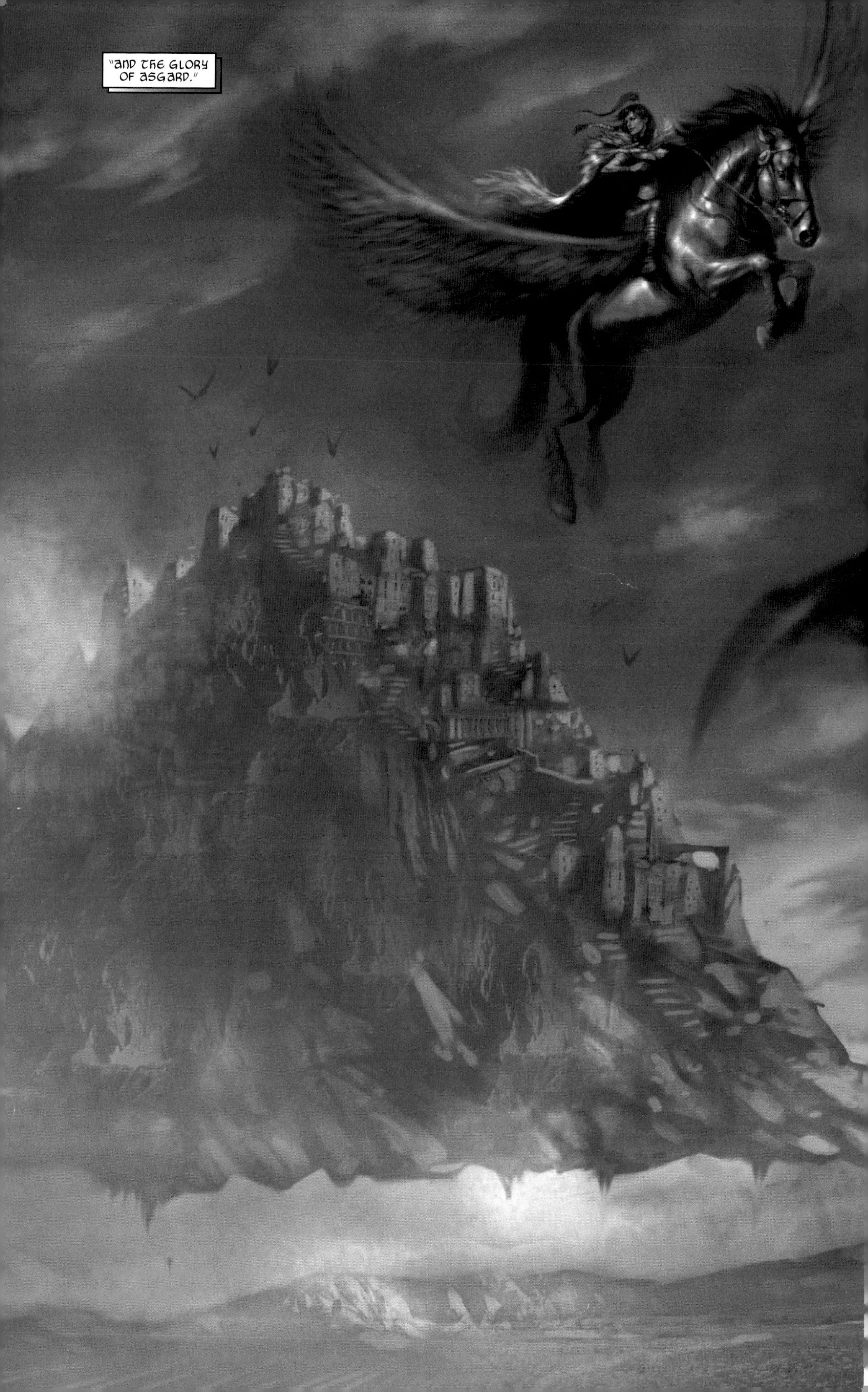
"AND THE GLORY OF ASGARD."

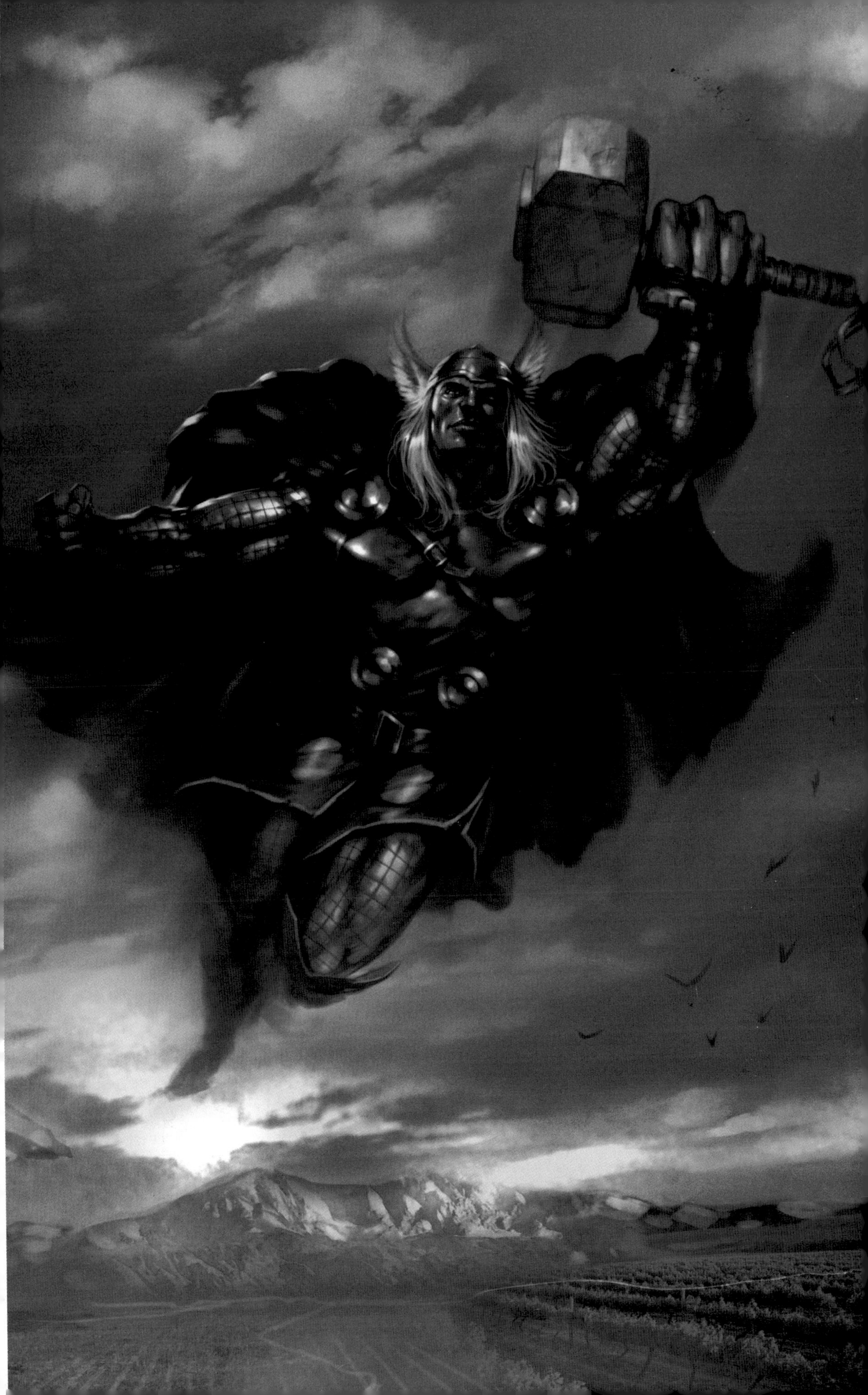

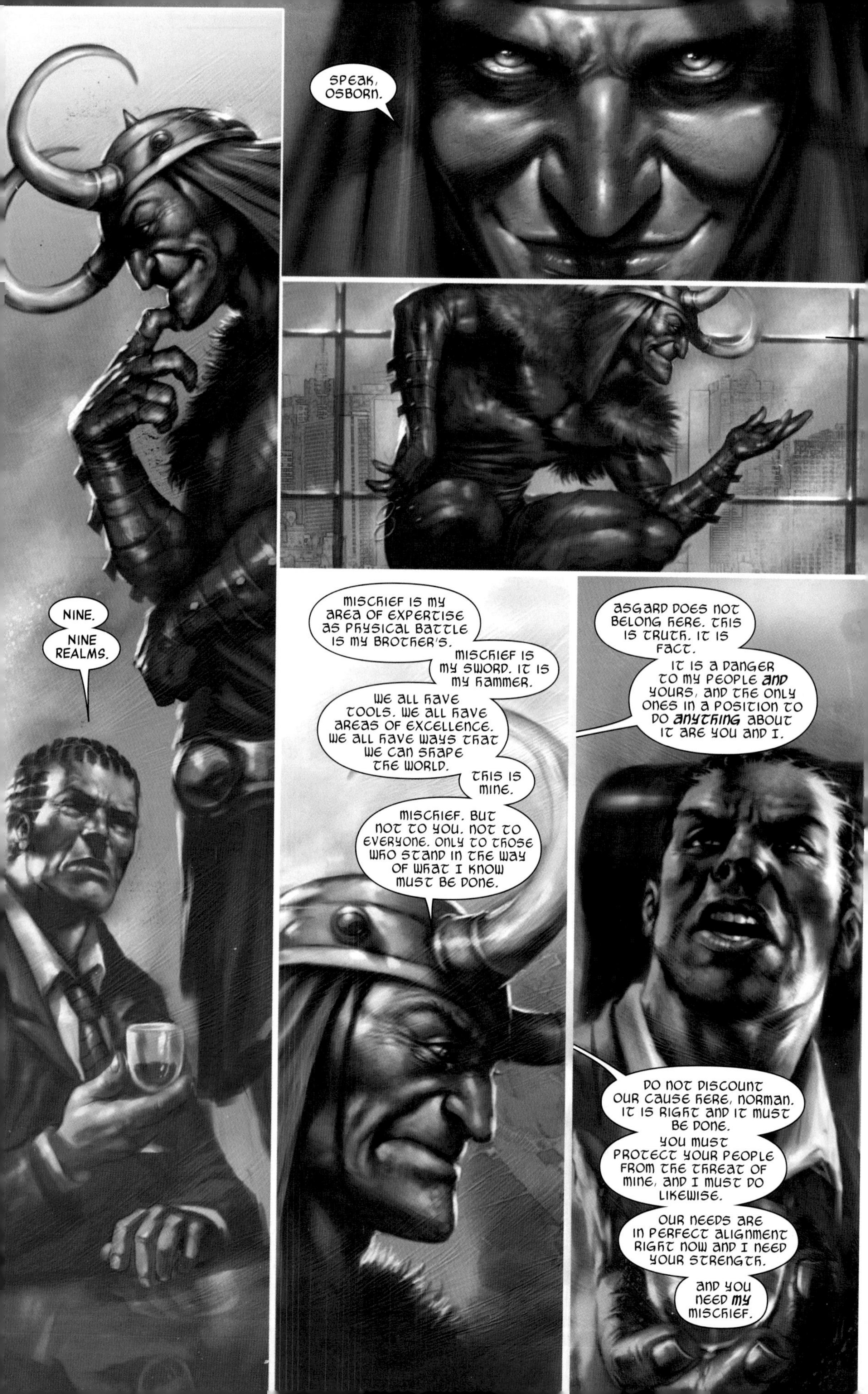

SPEAK, OSBORN.
NINE.
NINE REALMS.
MISCHIEF IS MY AREA OF EXPERTISE AS PHYSICAL BATTLE IS MY BROTHER'S.
MISCHIEF IS MY SWORD. IT IS MY HAMMER.
WE ALL HAVE TOOLS. WE ALL HAVE AREAS OF EXCELLENCE. WE ALL HAVE WAYS THAT WE CAN SHAPE THE WORLD.
THIS IS MINE.
MISCHIEF. BUT NOT TO YOU. NOT TO EVERYONE. ONLY TO THOSE WHO STAND IN THE WAY OF WHAT I KNOW MUST BE DONE.
ASGARD DOES NOT BELONG HERE. THIS IS TRUTH. IT IS FACT.
IT IS A DANGER TO MY PEOPLE AND YOURS, AND THE ONLY ONES IN A POSITION TO DO ANYTHING ABOUT IT ARE YOU AND I.
DO NOT DISCOUNT OUR CAUSE HERE, NORMAN. IT IS RIGHT AND IT MUST BE DONE.
YOU MUST PROTECT YOUR PEOPLE FROM THE THREAT OF MINE, AND I MUST DO LIKEWISE.
OUR NEEDS ARE IN PERFECT ALIGNMENT RIGHT NOW AND I NEED YOUR STRENGTH.
AND YOU NEED MY MISCHIEF.

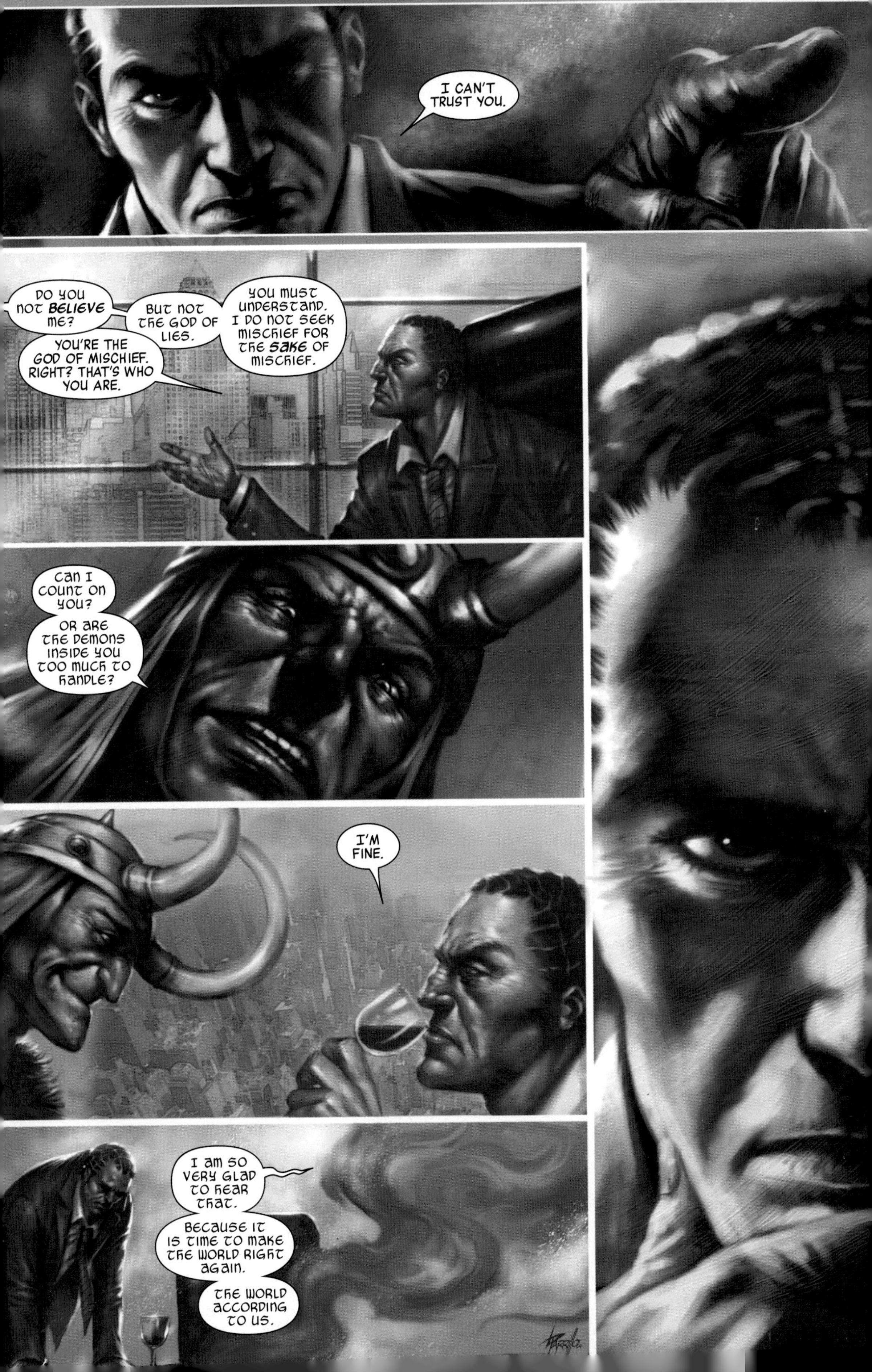
I CAN'T TRUST YOU.
DO YOU NOT BELIEVE ME?
BUT NOT THE GOD OF LIES.
YOU'RE THE GOD OF MISCHIEF. RIGHT? THAT'S WHO YOU ARE.
YOU MUST UNDERSTAND. I DO NOT SEEK MISCHIEF FOR THE SAKE OF MISCHIEF.
CAN I COUNT ON YOU?
OR ARE THE DEMONS INSIDE YOU TOO MUCH TO HANDLE?
I'M FINE.
I AM SO VERY GLAD TO HEAR THAT.
BECAUSE IT IS TIME TO MAKE THE WORLD RIGHT AGAIN.
THE WORLD ACCORDING TO US.

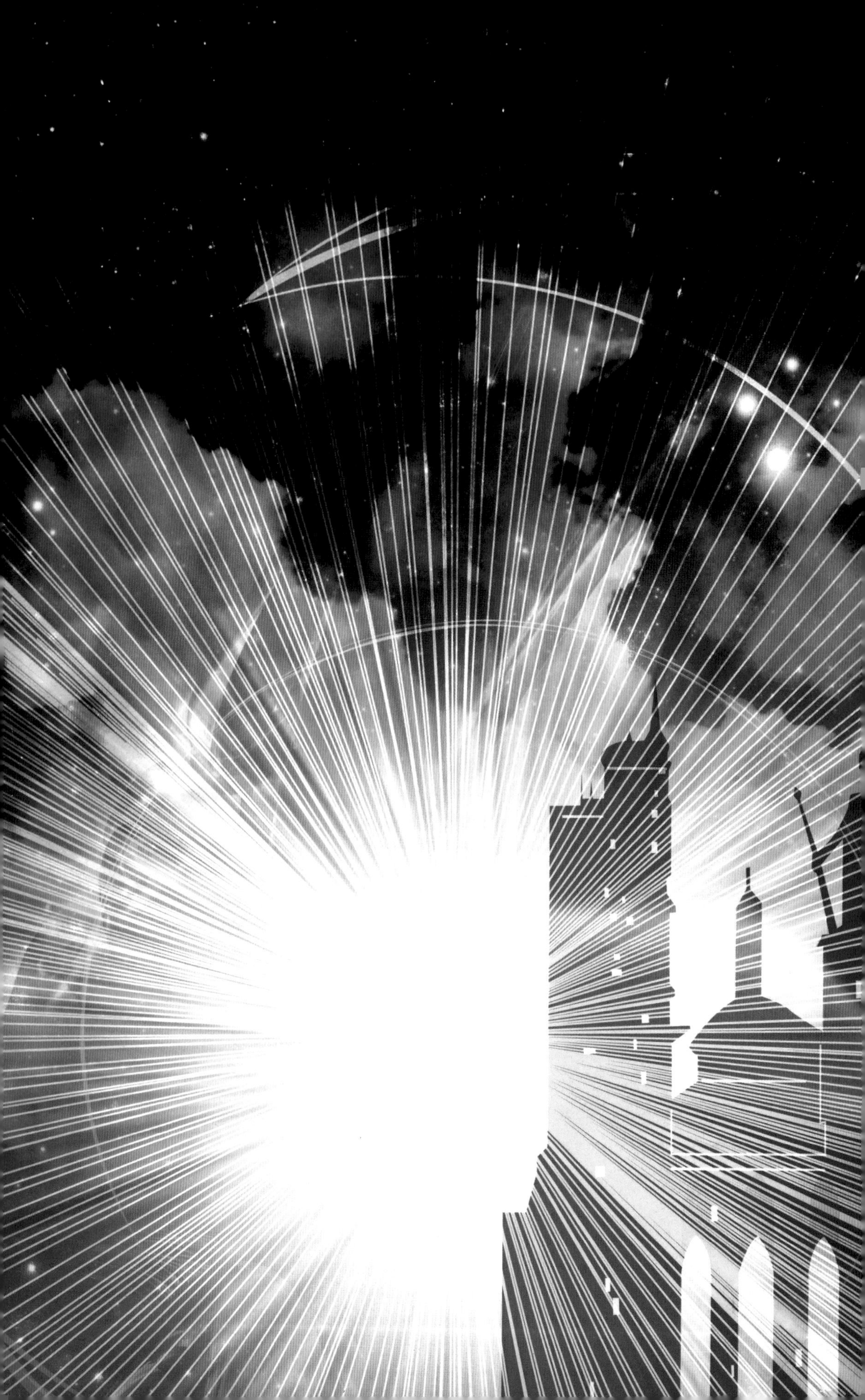

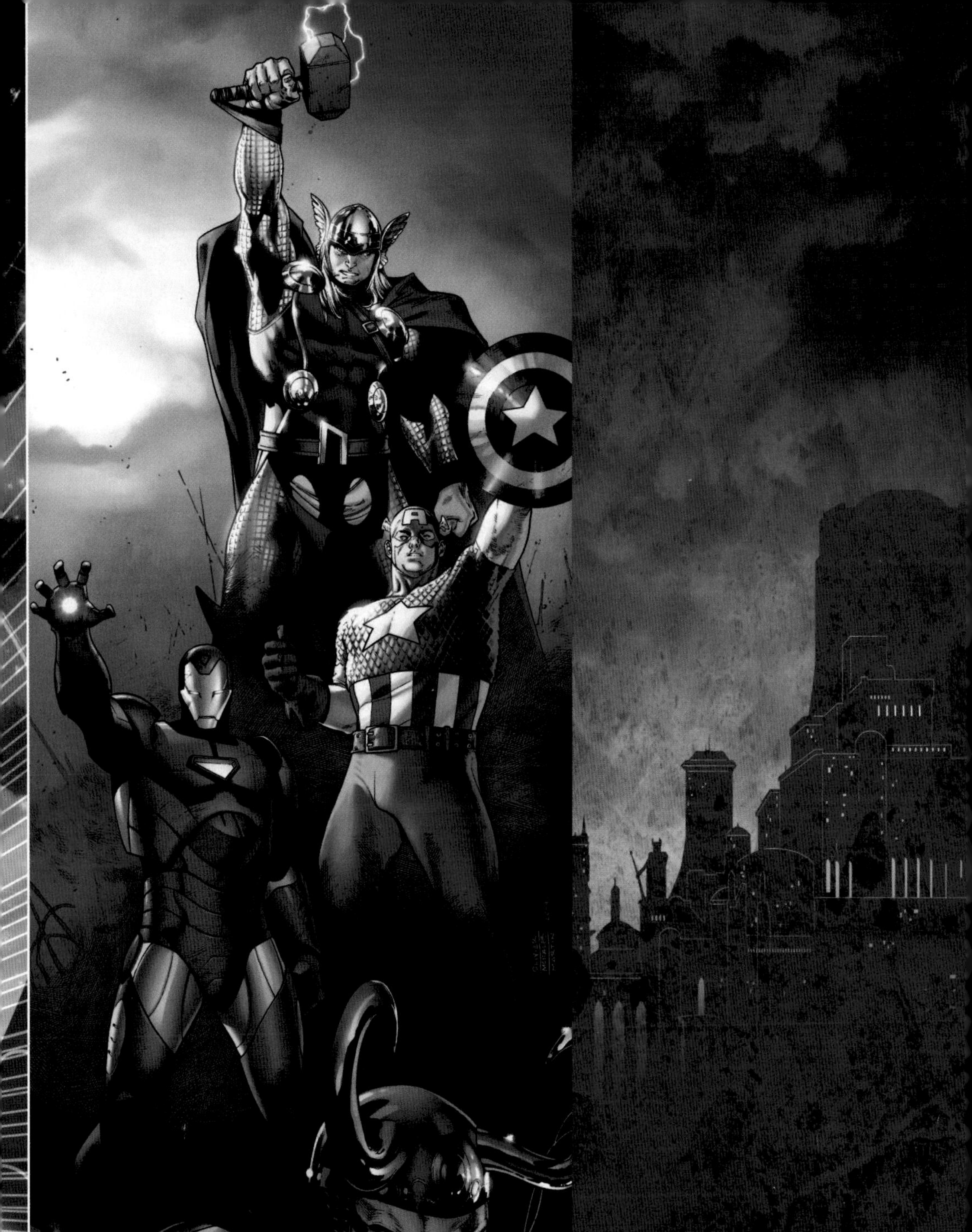

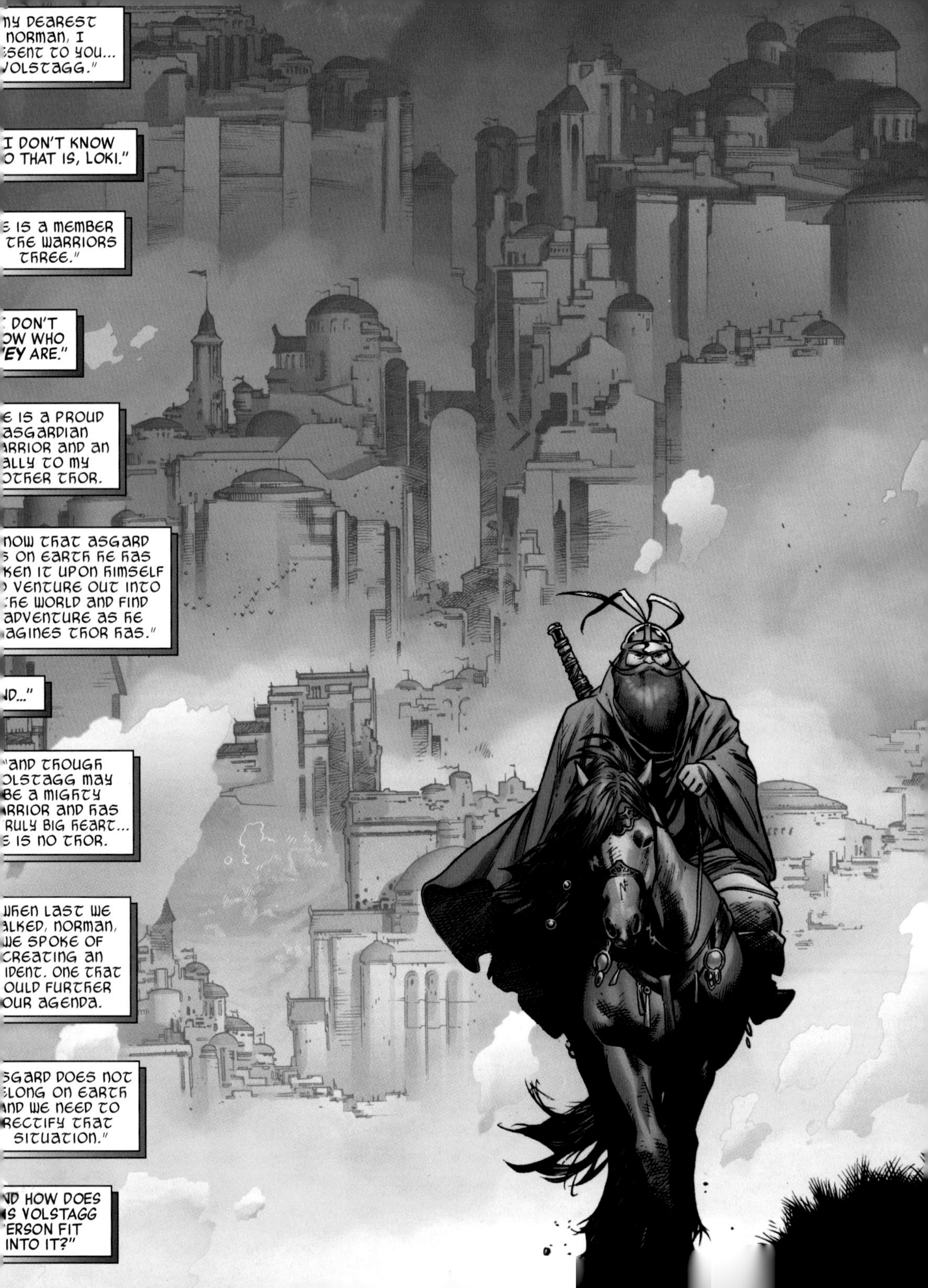
MY DEAREST NORMAN, I SENT TO YOU... VOLSTAGG."
I DON'T KNOW O THAT IS, LOKI."
E IS A MEMBER THE WARRIORS THREE."
DON'T OW WHO EY ARE."
E IS A PROUD ASGARDIAN ARRIOR AND AN ALLY TO MY OTHER THOR.
NOW THAT ASGARD S ON EARTH HE HAS KEN IT UPON HIMSELF O VENTURE OUT INTO HE WORLD AND FIND ADVENTURE AS HE AGINES THOR HAS."
ND..."
"AND THOUGH OLSTAGG MAY BE A MIGHTY ARRIOR AND HAS RULY BIG HEART... E IS NO THOR.
WHEN LAST WE ALKED, NORMAN, WE SPOKE OF CREATING AN IDENT. ONE THAT OULD FURTHER OUR AGENDA.
SGARD DOES NOT ELONG ON EARTH AND WE NEED TO RECTIFY THAT SITUATION."
ND HOW DOES S VOLSTAGG ERSON FIT INTO IT?"

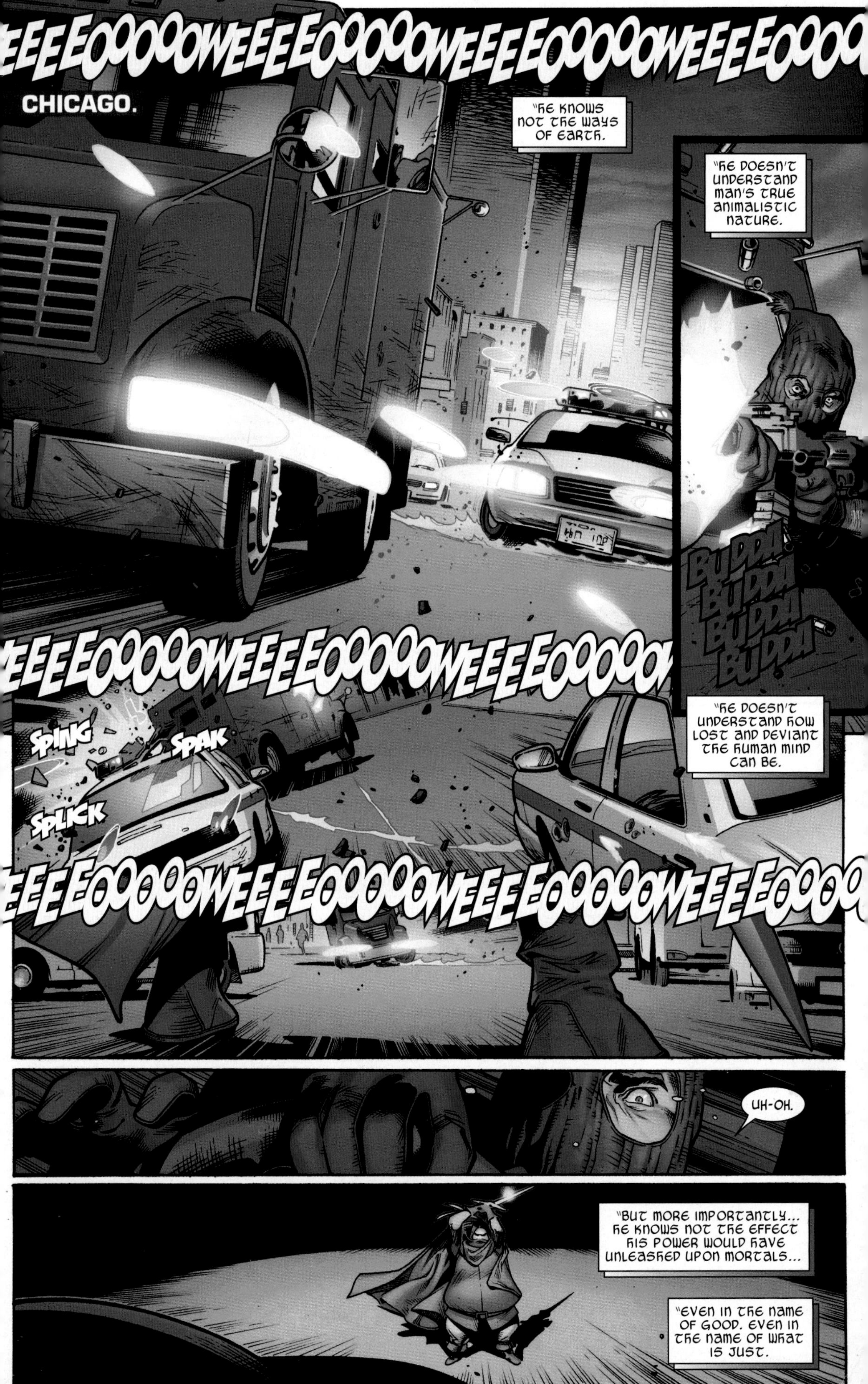
EEEEOOOOOWEEEEOOOOOWEEEEOOOOOWEEEEOOOO
CHICAGO.
"HE KNOWS NOT THE WAYS OF EARTH.
"HE DOESN'T UNDERSTAND MAN'S TRUE ANIMALISTIC NATURE.
BUDDA BUDDA BUDDA BUDDA
EEEEOOOOOWEEEEOOOOOWEEEEOOOOO
"HE DOESN'T UNDERSTAND HOW LOST AND DEVIANT THE HUMAN MIND CAN BE.
SPING
SPAK
SPLICK
EEEEOOOOOWEEEEOOOOOWEEEEOOOOOWEEEEOOOO
UH-OH.
"BUT MORE IMPORTANTLY... HE KNOWS NOT THE EFFECT HIS POWER WOULD HAVE UNLEASHED UPON MORTALS...
"EVEN IN THE NAME OF GOOD. EVEN IN THE NAME OF WHAT IS JUST.

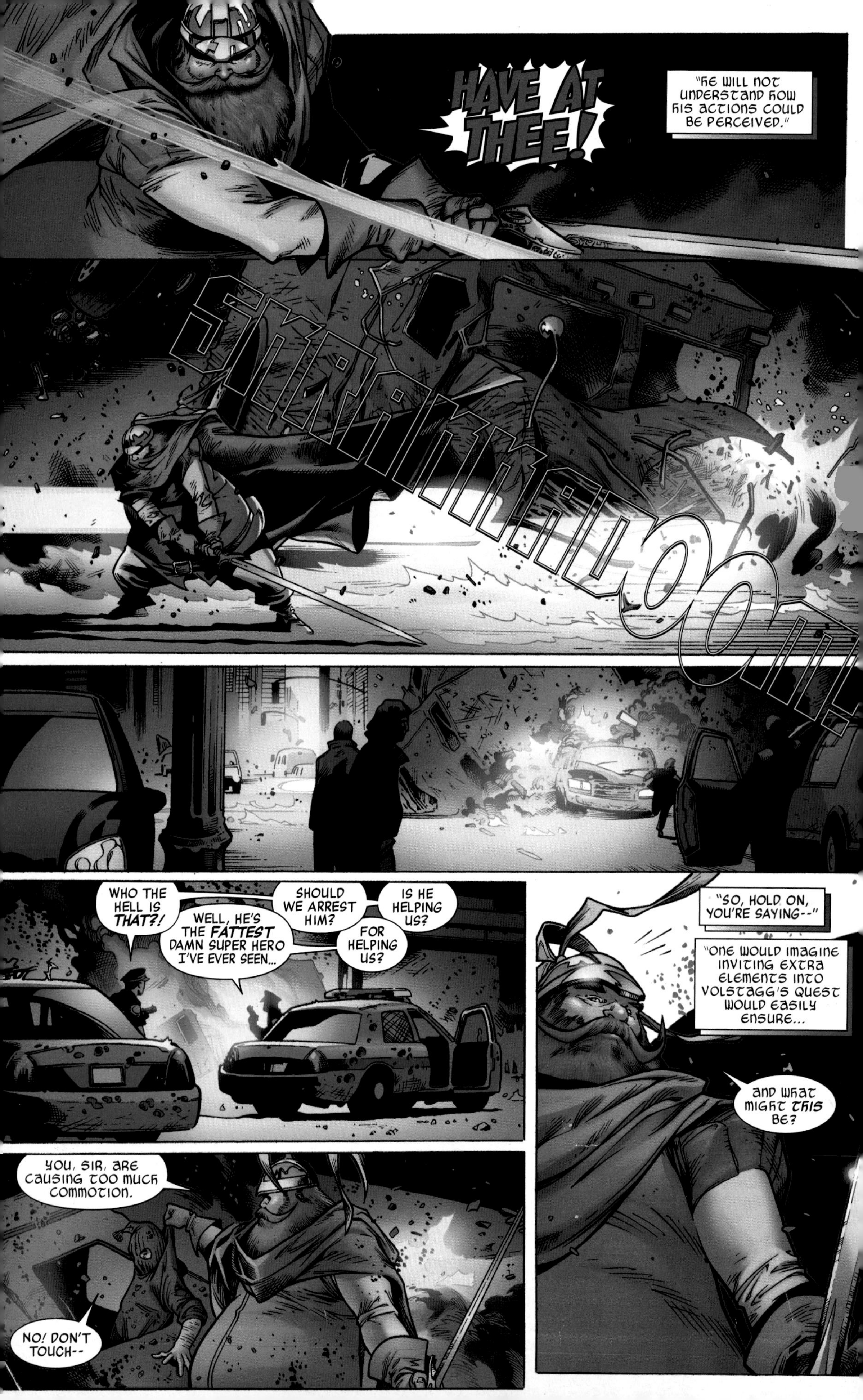
HAVE AT THEE!
"HE WILL NOT UNDERSTAND HOW HIS ACTIONS COULD BE PERCEIVED."
WHO THE HELL IS THAT?!
SHOULD WE ARREST HIM?
IS HE HELPING US?
WELL, HE'S THE FATTEST DAMN SUPER HERO I'VE EVER SEEN...
FOR HELPING US?
"SO, HOLD ON, YOU'RE SAYING--"
"ONE WOULD IMAGINE INVITING EXTRA ELEMENTS INTO VOLSTAGG'S QUEST WOULD EASILY ENSURE...
AND WHAT MIGHT THIS BE?
YOU, SIR, ARE CAUSING TOO MUCH COMMOTION.
NO! DON'T TOUCH--

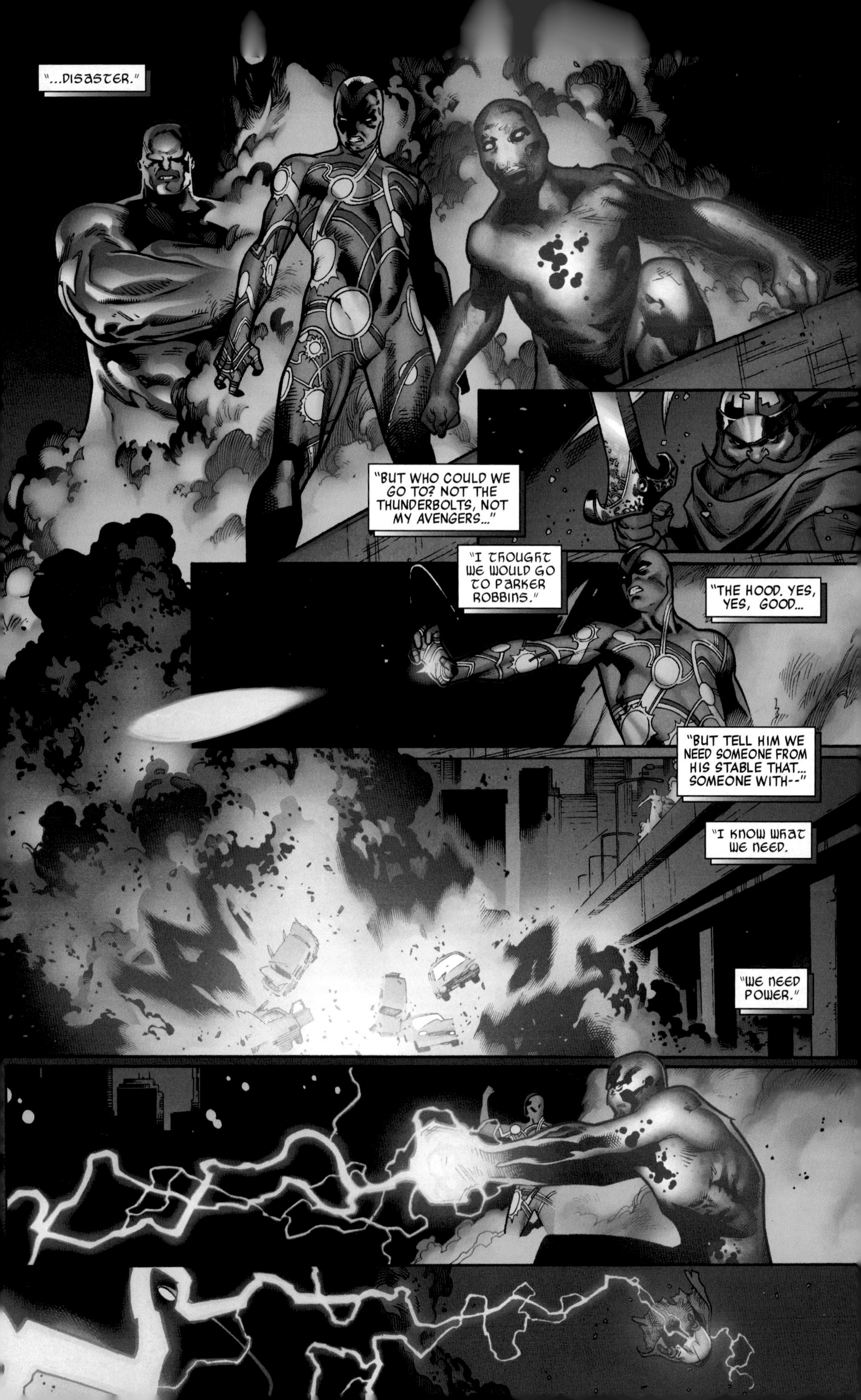
"...DISASTER."
"BUT WHO COULD WE GO TO? NOT THE THUNDERBOLTS, NOT MY AVENGERS..."
"I THOUGHT WE WOULD GO TO PARKER ROBBINS."
"THE HOOD. YES, YES, GOOD...
"BUT TELL HIM WE NEED SOMEONE FROM HIS STABLE THAT... SOMEONE WITH--"
"I KNOW WHAT WE NEED.
"WE NEED POWER."

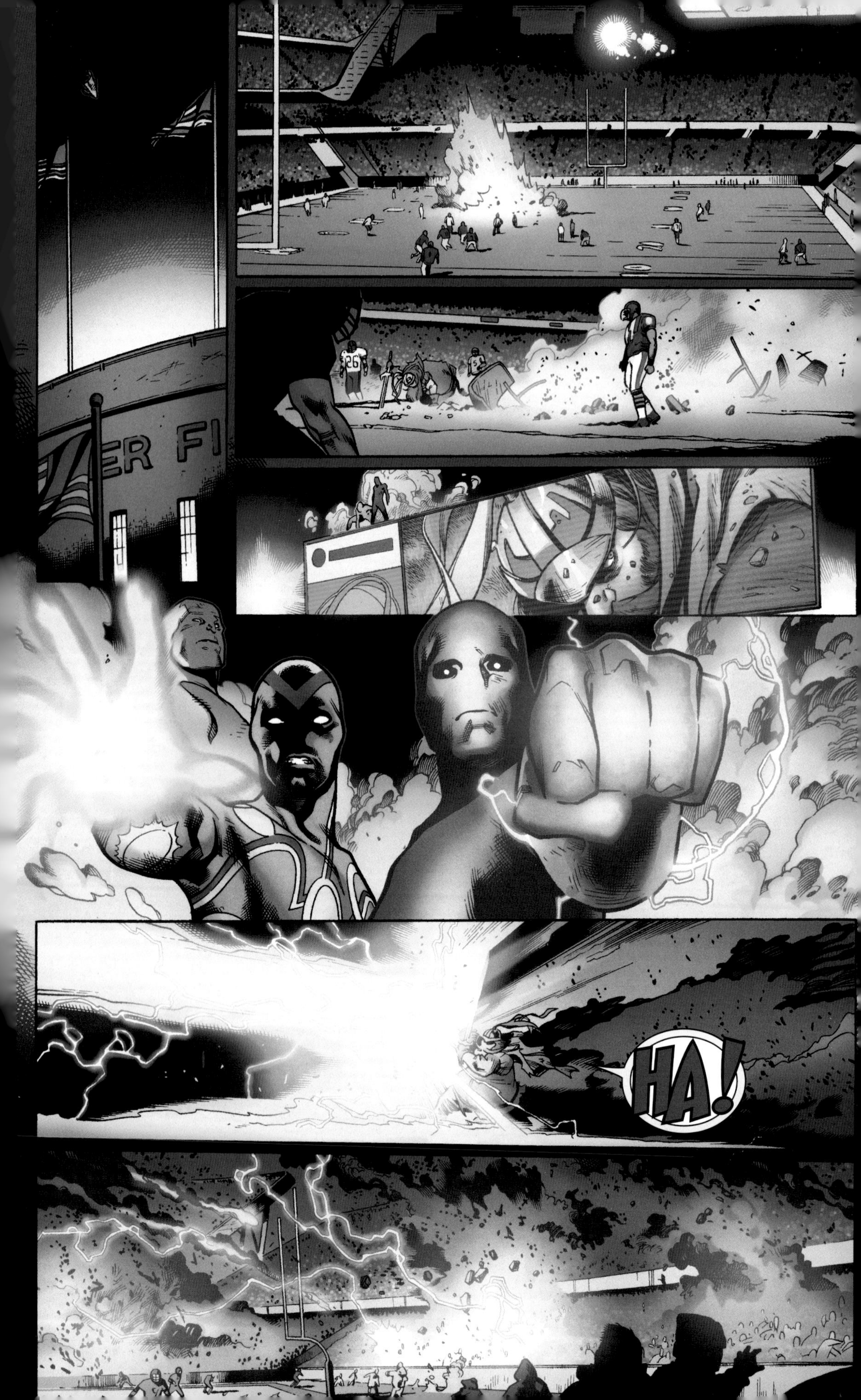
ER FI
HA!

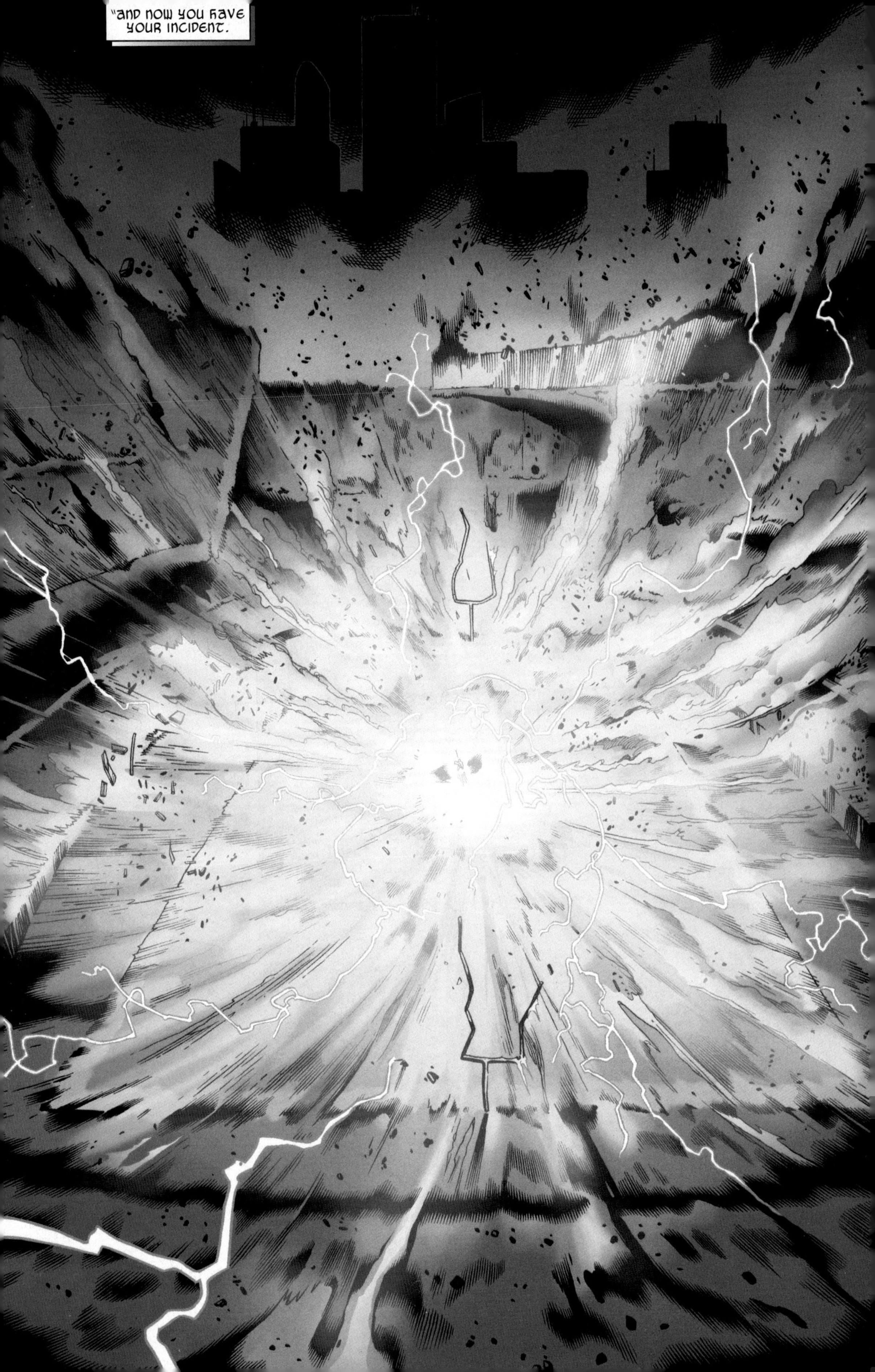
"AND NOW YOU HAVE YOUR INCIDENT.

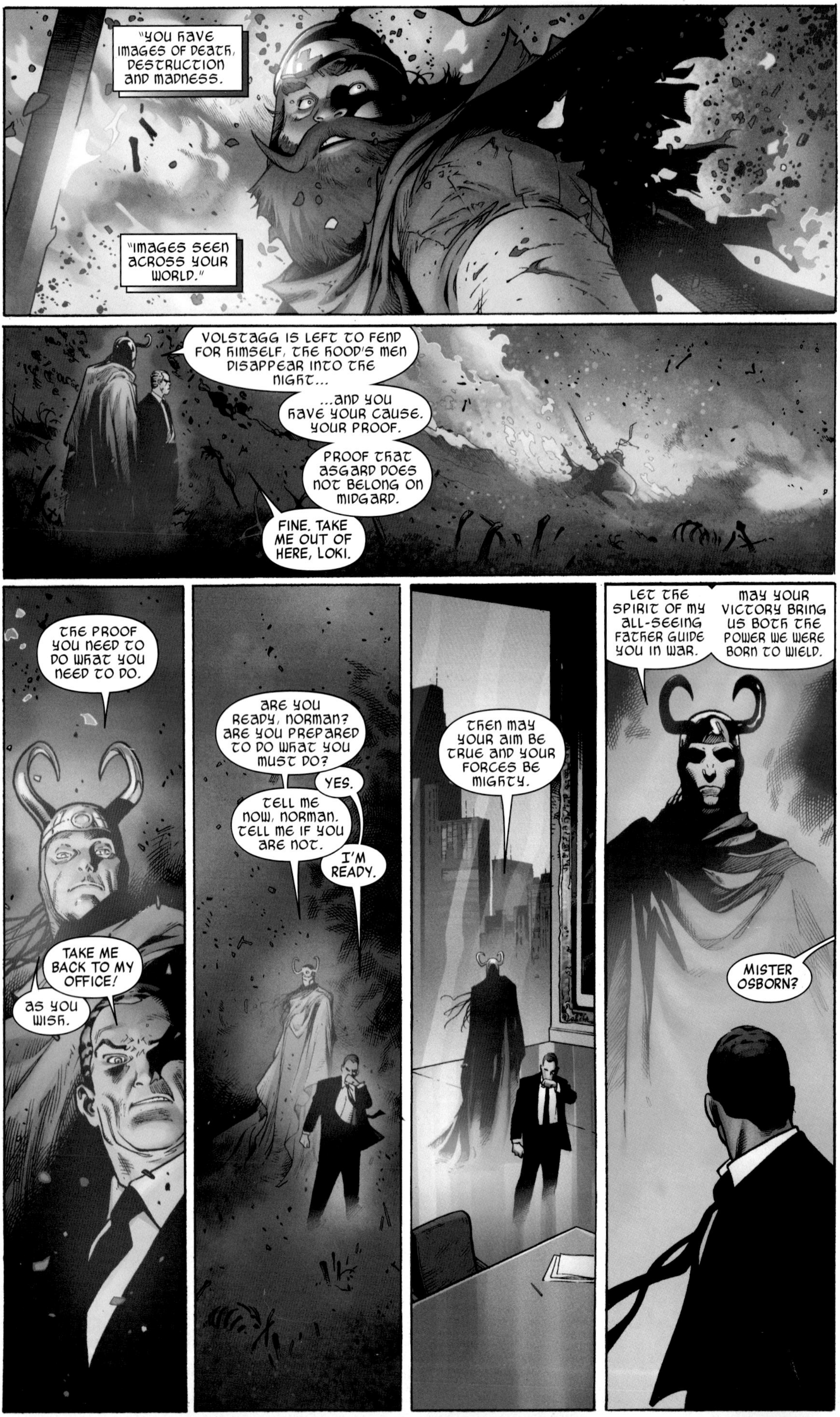
"YOU HAVE IMAGES OF DEATH, DESTRUCTION AND MADNESS.
"IMAGES SEEN ACROSS YOUR WORLD."
VOLSTAGG IS LEFT TO FEND FOR HIMSELF, THE HOOD'S MEN DISAPPEAR INTO THE NIGHT...
...AND YOU HAVE YOUR CAUSE. YOUR PROOF.
PROOF THAT ASGARD DOES NOT BELONG ON MIDGARD.
FINE. TAKE ME OUT OF HERE, LOKI.
THE PROOF YOU NEED TO DO WHAT YOU NEED TO DO.
TAKE ME BACK TO MY OFFICE!
AS YOU WISH.
ARE YOU READY, NORMAN? ARE YOU PREPARED TO DO WHAT YOU MUST DO?
YES.
TELL ME NOW, NORMAN. TELL ME IF YOU ARE NOT.
I'M READY.
THEN MAY YOUR AIM BE TRUE AND YOUR FORCES BE MIGHTY.
LET THE SPIRIT OF MY ALL-SEEING FATHER GUIDE YOU IN WAR.
MAY YOUR VICTORY BRING US BOTH THE POWER WE WERE BORN TO WIELD.
MISTER OSBORN?

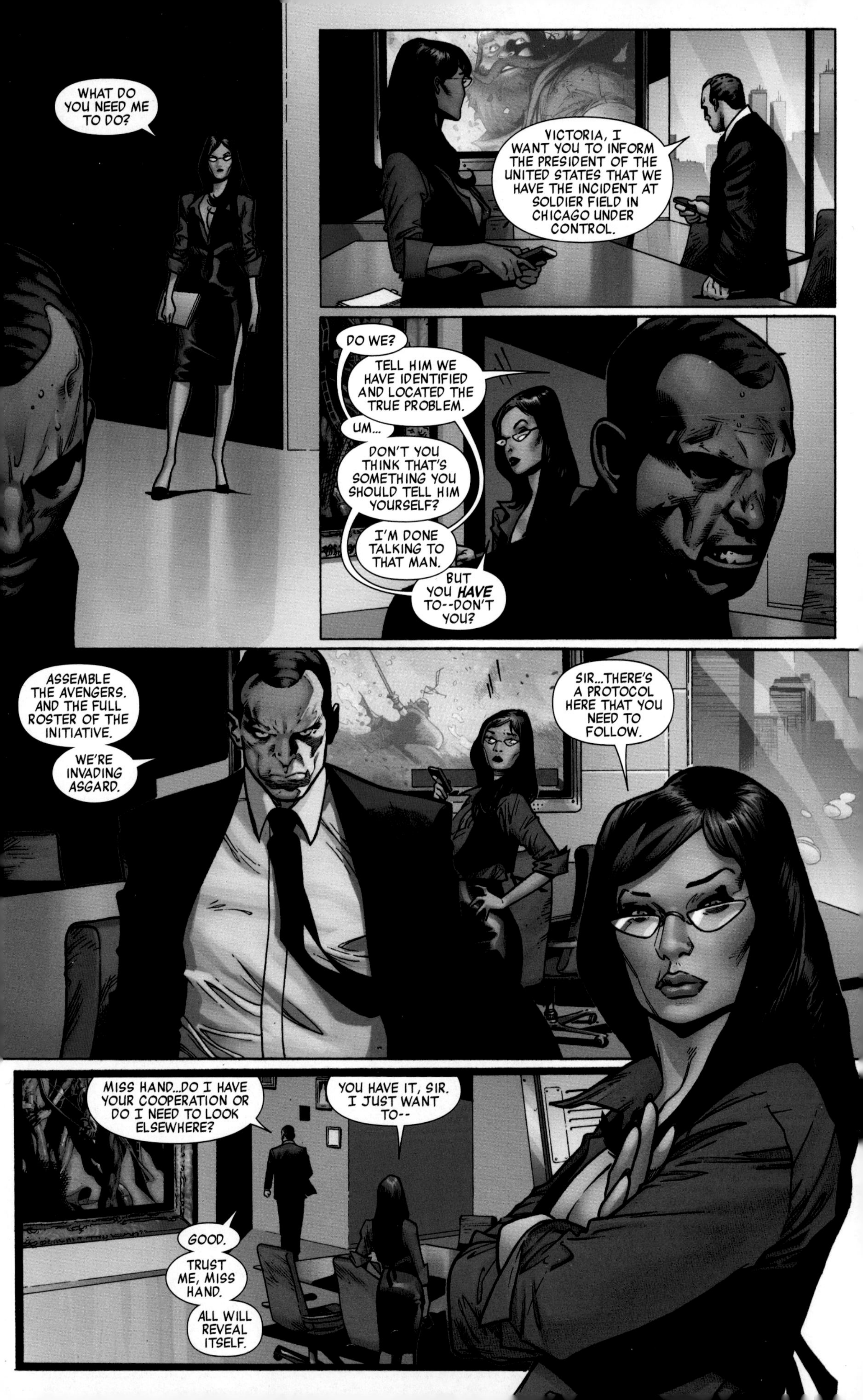

WHAT DO YOU NEED ME TO DO?
VICTORIA, I WANT YOU TO INFORM THE PRESIDENT OF THE UNITED STATES THAT WE HAVE THE INCIDENT AT SOLDIER FIELD IN CHICAGO UNDER CONTROL.
DO WE?
TELL HIM WE HAVE IDENTIFIED AND LOCATED THE TRUE PROBLEM.
UM...
DON'T YOU THINK THAT'S SOMETHING YOU SHOULD TELL HIM YOURSELF?
I'M DONE TALKING TO THAT MAN.
BUT YOU **HAVE** TO--DON'T YOU?
ASSEMBLE THE AVENGERS. AND THE FULL ROSTER OF THE INITIATIVE.
WE'RE INVADING ASGARD.
SIR...THERE'S A PROTOCOL HERE THAT YOU NEED TO FOLLOW.
MISS HAND...DO I HAVE YOUR COOPERATION OR DO I NEED TO LOOK ELSEWHERE?
YOU HAVE IT, SIR. I JUST WANT TO--
GOOD.
TRUST ME, MISS HAND.
ALL WILL REVEAL ITSELF.

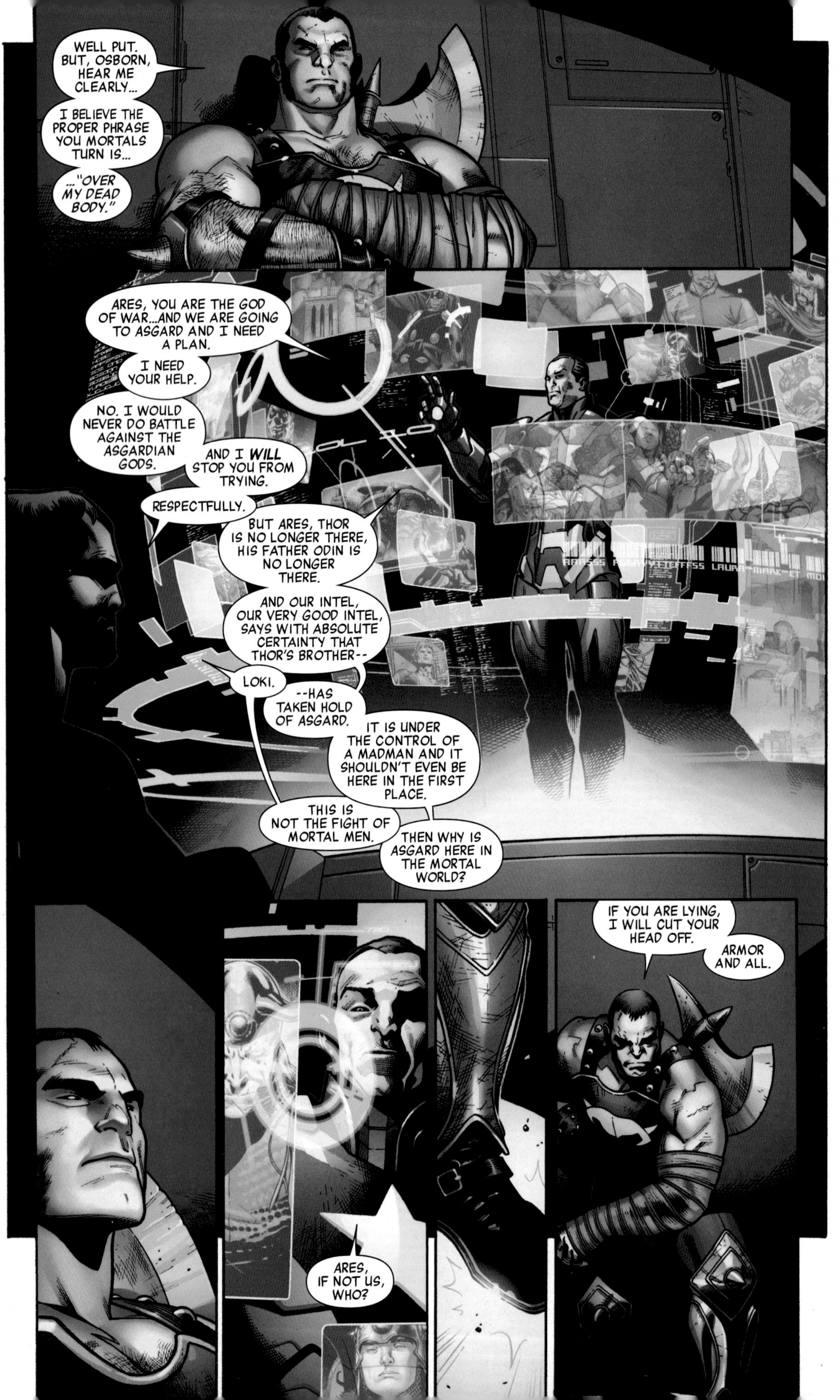
WELL PUT. BUT, OSBORN, HEAR ME CLEARLY...
I BELIEVE THE PROPER PHRASE YOU MORTALS TURN IS...
..."OVER MY DEAD BODY."
ARES, YOU ARE THE GOD OF WAR...AND WE ARE GOING TO ASGARD AND I NEED A PLAN.
I NEED YOUR HELP.
NO. I WOULD NEVER DO BATTLE AGAINST THE ASGARDIAN GODS.
AND I WILL STOP YOU FROM TRYING.
RESPECTFULLY.
BUT ARES, THOR IS NO LONGER THERE, HIS FATHER ODIN IS NO LONGER THERE.
AND OUR INTEL, OUR VERY GOOD INTEL, SAYS WITH ABSOLUTE CERTAINTY THAT THOR'S BROTHER--
LOKI.
--HAS TAKEN HOLD OF ASGARD.
IT IS UNDER THE CONTROL OF A MADMAN AND IT SHOULDN'T EVEN BE HERE IN THE FIRST PLACE.
THIS IS NOT THE FIGHT OF MORTAL MEN.
THEN WHY IS ASGARD HERE IN THE MORTAL WORLD?
ARES, IF NOT US, WHO?
IF YOU ARE LYING, I WILL CUT YOUR HEAD OFF.
ARMOR AND ALL.

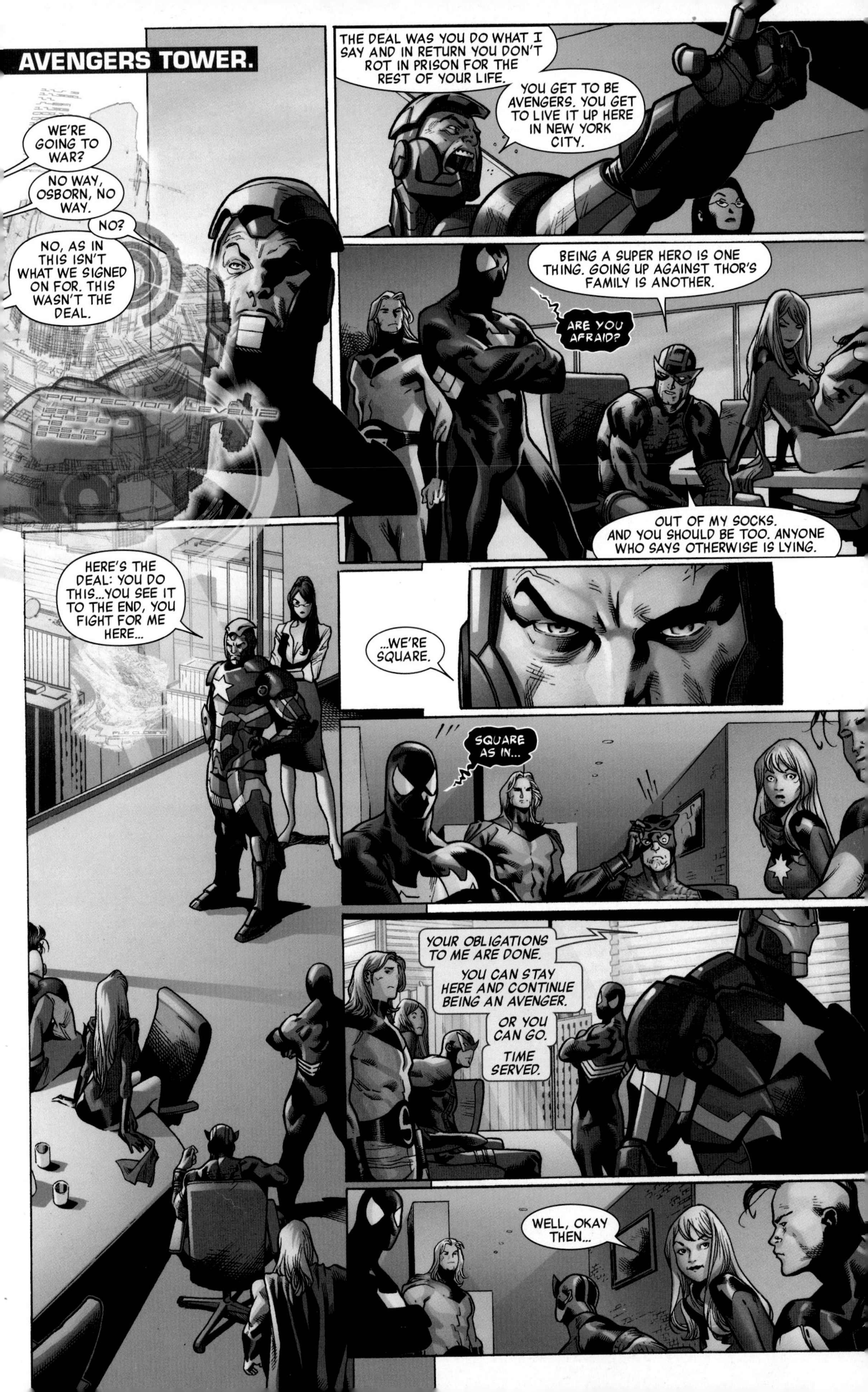

AVENGERS TOWER.
WE'RE GOING TO WAR?
NO WAY, OSBORN, NO WAY.
NO?
NO, AS IN THIS ISN'T WHAT WE SIGNED ON FOR. THIS WASN'T THE DEAL.
THE DEAL WAS YOU DO WHAT I SAY AND IN RETURN YOU DON'T ROT IN PRISON FOR THE REST OF YOUR LIFE.
YOU GET TO BE AVENGERS. YOU GET TO LIVE IT UP HERE IN NEW YORK CITY.
BEING A SUPER HERO IS ONE THING. GOING UP AGAINST THOR'S FAMILY IS ANOTHER.
ARE YOU AFRAID?
OUT OF MY SOCKS. AND YOU SHOULD BE TOO. ANYONE WHO SAYS OTHERWISE IS LYING.
HERE'S THE DEAL: YOU DO THIS...YOU SEE IT TO THE END, YOU FIGHT FOR ME HERE...
...WE'RE SQUARE.
SQUARE AS IN...
YOUR OBLIGATIONS TO ME ARE DONE.
YOU CAN STAY HERE AND CONTINUE BEING AN AVENGER.
OR YOU CAN GO.
TIME SERVED.
WELL, OKAY THEN...

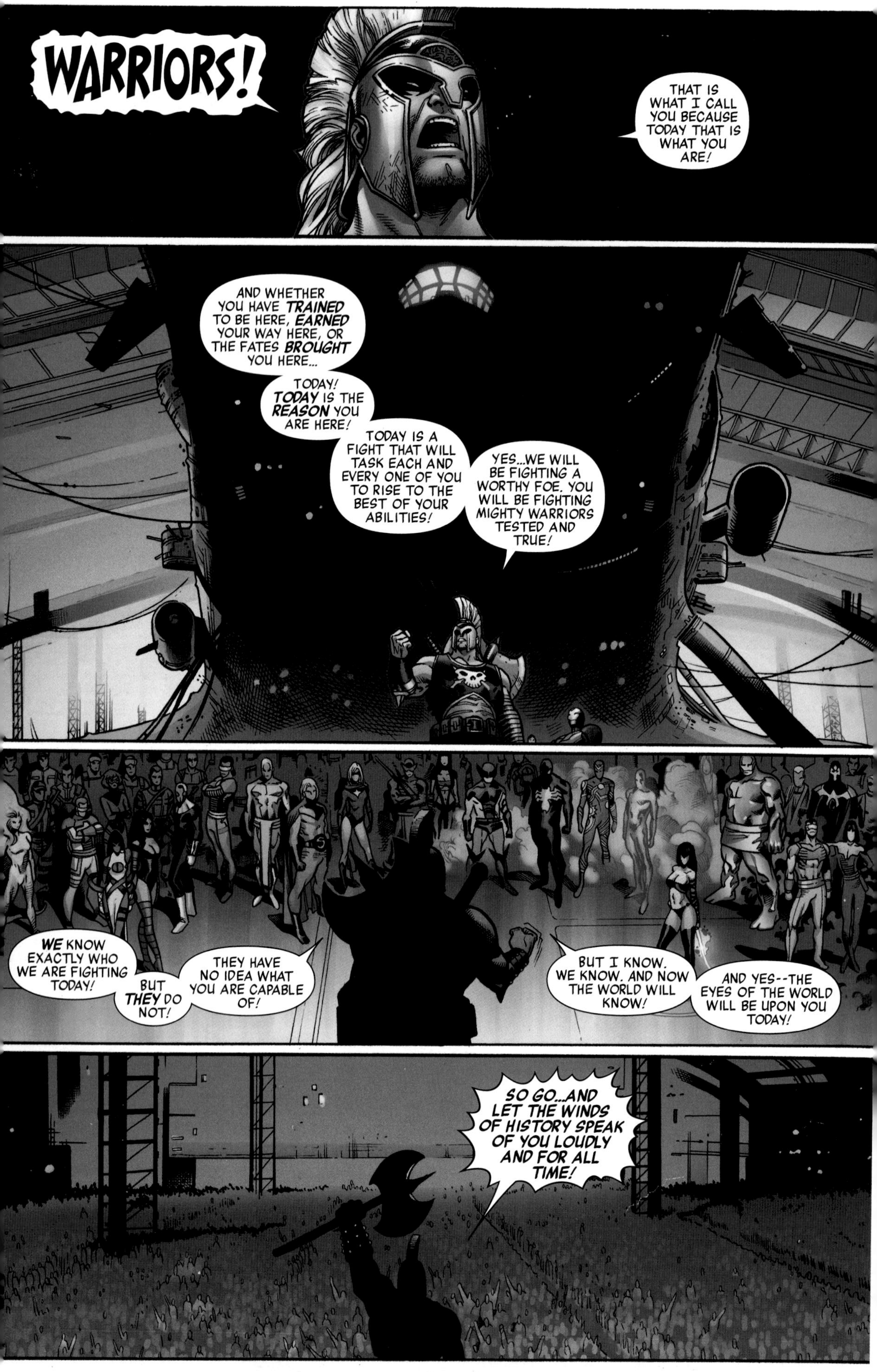
WARRIORS!
THAT IS WHAT I CALL YOU BECAUSE TODAY THAT IS WHAT YOU ARE!
AND WHETHER YOU HAVE TRAINED TO BE HERE, EARNED YOUR WAY HERE, OR THE FATES BROUGHT YOU HERE...
TODAY! TODAY IS THE REASON YOU ARE HERE!
TODAY IS A FIGHT THAT WILL TASK EACH AND EVERY ONE OF YOU TO RISE TO THE BEST OF YOUR ABILITIES!
YES...WE WILL BE FIGHTING A WORTHY FOE. YOU WILL BE FIGHTING MIGHTY WARRIORS TESTED AND TRUE!
WE KNOW EXACTLY WHO WE ARE FIGHTING TODAY!
BUT THEY DO NOT!
THEY HAVE NO IDEA WHAT YOU ARE CAPABLE OF!
BUT I KNOW. WE KNOW. AND NOW THE WORLD WILL KNOW!
AND YES--THE EYES OF THE WORLD WILL BE UPON YOU TODAY!
SO GO...AND LET THE WINDS OF HISTORY SPEAK OF YOU LOUDLY AND FOR ALL TIME!

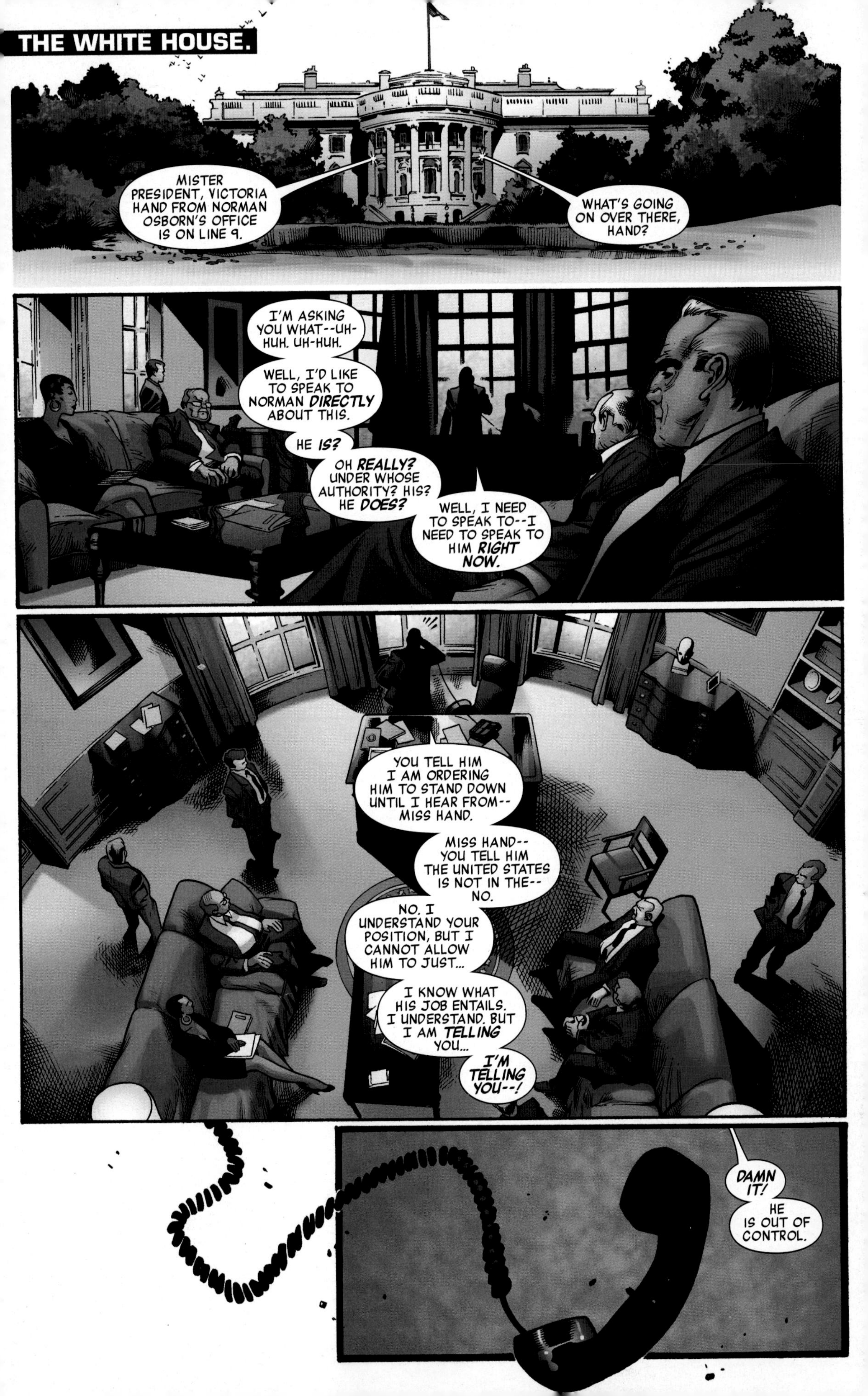
THE WHITE HOUSE.
MISTER PRESIDENT, VICTORIA HAND FROM NORMAN OSBORN'S OFFICE IS ON LINE 9.
WHAT'S GOING ON OVER THERE, HAND?
I'M ASKING YOU WHAT--UH-HUH. UH-HUH.
WELL, I'D LIKE TO SPEAK TO NORMAN DIRECTLY ABOUT THIS.
HE IS?
OH REALLY? UNDER WHOSE AUTHORITY? HIS? HE DOES?
WELL, I NEED TO SPEAK TO--I NEED TO SPEAK TO HIM RIGHT NOW.
YOU TELL HIM I AM ORDERING HIM TO STAND DOWN UNTIL I HEAR FROM--MISS HAND.
MISS HAND--YOU TELL HIM THE UNITED STATES IS NOT IN THE--NO.
NO. I UNDERSTAND YOUR POSITION, BUT I CANNOT ALLOW HIM TO JUST...
I KNOW WHAT HIS JOB ENTAILS. I UNDERSTAND. BUT I AM TELLING YOU...
I'M TELLING YOU--!
DAMN IT!
HE IS OUT OF CONTROL.

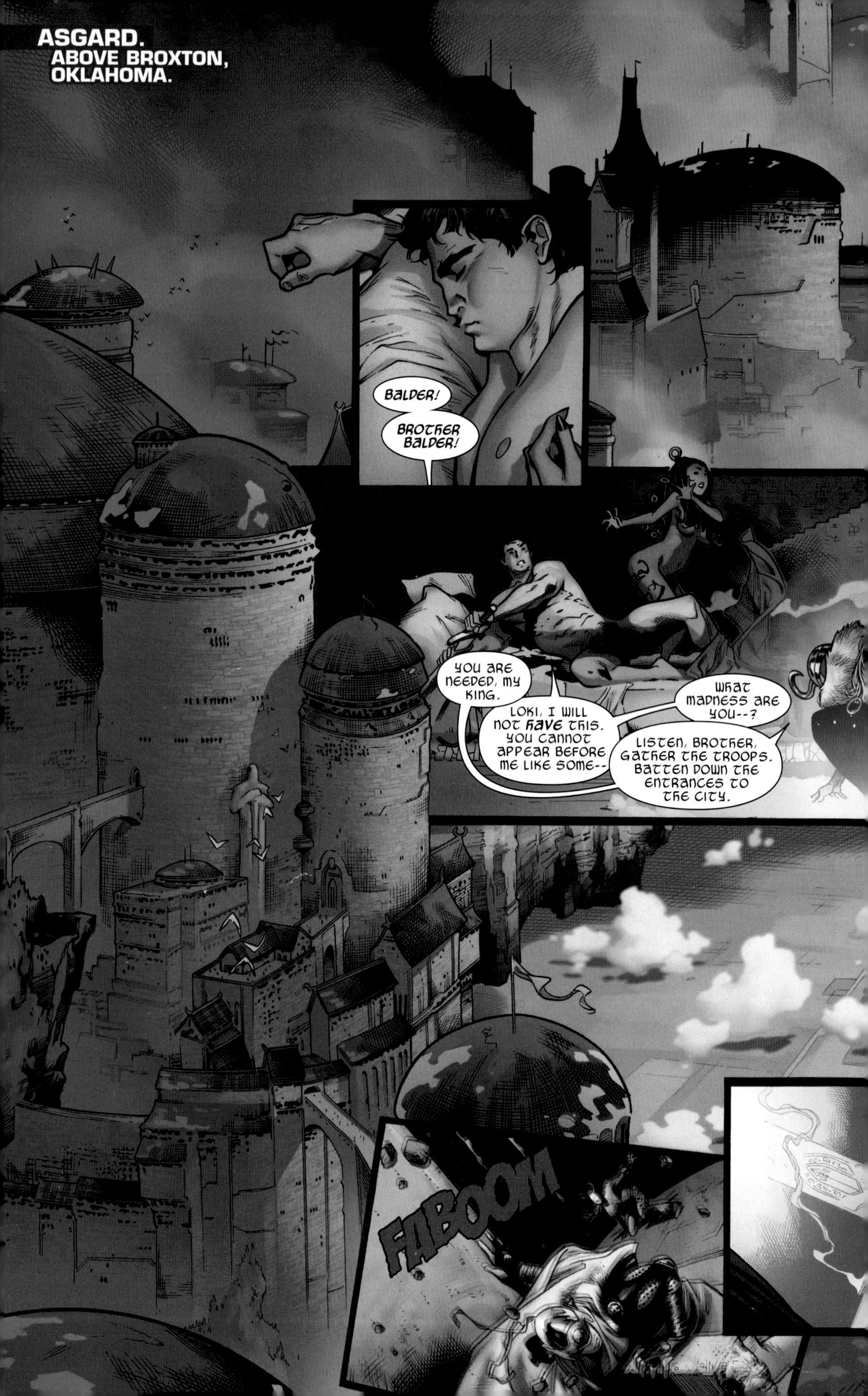
ASGARD.
ABOVE BROXTON, OKLAHOMA.
BALDER!
BROTHER BALDER!
YOU ARE NEEDED, MY KING.
LOKI, I WILL NOT HAVE THIS. YOU CANNOT APPEAR BEFORE ME LIKE SOME--
WHAT MADNESS ARE YOU--?
LISTEN, BROTHER, GATHER THE TROOPS. BATTEN DOWN THE ENTRANCES TO THE CITY.
FABOOM

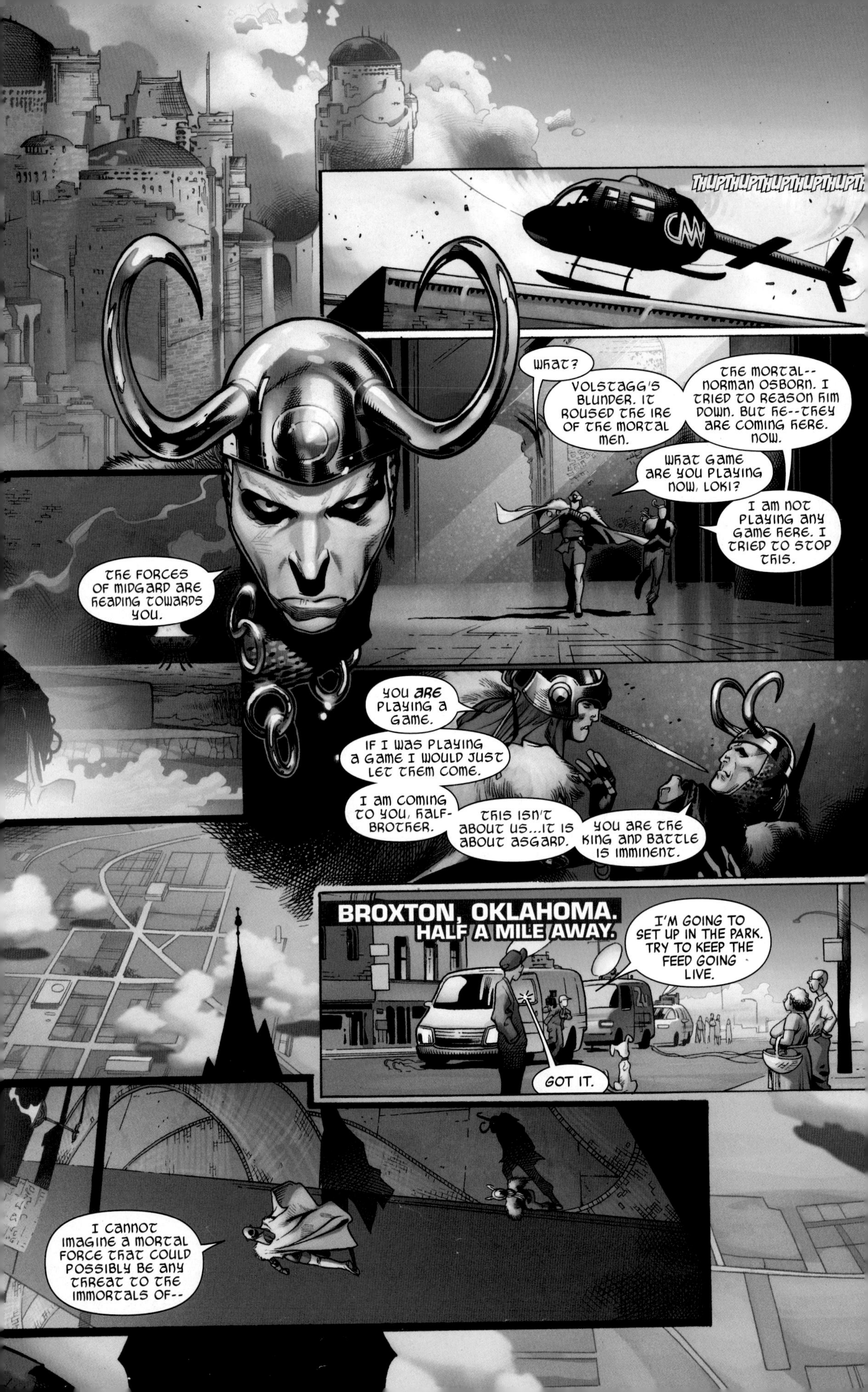
THUPTHUPTHUPTHUPTHUPTH
WHAT?
VOLSTAGG'S BLUNDER. IT ROUSED THE IRE OF THE MORTAL MEN.
THE MORTAL--NORMAN OSBORN. I TRIED TO REASON HIM DOWN. BUT HE--THEY ARE COMING HERE. NOW.
WHAT GAME ARE YOU PLAYING NOW, LOKI?
I AM NOT PLAYING ANY GAME HERE. I TRIED TO STOP THIS.
THE FORCES OF MIDGARD ARE HEADING TOWARDS YOU.
YOU ARE PLAYING A GAME.
IF I WAS PLAYING A GAME I WOULD JUST LET THEM COME.
I AM COMING TO YOU, HALF-BROTHER.
THIS ISN'T ABOUT US...IT IS ABOUT ASGARD.
YOU ARE THE KING AND BATTLE IS IMMINENT.
BROXTON, OKLAHOMA. HALF A MILE AWAY.
I'M GOING TO SET UP IN THE PARK. TRY TO KEEP THE FEED GOING LIVE.
GOT IT.
I CANNOT IMAGINE A MORTAL FORCE THAT COULD POSSIBLY BE ANY THREAT TO THE IMMORTALS OF--

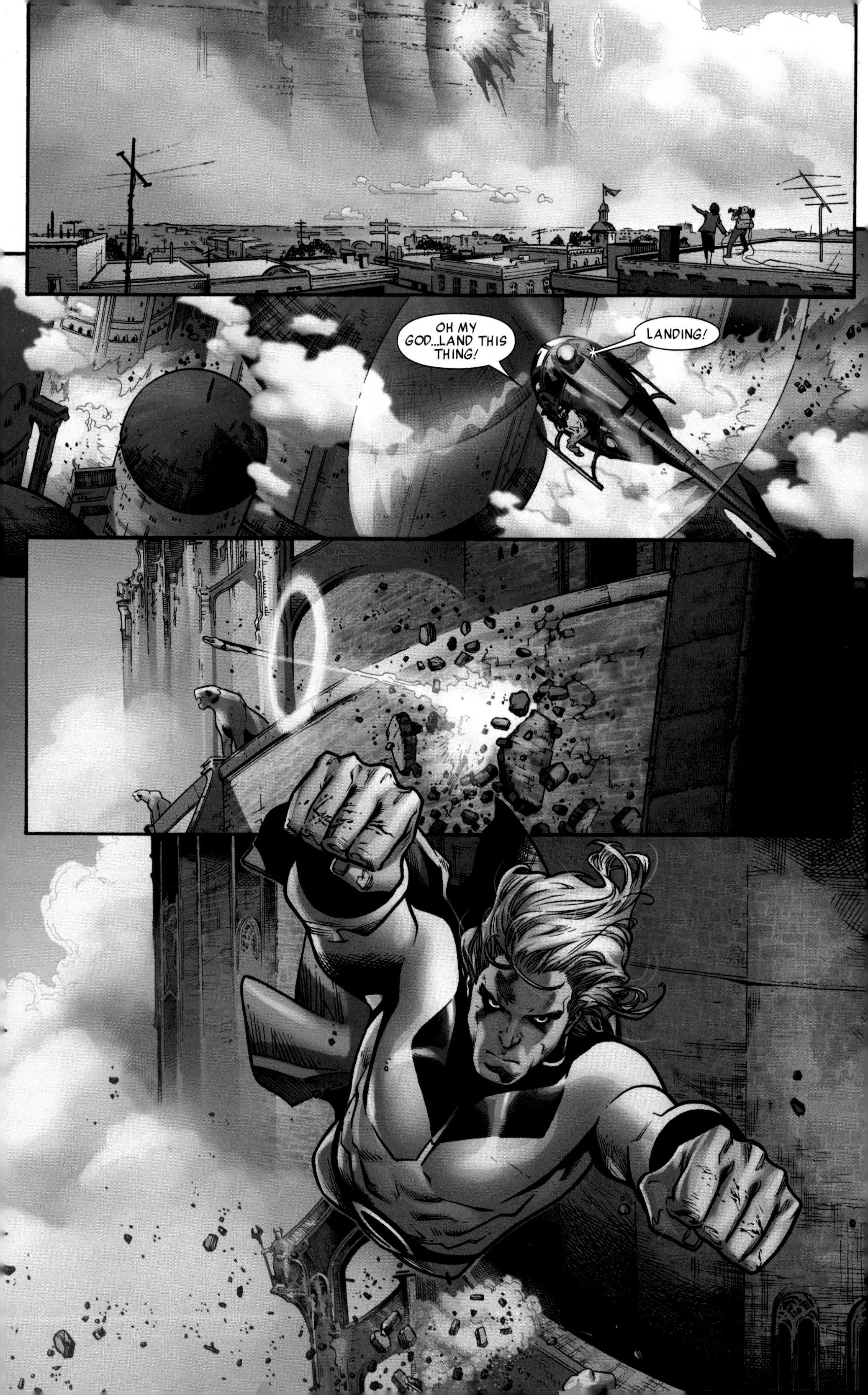
OH MY GOD...LAND THIS THING!
LANDING!

THE SIEGE OF ASGARD-PHASE ONE

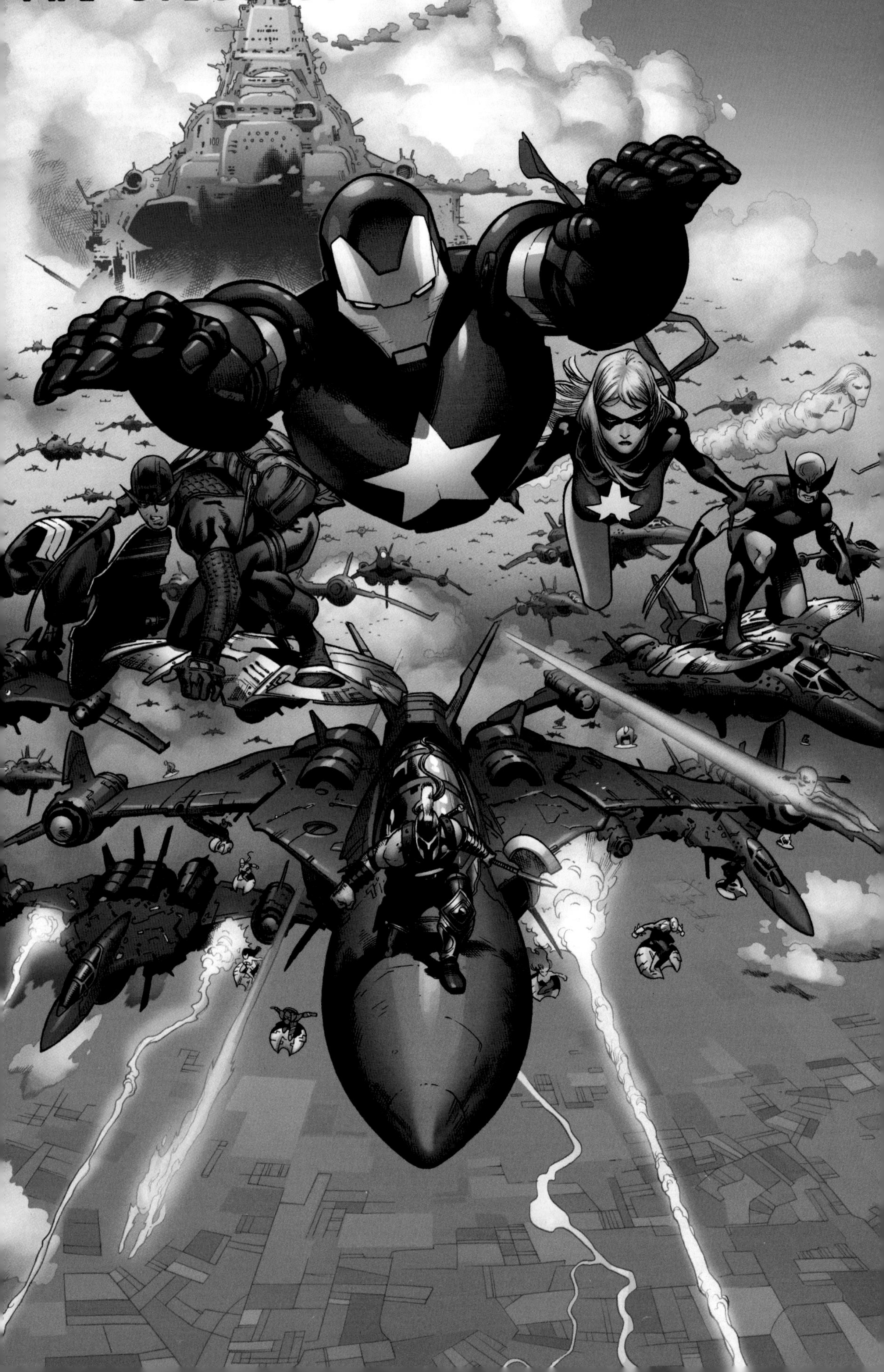

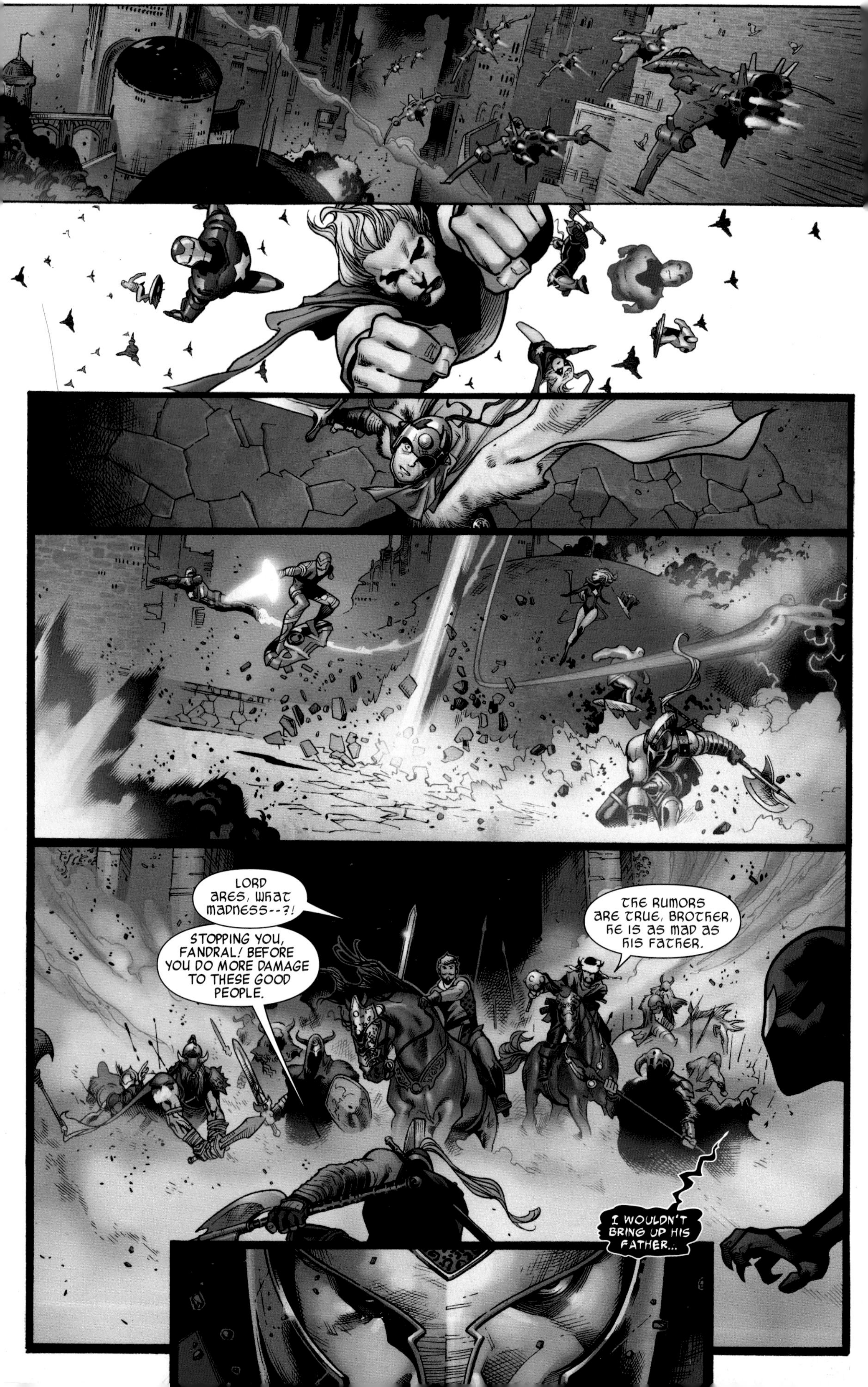
LORD ARES, WHAT MADNESS--?!
STOPPING YOU, FANDRAL! BEFORE YOU DO MORE DAMAGE TO THESE GOOD PEOPLE.
THE RUMORS ARE TRUE, BROTHER, HE IS AS MAD AS HIS FATHER.
I WOULDN'T BRING UP HIS FATHER...

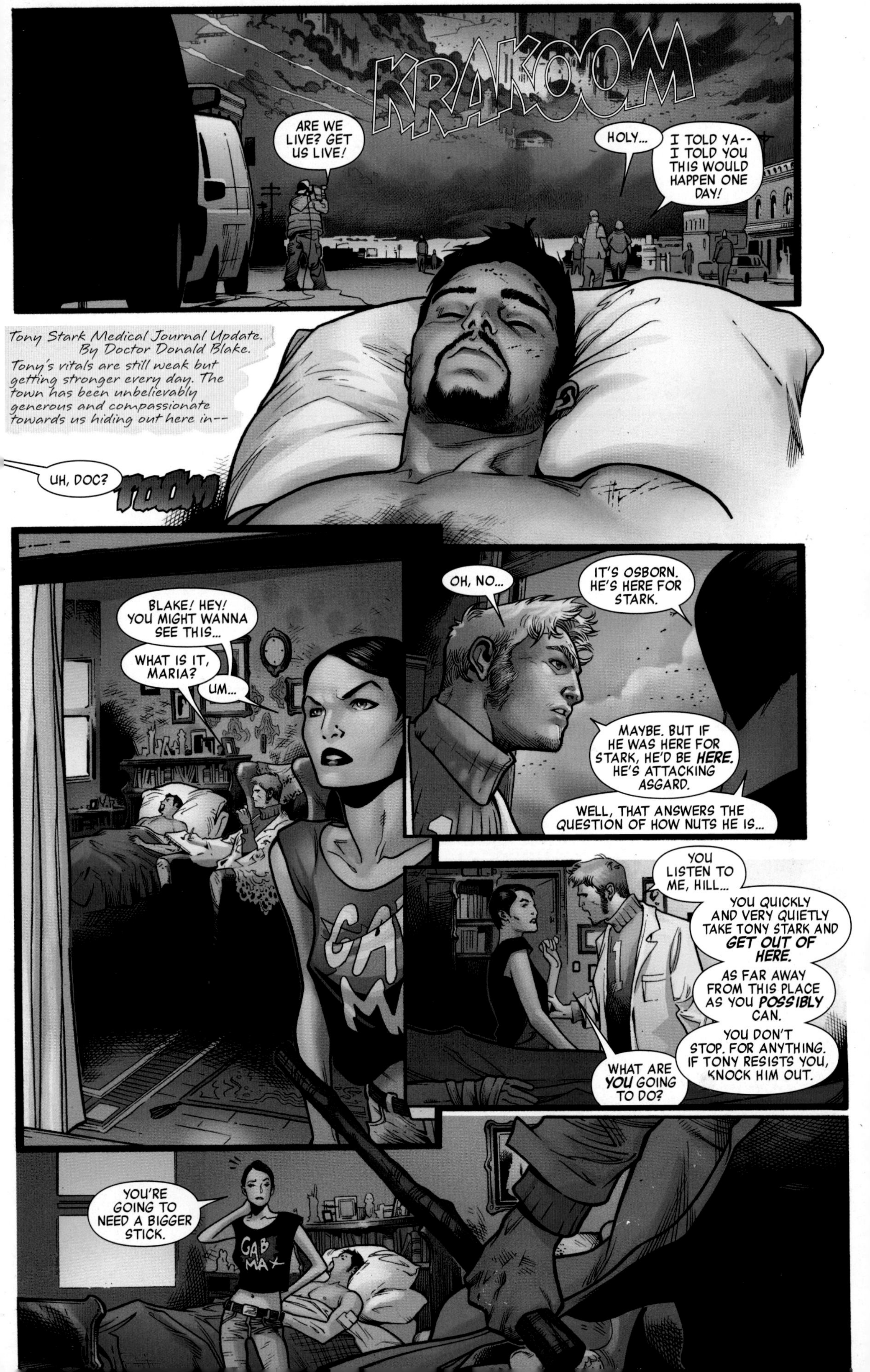
KRAKOOM
ARE WE LIVE? GET US LIVE!
HOLY...
I TOLD YA-- I TOLD YOU THIS WOULD HAPPEN ONE DAY!
Tony Stark Medical Journal Update. By Doctor Donald Blake.
Tony's vitals are still weak but getting stronger every day. The town has been unbelievably generous and compassionate towards us hiding out here in--
UH, DOC?
BLAKE! HEY! YOU MIGHT WANNA SEE THIS...
WHAT IS IT, MARIA?
UM...
OH, NO...
IT'S OSBORN. HE'S HERE FOR STARK.
MAYBE. BUT IF HE WAS HERE FOR STARK, HE'D BE HERE. HE'S ATTACKING ASGARD.
WELL, THAT ANSWERS THE QUESTION OF HOW NUTS HE IS...
YOU LISTEN TO ME, HILL...
YOU QUICKLY AND VERY QUIETLY TAKE TONY STARK AND GET OUT OF HERE.
AS FAR AWAY FROM THIS PLACE AS YOU POSSIBLY CAN.
YOU DON'T STOP. FOR ANYTHING. IF TONY RESISTS YOU, KNOCK HIM OUT.
WHAT ARE YOU GOING TO DO?
YOU'RE GOING TO NEED A BIGGER STICK.

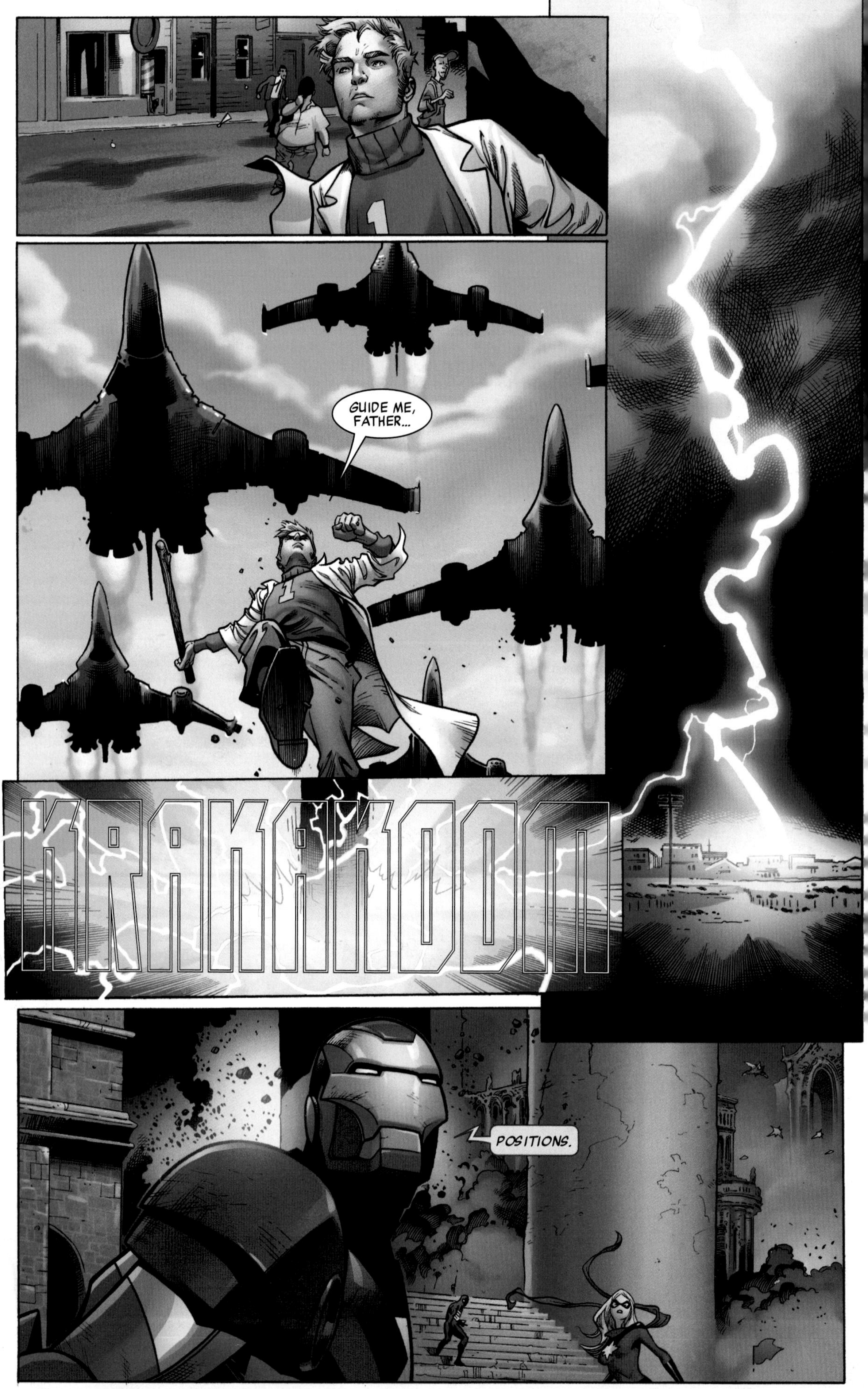
GUIDE ME, FATHER...
KRAKAKOOM
POSITIONS.

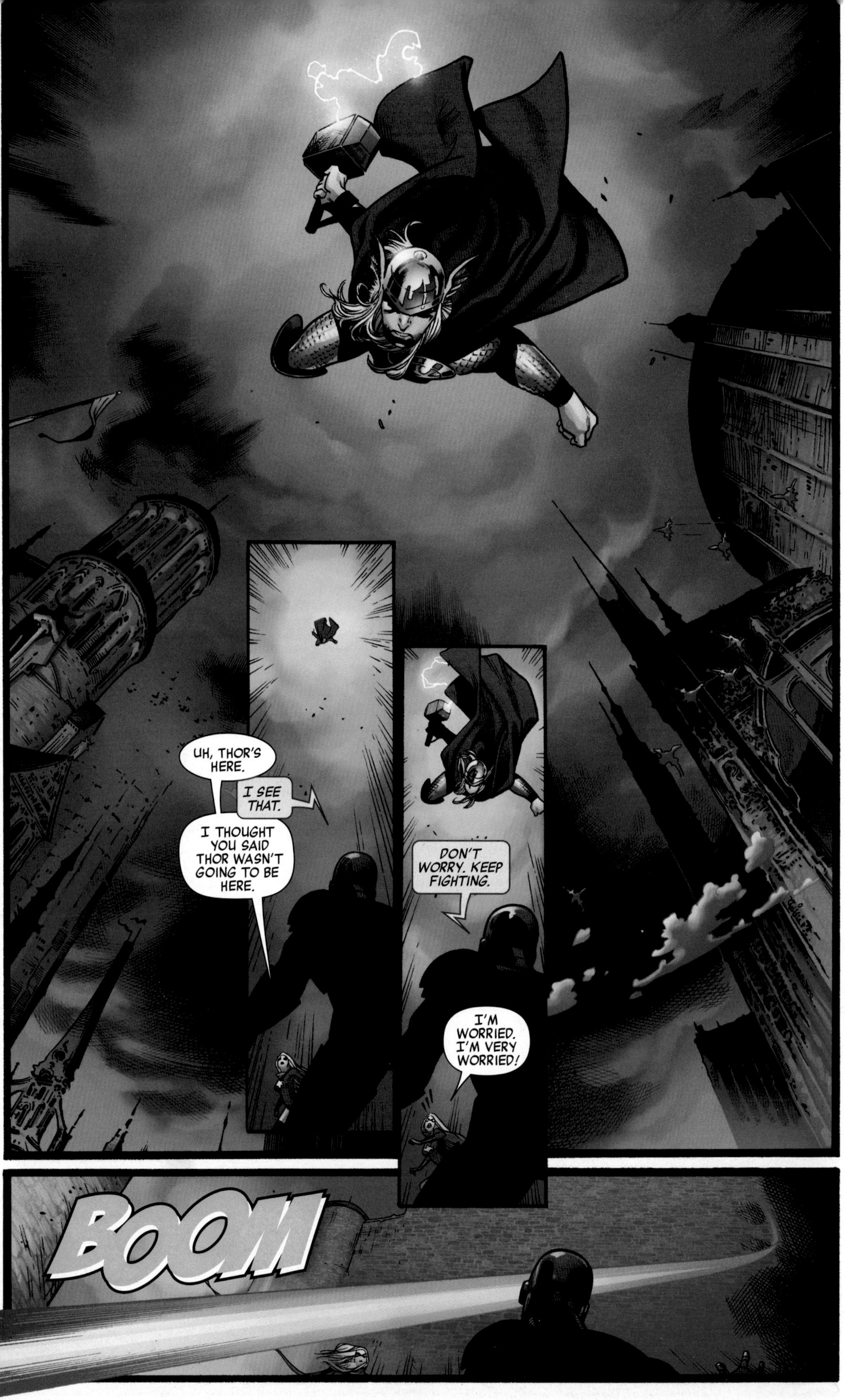
UH, THOR'S HERE.
I SEE THAT.
I THOUGHT YOU SAID THOR WASN'T GOING TO BE HERE.
DON'T WORRY. KEEP FIGHTING.
I'M WORRIED. I'M VERY WORRIED!
BOOM

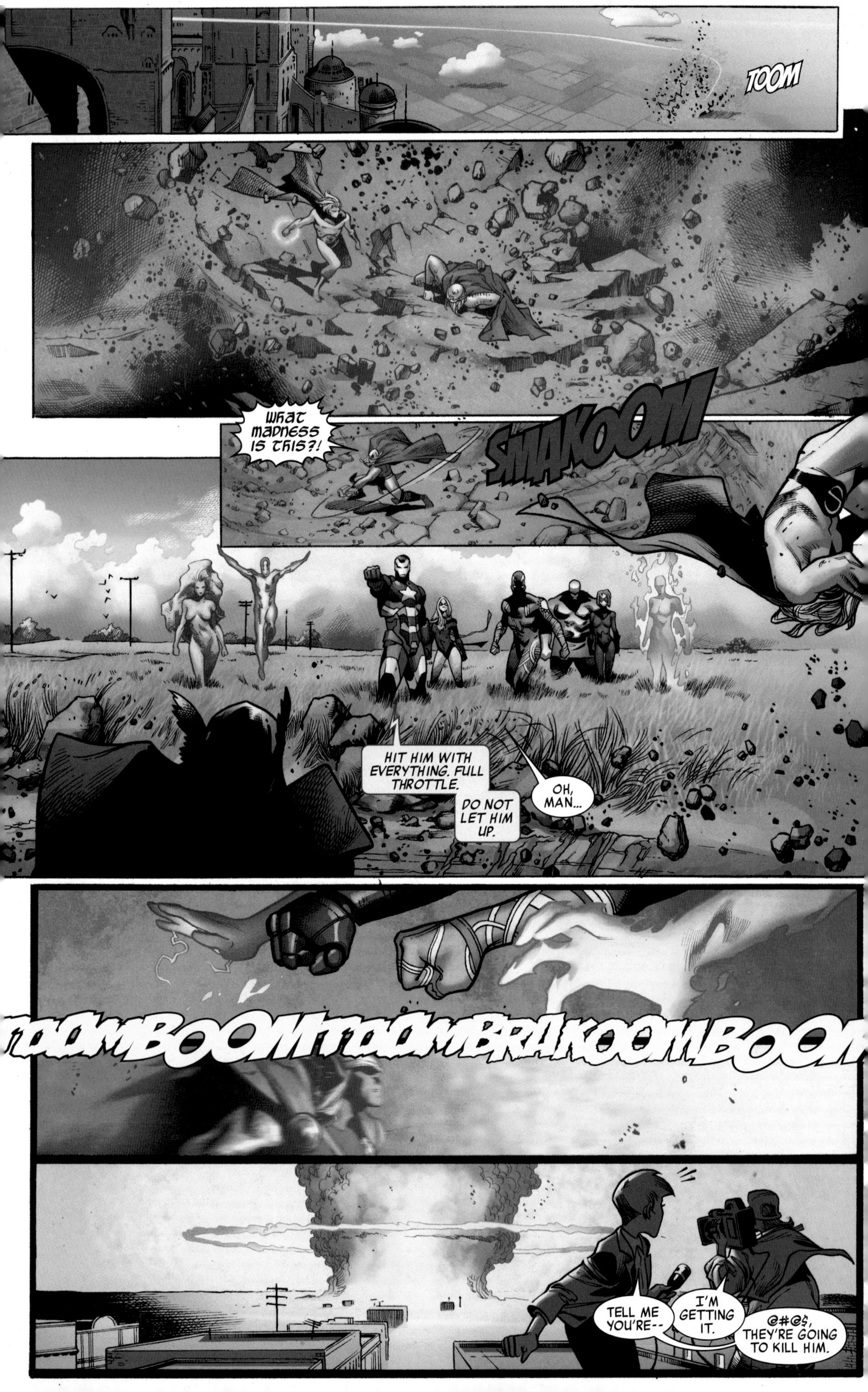
TOOM
WHAT MADNESS IS THIS?!
SMAKOOM
HIT HIM WITH EVERYTHING. FULL THROTTLE.
DO NOT LET HIM UP.
OH, MAN...
TOOMBOOMTOOMBRAKOOMBOOM
TELL ME YOU'RE--
I'M GETTING IT.
@#@$, THEY'RE GOING TO KILL HIM.

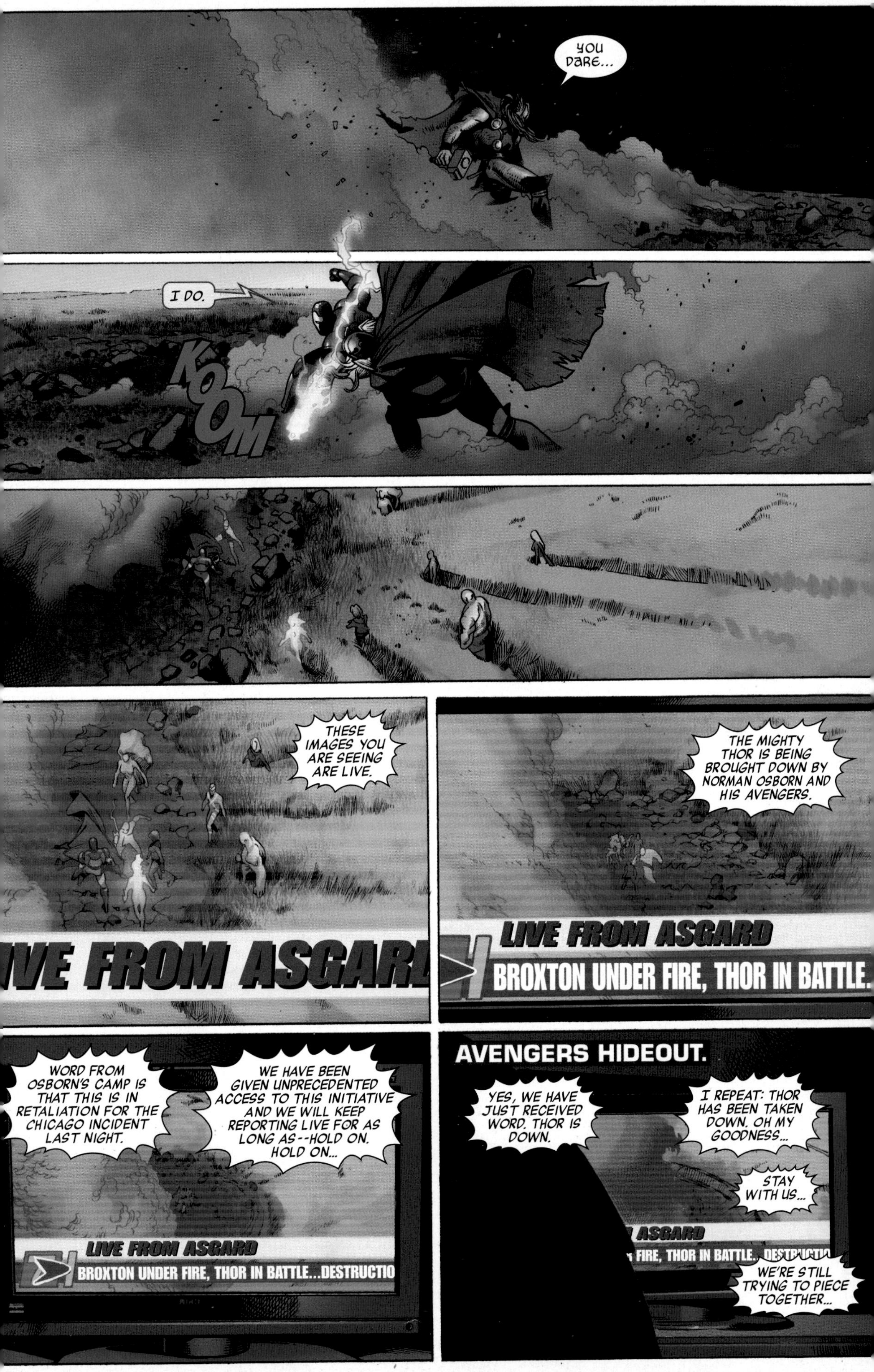
YOU DARE...
I DO.
KOOM
THESE IMAGES YOU ARE SEEING ARE LIVE.
IVE FROM ASGARD
THE MIGHTY THOR IS BEING BROUGHT DOWN BY NORMAN OSBORN AND HIS AVENGERS.
LIVE FROM ASGARD
BROXTON UNDER FIRE, THOR IN BATTLE.
WORD FROM OSBORN'S CAMP IS THAT THIS IS IN RETALIATION FOR THE CHICAGO INCIDENT LAST NIGHT.
WE HAVE BEEN GIVEN UNPRECEDENTED ACCESS TO THIS INITIATIVE AND WE WILL KEEP REPORTING LIVE FOR AS LONG AS--HOLD ON. HOLD ON...
LIVE FROM ASGARD
BROXTON UNDER FIRE, THOR IN BATTLE...DESTRUCTIO
AVENGERS HIDEOUT.
YES, WE HAVE JUST RECEIVED WORD. THOR IS DOWN.
I REPEAT: THOR HAS BEEN TAKEN DOWN. OH MY GOODNESS...
STAY WITH US...
ASGARD
FIRE, THOR IN BATTLE...DESTRUCTIO
WE'RE STILL TRYING TO PIECE TOGETHER...

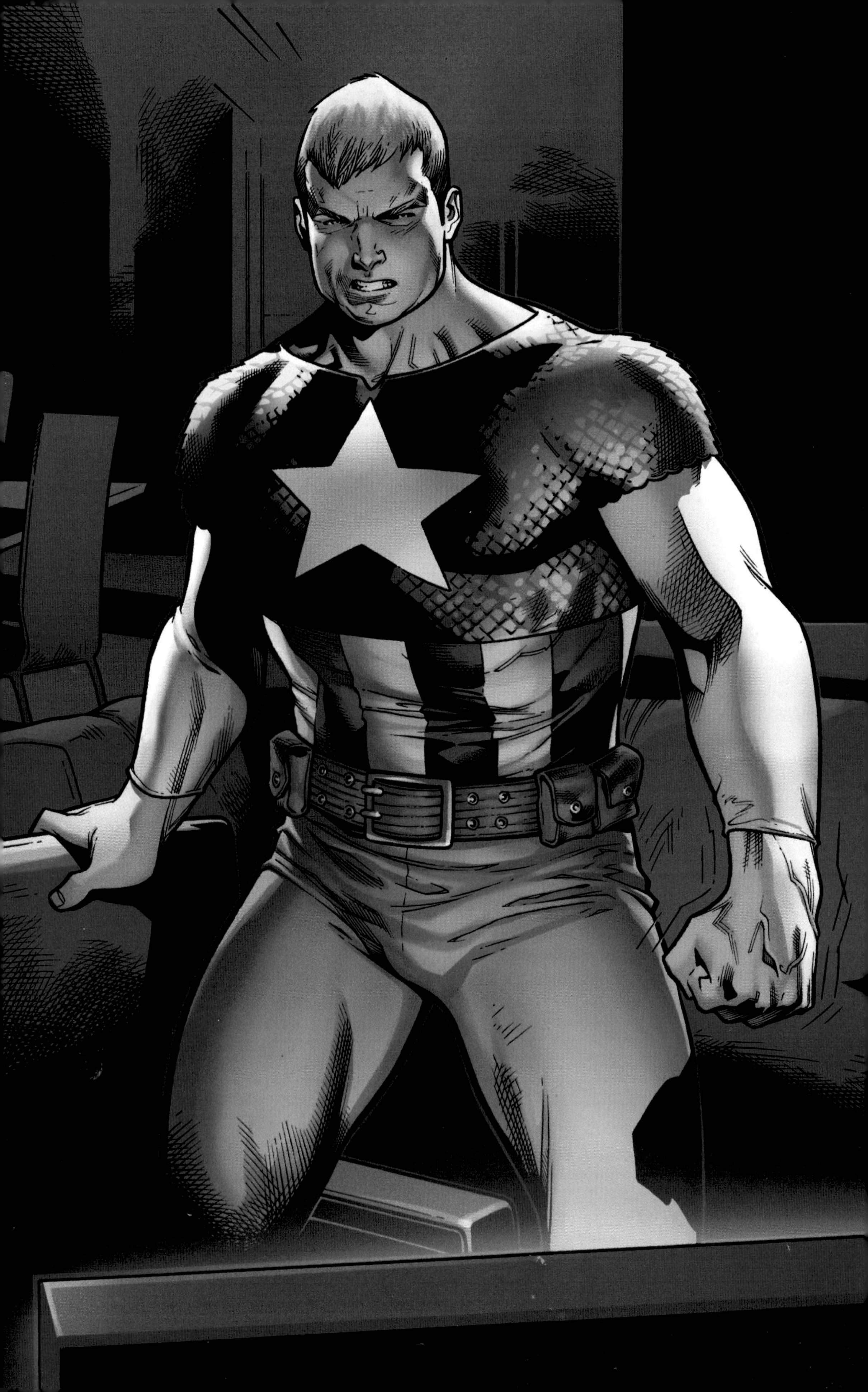

HAMMER DOCUMENT 68785895-78795 GDFBCV
TOP SECRET CODE-WHITE

ARES WAR PLAN TRANSCRIPT

MEETING CONDUCTED BY
HAMMER COMMANDER NORMAN OSBORN (IRON PATRIOT)
SECURITY LEVEL **TEN.** CODE CLEARANCE **WHITE.**
MEETING ATTENDED AND OBSERVED BY
DEPUTY DIRECTOR VICTORIA HAND
(SECURITY CLEARANCE LEVEL 9),
DR. KARLA SOFEN (MS. MARVEL), **DAKEN AKIHIRO** (WOLVERINE)
BENJAMIN POINDEXTER (HAWKEYE), **MACDONALD GARGAN** (SPIDER-MAN)
(SECURITY CLEARANCE LEVEL 5),
ROBERT REYNOLDS (THE SENTRY)
(SECURITY CLEARANCE LEVEL 2),
AND **TONY MASTERS** (TASKMASTER), **INITIATIVE COMMANDER**
(SECURITY LEVEL 4).

RECORDING DATE: 4/5/2010

PLACE: **AVENGERS TOWER MEETING ROOM. NEW YORK CITY.**

SIEGE

NORMAN OSBORN: What we're talking about here does not leave this room.

MS. MARVEL: We're not allowed to leave this room.

NORMAN OSBORN: Good point. Ares...

ARES: Osborn has asked me to put together invasion scenarios for dealing with the floating city of Asgard currently located here on Earth.

HAWKEYE: I'm sorry, what?

SPIDER-MAN: When did we agree to that? I didn't agree to that.

NORMAN OSBORN: Settle.

SPIDER-MAN: I thought this was in theory.

NORMAN OSBORN: Settle.

VICTORIA HAND: People, sit and listen.

SPIDER-MAN: But--

VICTORIA HAND: You're not here to give us a but, you're here to listen and do. That's the deal.

ARES: The city is currently hovering 12 feet off the ground over the farmer's fields of--

HAWKEYE: I'm sorry, hold on.

VICTORIA HAND: Hawkeye, we need you to pay attention.

HAWKEYE: Oh, I'm paying attention. You expect us...all of us to go in there and start tussling with those guys?

NORMAN OSBORN: Asgard is in a position to threaten America and the American way of life.

HAWKEYE: So is McDonald's. Should we invade that too?

WOLVERINE: I think what Hawkeye is trying to say is there are Asgardian gods living there. A city of Asgardian gods. Am I right?

NORMAN OSBORN: Yes. And if you feel threatened by that, you should go with that feeling.

HAWKEYE: Exactly.

NORMAN OSBORN: There is a threat. Not only to our well-being, but to the natural order of

HAMMER IMAGE FILE 68785895-78795-A:
GROUND VIEW – ASGARD

HAMMER IMAGE FILE 68785895-78795-B:
STREET VIEW – BROXTON, OK, USA

HAMMER DOCUMENT 68785895-78795 GDFBCV
TOP SECRET CODE - WHITE

SIEGE

HAMMER IMAGE FILE 68785895-78795-C:
AERIAL VIEW – ASGARD

things. This Asgard, it doesn't belong here. It's upsetting to the order of things.

SPIDER-MAN: Says who?

NORMAN OSBORN: Excuse me?

SPIDER-MAN: I mean, who says it ain't supposed to be here. It was there and now it's here. Who says no?

NORMAN OSBORN: God.

SPIDER-MAN: Really? Because I bet those guys kinda know more about God than you.

NORMAN OSBORN: It's not supposed to be here on Earth. It's not supposed to be in the United States.

HAWKEYE: How do you know?

ARES: Osborn is right. And I, son of Zeus, prince of Olympus, do know the true way of things. Asgard is part of a realm and it does not belong here. Something is wrong. The balance of the universe is upset.

HAWKEYE: And it's our problem how?

ARES: We're the Avengers. We're the protectors of this realm.

HAWKEYE: Uh-huh.

MS. MARVEL: It does seem sort of beyond our pay grade, Norman. Mathematically.

NORMAN OSBORN: You agreed to the role of the Avengers. This--this is what the Avengers do.

SPIDER-MAN: That's what those Avengers did. The old ones. And if you'll notice they ain't exactly Avengers no more.

HAWKEYE: Exactly, this is the kind of crap we should be avoiding.

SPIDER-MAN: There's no win.

HAWKEYE: There's no angle. It's just picking a fight.

ARES: You call yourself a man?

HAWKEYE: I do.

ARES: Then why do you speak as a child?

HAWKEYE: Yeah. See...he is the god of war. And there's just one of him. And I am now shutting my ass up. And I am a badass man. I'm known, specifically, as a badass. And one of them, just one, got me to shut the hell up.

NORMAN OSBORN: I'm ignoring you and moving forward.

HAWKEYE: Ignoring me?

THE SENTRY: And the idea of us living together in harmony is a stupid idea because...?

NORMAN OSBORN: We have to assume that the Asgardians, with their superior strength, technology and everything else, are a threat to us

HAMMER DOCUMENT 68785895-78795 GDFBCV
TOP SECRET CODE - WHITE

and our way of life.
THE SENTRY: Because?
NORMAN OSBORN: Yes. There are other ways to look at it. But that's not what we are here to do. We are put on this Earth to see a thing like this as a threat and a threat that needs to be dealt with. That is what we are charged to do. Others can sit back and fantasize about a world of immortals and mortals cohabitating together in Xanadu and euphoria. We do not get to do that. We are men of war. Ares?
ARES: We will have one chance at a surprise attack. One and one only. The target of the attack is clear. You see the outpost? There.
ARES: There is our primary target.
TASKMASTER: What is it?
ARES: That is Heimdall's observatory. Heimdall is their protector. He protects the gates of the realm and watches over all others. He can see and hear as far as creation.
TASKMASTER: So maybe he's watching us?
ARES: One would surmise no. One would imagine he sees no threat here.
HAWKEYE: And he'd be right.
ARES: But the observatory also holds, or once held, the entrance to the Bifröst. The legendary rainbow bridge that allows any Asgardian under Odin's rule to travel from one realm to the next. I do not know if this new Asgard still uses Bifröst but if they do, and I would assume so, then the observatory has to be destroyed in our first strike. It is the only chance those living on Asgard will have to call in reinforcements. Asgard has to be cut off. No way in and no way out. You, Robert, you will strike the observatory like a golden bullet. You will destroy it and anyone in it. This will cut them off from calling in reserves and give up the momentary upper hand. From there, we will head as one, as a frontline, toward's Odin's throneroom.
WOLVERINE: And bombing the hell out of the place is out of the question because...?
NORMAN OSBORN: Asgard is right next to, and I mean on top of, a small, all-American town. We are not going to take that risk.
HAWKEYE: Why don't we just use

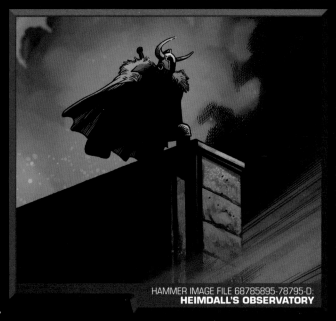

HAMMER IMAGE FILE 68785895-78795-D:
HEIMDALL'S OBSERVATORY

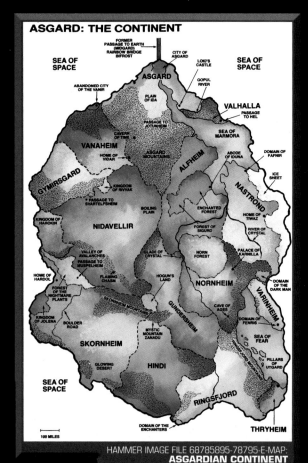

ASGARD: THE CONTINENT
FORMER PASSAGE TO EARTH (MIDGARD) RAINBOW BRIDGE BIFROST
CITY OF ASGARD
SEA OF SPACE
LOKI'S CASTLE
SEA OF SPACE
ASGARD
GOPUL RIVER
ABANDONED CITY OF THE VANIR
PLAIN OF IDA
VALHALLA
PASSAGE TO HEL
PASSAGE TO JOTUNHEIM
CAVERN OF TIME
SEA OF MARMORA
VANAHEIM
ASGARD MOUNTAINS
ALFHEIM
ABODE OF IDUNA
DOMAIN OF FAFNIR
HOME OF VIDAR
ICE SHEET
GYMIRSGARD
KINGDOM OF RIVVAK
NASTROND
PASSAGE TO SVARTELFSHEIM
BOILING PLAIN
ENCHANTED FOREST
HOME OF TIWAZ
KINGDOM OF HAROKIN
NIDAVELLIR
FOREST OF SIGURD
RIVER OF CRYSTAL
VALLEY OF AVALANCHES
GLADE OF CRYSTAL
NORN FOREST
PALACE OF KARNILLA
PASSAGE TO MUSPELHEIM
HOME OF HARDOL
FLAMING CHASM
HOGUN'S LAND
NORNHEIM
DOMAIN OF THE DARK MAN
FOREST OF THE NIGHTMARE PLANTS
SKORNHEIM MOUNTAINS
VARINHEIM
GUNDERSHEIM
CAVE OF AGES
KINGDOM OF JOLENA
BOULDER ROAD
MYSTIC MOUNTAIN ZANADU
DOMAIN OF FENRIS
SEA OF FEAR
SKORNHEIM
RINGSFJORD MOUNTAINS
PILLARS OF UTGARD
GLOWING DESERT
HINDI
SEA OF SPACE
RINGSFJORD
DOMAIN OF THE ENCHANTERS
THRYHEIM
100 MILES

HAMMER IMAGE FILE 68785895-78795-E-MAP:
ASGARDIAN CONTINENT

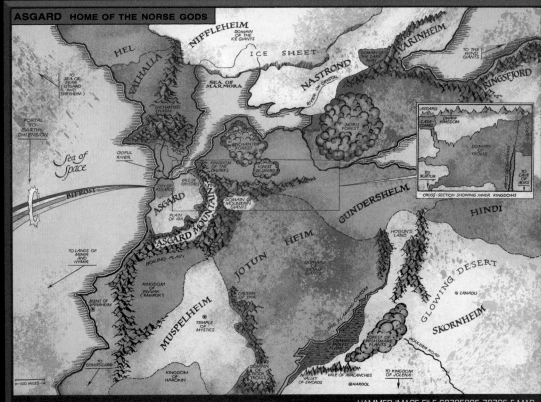

ASGARD HOME OF THE NORSE GODS
NIFFLEHEIM
DOMAIN OF THE ICE GIANTS
ICE SHEET
HEL
VALHALLA
SEA OF MARMORA
NASTROND
RIVER OF CRYSTAL
VARINHEIM
TO THE WIND GIANTS
RINGSEJORD
DOMAIN OF THE DARK MAN
TO SEA OF FEAR (UTGARD AND THRYHEIM)
PORTAL TO EARTH-DIMENSION
ENCHANTED CHASM
NORN FOREST
ENCHANTED FOREST
Sea of Space
GOPUL RIVER
KINGDOM OF THE DWARFS
FOREST OF SIGURD
VALE OF CRYSTALS
CITY OF ASGARD
BIFROST
ASGARD
DOMAIN OF MOUNTAIN GIANTS
PLAIN OF IDA
ASGARD MOUNTAINS
GUNDERSHELM
HINDI
ASGARD
DWARF KINGDOM
CATA-COMBS
DOMAIN OF TROLLS
NORNS
ABYSS OF SHADOWS
TO SURTUR
TO CAVE OF AGES
CROSS-SECTION SHOWING INNER KINGDOMS
HOGUN'S LAND
TO LANDS OF MIMIR AND HYMIR
BOILING PLAIN
JOTUN
HEIM
DOMAIN OF STORM GIANTS
GLOWING DESERT
ZANADU
KINGDOM OF RIVVAK (RAMPOK)
CAVERN OF TIME
RUINS OF VANAHEIM
MUSPELHEIM
TEMPLE OF MYSTICS
THE FLAMING CHASM
SKORNHEIM
SWAMPS OF ENDLESS FLAME
FOREST OF NIGHTMARE PLANTS
BOULDER ROAD
TO GYMIRSGARD
DOMAIN OF ROCK TROLLS
KINGDOM OF HAROKIN
VALLEY OF SWORDS
VALE OF AVALANCHES
HARDOL
TO KINGDOM OF JOLENA
100 MILES

HAMMER IMAGE FILE 68785895-78795-F-MAP:
ASGARDIAN CONTINENT, DETAIL

blondie here to golden bullet the hell out of the place until he's out of steam?

ARES: Because that is not a plan.

HAWKEYE: Okay, Mister Plan, what happens when the Asgardians mop the floor with us?

NORMAN OSBORN: We're the first wave. There are others. There is back-up.

HAWKEYE: And I'll just ask so I can tell myself I asked: and who would that be?

NORMAN OSBORN: It's top secret.

HAWKEYE: Of course it is.

WOLVERINE: Is it someone who will make a difference?

NORMAN OSBORN: It's someone who can fight this fight.

MS. MARVEL: On an Asgardian level.

NORMAN OSBORN: Exactly at that level.

HAWKEYE: Then why not send them in as the front line?

NORMAN OSBORN: Because this win has to be our win. It has to be us. Or it doesn't count.

SPIDER-MAN: And we do this, we're done. That's the deal. We're free to go.

NORMAN OSBORN: That is the deal.

MS. MARVEL: The fact that you are ready to offer that makes us feel like you don't think there's a chance we're going to make it out of there alive.

NORMAN OSBORN: Quite the contrary. I have all the faith in the world. There's a lot more riding on this than just your wasted-up-until-now lives.

VICTORIA HAND: We want you, each of you, to study these maps and intel. In this room. You don't leave the room. Study them. Find positions for yourselves once the battle has started. We'll need people in the air, on the ground. We'll need ground troops and snipers. Study. We're doing this smart. I'd ask if anyone had any questions but you've already asked more than any of us wanted to hear.

SPIDER-MAN: But what about--

VICTORIA HAND: No. Stop. No talking. It's reading time.

SPIDER-MAN: But--

VICTORIA HAND: Do you need a time-out?

End of transmission.

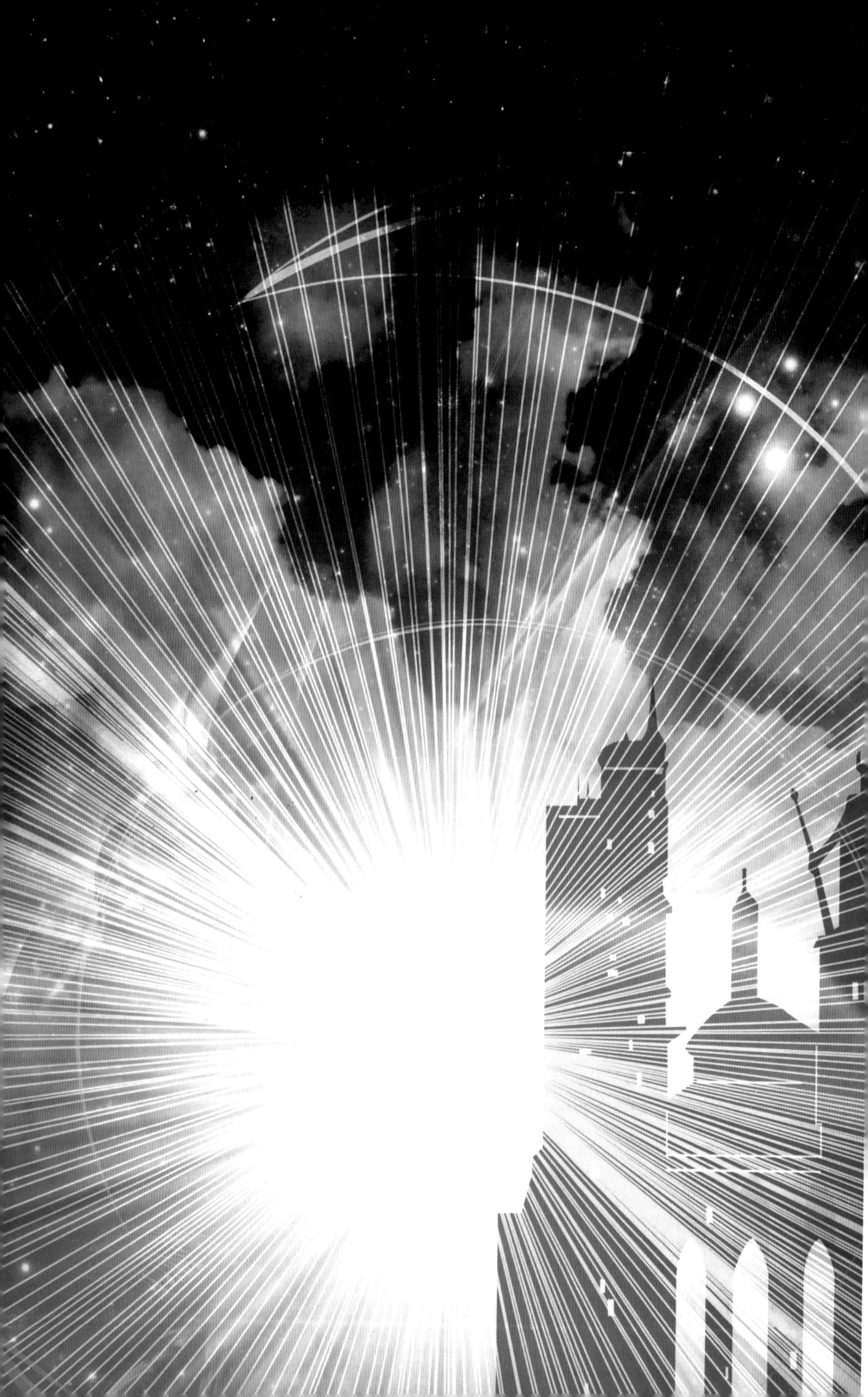

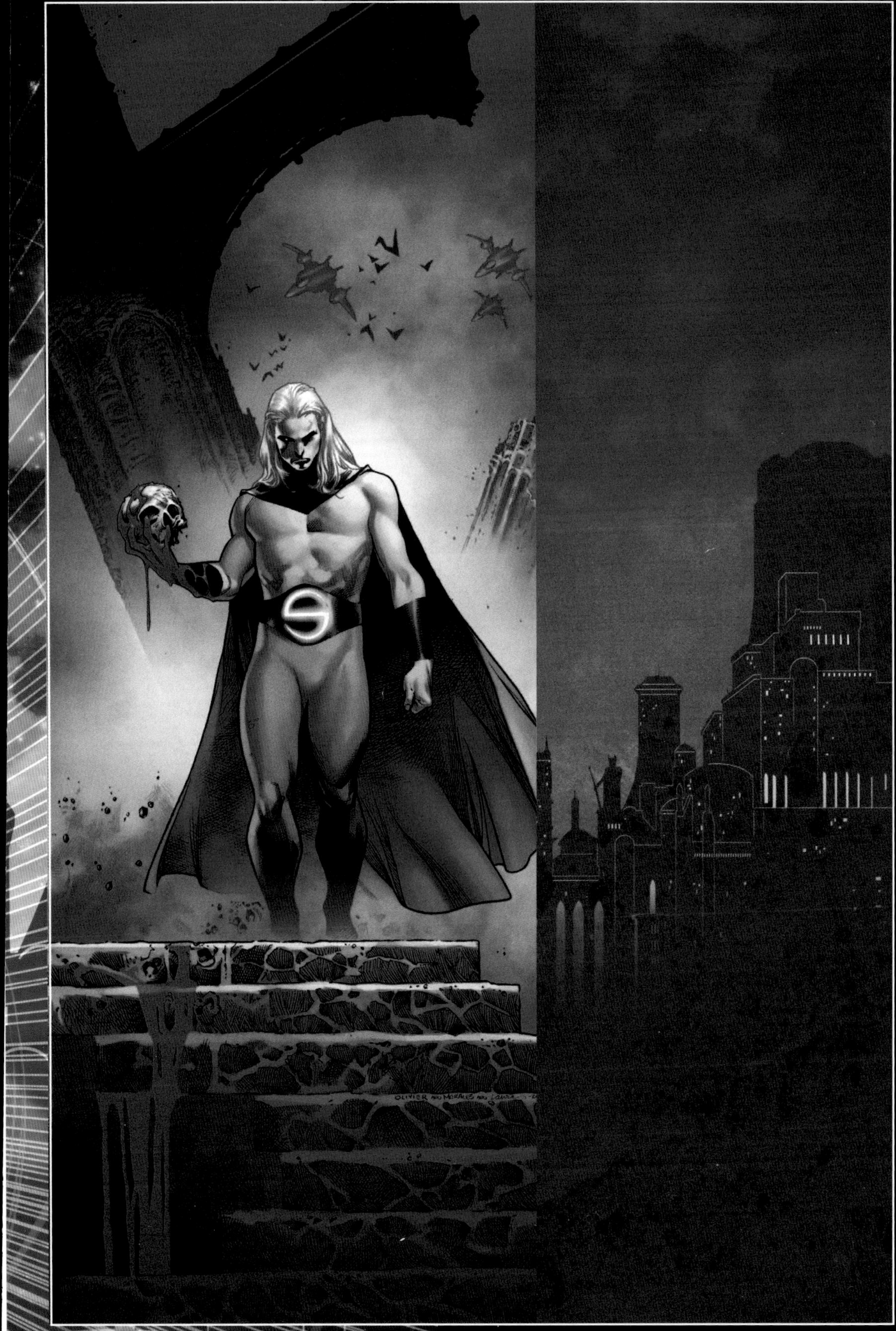

2

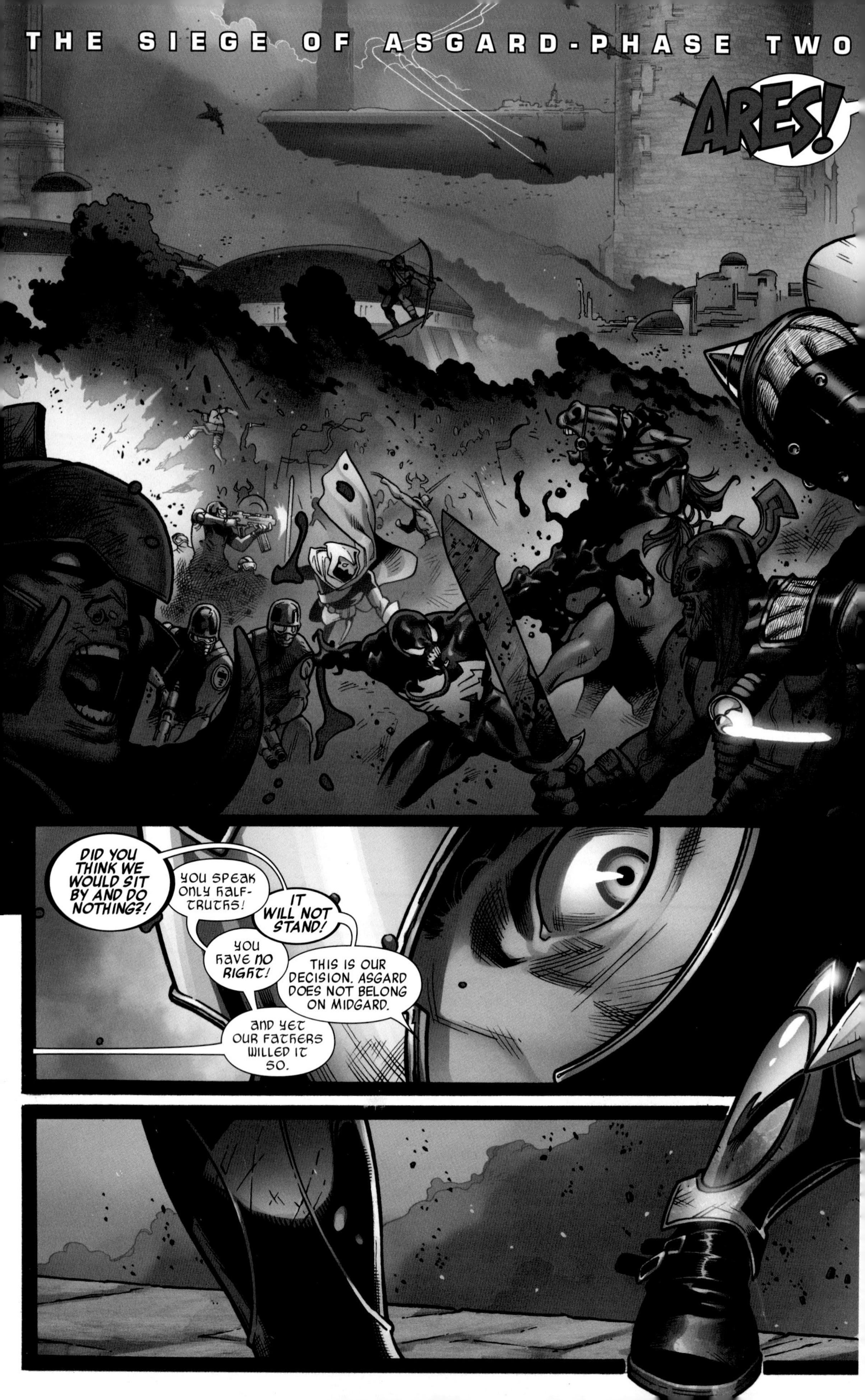
THE SIEGE OF ASGARD-PHASE TWO
ARES!
DID YOU THINK WE WOULD SIT BY AND DO NOTHING?!
YOU SPEAK ONLY HALF-TRUTHS!
IT WILL NOT STAND!
YOU HAVE NO RIGHT!
THIS IS OUR DECISION. ASGARD DOES NOT BELONG ON MIDGARD.
AND YET OUR FATHERS WILLED IT SO.

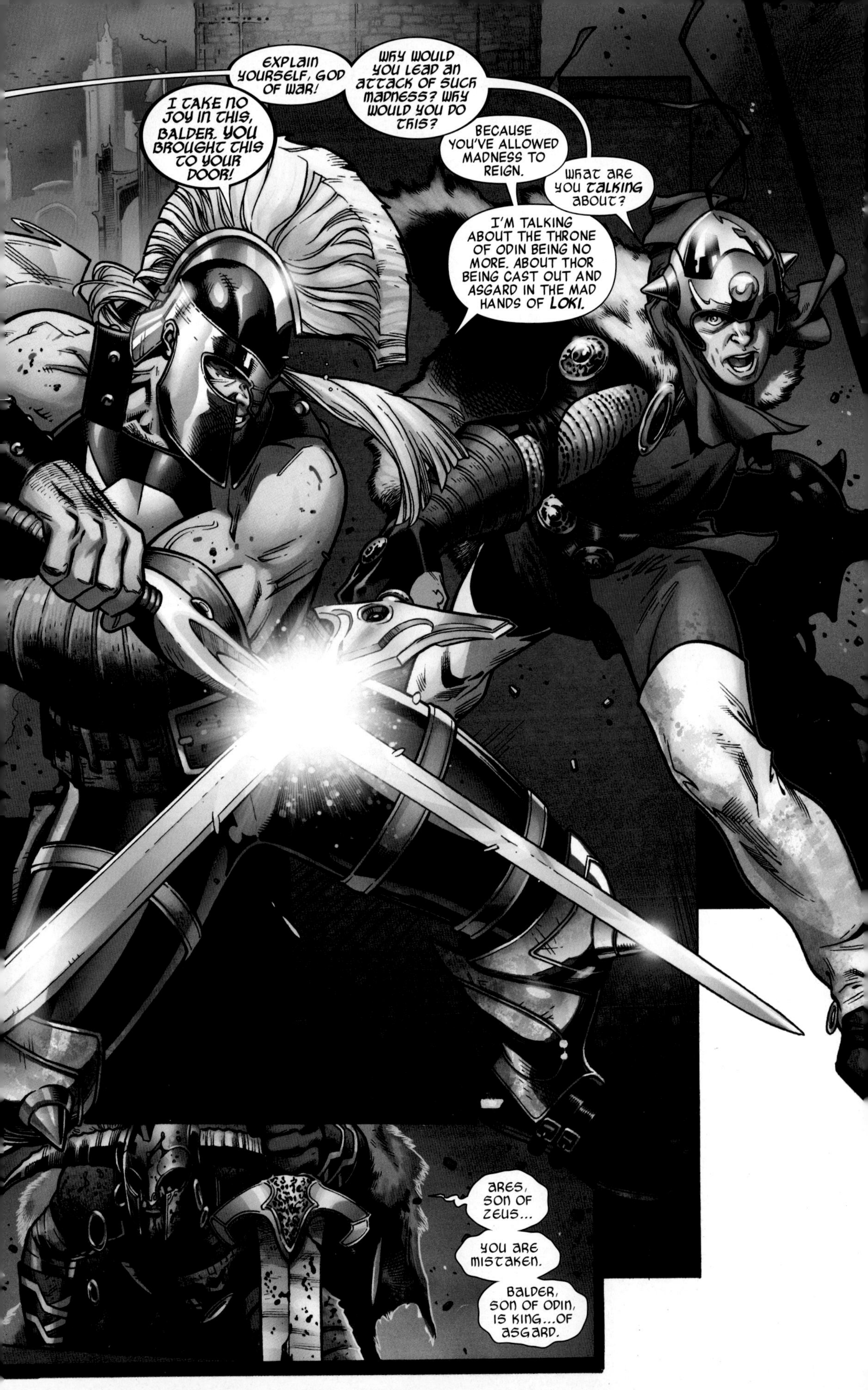
EXPLAIN YOURSELF, GOD OF WAR!
WHY WOULD YOU LEAD AN ATTACK OF SUCH MADNESS? WHY WOULD YOU DO THIS?
I TAKE NO JOY IN THIS, BALDER. YOU BROUGHT THIS TO YOUR DOOR!
BECAUSE YOU'VE ALLOWED MADNESS TO REIGN.
WHAT ARE YOU TALKING ABOUT?
I'M TALKING ABOUT THE THRONE OF ODIN BEING NO MORE. ABOUT THOR BEING CAST OUT AND ASGARD IN THE MAD HANDS OF LOKI.
ARES, SON OF ZEUS...
YOU ARE MISTAKEN.
BALDER, SON OF ODIN, IS KING...OF ASGARD.

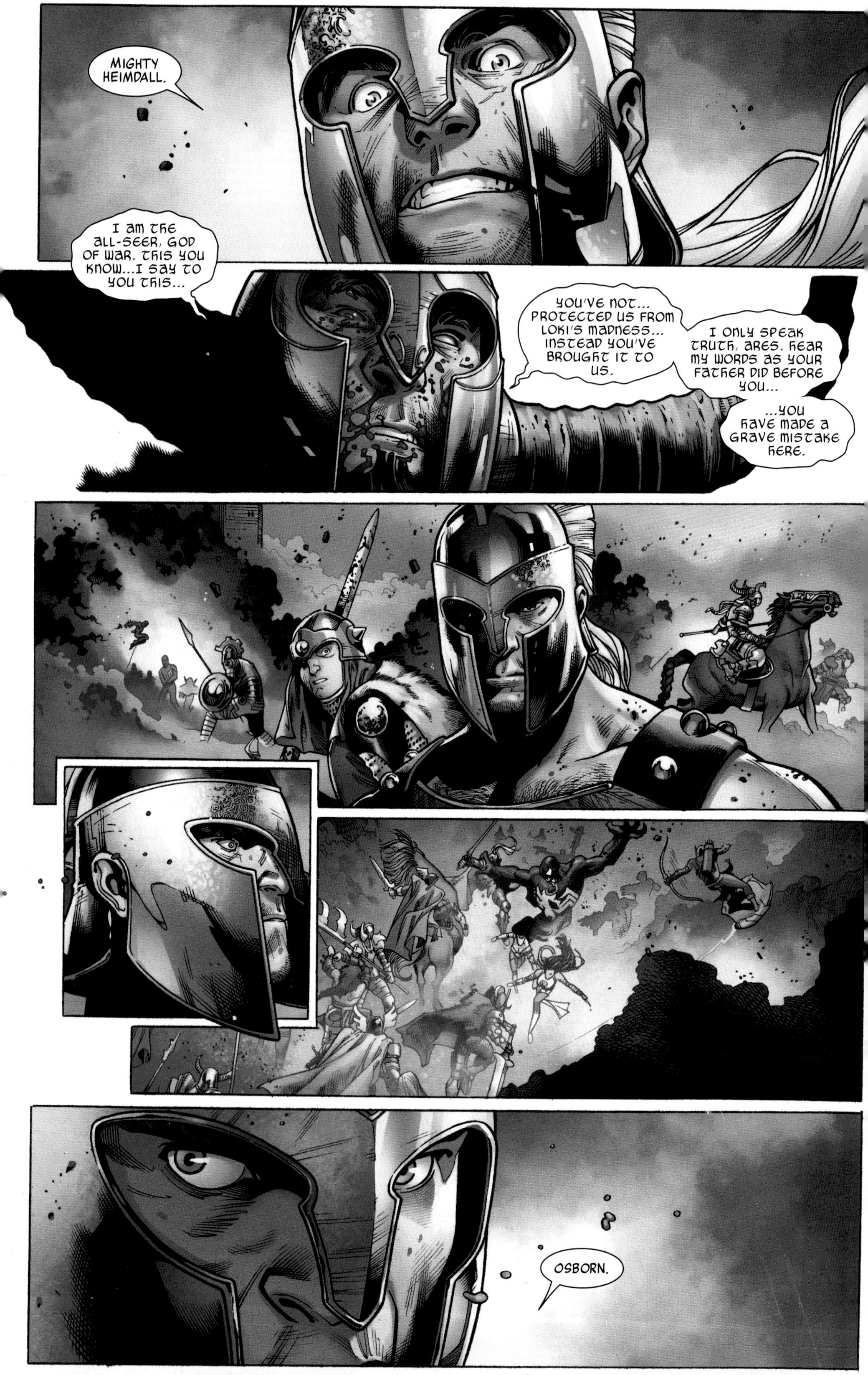
MIGHTY HEIMDALL.
I AM THE ALL-SEER, GOD OF WAR. THIS YOU KNOW...I SAY TO YOU THIS...
YOU'VE NOT... PROTECTED US FROM LOKI'S MADNESS... INSTEAD YOU'VE BROUGHT IT TO US.
I ONLY SPEAK TRUTH, ARES. HEAR MY WORDS AS YOUR FATHER DID BEFORE YOU...
...YOU HAVE MADE A GRAVE MISTAKE HERE.
OSBORN.

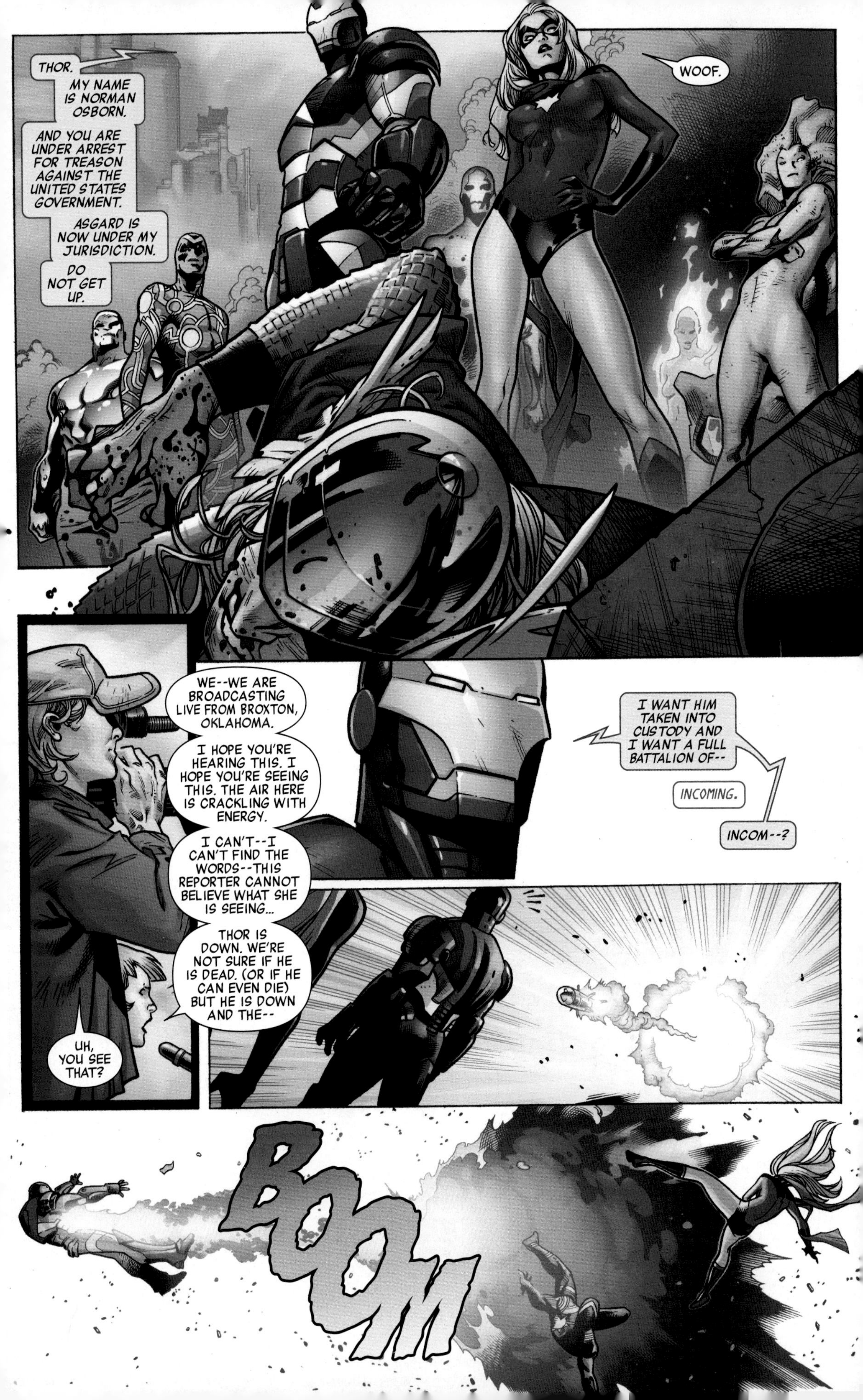
THOR.
MY NAME IS NORMAN OSBORN.
AND YOU ARE UNDER ARREST FOR TREASON AGAINST THE UNITED STATES GOVERNMENT.
ASGARD IS NOW UNDER MY JURISDICTION.
DO NOT GET UP.
WOOF.
WE--WE ARE BROADCASTING LIVE FROM BROXTON, OKLAHOMA.
I HOPE YOU'RE HEARING THIS. I HOPE YOU'RE SEEING THIS. THE AIR HERE IS CRACKLING WITH ENERGY.
I CAN'T--I CAN'T FIND THE WORDS--THIS REPORTER CANNOT BELIEVE WHAT SHE IS SEEING...
THOR IS DOWN. WE'RE NOT SURE IF HE IS DEAD. (OR IF HE CAN EVEN DIE) BUT HE IS DOWN AND THE--
UH, YOU SEE THAT?
I WANT HIM TAKEN INTO CUSTODY AND I WANT A FULL BATTALION OF--
INCOMING.
INCOM--?
BOOM

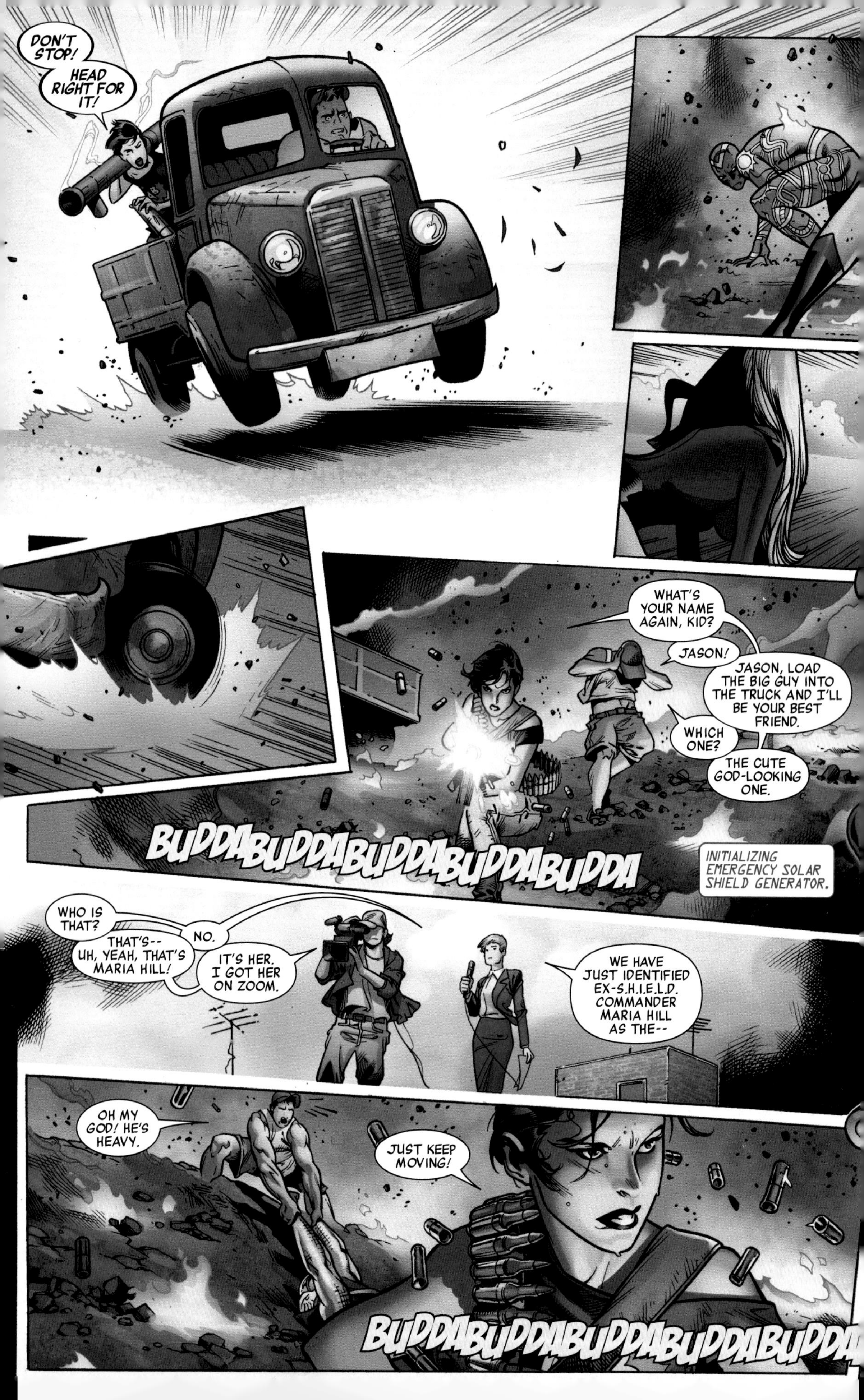

DON'T STOP! HEAD RIGHT FOR IT!
WHAT'S YOUR NAME AGAIN, KID?
JASON!
JASON, LOAD THE BIG GUY INTO THE TRUCK AND I'LL BE YOUR BEST FRIEND.
WHICH ONE?
THE CUTE GOD-LOOKING ONE.
BUDDABUDDABUDDABUDDABUDDA
INITIALIZING EMERGENCY SOLAR SHIELD GENERATOR.
WHO IS THAT?
THAT'S-- UH, YEAH, THAT'S MARIA HILL!
NO.
IT'S HER. I GOT HER ON ZOOM.
WE HAVE JUST IDENTIFIED EX-S.H.I.E.L.D. COMMANDER MARIA HILL AS THE--
OH MY GOD! HE'S HEAVY.
JUST KEEP MOVING!
BUDDABUDDABUDDABUDDABUDDA

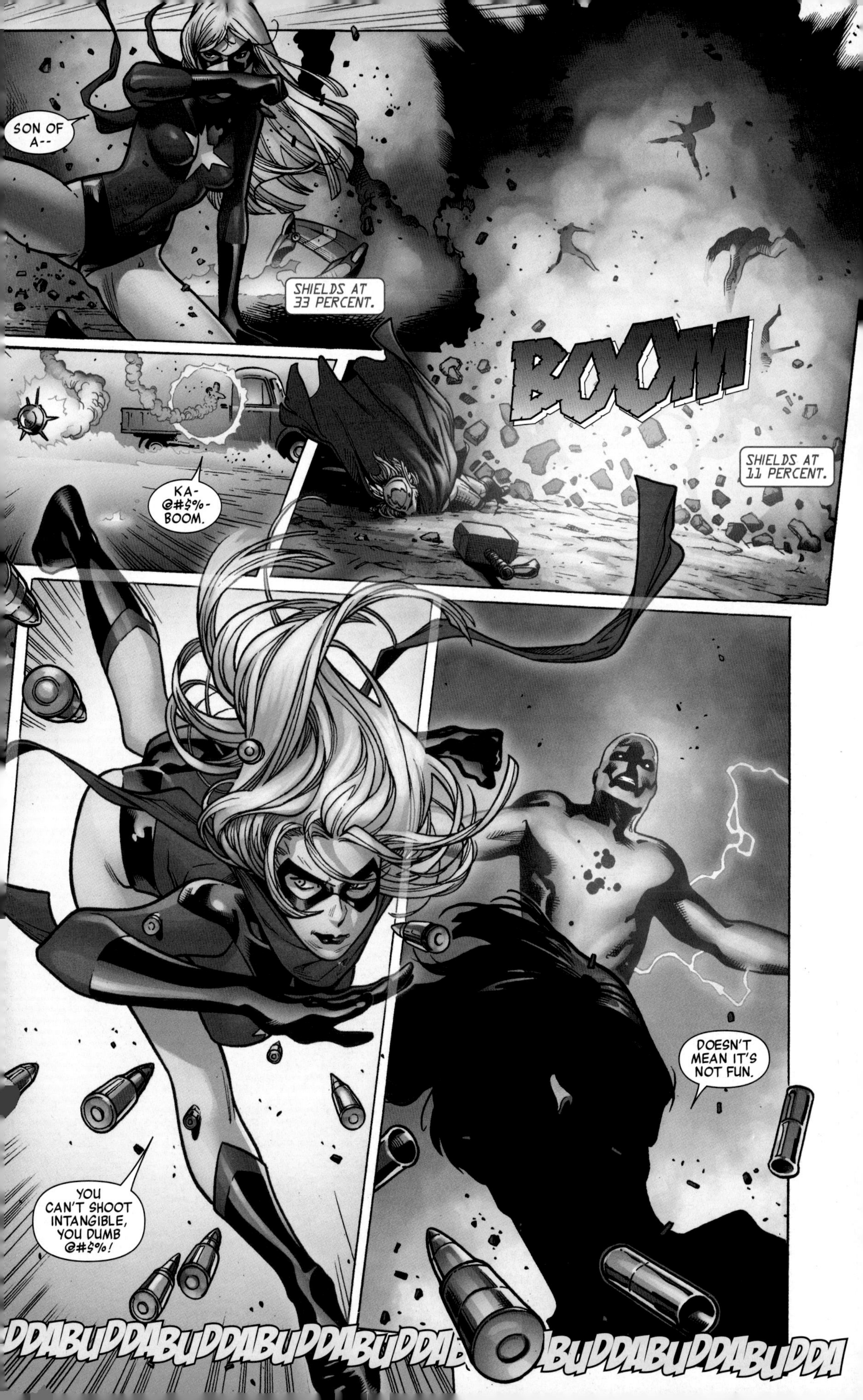
SON OF A--
SHIELDS AT 33 PERCENT.
BOOM
SHIELDS AT 11 PERCENT.
KA-@#$%-BOOM.
YOU CAN'T SHOOT INTANGIBLE, YOU DUMB @#$%!
DOESN'T MEAN IT'S NOT FUN.
DDABUDDABUDDABUDDABUDDAB BUDDABUDDABUDDA

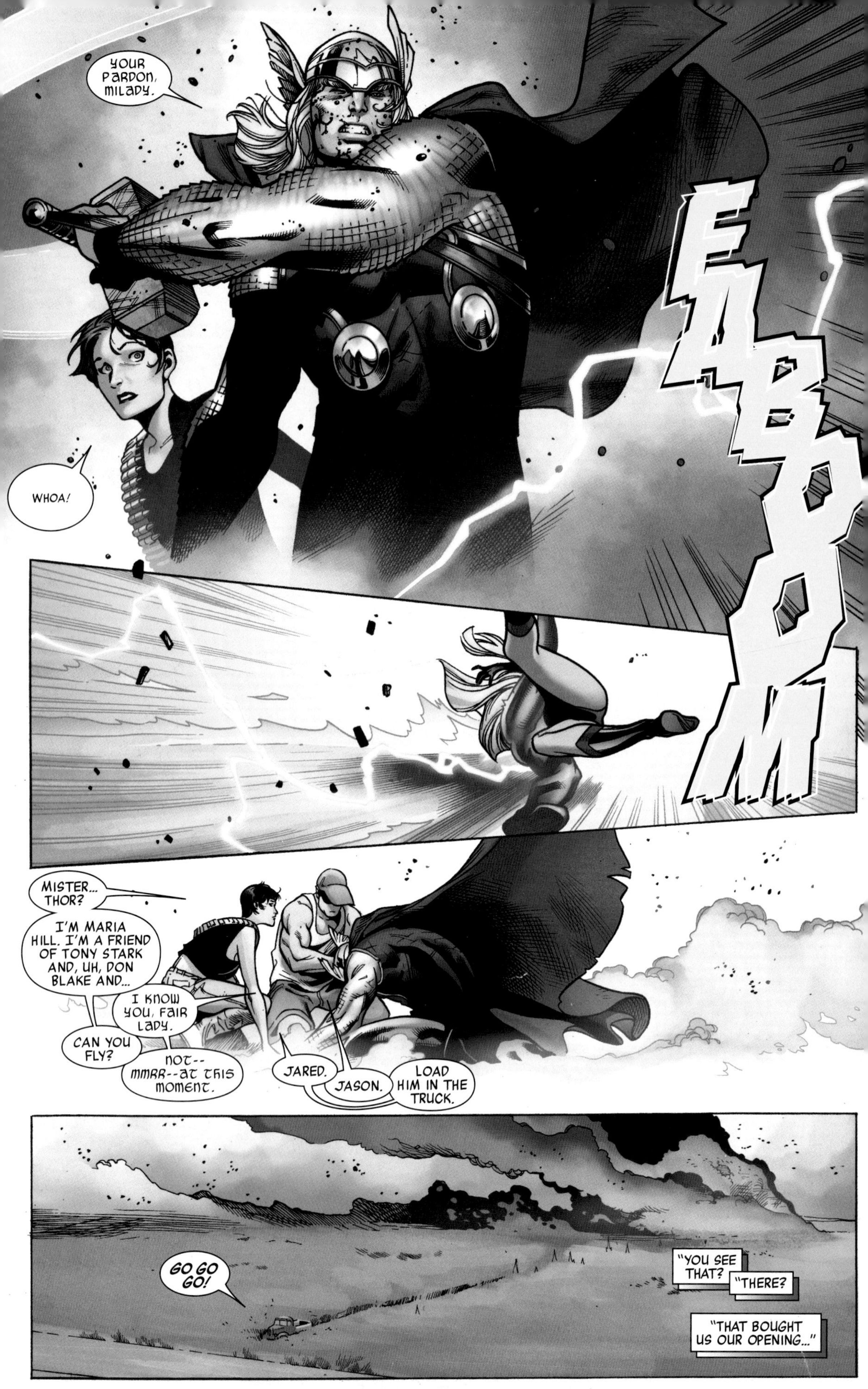
YOUR PARDON, MILADY.
WHOA!
KABOOM
MISTER... THOR?
I'M MARIA HILL. I'M A FRIEND OF TONY STARK AND, UH, DON BLAKE AND...
I KNOW YOU, FAIR LADY.
CAN YOU FLY?
NOT-- MMRR--AT THIS MOMENT.
JARED.
JASON.
LOAD HIM IN THE TRUCK.
GO GO GO!
"YOU SEE THAT?
"THERE?
"THAT BOUGHT US OUR OPENING..."

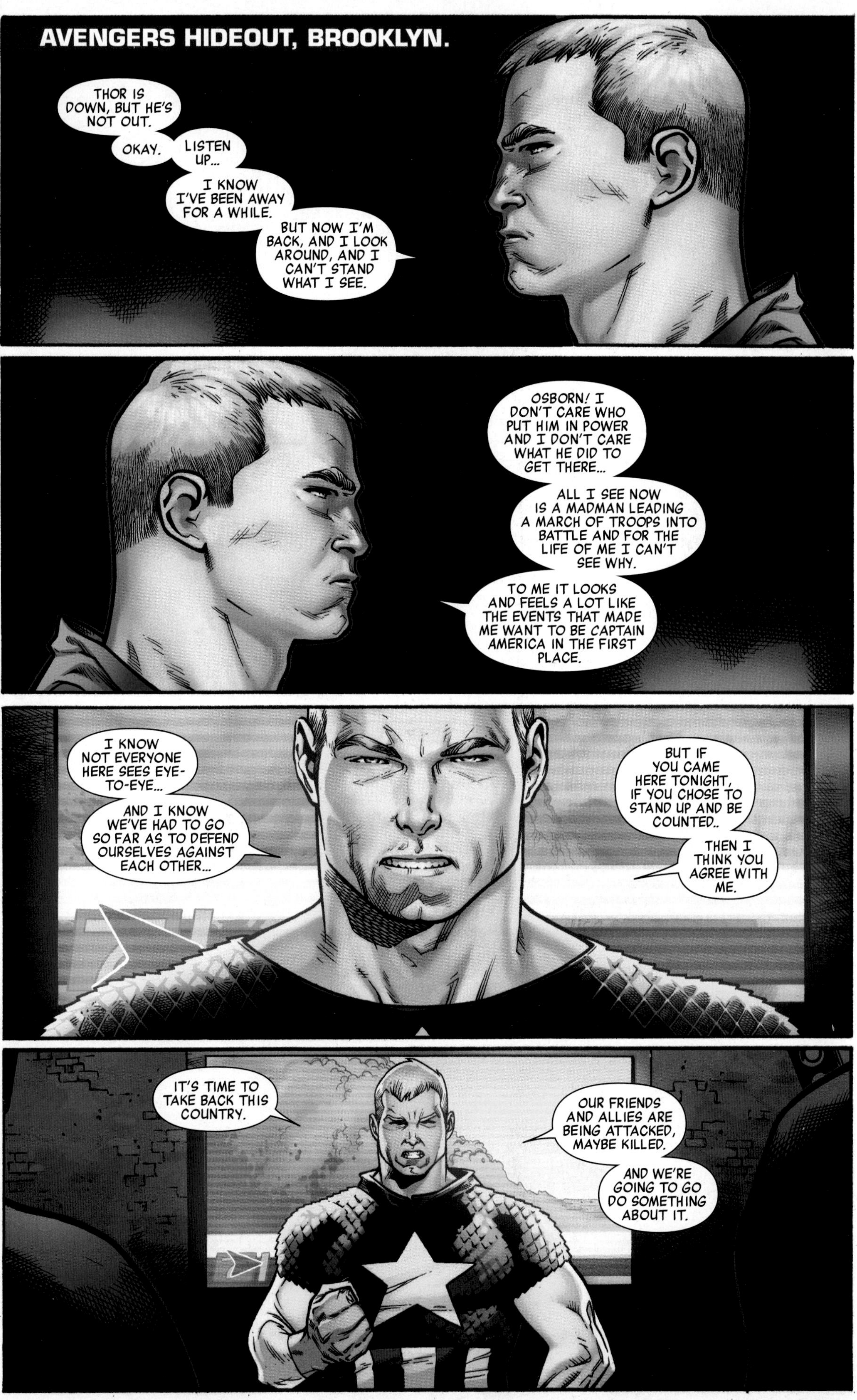
AVENGERS HIDEOUT, BROOKLYN.
THOR IS DOWN, BUT HE'S NOT OUT.
OKAY.
LISTEN UP...
I KNOW I'VE BEEN AWAY FOR A WHILE.
BUT NOW I'M BACK, AND I LOOK AROUND, AND I CAN'T STAND WHAT I SEE.
OSBORN! I DON'T CARE WHO PUT HIM IN POWER AND I DON'T CARE WHAT HE DID TO GET THERE...
ALL I SEE NOW IS A MADMAN LEADING A MARCH OF TROOPS INTO BATTLE AND FOR THE LIFE OF ME I CAN'T SEE WHY.
TO ME IT LOOKS AND FEELS A LOT LIKE THE EVENTS THAT MADE ME WANT TO BE CAPTAIN AMERICA IN THE FIRST PLACE.
I KNOW NOT EVERYONE HERE SEES EYE-TO-EYE...
AND I KNOW WE'VE HAD TO GO SO FAR AS TO DEFEND OURSELVES AGAINST EACH OTHER...
BUT IF YOU CAME HERE TONIGHT, IF YOU CHOSE TO STAND UP AND BE COUNTED..
THEN I THINK YOU AGREE WITH ME.
IT'S TIME TO TAKE BACK THIS COUNTRY.
OUR FRIENDS AND ALLIES ARE BEING ATTACKED, MAYBE KILLED.
AND WE'RE GOING TO GO DO SOMETHING ABOUT IT.

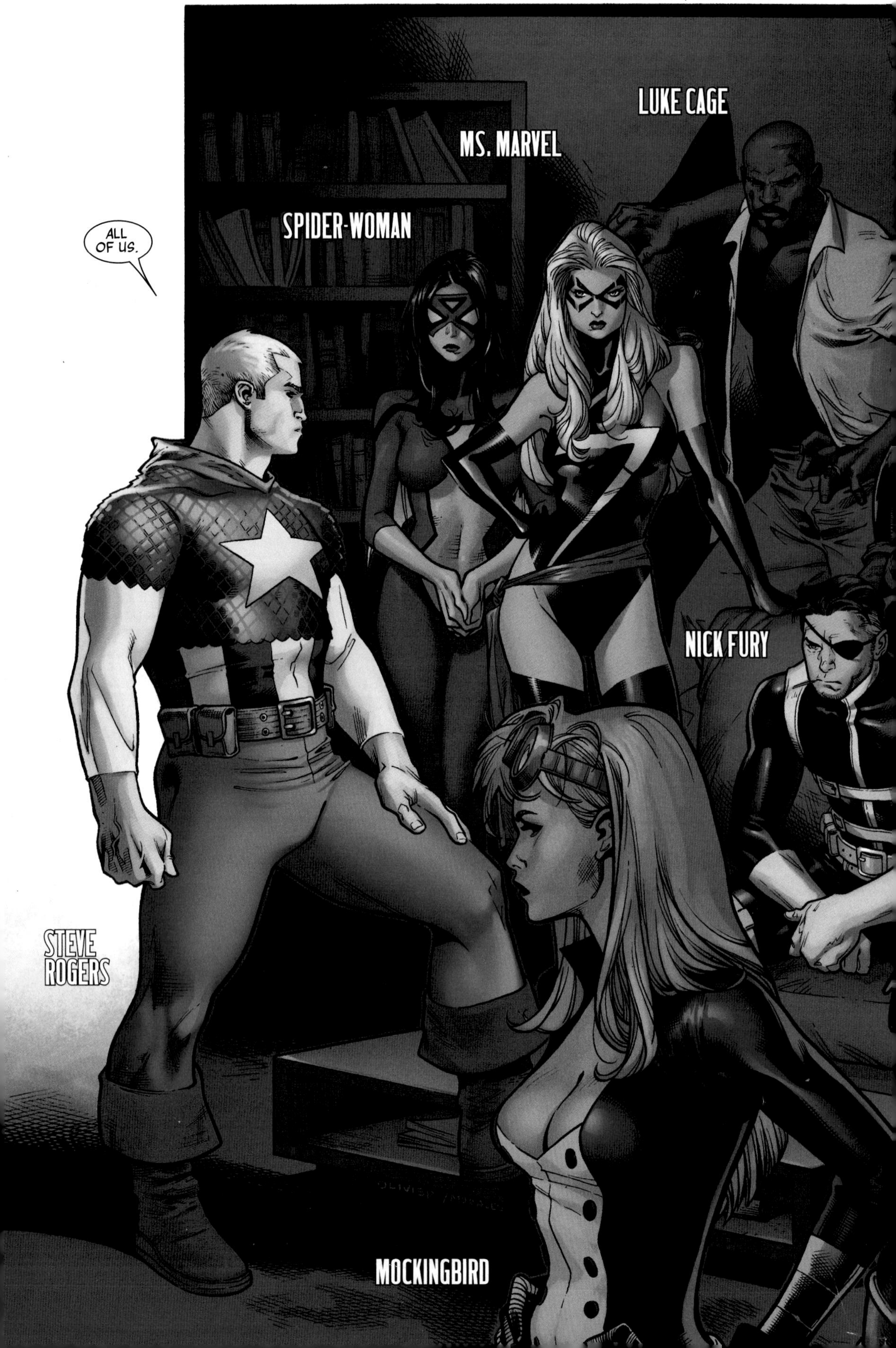
ALL OF US.
LUKE CAGE
MS. MARVEL
SPIDER-WOMAN
NICK FURY
STEVE ROGERS
MOCKINGBIRD

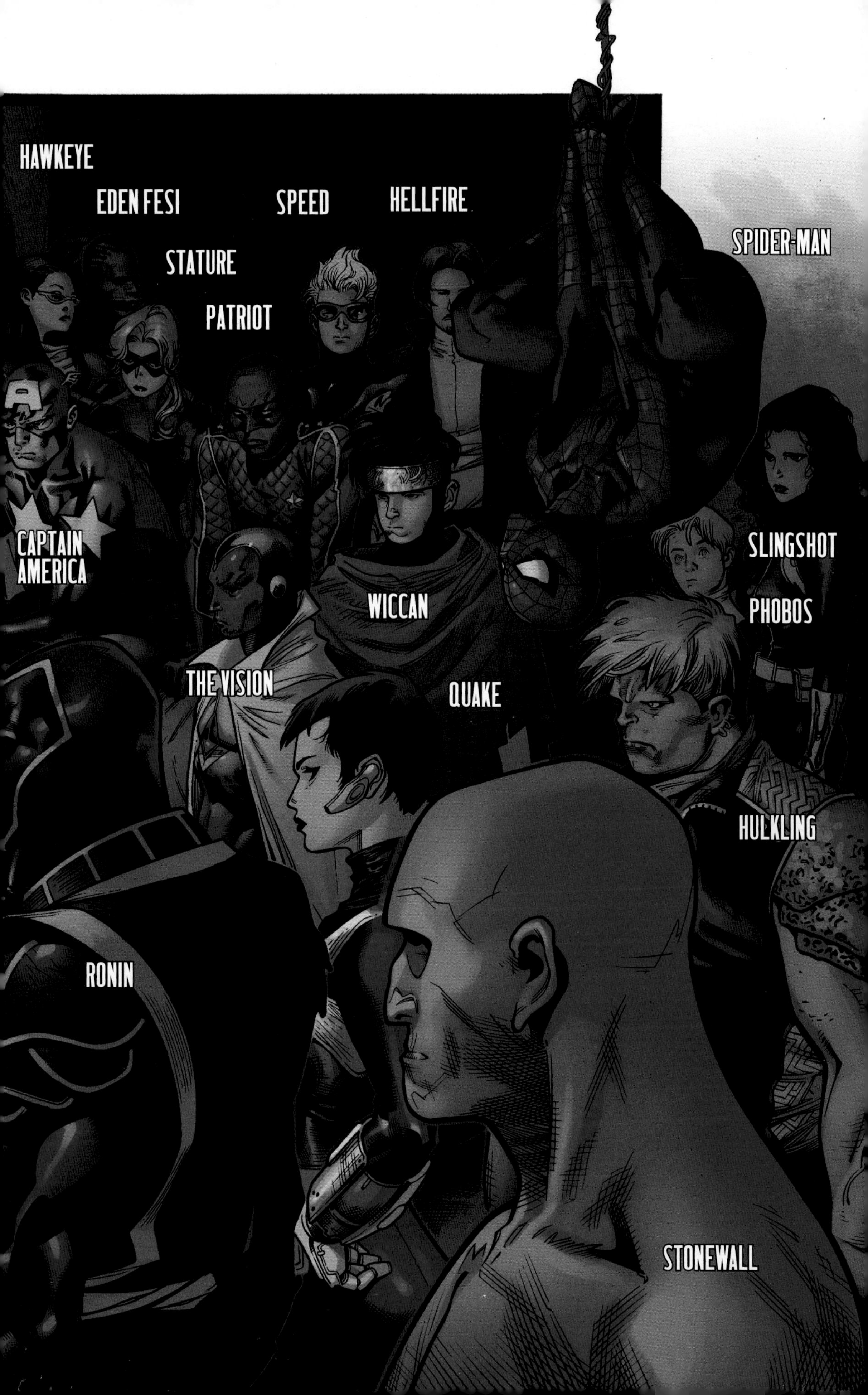
HAWKEYE
EDEN FESI
SPEED
HELLFIRE
SPIDER-MAN
STATURE
PATRIOT
CAPTAIN AMERICA
SLINGSHOT
WICCAN
PHOBOS
THE VISION
QUAKE
HULKING
RONIN
STONEWALL

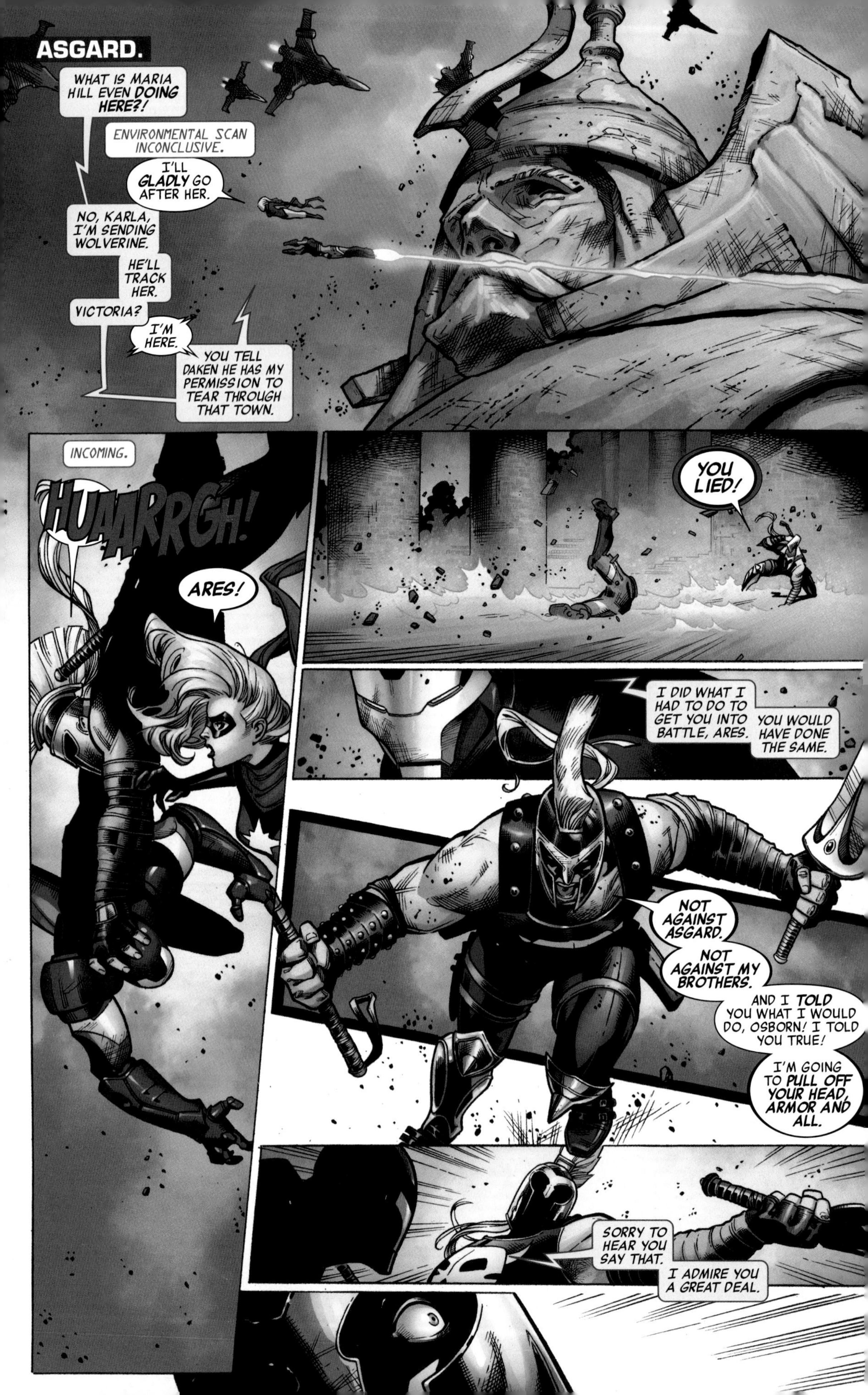
ASGARD.
WHAT IS MARIA HILL EVEN DOING HERE?!
ENVIRONMENTAL SCAN INCONCLUSIVE.
I'LL GLADLY GO AFTER HER.
NO, KARLA, I'M SENDING WOLVERINE.
HE'LL TRACK HER.
VICTORIA?
I'M HERE.
YOU TELL DAKEN HE HAS MY PERMISSION TO TEAR THROUGH THAT TOWN.
INCOMING.
HUAARRGH!
ARES!
YOU LIED!
I DID WHAT I HAD TO DO TO GET YOU INTO BATTLE, ARES.
YOU WOULD HAVE DONE THE SAME.
NOT AGAINST ASGARD.
NOT AGAINST MY BROTHERS.
AND I TOLD YOU WHAT I WOULD DO, OSBORN! I TOLD YOU TRUE!
I'M GOING TO PULL OFF YOUR HEAD, ARMOR AND ALL.
SORRY TO HEAR YOU SAY THAT.
I ADMIRE YOU A GREAT DEAL.

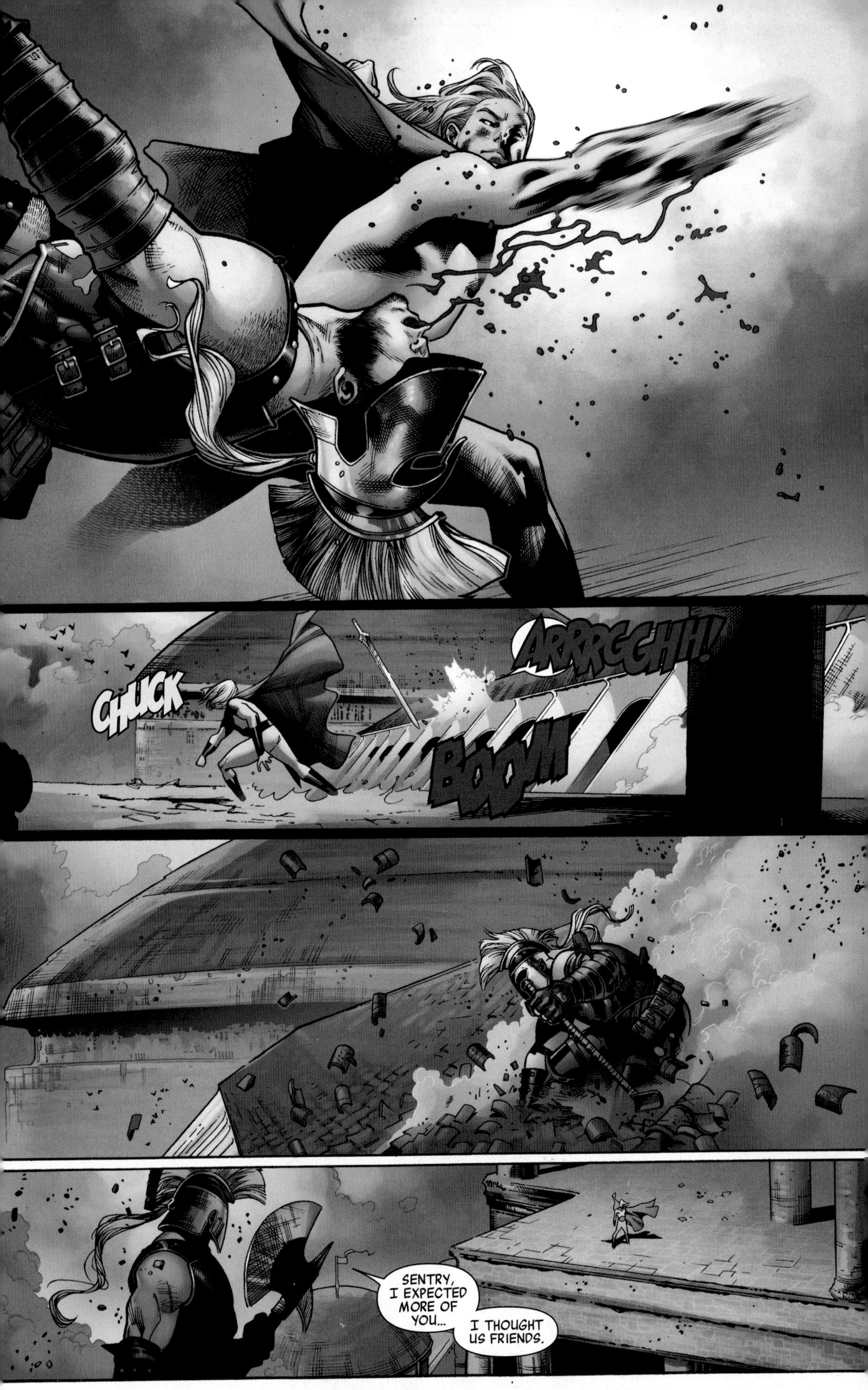
CHUCK
ARRRGGHH!
BOOM
SENTRY, I EXPECTED MORE OF YOU...
I THOUGHT US FRIENDS.

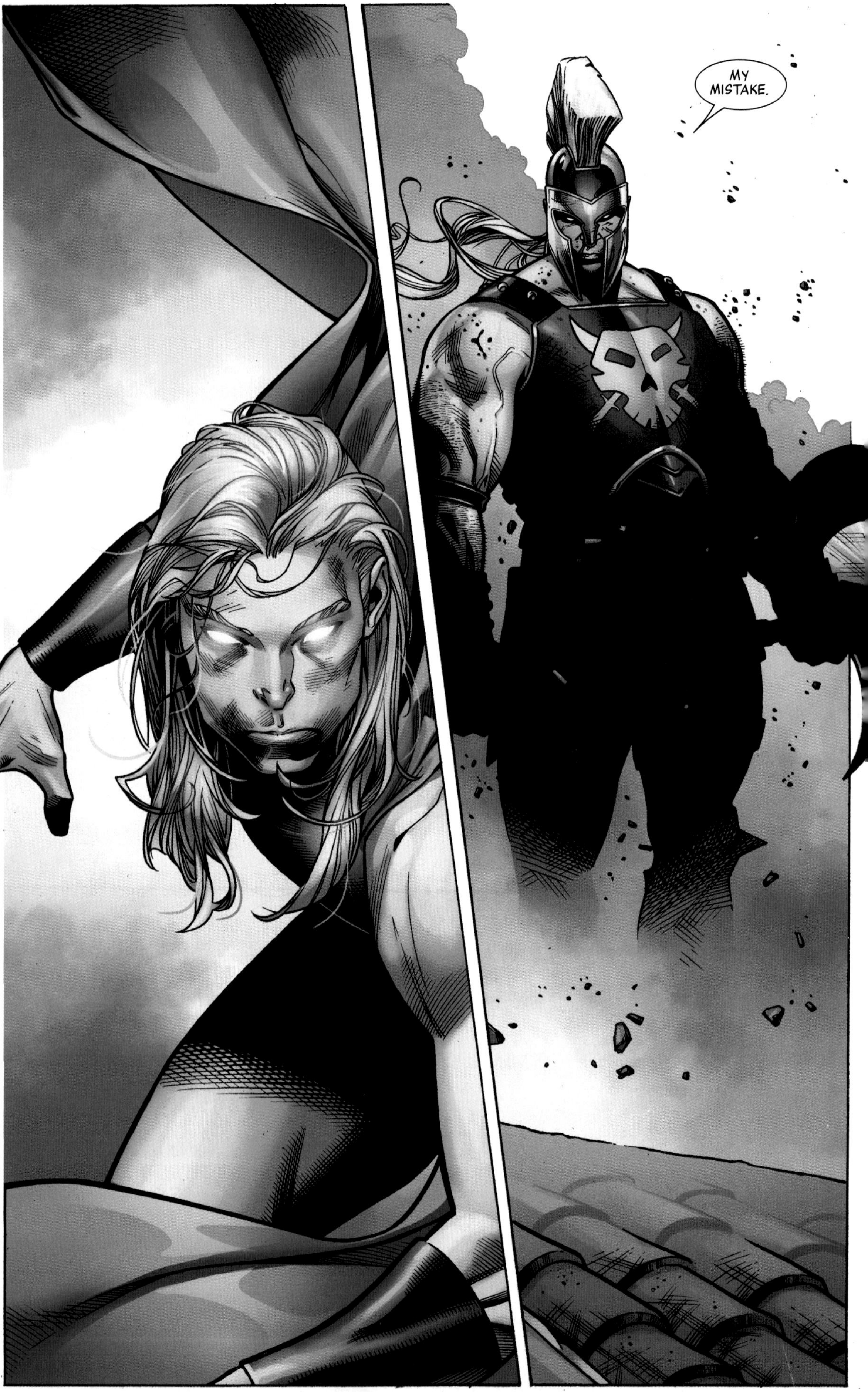
MY MISTAKE.

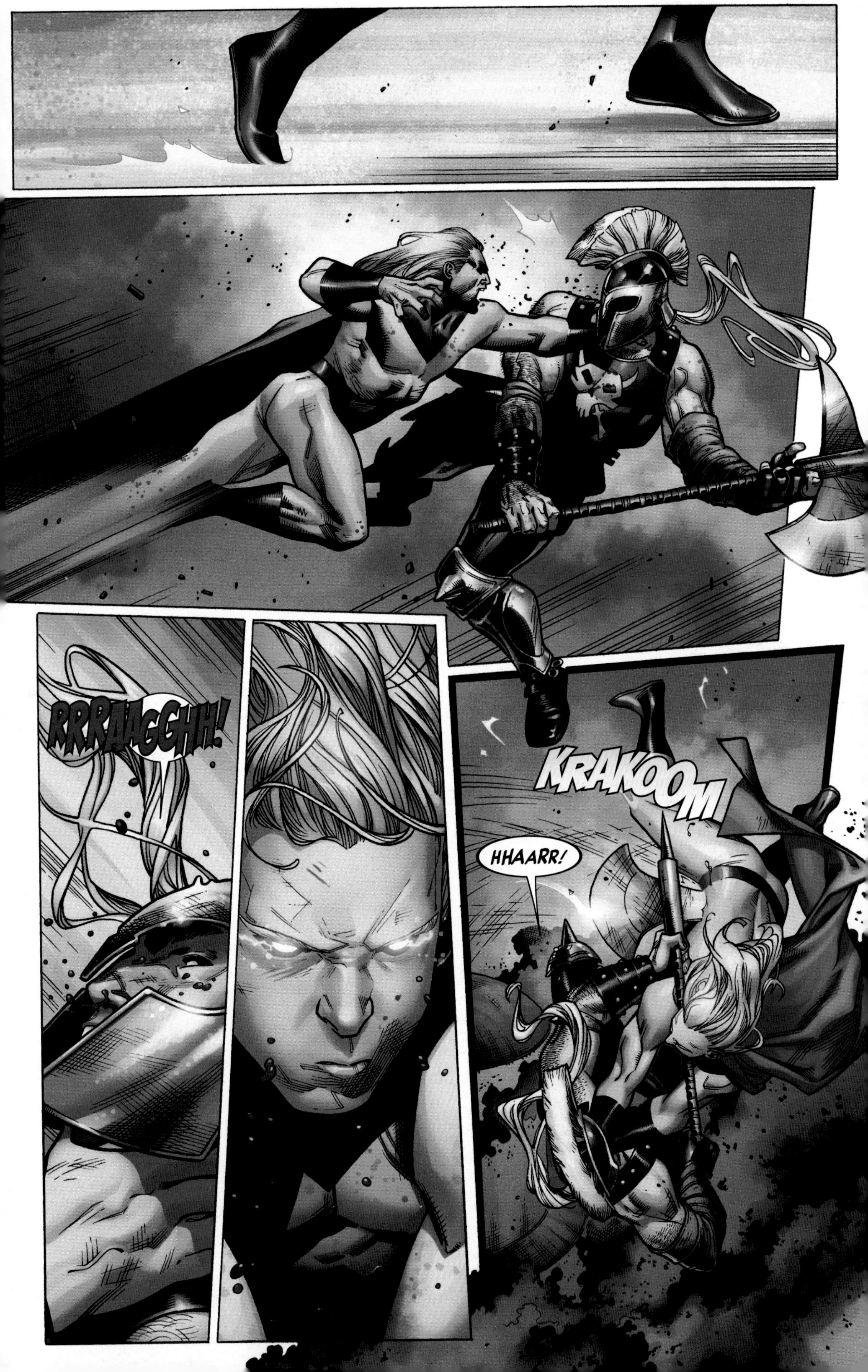
RRRAAGGHH!
KRAKOOM
HHAARR!

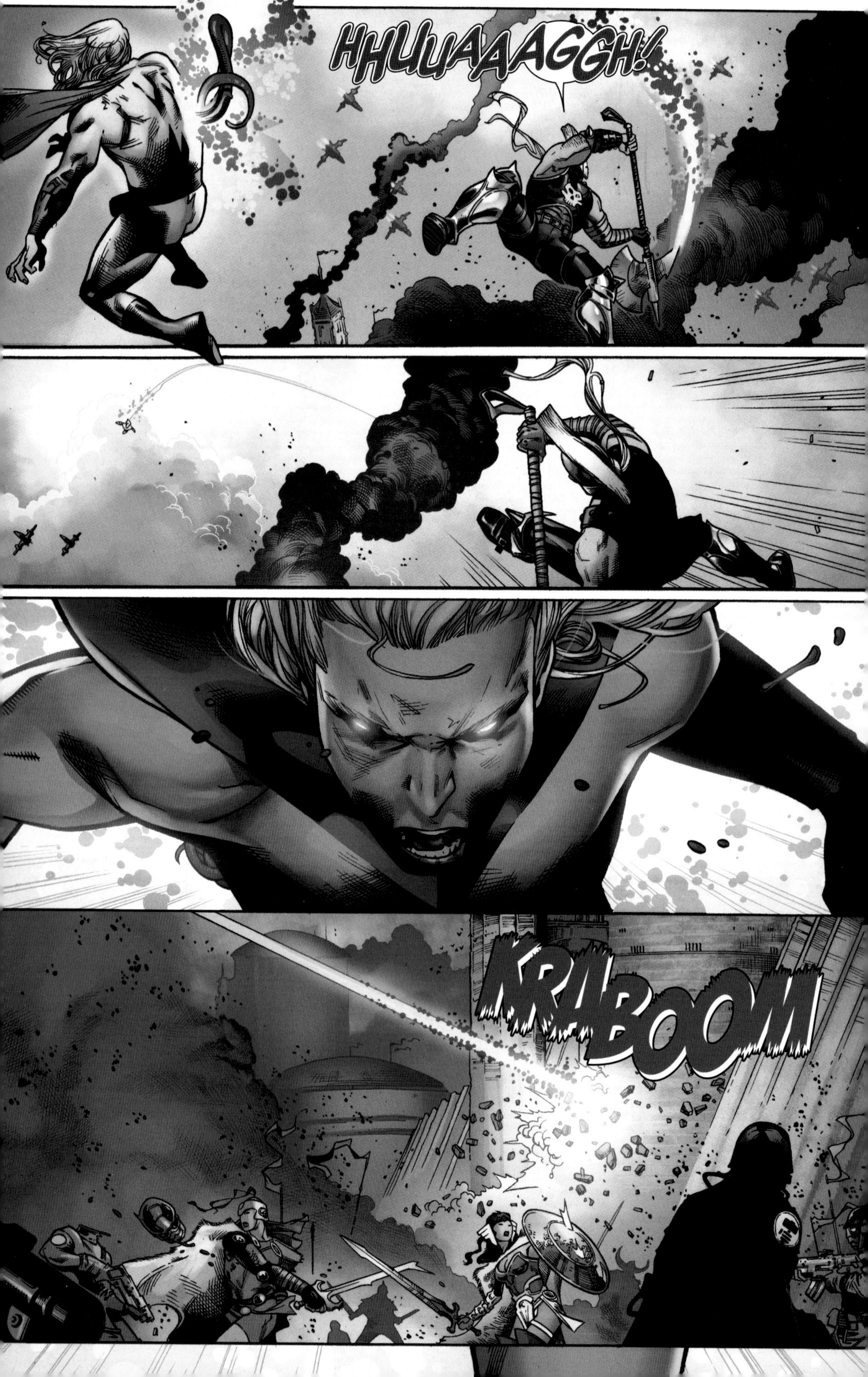
HHUUAAAAGGH!
KRABOOM

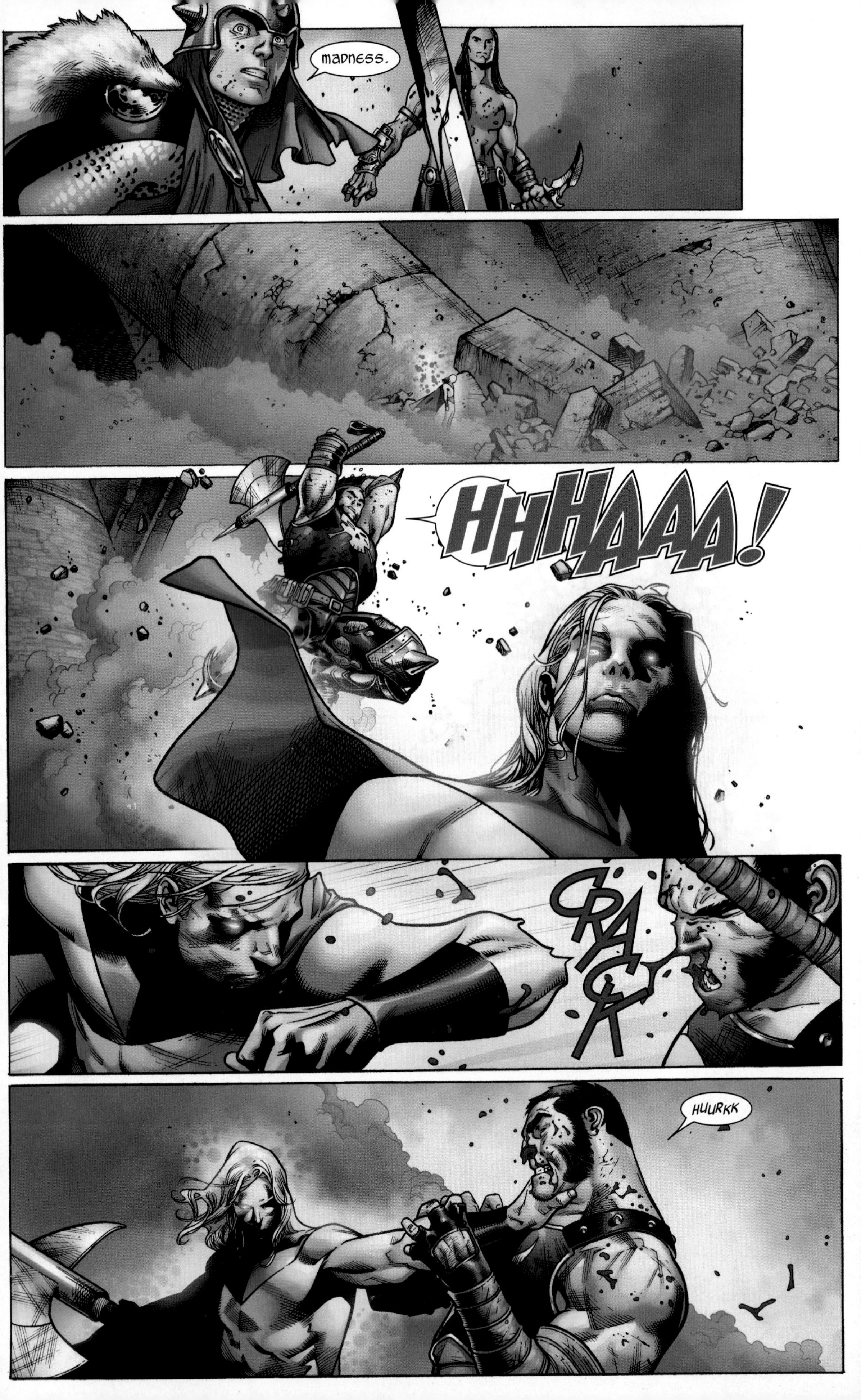
MADNESS.
HHHAAAA!
CRACK
HUURKK

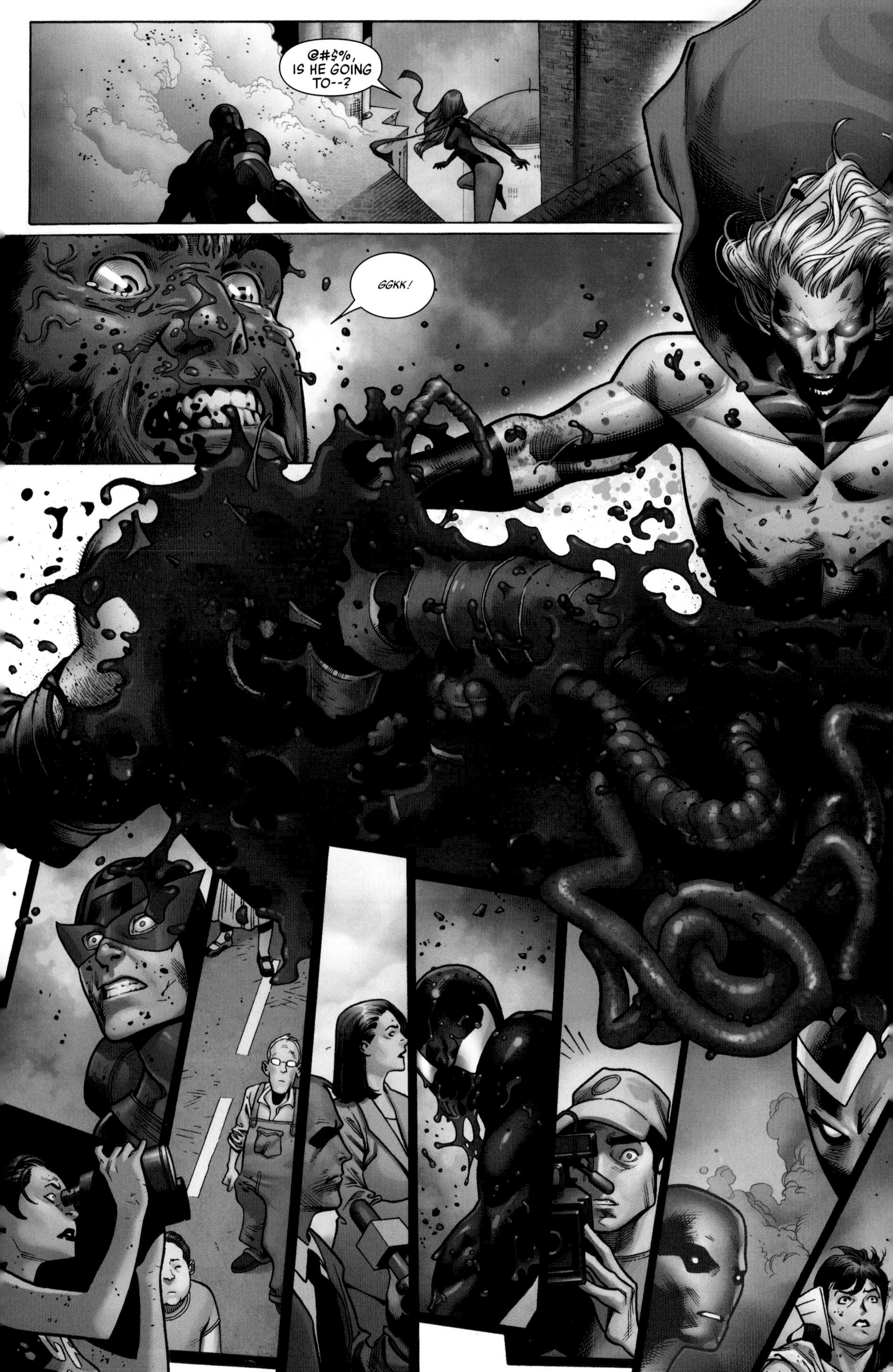
@#$%, IS HE GOING TO--?
GGKK!

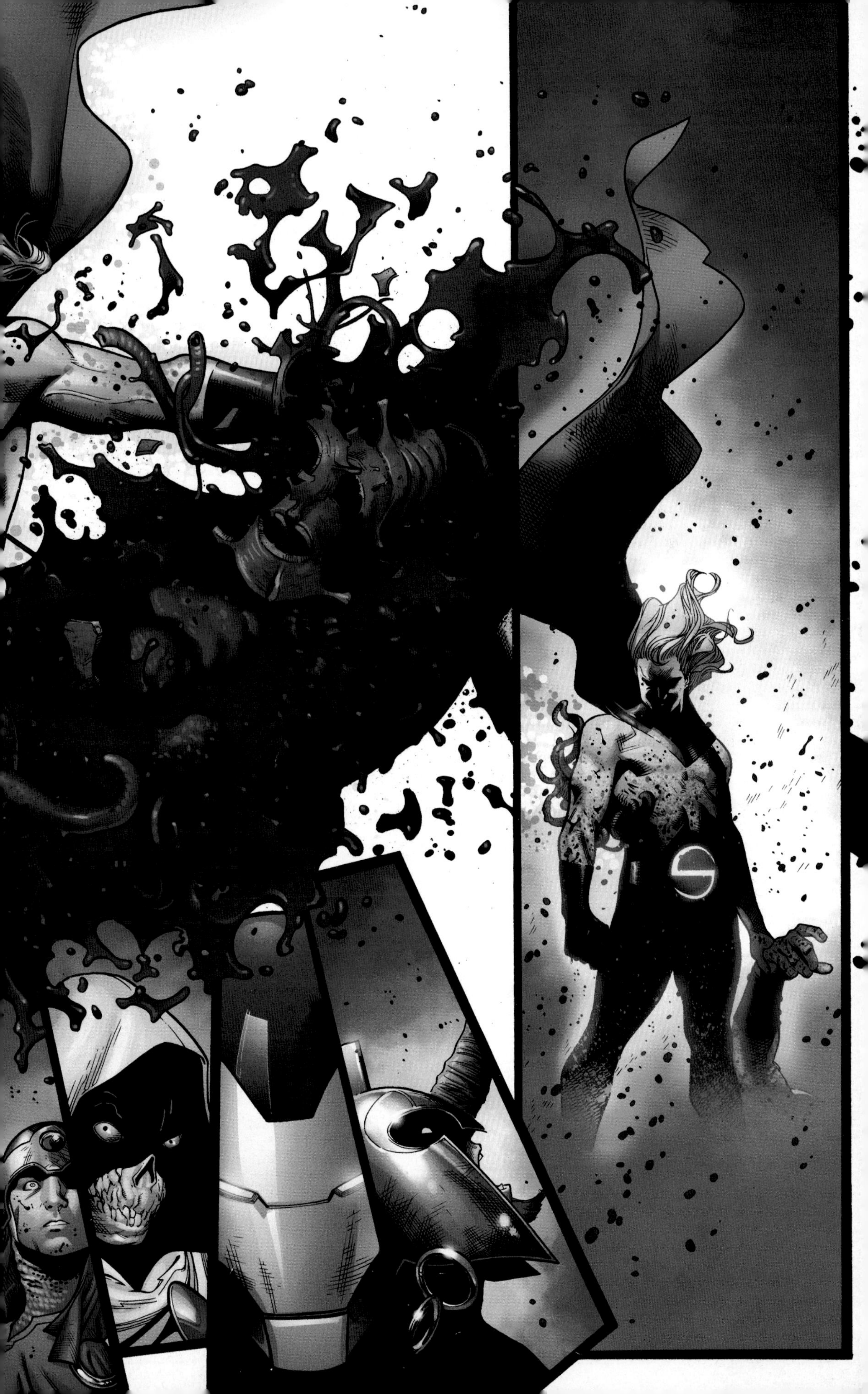

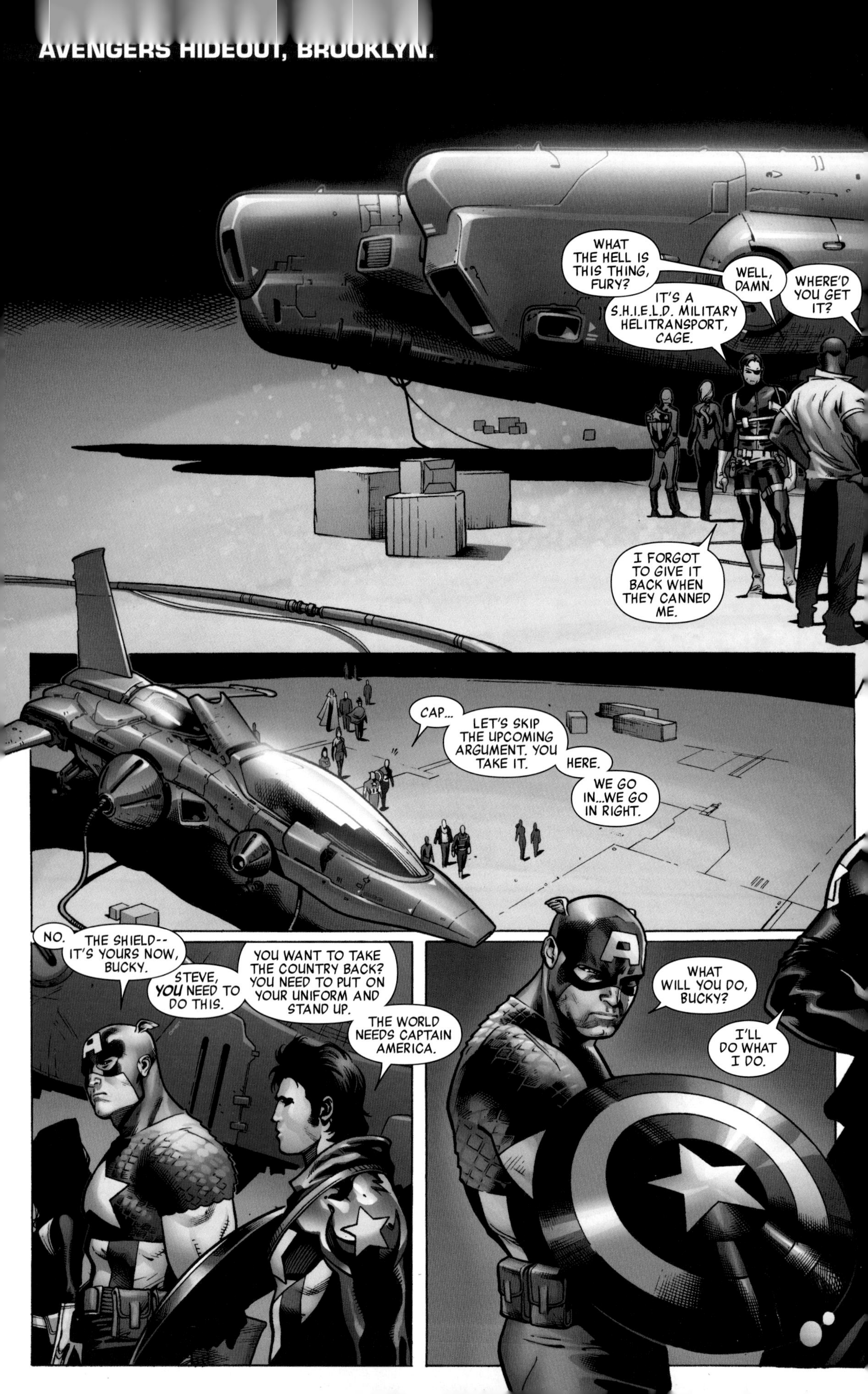
AVENGERS HIDEOUT, BROOKLYN.
WHAT THE HELL IS THIS THING, FURY?
IT'S A S.H.I.E.L.D. MILITARY HELITRANSPORT, CAGE.
WELL, DAMN.
WHERE'D YOU GET IT?
I FORGOT TO GIVE IT BACK WHEN THEY CANNED ME.
CAP...
LET'S SKIP THE UPCOMING ARGUMENT. YOU TAKE IT.
HERE.
WE GO IN...WE GO IN RIGHT.
NO.
THE SHIELD-- IT'S YOURS NOW, BUCKY.
STEVE, YOU NEED TO DO THIS.
YOU WANT TO TAKE THE COUNTRY BACK? YOU NEED TO PUT ON YOUR UNIFORM AND STAND UP.
THE WORLD NEEDS CAPTAIN AMERICA.
WHAT WILL YOU DO, BUCKY?
I'LL DO WHAT I DO.

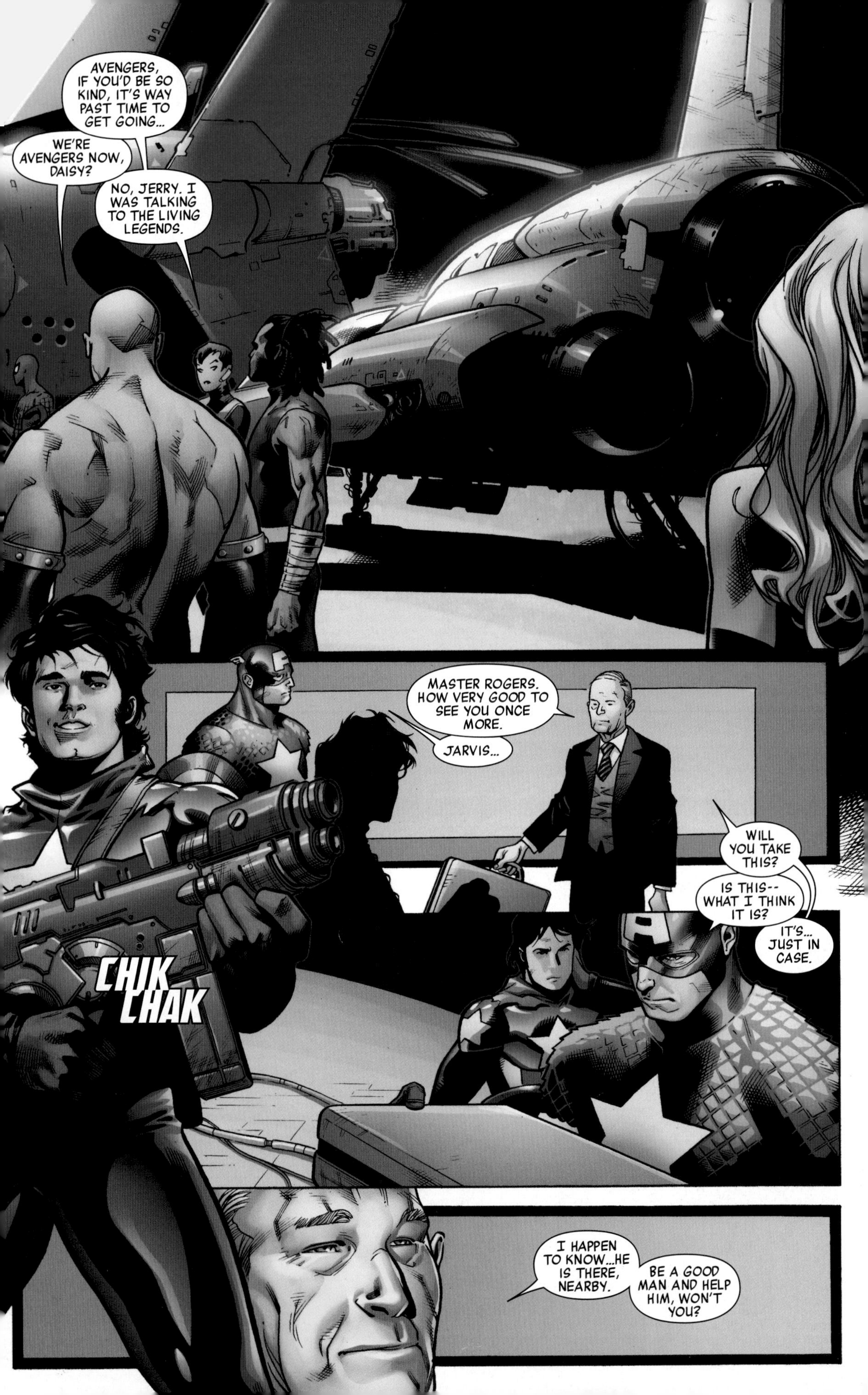

AVENGERS, IF YOU'D BE SO KIND, IT'S WAY PAST TIME TO GET GOING...
WE'RE AVENGERS NOW, DAISY?
NO, JERRY. I WAS TALKING TO THE LIVING LEGENDS.
MASTER ROGERS. HOW VERY GOOD TO SEE YOU ONCE MORE.
JARVIS...
WILL YOU TAKE THIS?
IS THIS--WHAT I THINK IT IS?
IT'S... JUST IN CASE.
CHIK CHAK
I HAPPEN TO KNOW...HE IS THERE, NEARBY.
BE A GOOD MAN AND HELP HIM, WON'T YOU?

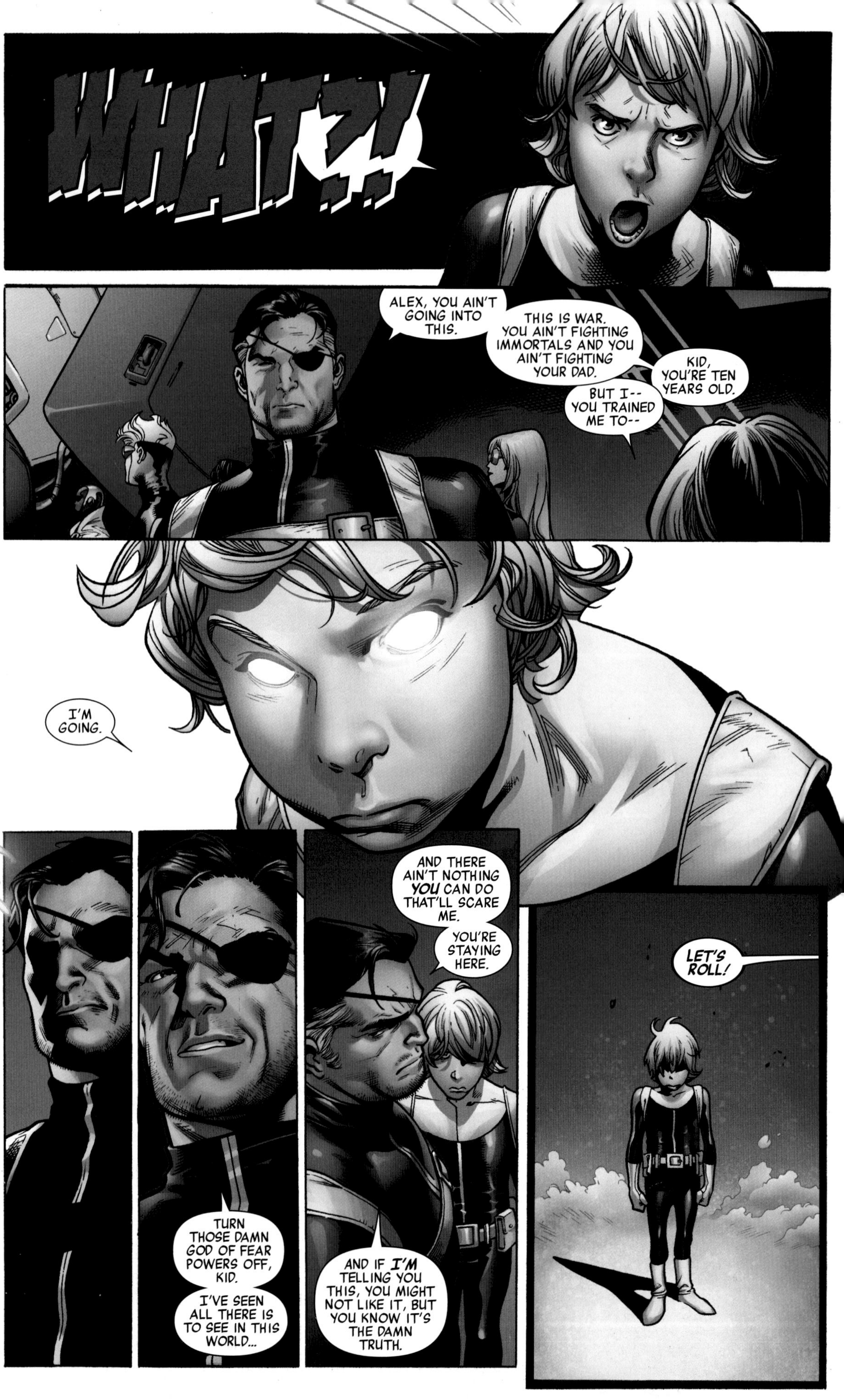
WHAT?!
ALEX, YOU AIN'T GOING INTO THIS.
THIS IS WAR. YOU AIN'T FIGHTING IMMORTALS AND YOU AIN'T FIGHTING YOUR DAD.
BUT I-- YOU TRAINED ME TO--
KID, YOU'RE TEN YEARS OLD.
I'M GOING.
TURN THOSE DAMN GOD OF FEAR POWERS OFF, KID.
I'VE SEEN ALL THERE IS TO SEE IN THIS WORLD...
AND THERE AIN'T NOTHING YOU CAN DO THAT'LL SCARE ME.
YOU'RE STAYING HERE.
AND IF I'M TELLING YOU THIS, YOU MIGHT NOT LIKE IT, BUT YOU KNOW IT'S THE DAMN TRUTH.
LET'S ROLL!

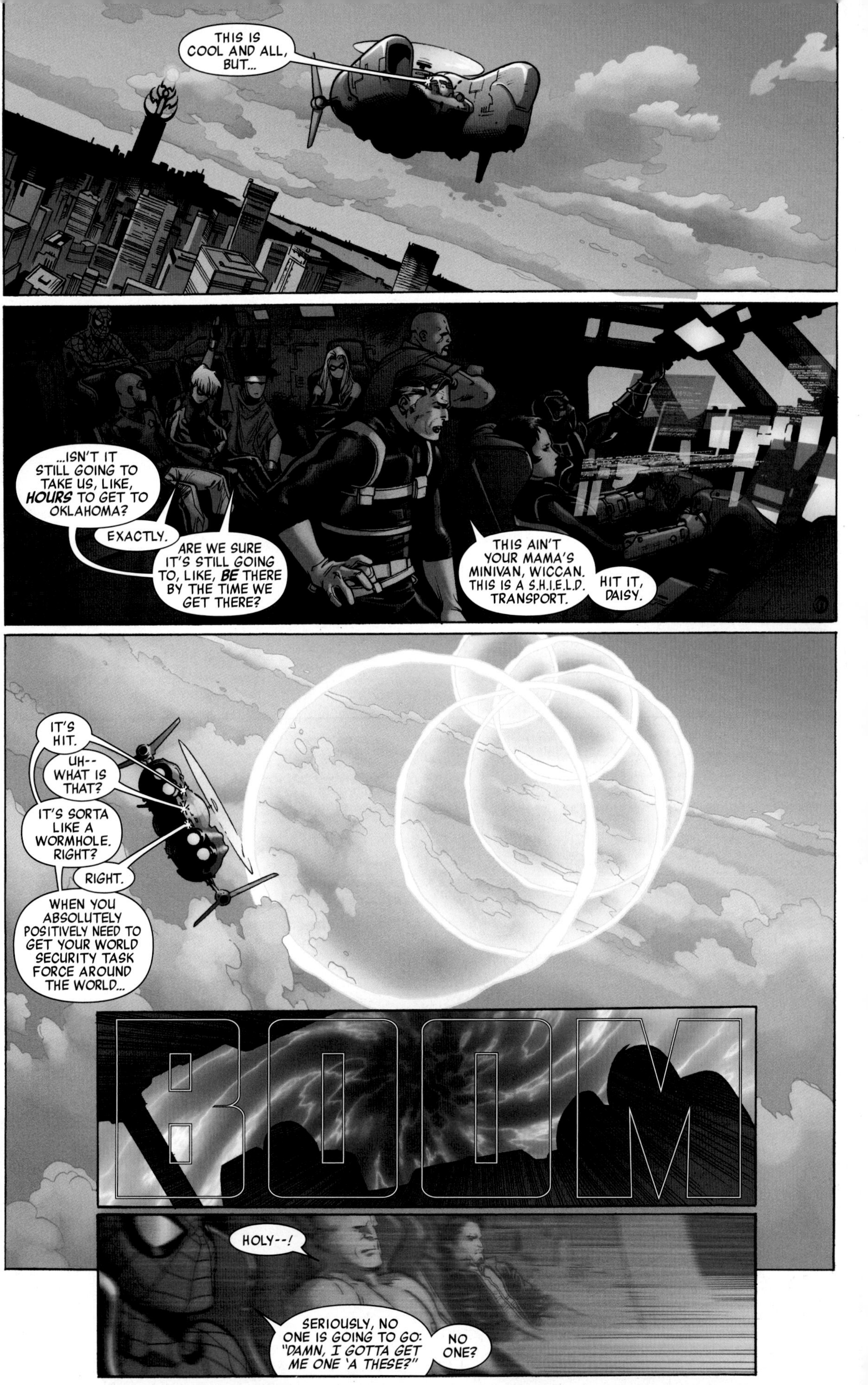
THIS IS COOL AND ALL, BUT...
...ISN'T IT STILL GOING TO TAKE US, LIKE, HOURS TO GET TO OKLAHOMA?
EXACTLY.
ARE WE SURE IT'S STILL GOING TO, LIKE, BE THERE BY THE TIME WE GET THERE?
THIS AIN'T YOUR MAMA'S MINIVAN, WICCAN. THIS IS A S.H.I.E.L.D. TRANSPORT.
HIT IT, DAISY.
IT'S HIT.
UH-- WHAT IS THAT?
IT'S SORTA LIKE A WORMHOLE. RIGHT?
RIGHT.
WHEN YOU ABSOLUTELY POSITIVELY NEED TO GET YOUR WORLD SECURITY TASK FORCE AROUND THE WORLD...
BOOM
HOLY--!
SERIOUSLY, NO ONE IS GOING TO GO: "DAMN, I GOTTA GET ME ONE 'A THESE?"
NO ONE?

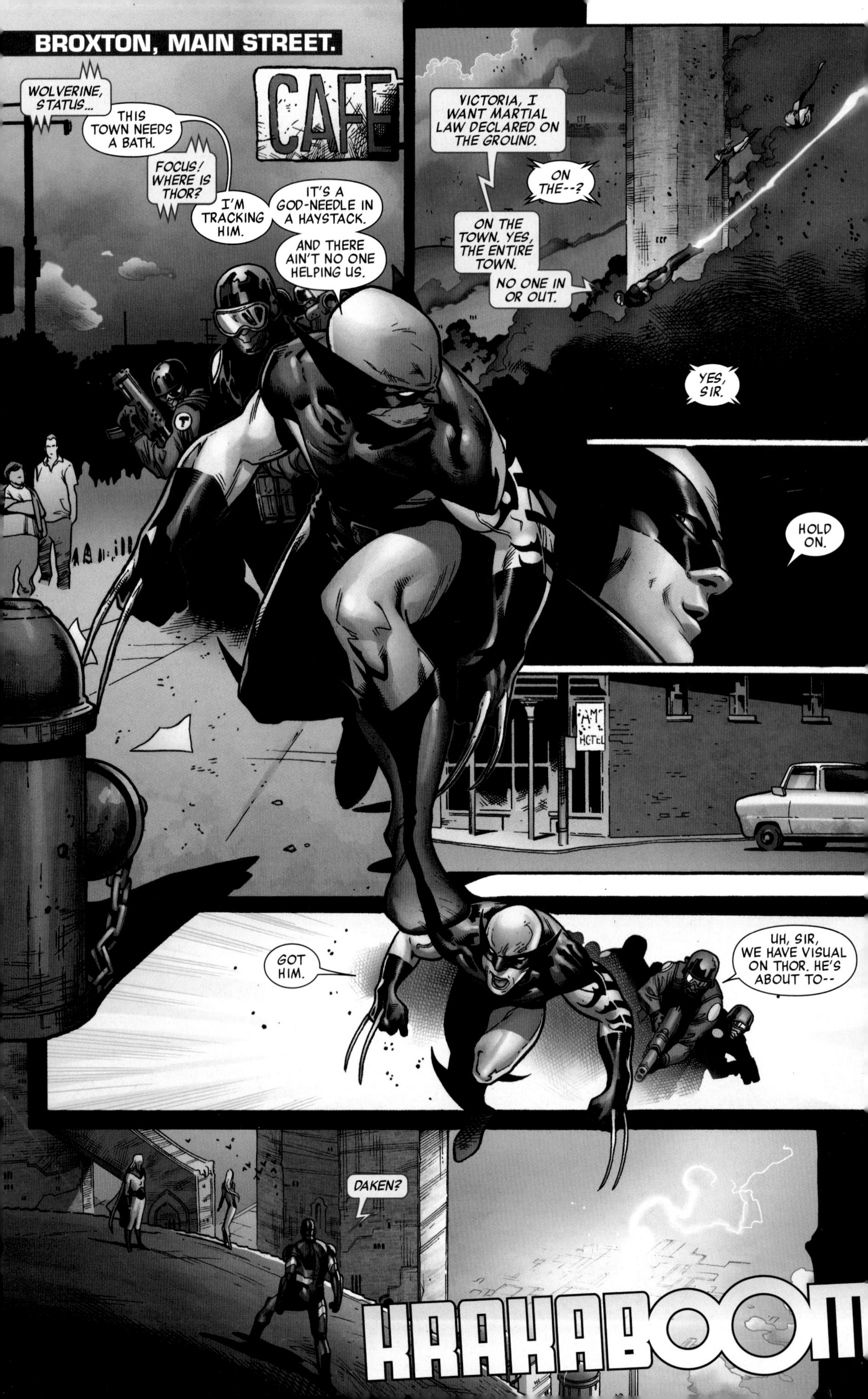
BROXTON, MAIN STREET.
CAFE
WOLVERINE, STATUS...
THIS TOWN NEEDS A BATH.
FOCUS! WHERE IS THOR?
I'M TRACKING HIM.
IT'S A GOD-NEEDLE IN A HAYSTACK.
AND THERE AIN'T NO ONE HELPING US.
VICTORIA, I WANT MARTIAL LAW DECLARED ON THE GROUND.
ON THE--?
ON THE TOWN. YES, THE ENTIRE TOWN.
NO ONE IN OR OUT.
YES, SIR.
HOLD ON.
HOTEL
GOT HIM.
UH, SIR, WE HAVE VISUAL ON THOR. HE'S ABOUT TO--
DAKEN?
KRAKABOOM

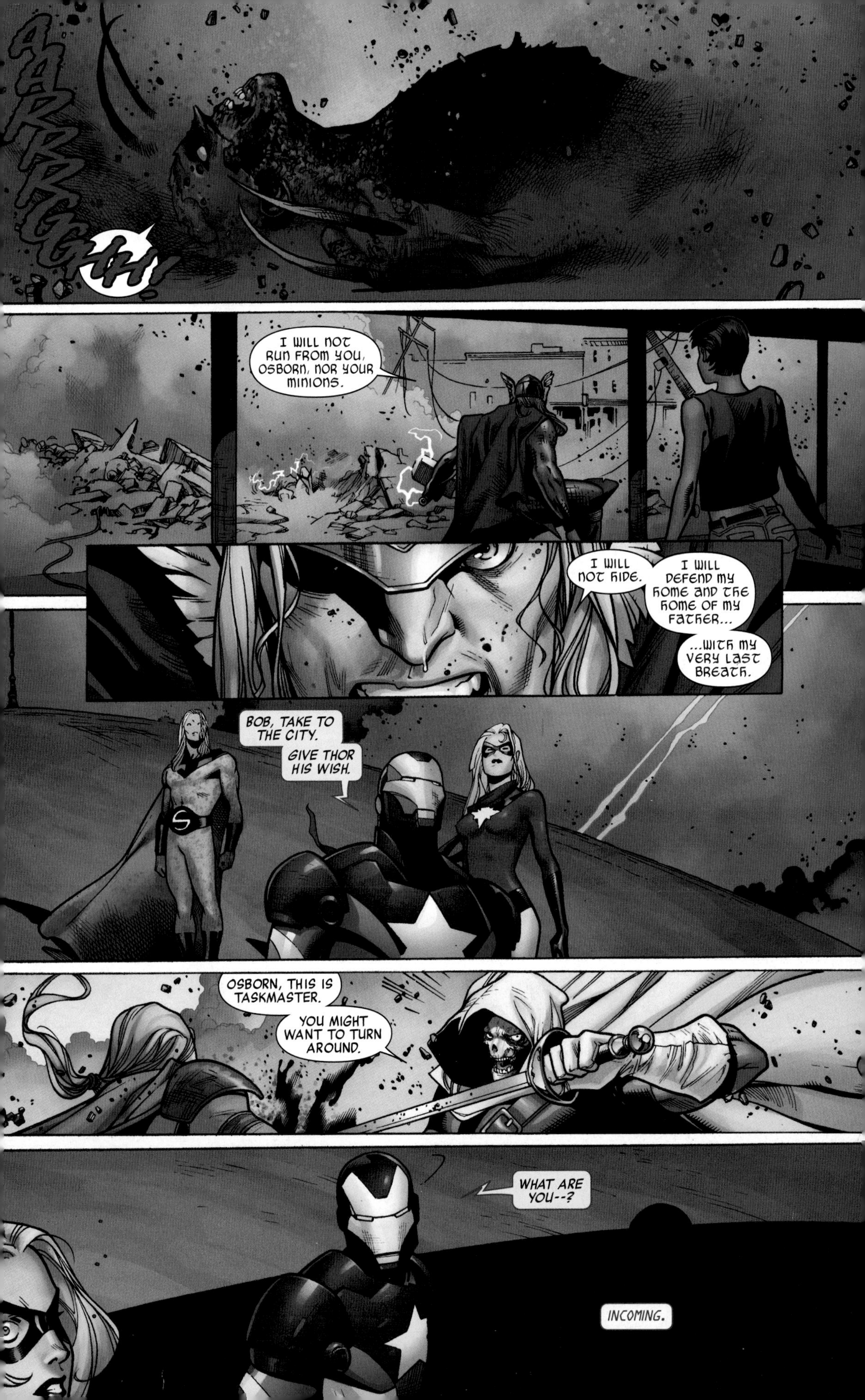
AARRGGHH!
I WILL NOT RUN FROM YOU, OSBORN, NOR YOUR MINIONS.
I WILL NOT HIDE.
I WILL DEFEND MY HOME AND THE HOME OF MY FATHER...
...WITH MY VERY LAST BREATH.
BOB, TAKE TO THE CITY.
GIVE THOR HIS WISH.
OSBORN, THIS IS TASKMASTER.
YOU MIGHT WANT TO TURN AROUND.
WHAT ARE YOU--?
INCOMING.

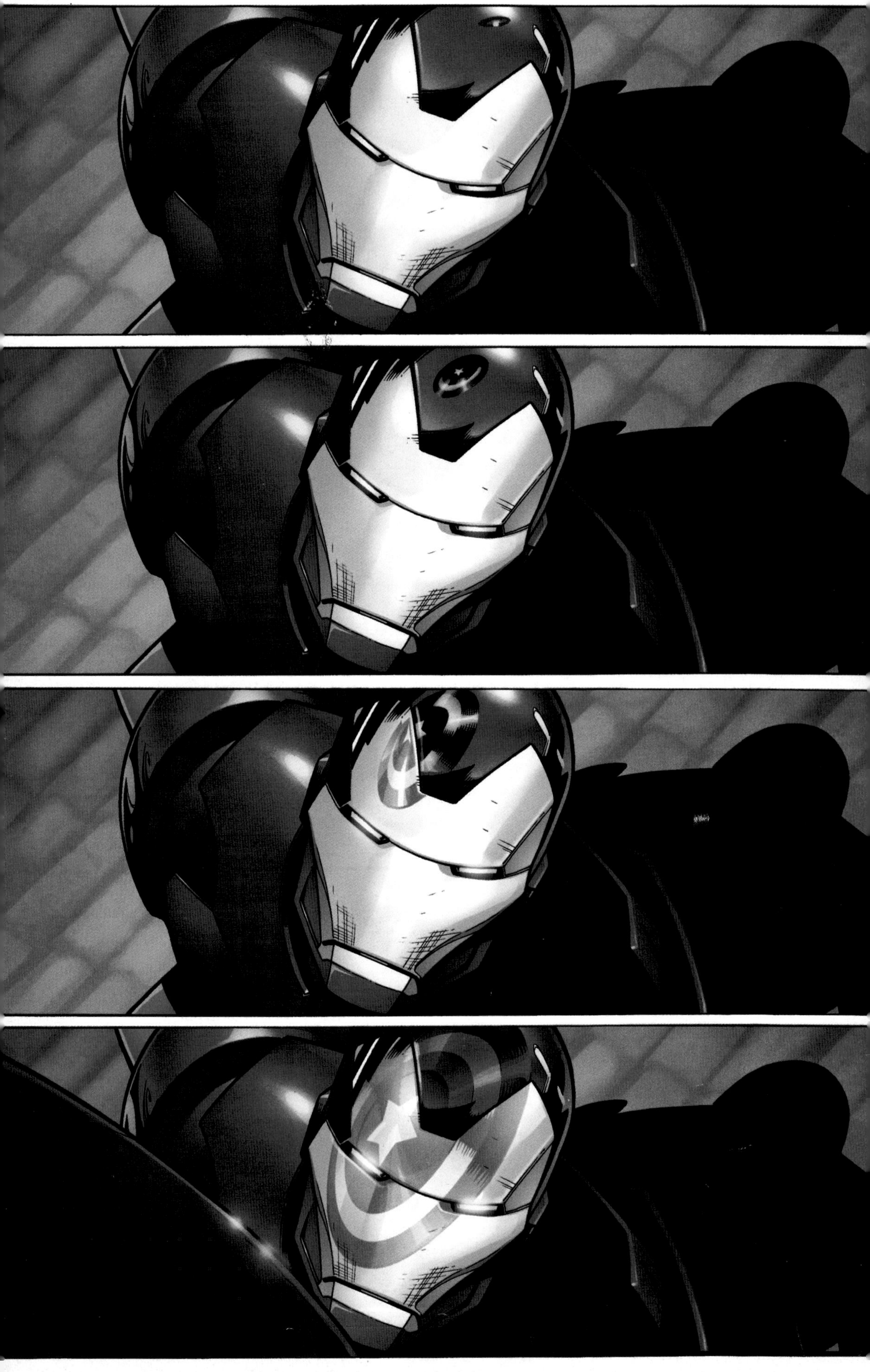

[FURY PROTOCOL 12]
BLACK WIDOW-EYES ONLY
ENCODED

LOGIN: BLACK WIDOW
PASSWORD: ***************

ONE EYE EAGLE DECRYPTION PACKAGE UPLOADED
SECRET WARRIORS DEBRIEFING
TOP SECRET CODE- WHITE
VIDEO TRANSCRIPT
RECORDING DATE: 4/6/ 2010

PLACE: FURY SECRET LOCATION 5. NEW YORK CITY

[IN ATTENDANCE]

● NICK FURY
QUAKE ●
AKA DAISY JOHNSON
● PHOBOS
AKA ALEXANDER AARON
THE DRUID ●
AKA SEBASTIAN DRUID
● SLINGSHOT
AKA YO-YO RODRIGUEZ
HELLFIRE ●
AKA J.T. SLADE
● STONEWALL
AKA JERRY SLEDGE
EDEN FESI ●

NICK FURY: Everyone sit down.

SLINGSHOT: Are we in trouble? Y'know, again?

NICK FURY: No.

HELLFIRE: Are you recording this?

NICK FURY: I am.

HELLFIRE: Why?

NICK FURY: This needs to be logged. There needs to be a record.

HELLFIRE: Doesn't that fly in the face of our whole "super secret agents in training" thing we got going?

NICK FURY: Not this time. Sit.

QUAKE: Sit.

HELLFIRE: Sitting. God.

NICK FURY: We've gotten the call.

HELLFIRE: From God?

QUAKE: Shut up.

NICK FURY: As far as you're concerned...yes.

SLINGSHOT: What's going on?

NICK FURY: Captain America. He's back and he is going after Osborn.

DRUID: Captain America's dead.

NICK FURY: Not so much.

HELLFIRE: Captain America? The real one?

NICK FURY: The real one.

HELLFIRE: Not that one hanging out with Luke Cage with the costume that points to his--

NICK FURY: The real one.

DRUID: He died right on the steps of the federal courthouse.

NICK FURY: Kid. You're going to learn, just 'cause you saw it on TV doesn't make it an actual thing.

DRUID: Looked pretty real.

NICK FURY: And yet.

QUAKE: What are we gonna do?

NICK FURY: We're going to team up with Cap's Avengers team and whoever else he can get his hands on and we're going to help him take down Osborn.

HELLFIRE: We're going to war?

NICK FURY: In every sense of the word.

STONEWALL: Are we ready for that?

NICK FURY: You are. You know how I know?

STONEWALL: How?

NICK FURY: 'Cause it's time and you have no other choice.

HELLFIRE: Wow. Well, okay.

QUAKE: What's the plan?

NICK FURY: We're heading over to the meet now. When we get there you're going to listen and follow orders. You do what I say or you do what Captain America says. You do exactly as told. None of this wise talk, double talk, sass or wise cracks. You do as you're told or you will die. When and if I fall, you follow Daisy. You do exactly as she says.

SLINGSHOT: But you're not going to fall.

NICK FURY: Honey, I will be a primary target. The minute I show my face on the battle-field, both me and Captain America will be the focus of all of Osborn's aggression. He will try to cut off the head of our resistance by cutting off our heads. Do not kid yourself... this is the real thing.

HELLFIRE: So, like, we may not all be coming back.

NICK FURY: True. But you can say that about any day doing anything.

SLINGSHOT: But you can say that doubly about doing things where large groups of super-powered adults are hitting you and trying to kill you.

NICK FURY: So you will do what you are told. You will, also, not gawk at or, I believe the term is, "geek out" when meeting the Avengers like you did after the Skrull invasion. That was embarrassing and non-productive.

HELLFIRE: I said one thing.

NICK FURY: I'm not talking about you. But watching you hit on Spider-Woman was one of the most embarrassing things I have ever seen and I've been alive for almost a hundred years. You need to grow up, grow a pair, and act like you actually belong in a room with adults. You need to listen and not talk.

HELLFIRE: But what if we--?

NICK FURY: I want you to see how the smart people in this room are not interrupting me and listening carefully. That's part of what makes them smart.

HELLFIRE: Okay, that time you were talking about me.

NICK FURY: The good news, kid, is you are always looking to beat the holy hell out of something and prove what a big boy you are. This is your chance. The leash is off. You take out that hell fire of yours and you burn the world. You, Daisy, Stonewall...you guys are the front line. We touch the ground and you go straight for Osborn. Daisy will try to clear the path, you guys follow Cap and his team and you run into it. Do not blink. Do not stop to look around. I will offer air support. Yo-Yo and Eden, you will help the wounded. If a hero falls, you get them the hell off the playing field. You do not let these nightmares get the killshot. You do not let them get in some torture. Because they will and they want to.

SLINGSHOT: Got it.

NICK FURY: The other good news is that no one will be paying one damn bit of attention to any of you. This is grudge match stuff. These players have been doing this dance with each other for years...and they will be focused on each other. Not you... that's why you will be the edge Captain America needs to win this war. You understand? No one expects a damn thing from you. So if you're smart enough to keep fighting you just might do something that defines your life.

QUAKE: Where are we going to? Where's the fight going to happen?

NICK FURY: Intel says we're going to Asgard.

STONEWALL: Whoa.

NICK FURY: Yeah. And all that said, do you guys remember the Sentry?

HELLFIRE: Sure.

NICK FURY: You do not engage him.

QUAKE: Even me?

NICK FURY: Even you. It's not a matter of being a coward or anything like that. It's math. You can't beat him. You just can't. You engage that maniac and you're dead. You're ripped in half.

STONEWALL: Then, wait, so how on earth are we going to win this thing?

NICK FURY: Let Thor worry about it.

PHOBOS: My dad's going to be there?

NICK FURY: Intel says Ares is leading the charge. Yes.

PHOBOS: You want me to fight my dad?

NICK FURY: I'll talk to you about that privately.

HELLFIRE: I don't get it...why are we recording this?

NICK FURY: Kid, what I just described to you is the textbook definition of treason. It ain't spy games and it ain't cutesy crap. We are declaring war on the United States. I want it on record it was me who did this. I want it known it was me.

HELLFIRE: Like, we're just kids under your scary influence.

NICK FURY: You are. Prepare to be taken as a prisoner of war if we fail. Prepare to be treated as an enemy of the state. If we do not win, and you live, that is what is coming. All the other things we've been working towards, all of it means nothing if we do not do this. Osborn has to be removed. He is a threat to the American way of life and that's that. Got it?

QUAKE: Yes sir.

NICK FURY: Good. Suit up. Shut up. We're leaving in five.

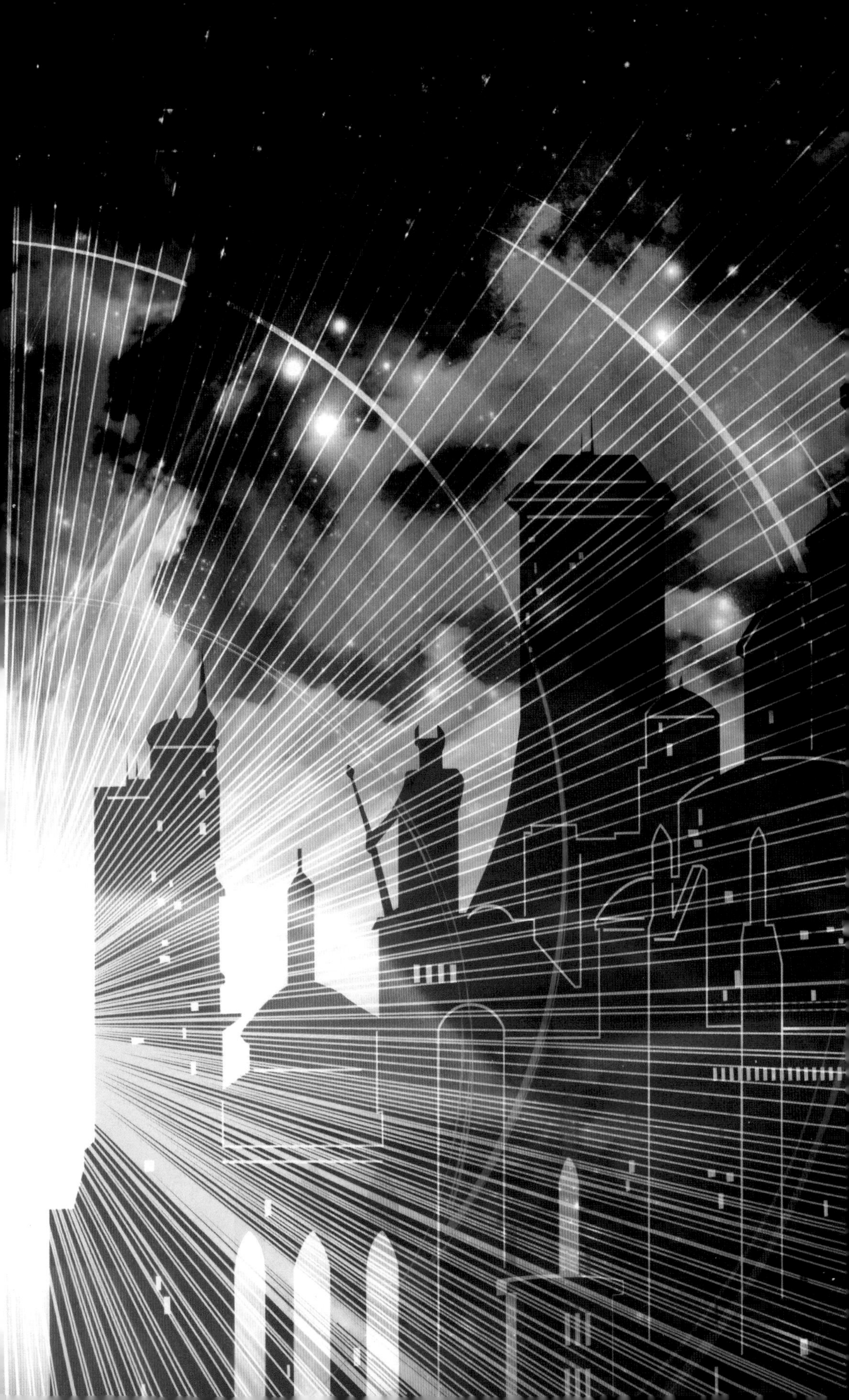

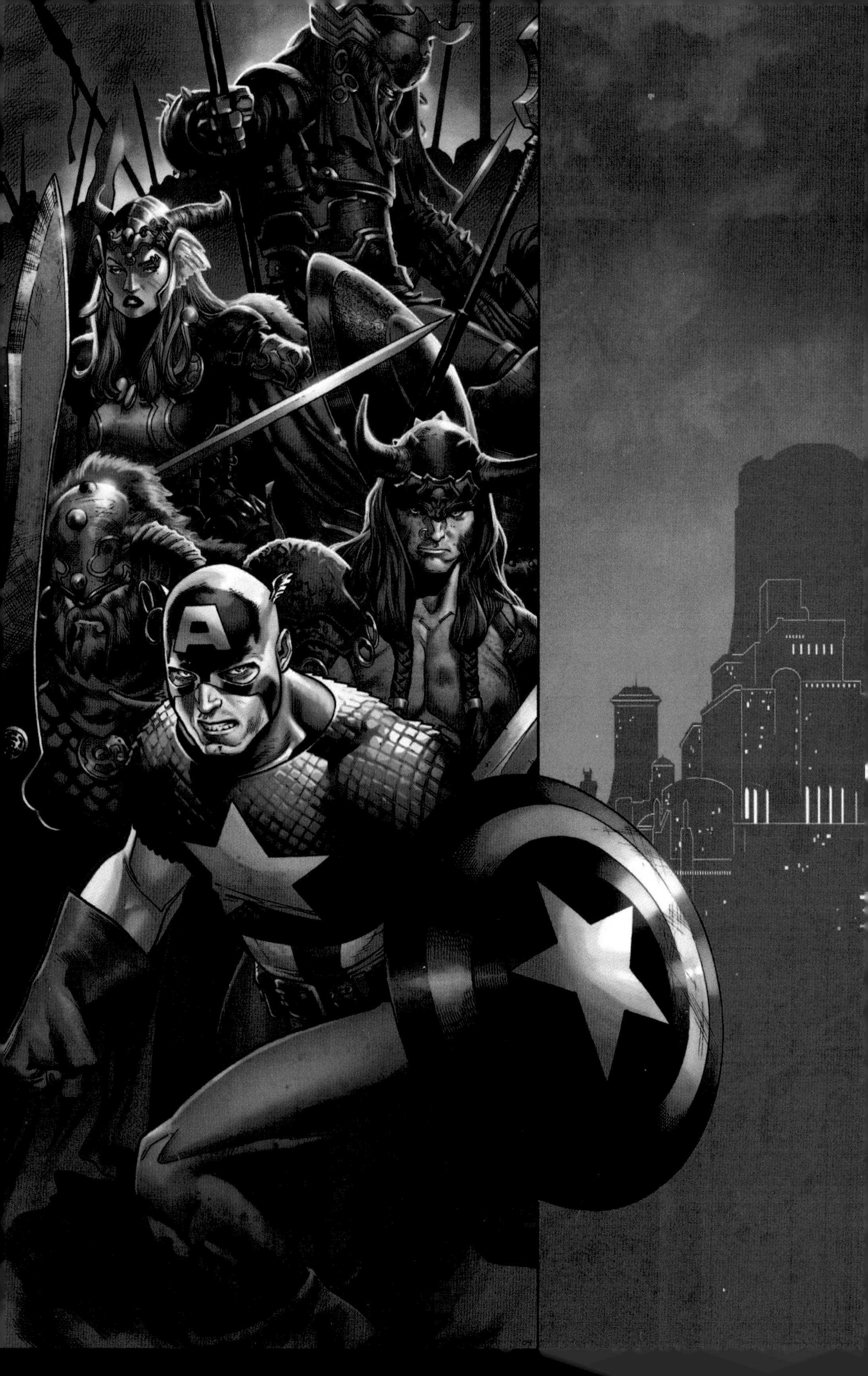

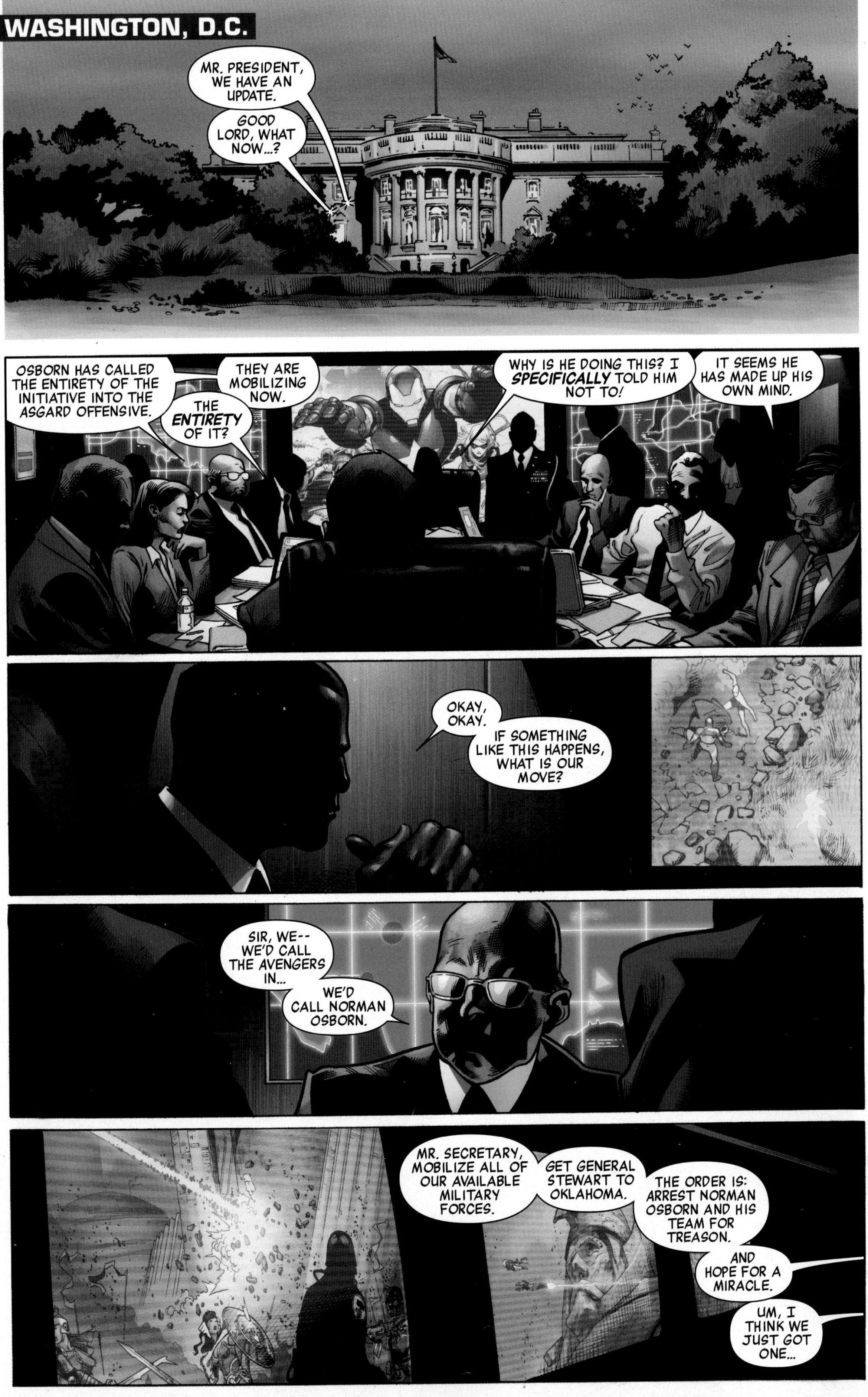
WASHINGTON, D.C.
MR. PRESIDENT, WE HAVE AN UPDATE.
GOOD LORD, WHAT NOW...?
OSBORN HAS CALLED THE ENTIRETY OF THE INITIATIVE INTO THE ASGARD OFFENSIVE.
THEY ARE MOBILIZING NOW.
THE ENTIRETY OF IT?
WHY IS HE DOING THIS? I SPECIFICALLY TOLD HIM NOT TO!
IT SEEMS HE HAS MADE UP HIS OWN MIND.
OKAY, OKAY.
IF SOMETHING LIKE THIS HAPPENS, WHAT IS OUR MOVE?
SIR, WE-- WE'D CALL THE AVENGERS IN...
WE'D CALL NORMAN OSBORN.
MR. SECRETARY, MOBILIZE ALL OF OUR AVAILABLE MILITARY FORCES.
GET GENERAL STEWART TO OKLAHOMA.
THE ORDER IS: ARREST NORMAN OSBORN AND HIS TEAM FOR TREASON.
AND HOPE FOR A MIRACLE.
UM, I THINK WE JUST GOT ONE...

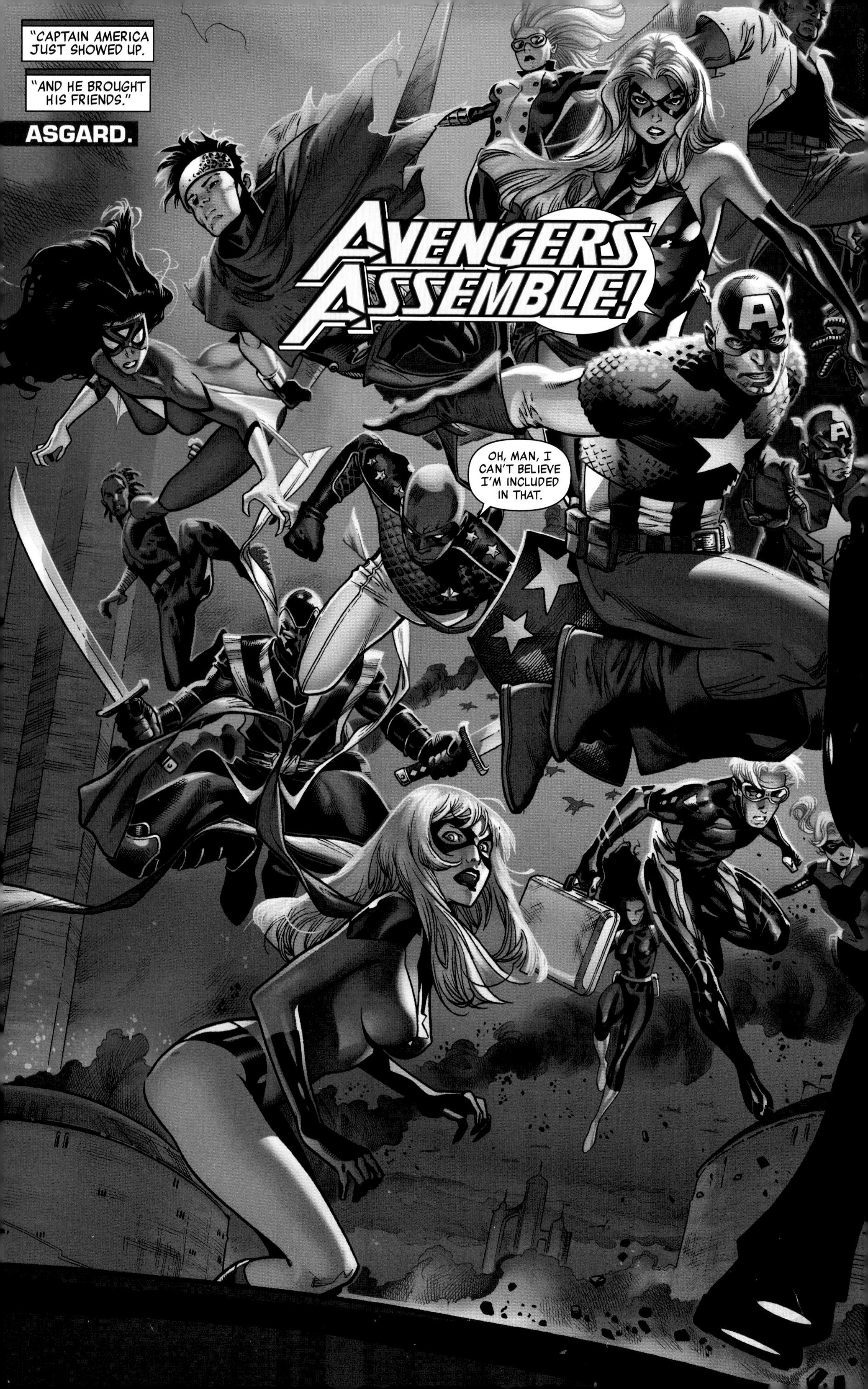
"CAPTAIN AMERICA JUST SHOWED UP.
"AND HE BROUGHT HIS FRIENDS."
ASGARD.
AVENGERS ASSEMBLE!
OH, MAN, I CAN'T BELIEVE I'M INCLUDED IN THAT.

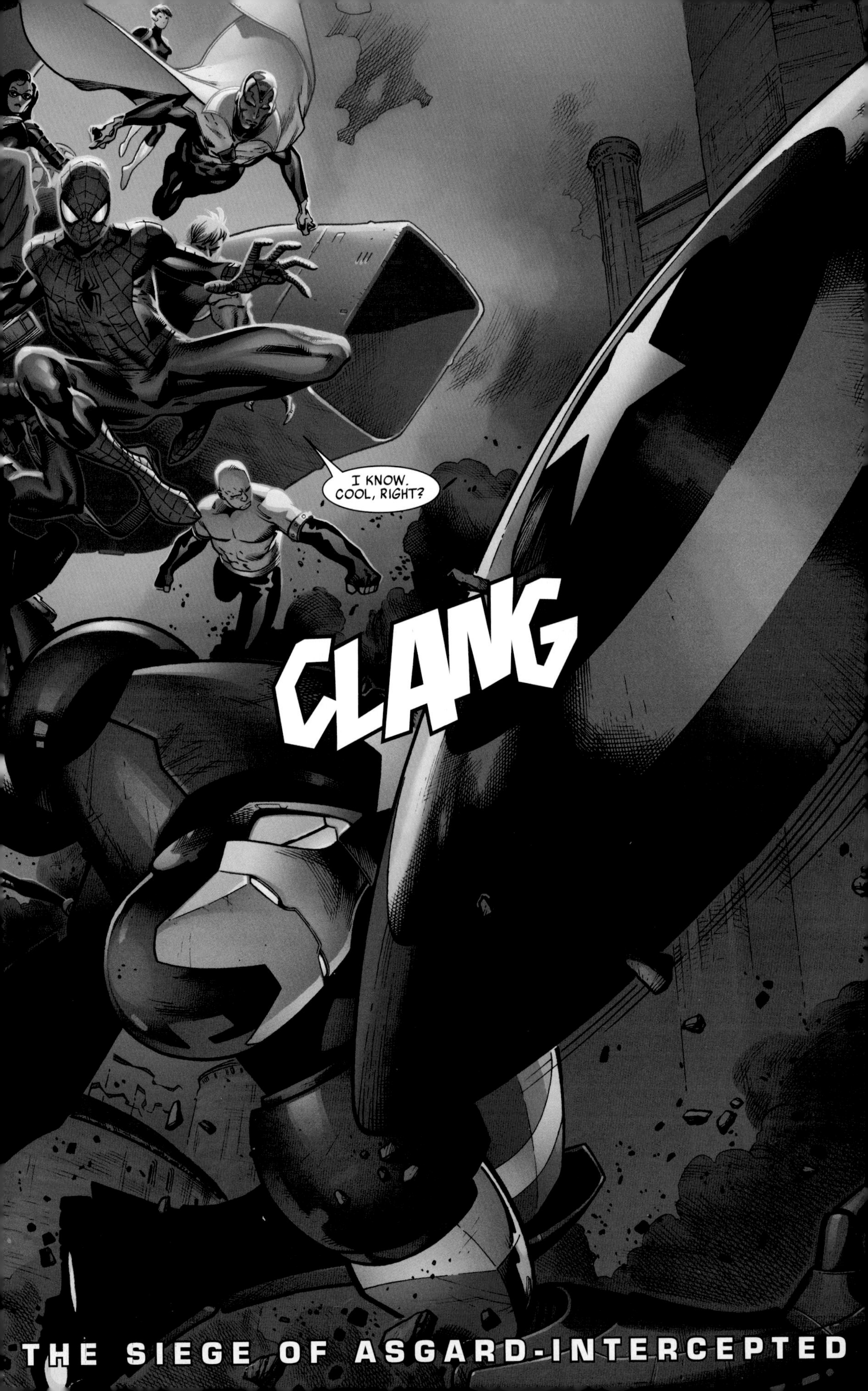
I KNOW. COOL, RIGHT?
CLANG
THE SIEGE OF ASGARD-INTERCEPTED

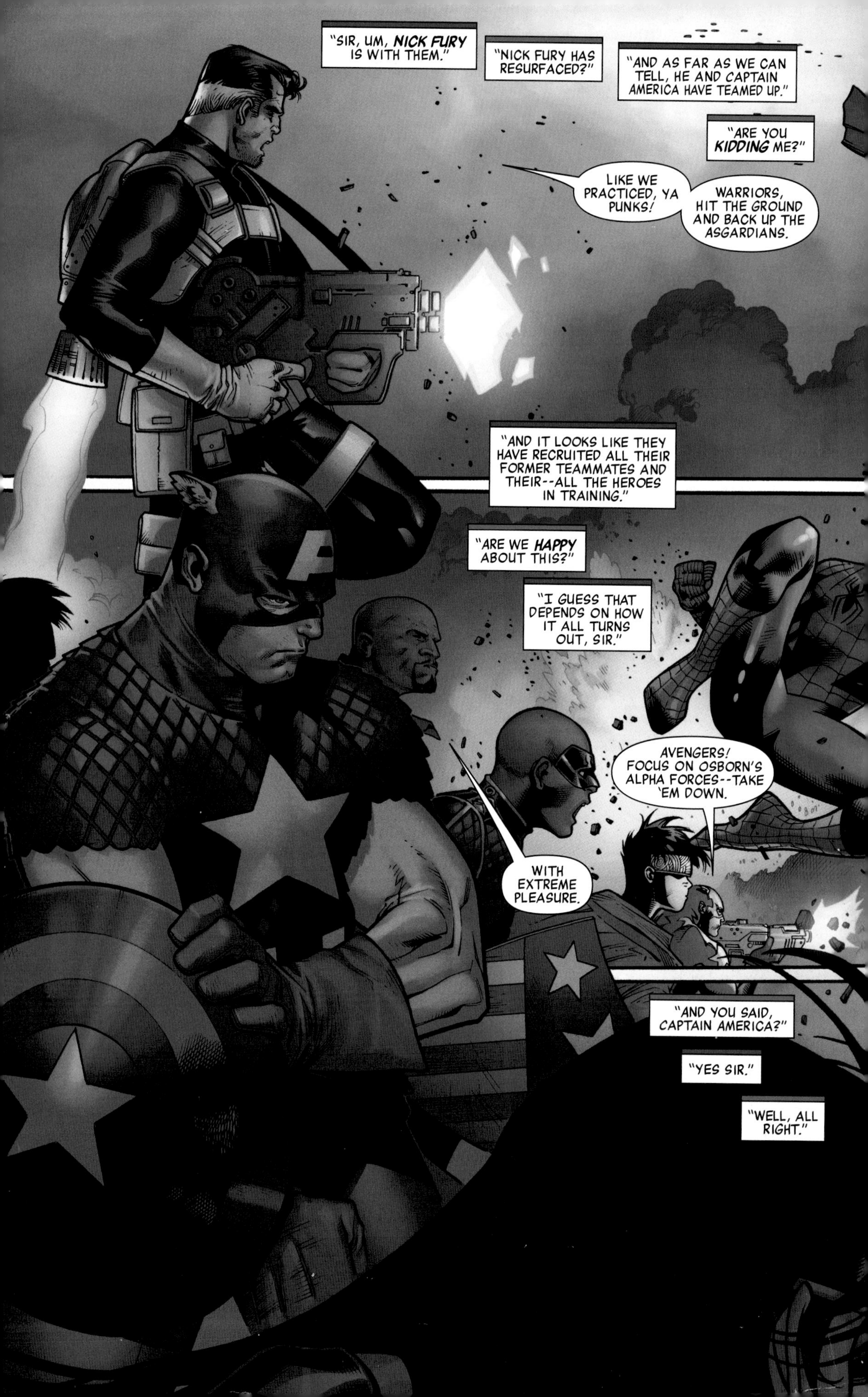

"SIR, UM, NICK FURY IS WITH THEM."
"NICK FURY HAS RESURFACED?"
"AND AS FAR AS WE CAN TELL, HE AND CAPTAIN AMERICA HAVE TEAMED UP."
"ARE YOU KIDDING ME?"
LIKE WE PRACTICED, YA PUNKS!
WARRIORS, HIT THE GROUND AND BACK UP THE ASGARDIANS.
"AND IT LOOKS LIKE THEY HAVE RECRUITED ALL THEIR FORMER TEAMMATES AND THEIR--ALL THE HEROES IN TRAINING."
"ARE WE HAPPY ABOUT THIS?"
"I GUESS THAT DEPENDS ON HOW IT ALL TURNS OUT, SIR."
AVENGERS! FOCUS ON OSBORN'S ALPHA FORCES--TAKE 'EM DOWN.
WITH EXTREME PLEASURE.
"AND YOU SAID, CAPTAIN AMERICA?"
"YES SIR."
"WELL, ALL RIGHT."

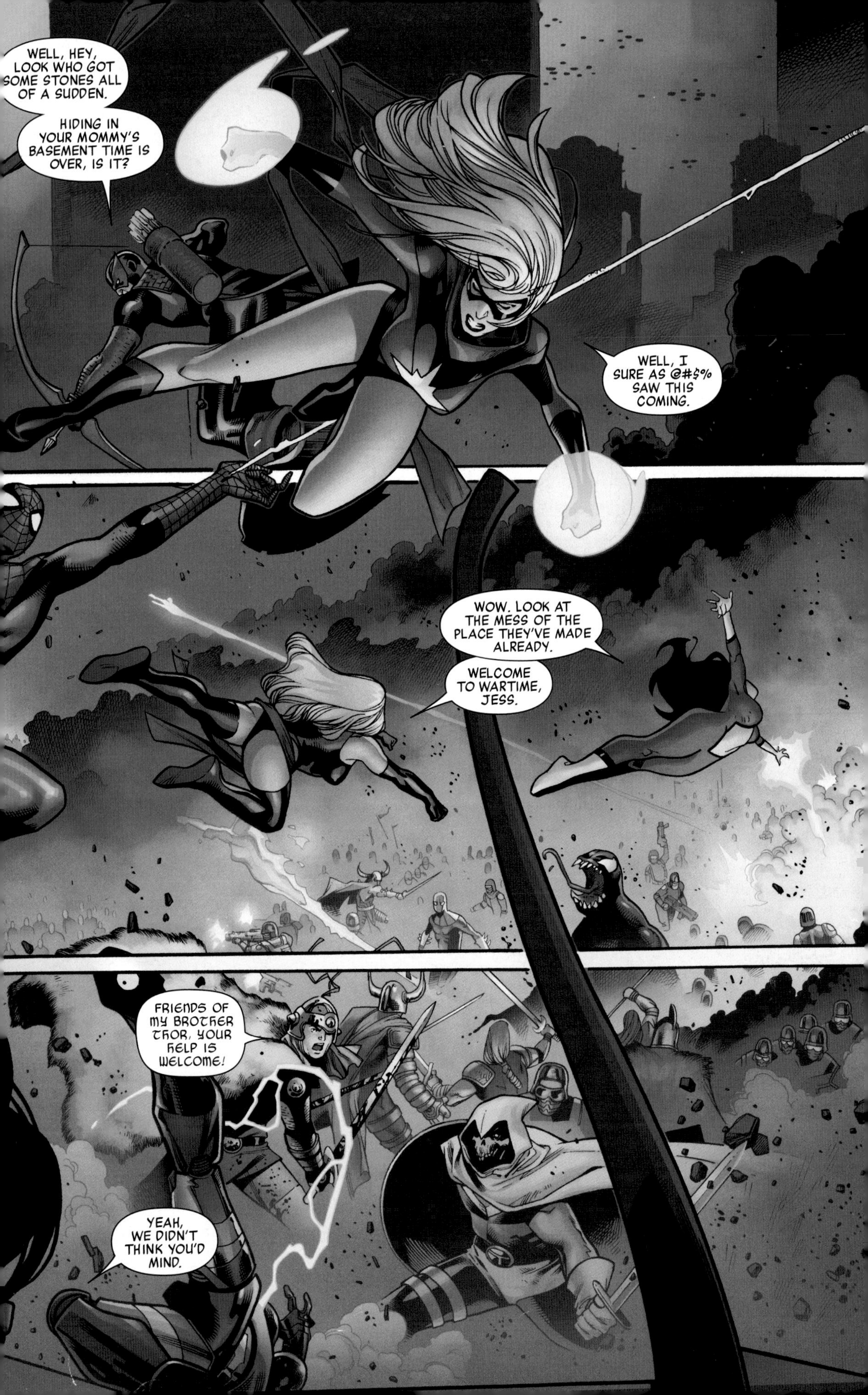
WELL, HEY, LOOK WHO GOT SOME STONES ALL OF A SUDDEN.
HIDING IN YOUR MOMMY'S BASEMENT TIME IS OVER, IS IT?
WELL, I SURE AS @#$% SAW THIS COMING.
WOW. LOOK AT THE MESS OF THE PLACE THEY'VE MADE ALREADY.
WELCOME TO WARTIME, JESS.
FRIENDS OF MY BROTHER THOR, YOUR HELP IS WELCOME!
YEAH, WE DIDN'T THINK YOU'D MIND.

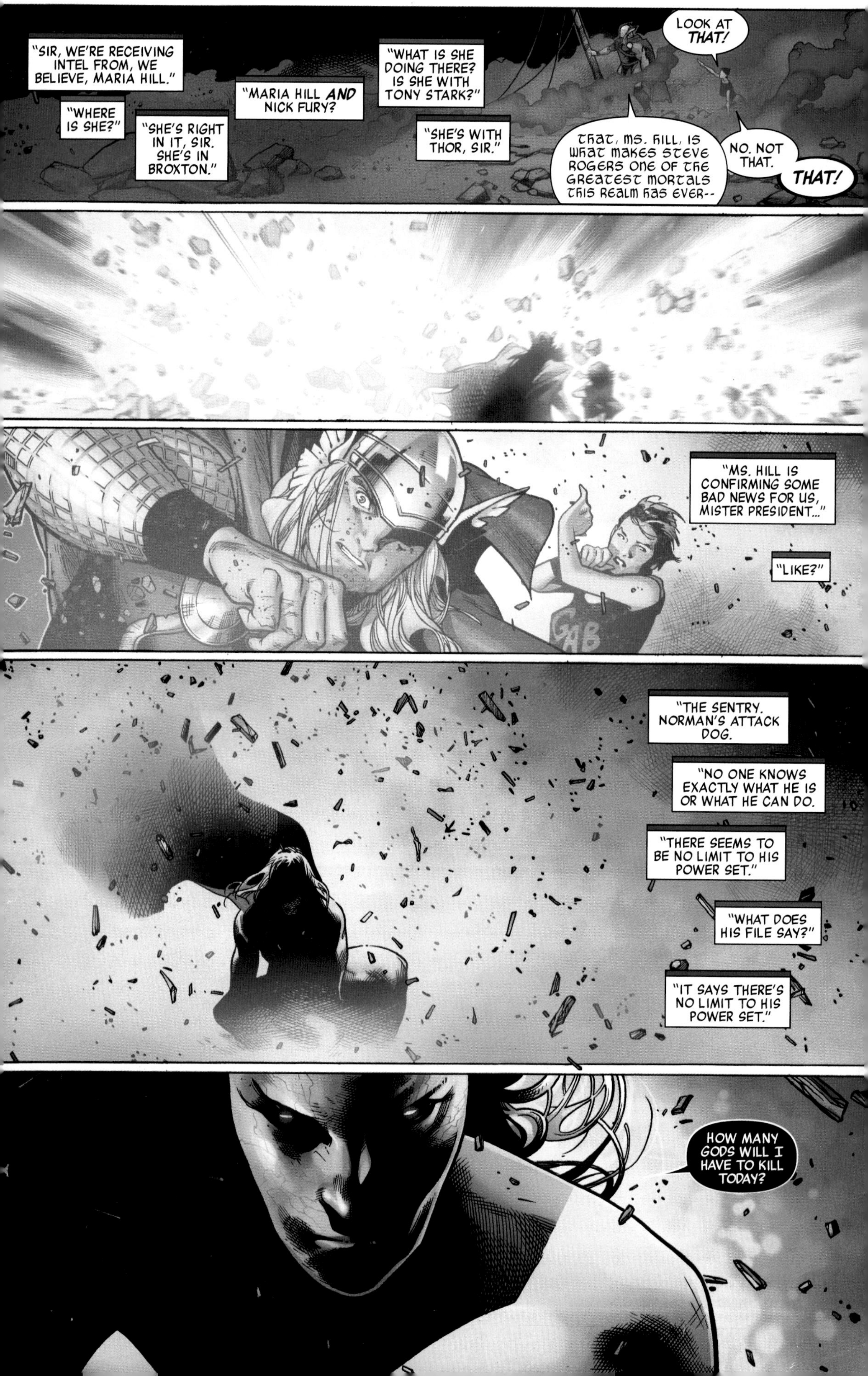
"SIR, WE'RE RECEIVING INTEL FROM, WE BELIEVE, MARIA HILL."
"WHERE IS SHE?"
"SHE'S RIGHT IN IT, SIR. SHE'S IN BROXTON."
"MARIA HILL AND NICK FURY?
"WHAT IS SHE DOING THERE? IS SHE WITH TONY STARK?"
"SHE'S WITH THOR, SIR."
LOOK AT THAT!
THAT, MS. HILL, IS WHAT MAKES STEVE ROGERS ONE OF THE GREATEST MORTALS THIS REALM HAS EVER--
NO. NOT THAT.
THAT!
"MS. HILL IS CONFIRMING SOME BAD NEWS FOR US, MISTER PRESIDENT..."
"LIKE?"
"THE SENTRY. NORMAN'S ATTACK DOG.
"NO ONE KNOWS EXACTLY WHAT HE IS OR WHAT HE CAN DO.
"THERE SEEMS TO BE NO LIMIT TO HIS POWER SET."
"WHAT DOES HIS FILE SAY?"
"IT SAYS THERE'S NO LIMIT TO HIS POWER SET."
HOW MANY GODS WILL I HAVE TO KILL TODAY?

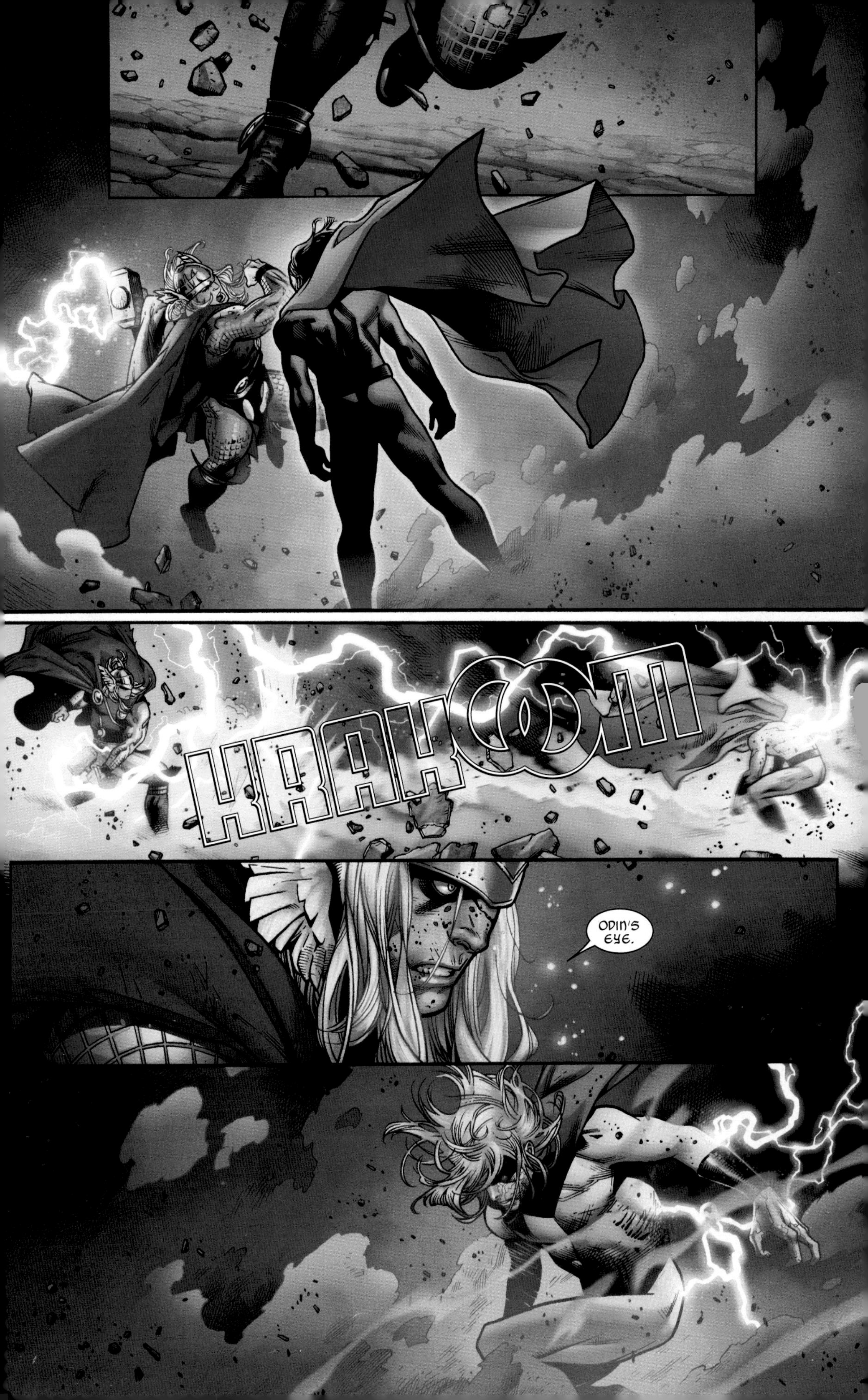
KRAKOOM
ODIN'S EYE.

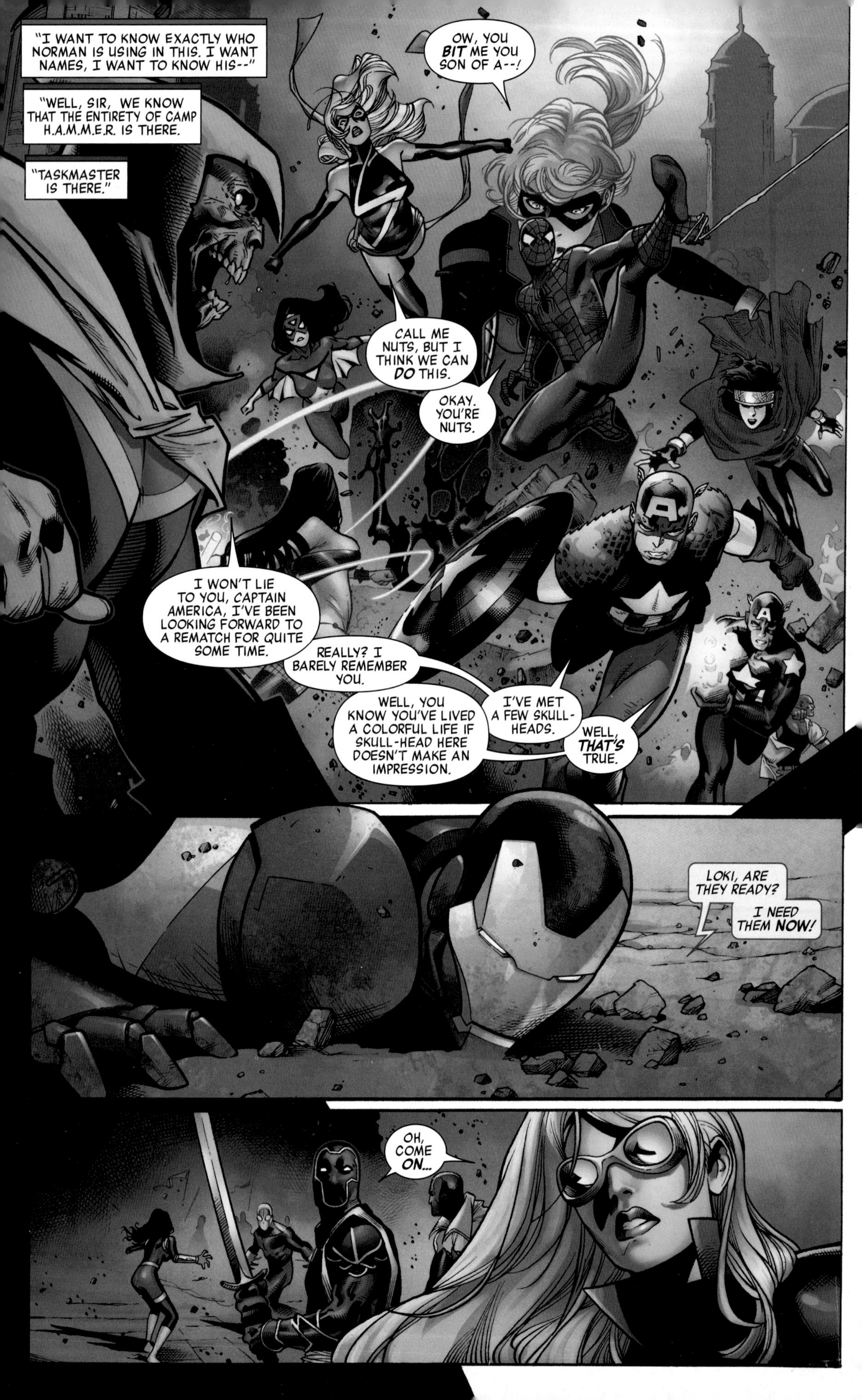
"I WANT TO KNOW EXACTLY WHO NORMAN IS USING IN THIS. I WANT NAMES, I WANT TO KNOW HIS--"
"WELL, SIR, WE KNOW THAT THE ENTIRETY OF CAMP H.A.M.M.E.R. IS THERE.
"TASKMASTER IS THERE."
OW, YOU BIT ME YOU SON OF A--!
CALL ME NUTS, BUT I THINK WE CAN DO THIS.
OKAY. YOU'RE NUTS.
I WON'T LIE TO YOU, CAPTAIN AMERICA, I'VE BEEN LOOKING FORWARD TO A REMATCH FOR QUITE SOME TIME.
REALLY? I BARELY REMEMBER YOU.
I'VE MET A FEW SKULL-HEADS.
WELL, YOU KNOW YOU'VE LIVED A COLORFUL LIFE IF SKULL-HEAD HERE DOESN'T MAKE AN IMPRESSION.
WELL, THAT'S TRUE.
LOKI, ARE THEY READY?
I NEED THEM NOW!
OH, COME ON...

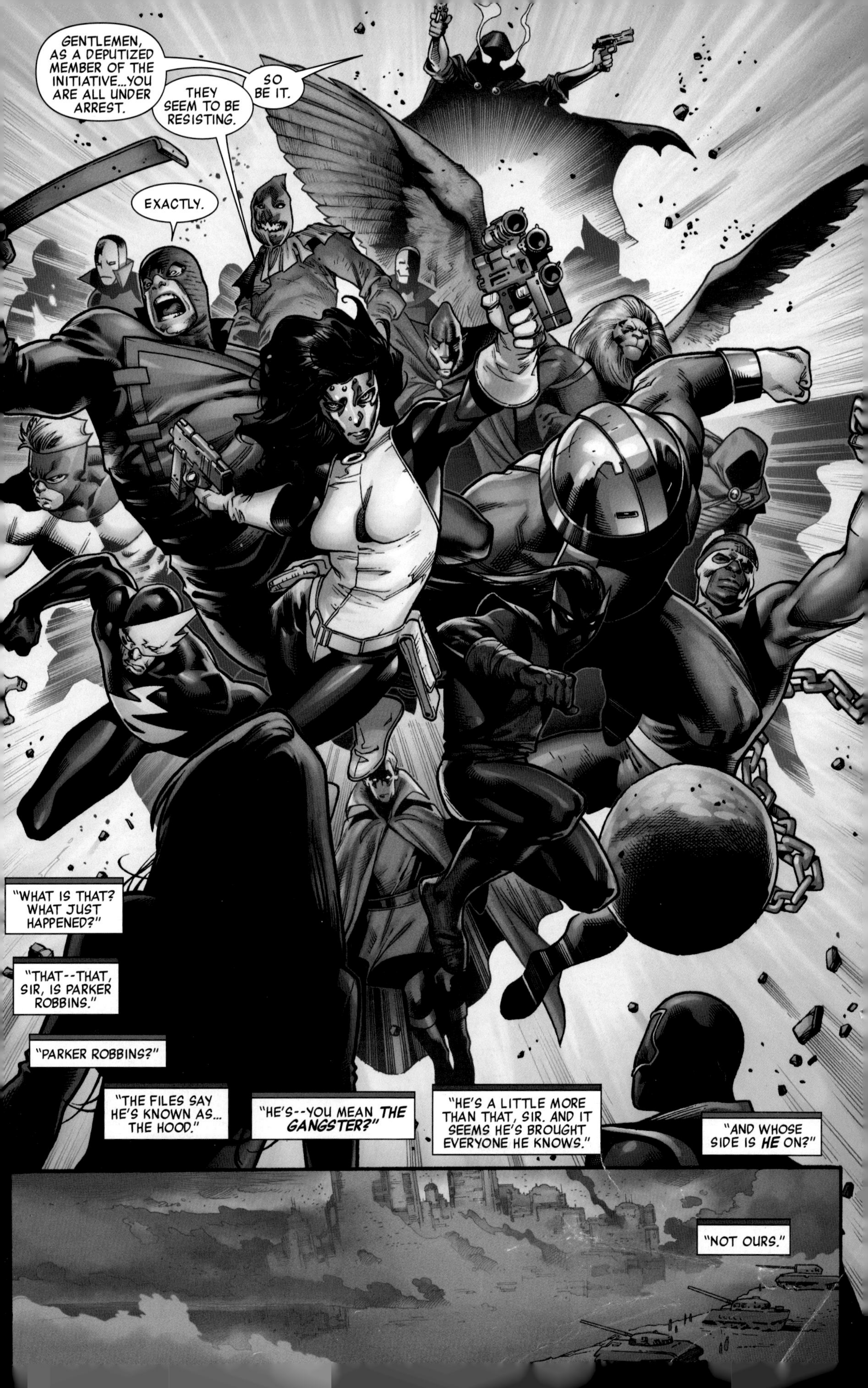
GENTLEMEN, AS A DEPUTIZED MEMBER OF THE INITIATIVE...YOU ARE ALL UNDER ARREST.
THEY SEEM TO BE RESISTING.
SO BE IT.
EXACTLY.
"WHAT IS THAT? WHAT JUST HAPPENED?"
"THAT--THAT, SIR, IS PARKER ROBBINS."
"PARKER ROBBINS?"
"THE FILES SAY HE'S KNOWN AS... THE HOOD."
"HE'S--YOU MEAN THE GANGSTER?"
"HE'S A LITTLE MORE THAN THAT, SIR. AND IT SEEMS HE'S BROUGHT EVERYONE HE KNOWS."
"AND WHOSE SIDE IS HE ON?"
"NOT OURS."

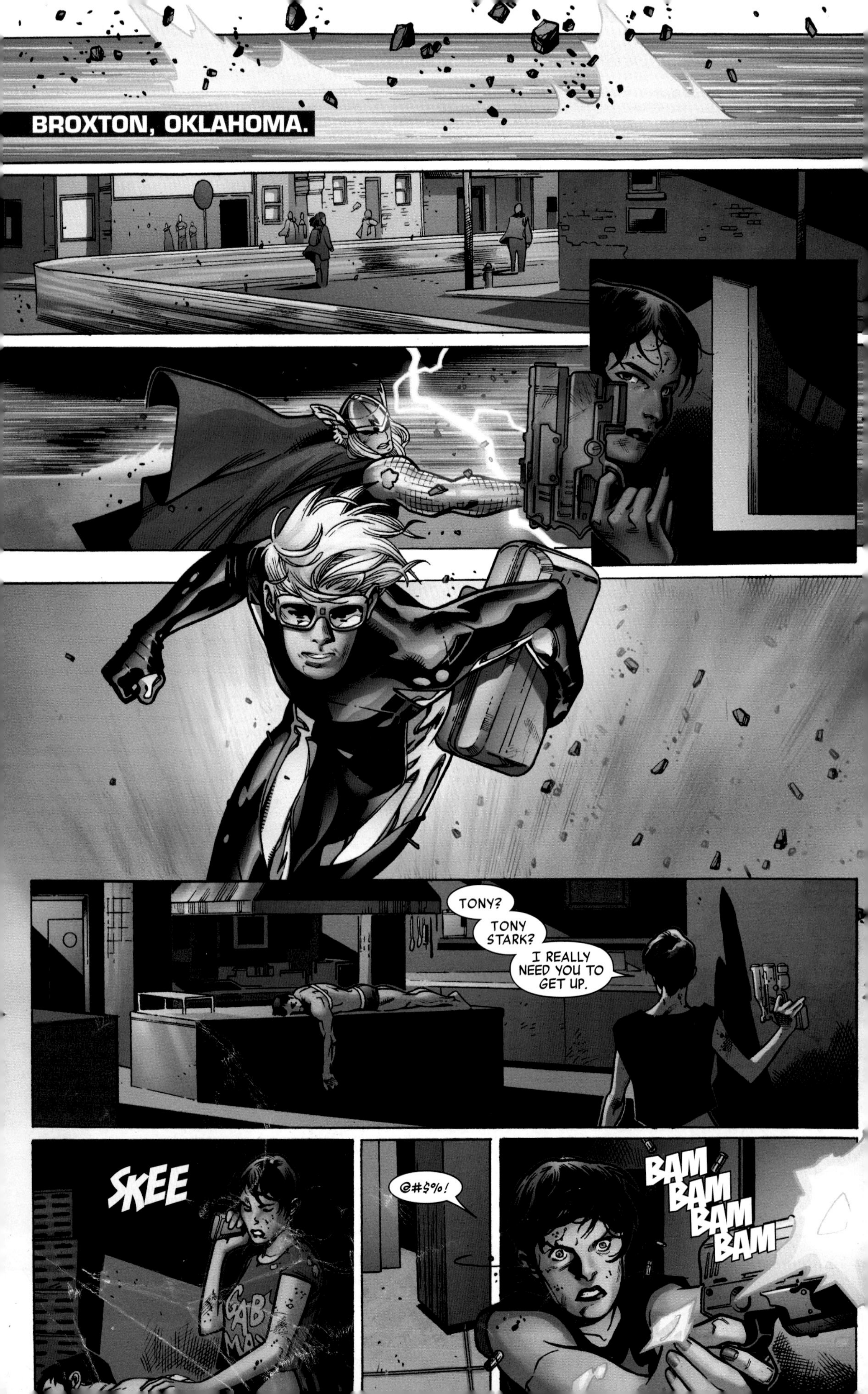
BROXTON, OKLAHOMA.
TONY?
TONY STARK?
I REALLY NEED YOU TO GET UP.
SKEE
@#$%!
BAM BAM BAM BAM

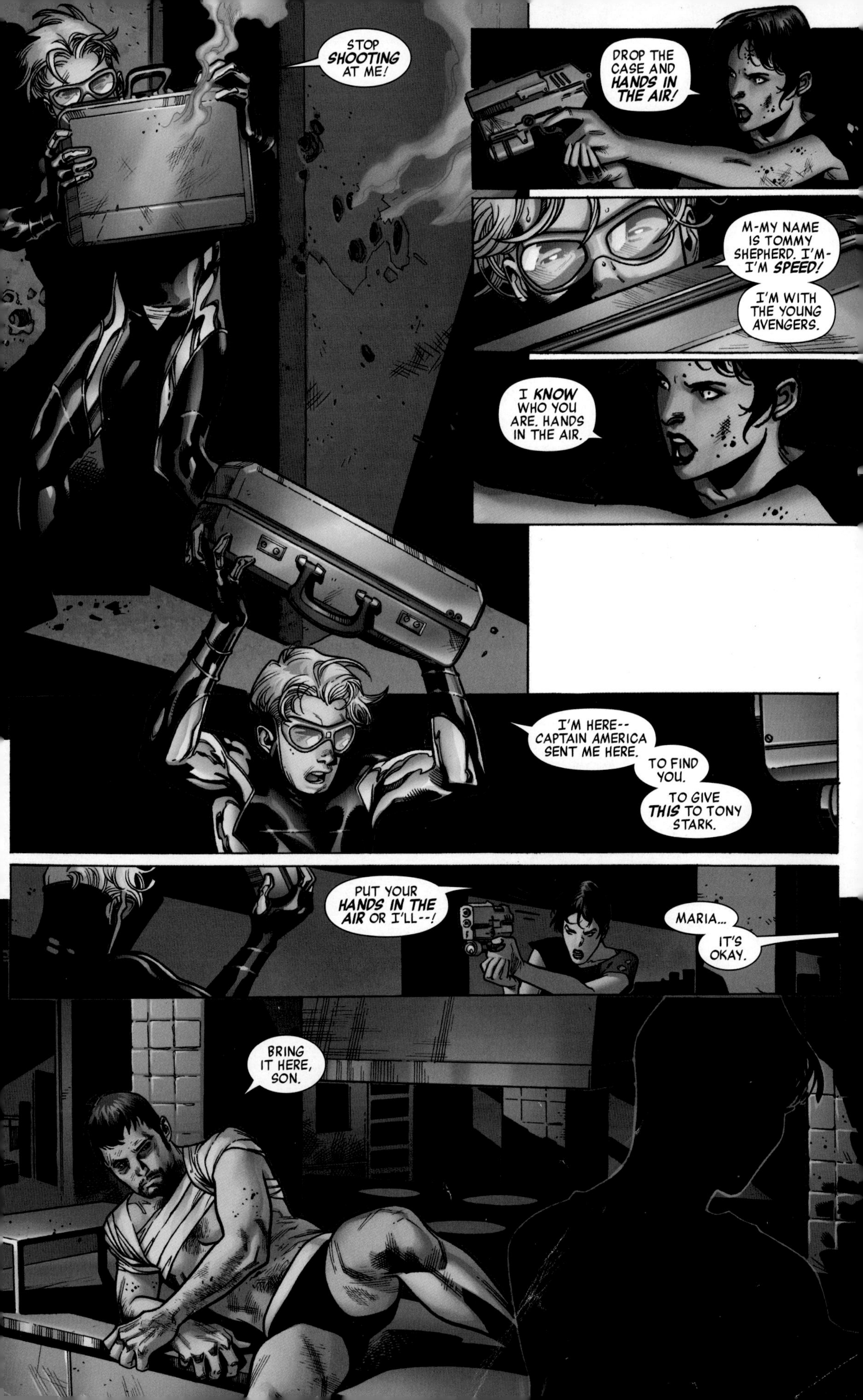
STOP SHOOTING AT ME!
DROP THE CASE AND HANDS IN THE AIR!
M-MY NAME IS TOMMY SHEPHERD. I'M-I'M SPEED!
I'M WITH THE YOUNG AVENGERS.
I KNOW WHO YOU ARE. HANDS IN THE AIR.
I'M HERE--CAPTAIN AMERICA SENT ME HERE.
TO FIND YOU.
TO GIVE THIS TO TONY STARK.
PUT YOUR HANDS IN THE AIR OR I'LL--!
MARIA...
IT'S OKAY.
BRING IT HERE, SON.

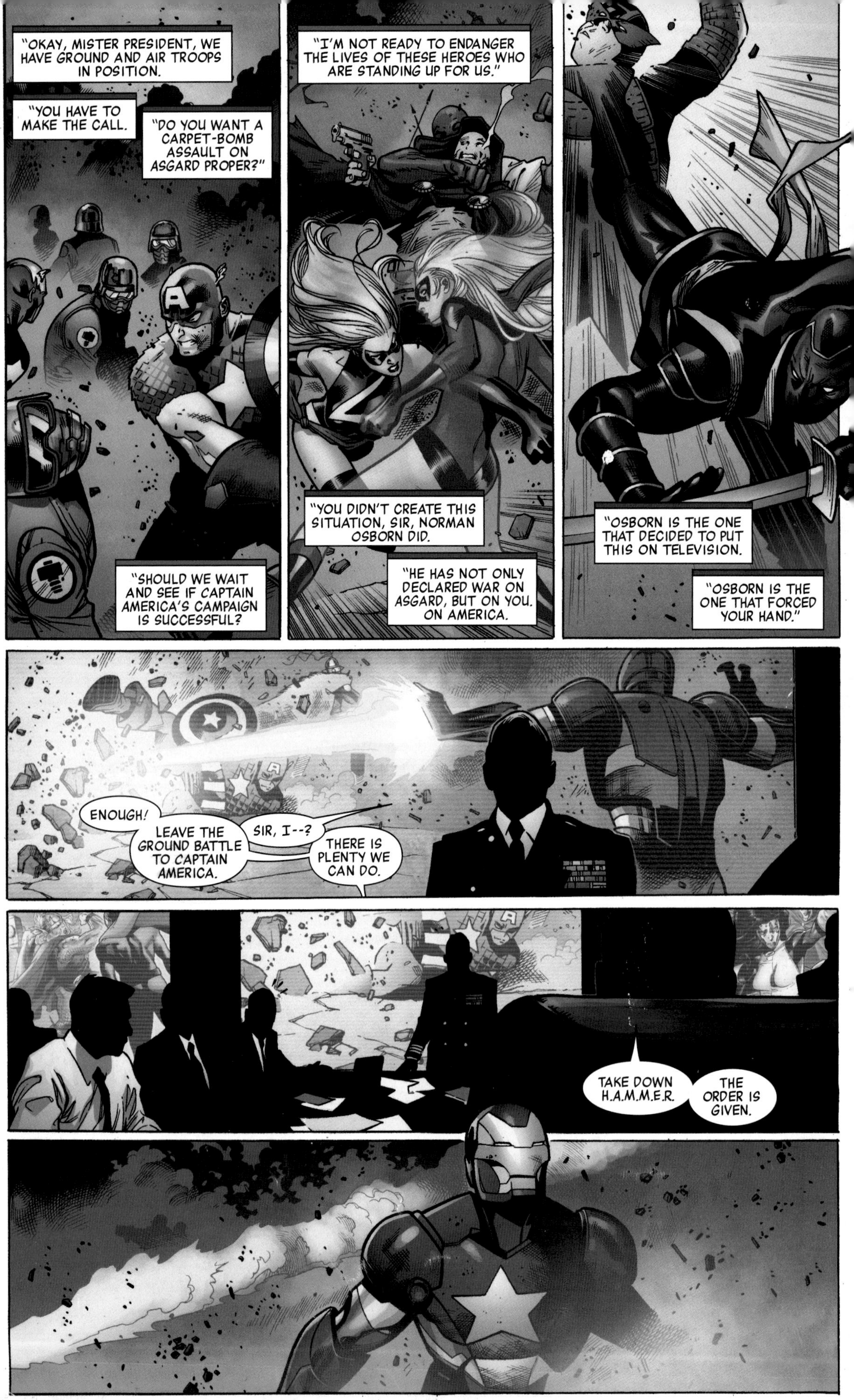
"OKAY, MISTER PRESIDENT, WE HAVE GROUND AND AIR TROOPS IN POSITION.
"YOU HAVE TO MAKE THE CALL.
"DO YOU WANT A CARPET-BOMB ASSAULT ON ASGARD PROPER?"
"SHOULD WE WAIT AND SEE IF CAPTAIN AMERICA'S CAMPAIGN IS SUCCESSFUL?
"I'M NOT READY TO ENDANGER THE LIVES OF THESE HEROES WHO ARE STANDING UP FOR US."
"YOU DIDN'T CREATE THIS SITUATION, SIR, NORMAN OSBORN DID.
"HE HAS NOT ONLY DECLARED WAR ON ASGARD, BUT ON YOU. ON AMERICA.
"OSBORN IS THE ONE THAT DECIDED TO PUT THIS ON TELEVISION.
"OSBORN IS THE ONE THAT FORCED YOUR HAND."
ENOUGH!
LEAVE THE GROUND BATTLE TO CAPTAIN AMERICA.
SIR, I--?
THERE IS PLENTY WE CAN DO.
TAKE DOWN H.A.M.M.E.R.
THE ORDER IS GIVEN.

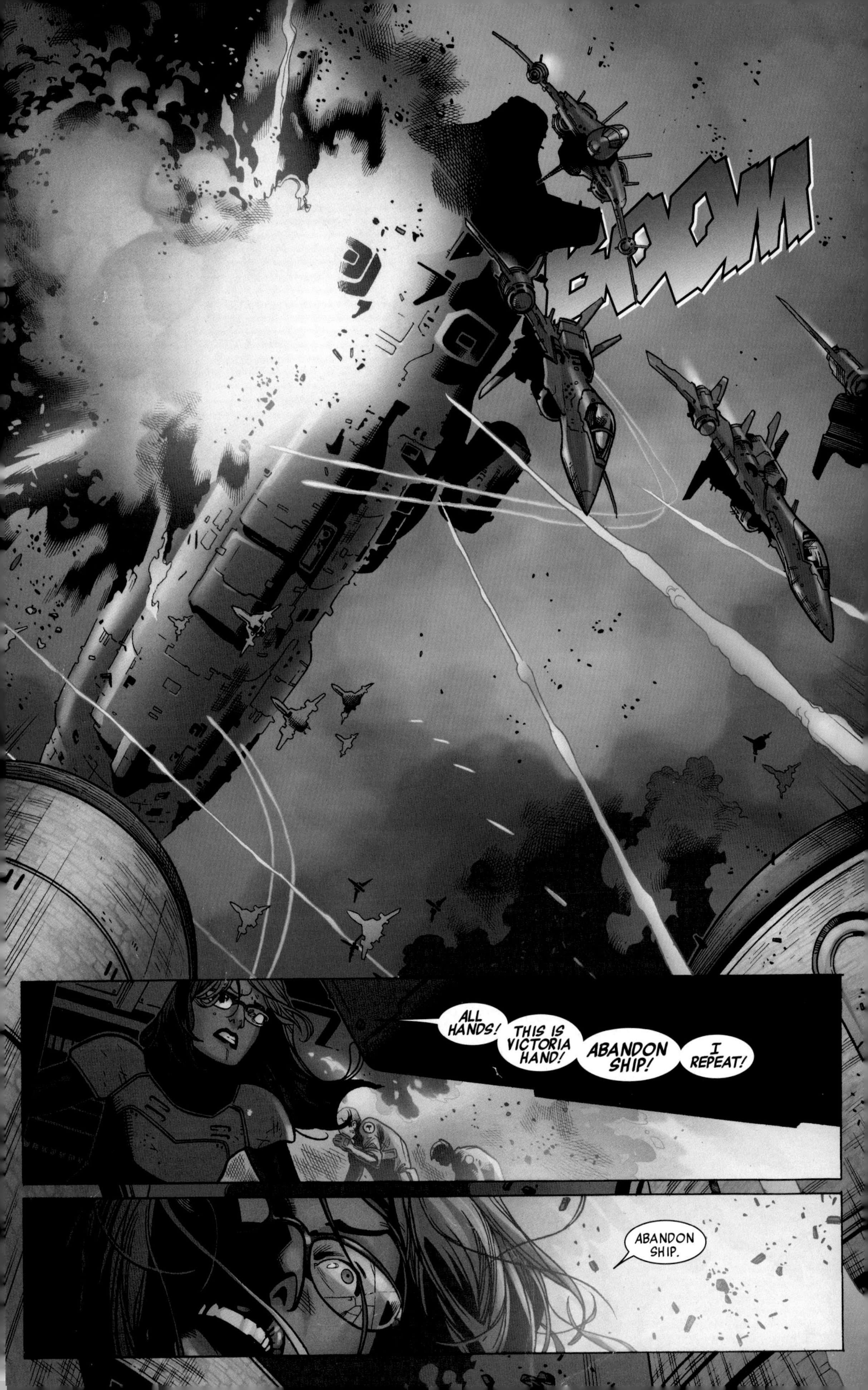
ALL HANDS!
THIS IS VICTORIA HAND!
ABANDON SHIP!
I REPEAT!
ABANDON SHIP.

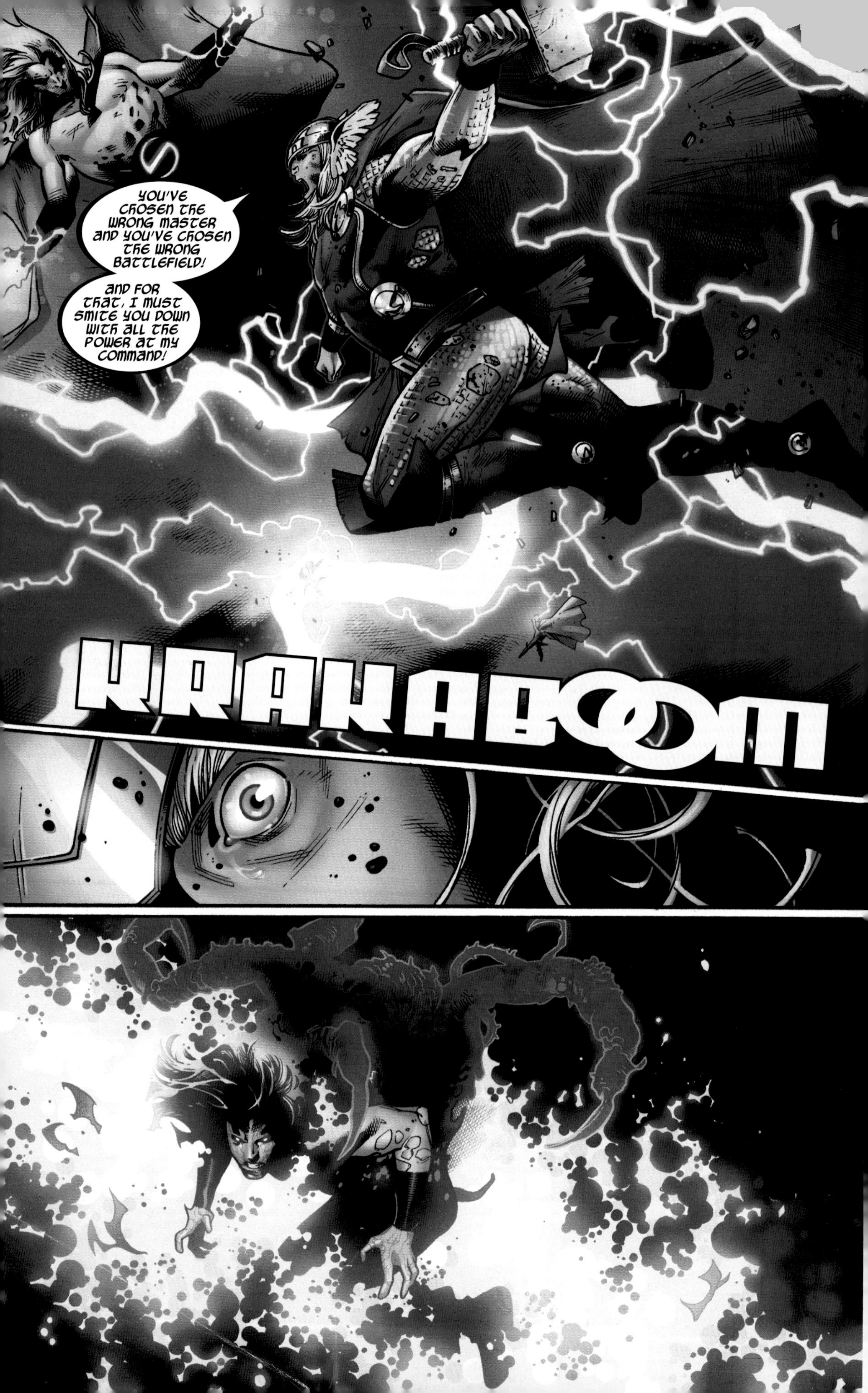
YOU'VE CHOSEN THE WRONG MASTER AND YOU'VE CHOSEN THE WRONG BATTLEFIELD!
AND FOR THAT, I MUST SMITE YOU DOWN WITH ALL THE POWER AT MY COMMAND!
KRAKABOOM

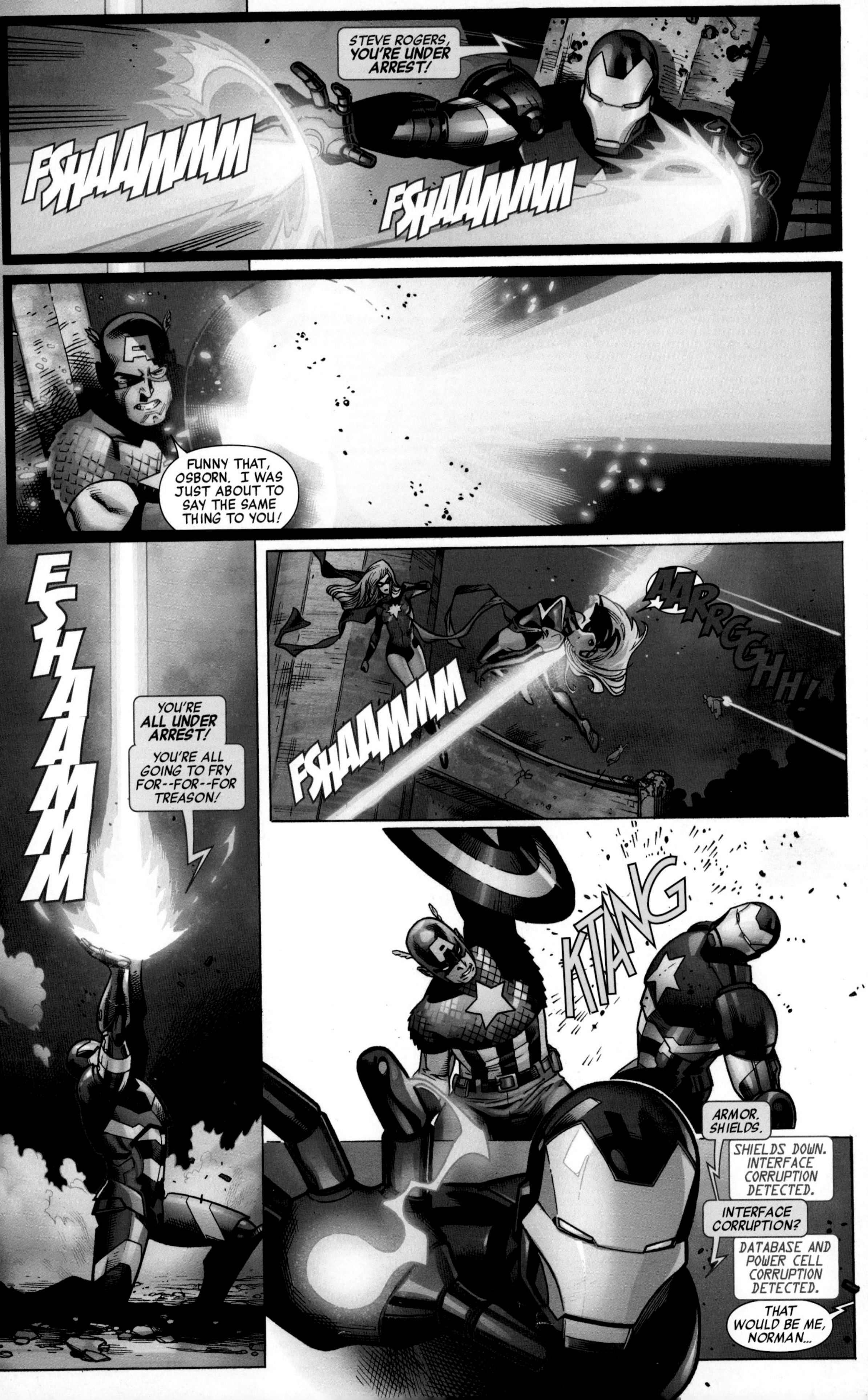
STEVE ROGERS, YOU'RE UNDER ARREST!
FSHAAMMM
FSHAAMMM
FUNNY THAT, OSBORN. I WAS JUST ABOUT TO SAY THE SAME THING TO YOU!
FSHAAMMM
YOU'RE ALL UNDER ARREST!
YOU'RE ALL GOING TO FRY FOR--FOR--FOR TREASON!
FSHAAMMM
AARRGGHH!
KTANG
ARMOR. SHIELDS.
SHIELDS DOWN. INTERFACE CORRUPTION DETECTED.
INTERFACE CORRUPTION?
DATABASE AND POWER CELL CORRUPTION DETECTED.
THAT WOULD BE ME, NORMAN...

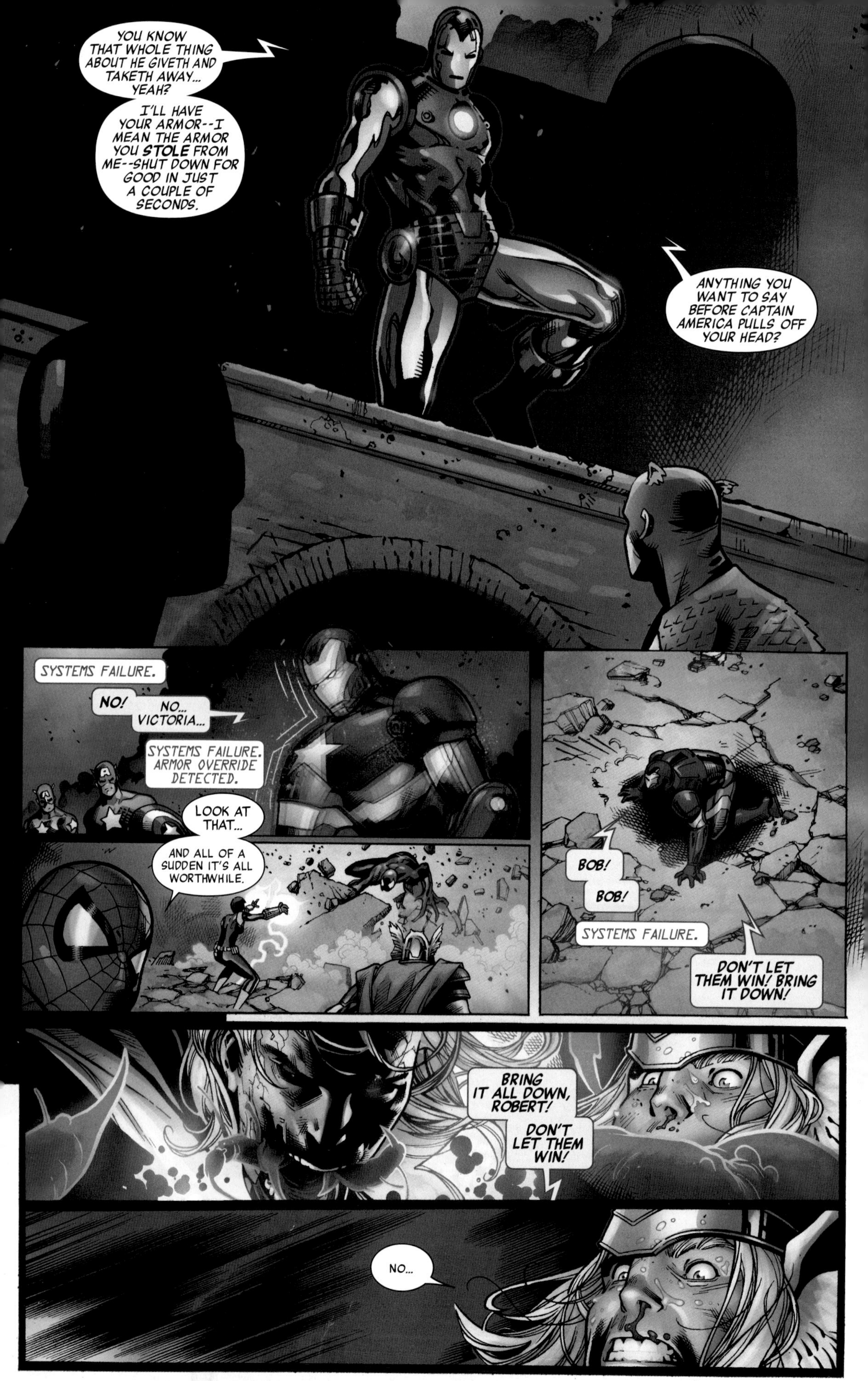

YOU KNOW THAT WHOLE THING ABOUT HE GIVETH AND TAKETH AWAY... YEAH?
I'LL HAVE YOUR ARMOR--I MEAN THE ARMOR YOU STOLE FROM ME--SHUT DOWN FOR GOOD IN JUST A COUPLE OF SECONDS.
ANYTHING YOU WANT TO SAY BEFORE CAPTAIN AMERICA PULLS OFF YOUR HEAD?
SYSTEMS FAILURE.
NO!
NO... VICTORIA...
SYSTEMS FAILURE. ARMOR OVERRIDE DETECTED.
LOOK AT THAT...
AND ALL OF A SUDDEN IT'S ALL WORTHWHILE.
BOB!
BOB!
SYSTEMS FAILURE.
DON'T LET THEM WIN! BRING IT DOWN!
BRING IT ALL DOWN, ROBERT!
DON'T LET THEM WIN!
NO...

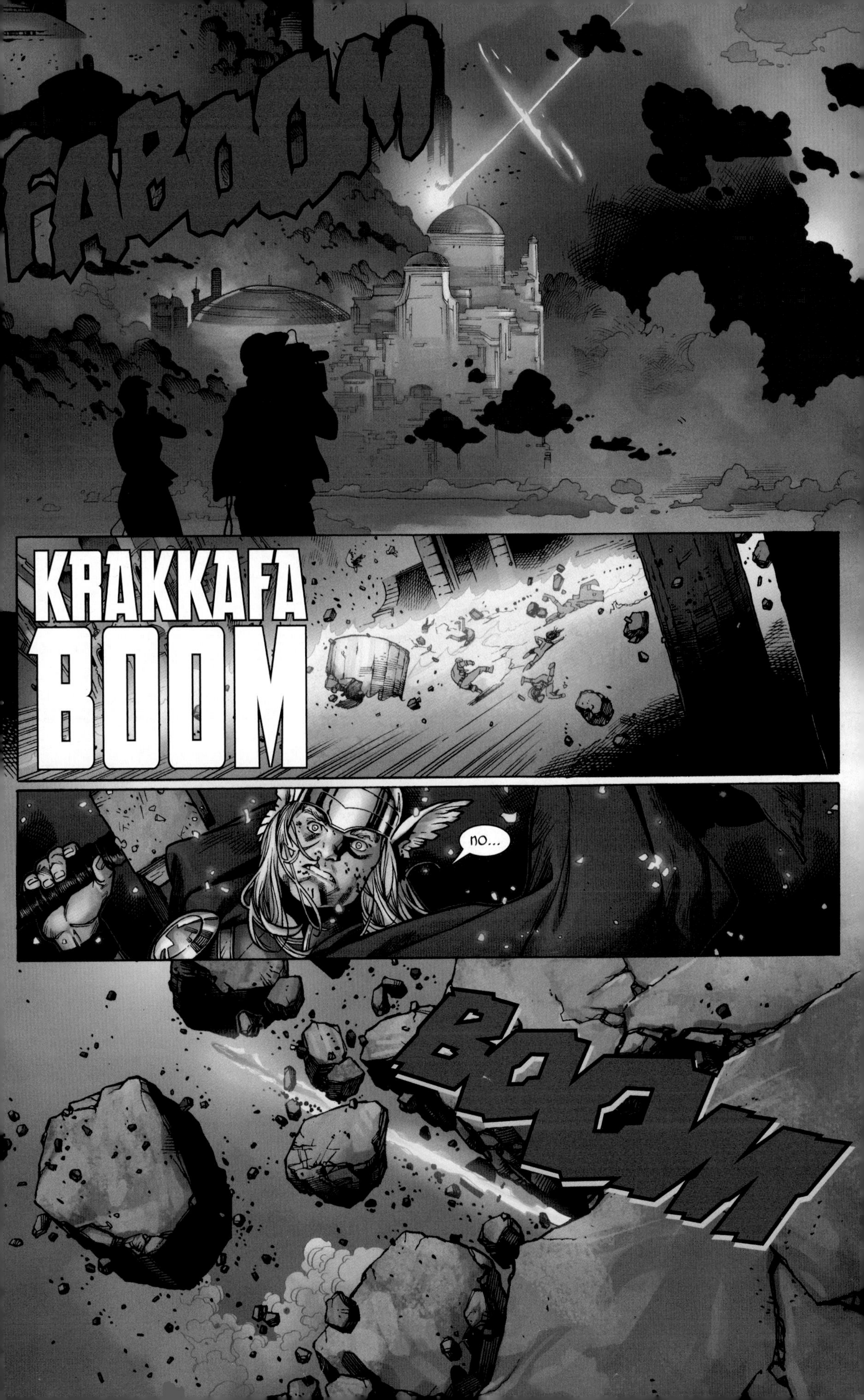
FABOOM
KRAKKAFA
BOOM
no...
BOOM

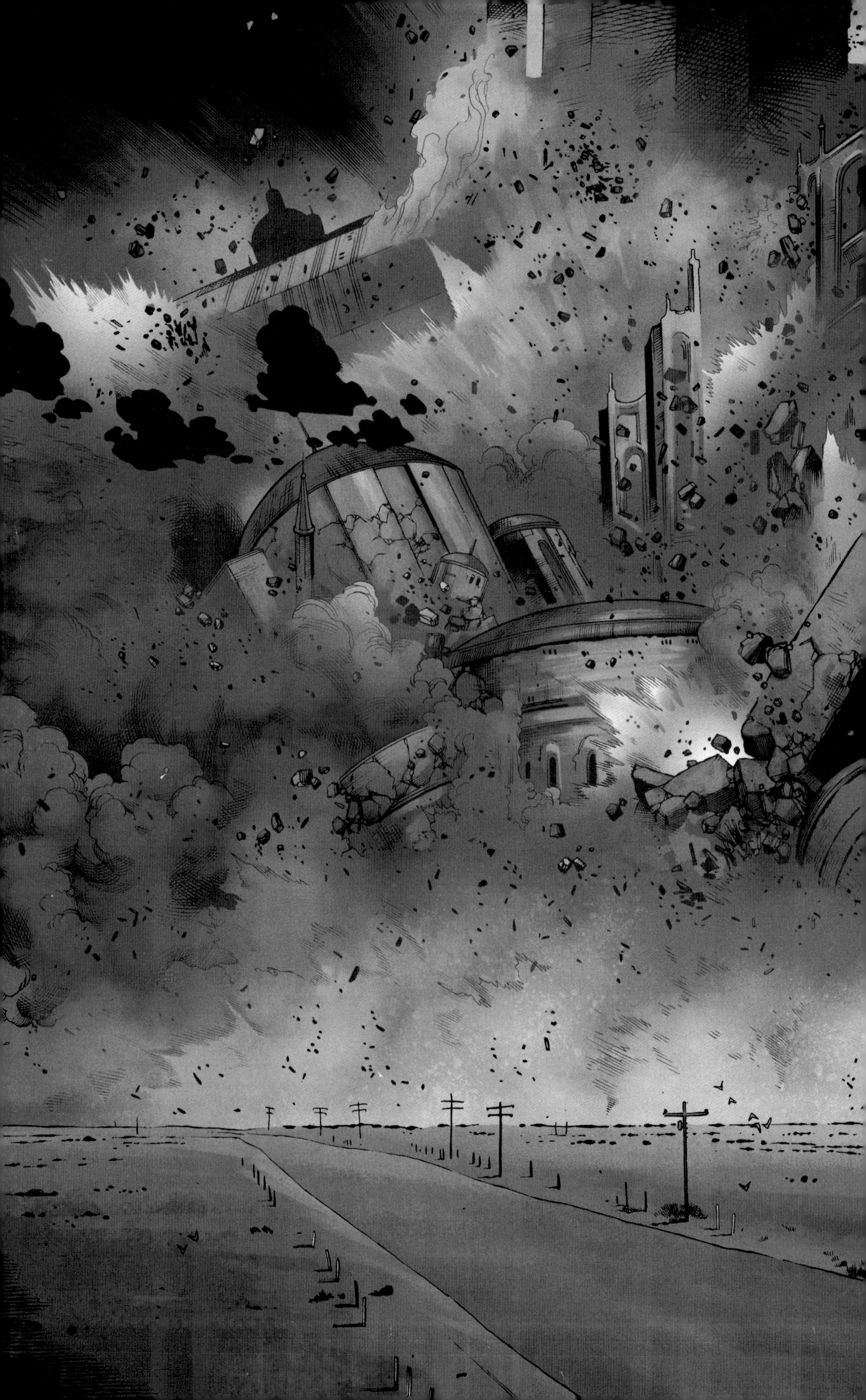

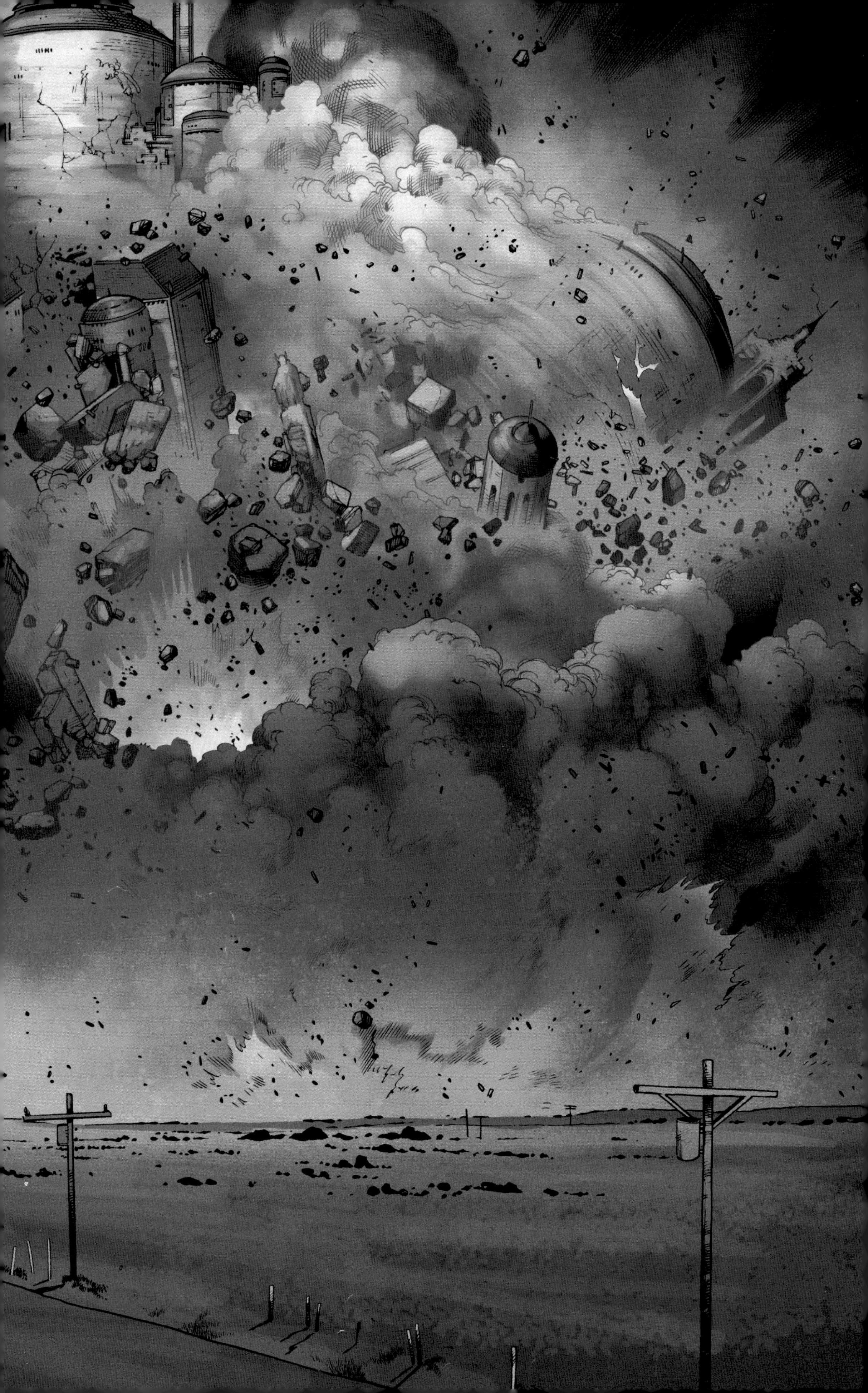

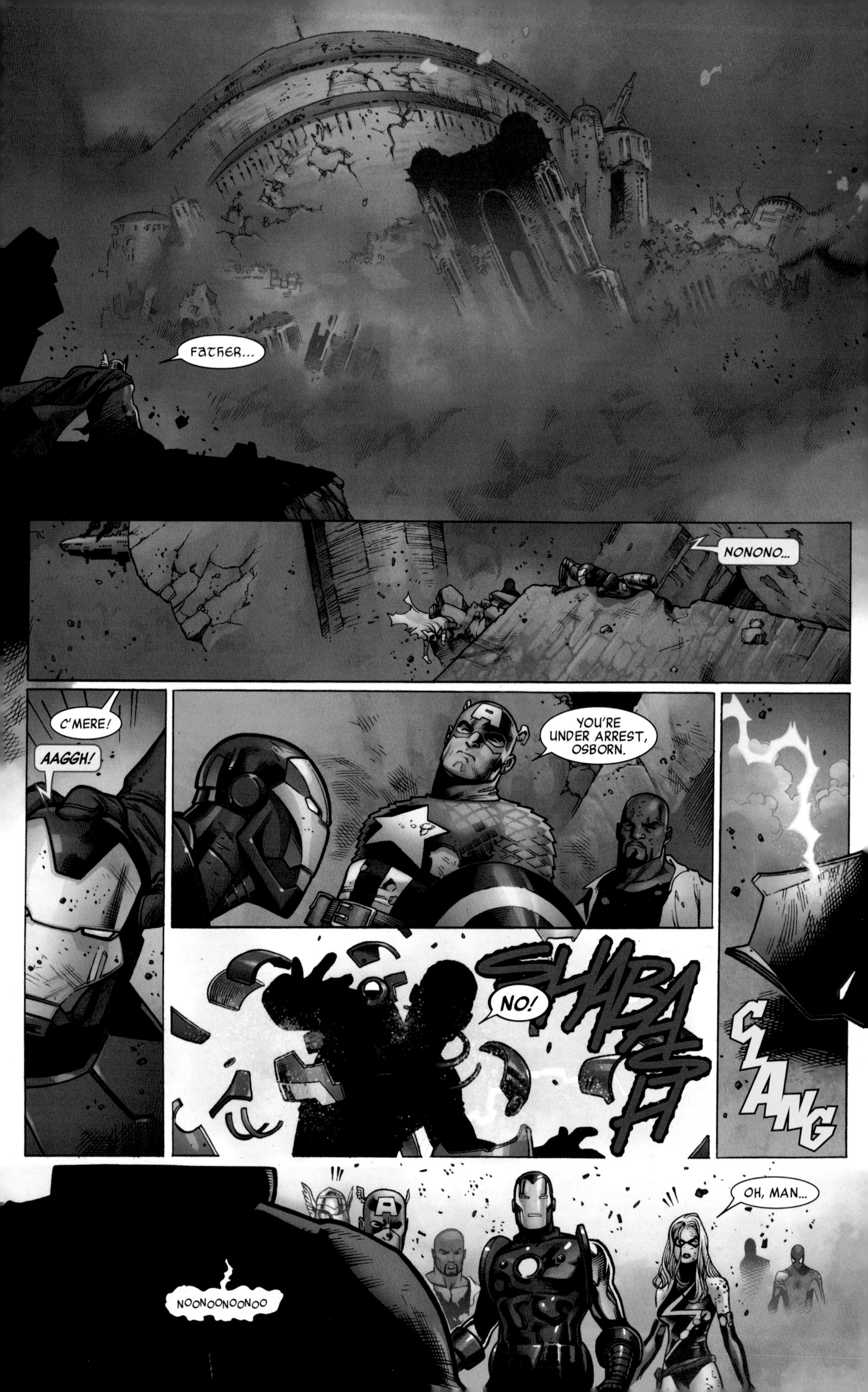
FATHER...
NONONO...
C'MERE!
AAGGH!
YOU'RE UNDER ARREST, OSBORN.
CLANG
NO!
SHABASH
OH, MAN...
NOONOONOONOO

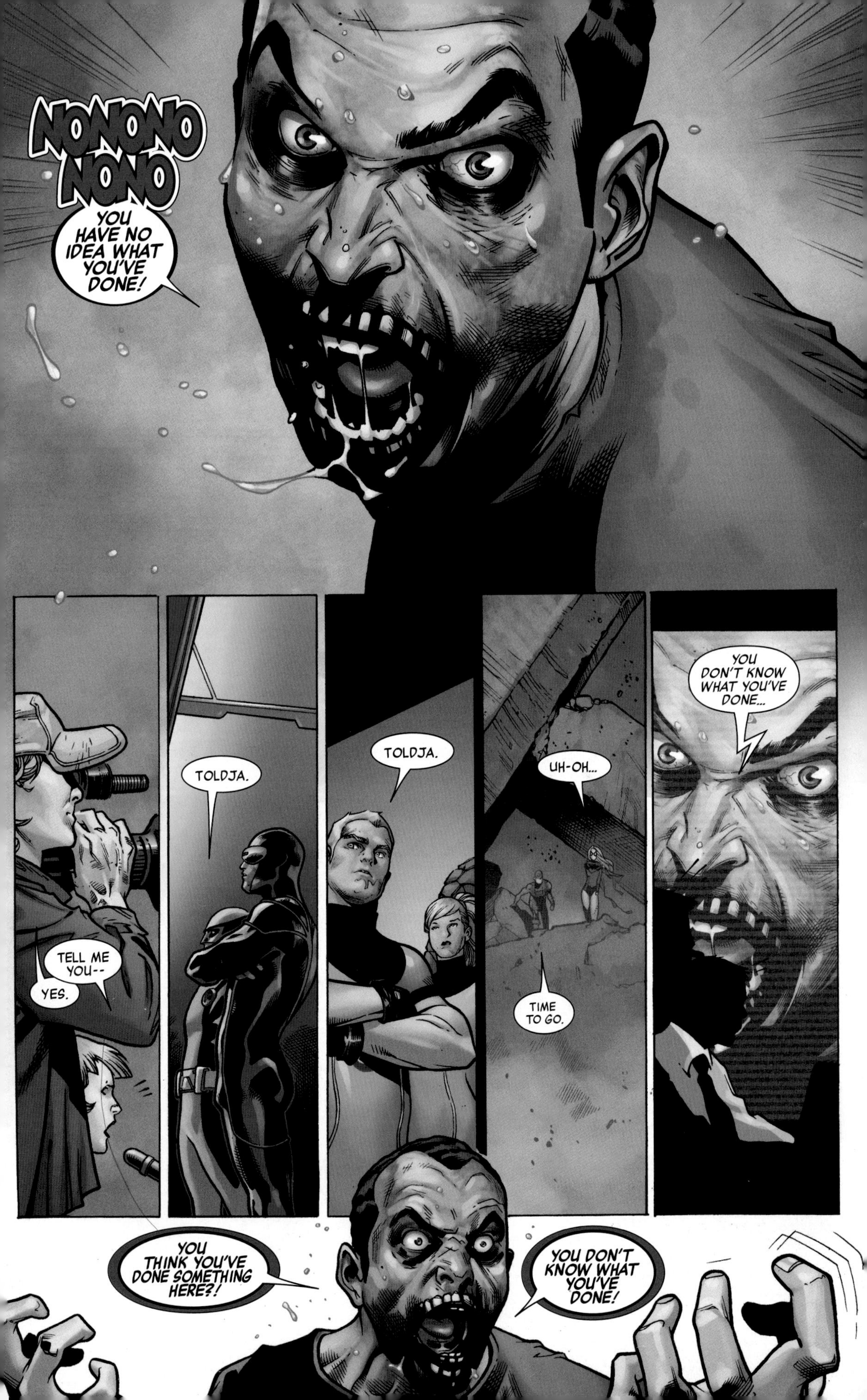
NONONO NONO
YOU HAVE NO IDEA WHAT YOU'VE DONE!
TELL ME YOU--
YES.
TOLDJA.
TOLDJA.
UH-OH...
TIME TO GO.
YOU DON'T KNOW WHAT YOU'VE DONE...
YOU THINK YOU'VE DONE SOMETHING HERE?!
YOU DON'T KNOW WHAT YOU'VE DONE!

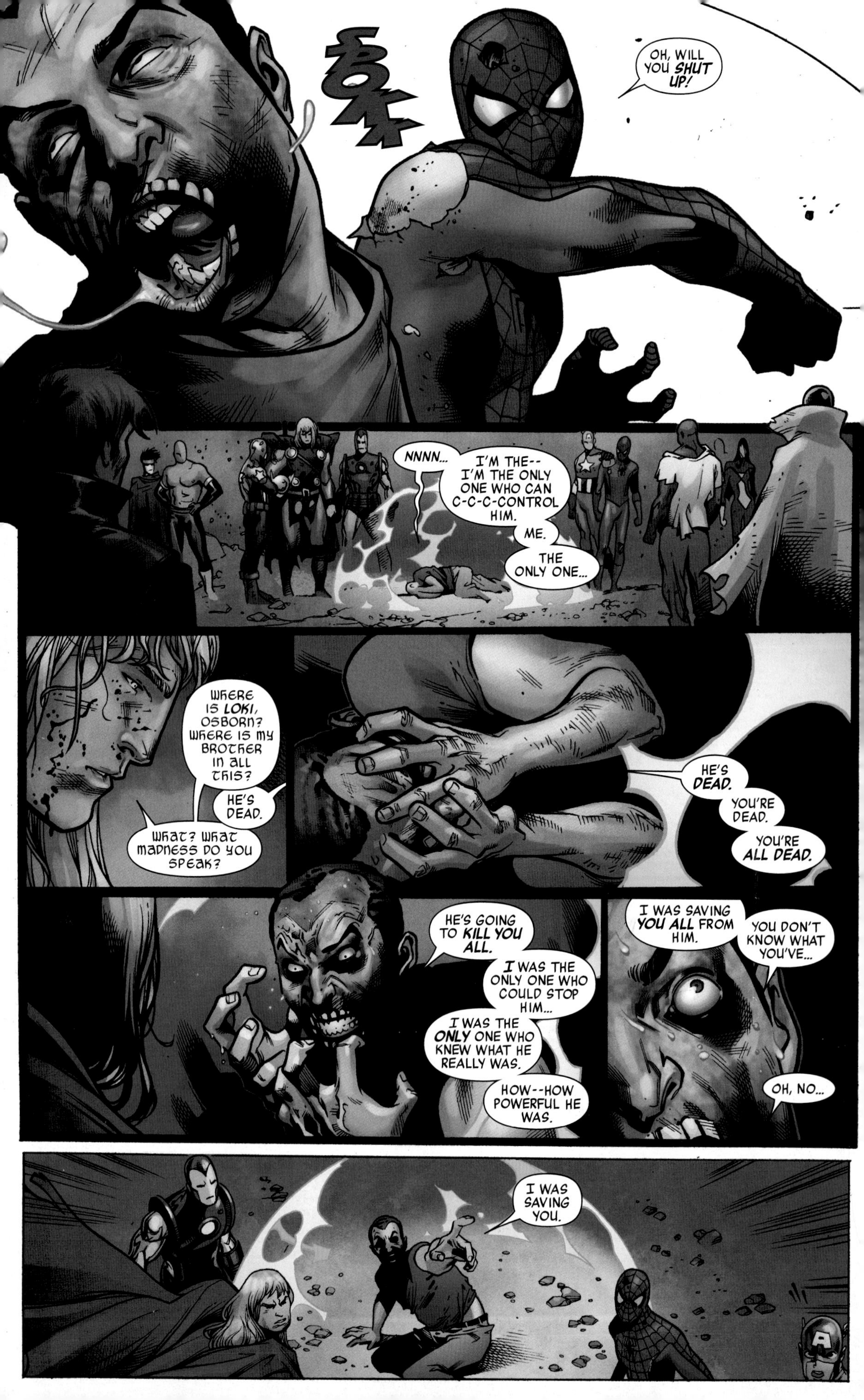

TOKK
OH, WILL YOU SHUT UP!
NNNN...
I'M THE-- I'M THE ONLY ONE WHO CAN C-C-C-CONTROL HIM.
ME.
THE ONLY ONE...
WHERE IS LOKI, OSBORN? WHERE IS MY BROTHER IN ALL THIS?
HE'S DEAD.
WHAT? WHAT MADNESS DO YOU SPEAK?
HE'S DEAD.
YOU'RE DEAD.
YOU'RE ALL DEAD.
HE'S GOING TO KILL YOU ALL.
I WAS THE ONLY ONE WHO COULD STOP HIM...
I WAS THE ONLY ONE WHO KNEW WHAT HE REALLY WAS.
HOW--HOW POWERFUL HE WAS.
I WAS SAVING YOU ALL FROM HIM.
YOU DON'T KNOW WHAT YOU'VE...
OH, NO...
I WAS SAVING YOU.

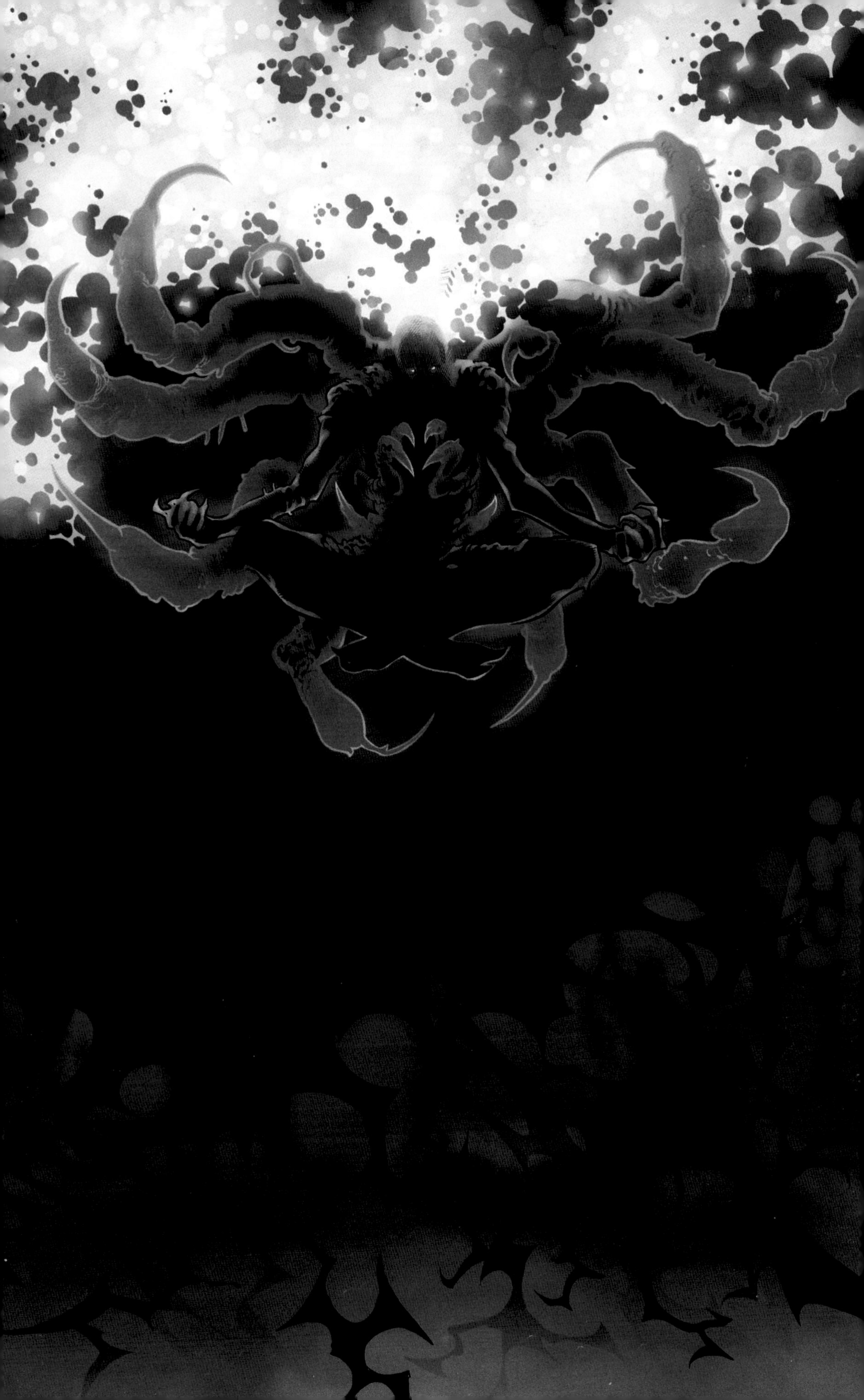

THE WHITE HOUSE

WASHINGTON

WHITE HOUSE PROTOCOL SERVER BETA 9-34234-45345

EYES ONLY. ENCODED

S.H.I.E.L.D. COMMAND DECRYPTION PACKAGE UPLOADED

MARIA HILL, COMMANDER OF S.H.I.E.L.D. (DECOMMISSIONED)
TRANSMITTING

TOP SECRET CODE- WHITE

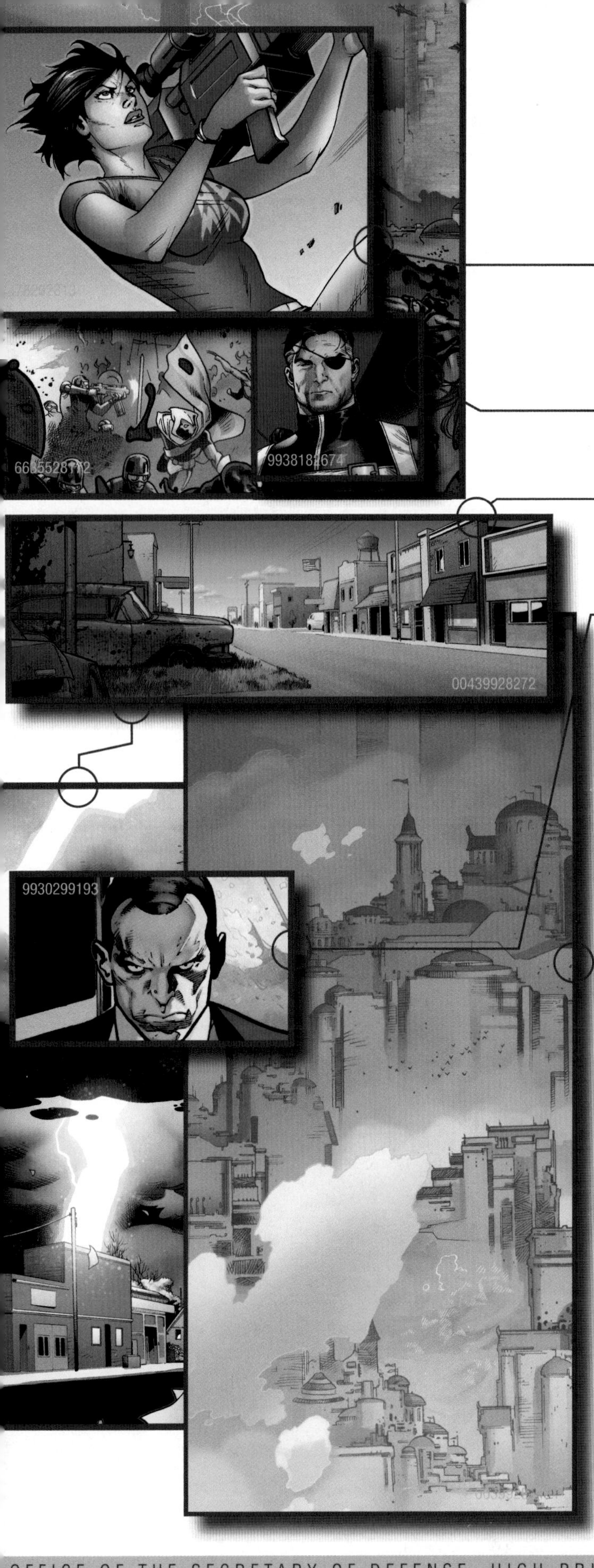
9938182674
00439928272
9930299193

TRANSMISSION TIME CODE
14:12

MARIA HILL

This is **Maria Hill** broadcasting on the secure S.H.I.E.L.D. Command Server. I know I do not have permission to use this server anymore and I am sorry I had to use an old **Nick Fury** trick to hack into it. But I need to get hold of you and I have no other choice. I am here in **Broxton, Oklahoma** caring for Tony Stark, who is out of commission. I have first-hand eyewitness testimony that **Norman Osborn** has taken an offensive stance against the colony of **Asgard.** This is a massive ground and air strike. I feel the entire city of Broxton is in jeopardy, thousands of American civilian lives, not to mention the countless Asgardians. I pray to God you did not approve this initiative. Something has to be done. Please advise. Is Osborn off the grid?

SECRETARY OF DEFENSE RIDELL

Miss Hill, your text transmission came in loud and clear. You have the ear of the entire situation room including the President and Vice President. Osborn is rogue. I repeat, Osborn is rogue. We are fully aware of the incident. It is broadcasting live on all commercial networks. Osborn called the press himself and we assume is using it to embolden his position. Be clear--he has no executive authority to act against Asgard. He is acting on his own. Your intel is welcome.

TRANSMISSION TIME CODE
15:02

MARIA HILL
This is Maria Hill. With the help of a local, I just rescued **Thor** from an assassination attempt by Osborn himself. I was able to get in and get out safely. I saved Thor but now **H.A.M.M.E.R.** ground units are in the city proper looking for us.

SECRETARY OF DEFENSE RIDELL
Hill, we witnessed the rescue. Job well done. The President has authorized you to take down Osborn if you have the shot. You have executive authority.

MARIA HILL
This is Maria Hill. I do not have the shot or firepower. I am in hiding with Thor until he recovers. Thor has a better chance of taking Osborn out than I do. With permission, I will transfer the President's order to him but I don't think he needs our permission to do what needs to be done to save his home.

SECRETARY OF DEFENSE RIDELL
Armed forces are on their way. Sit tight, agent.

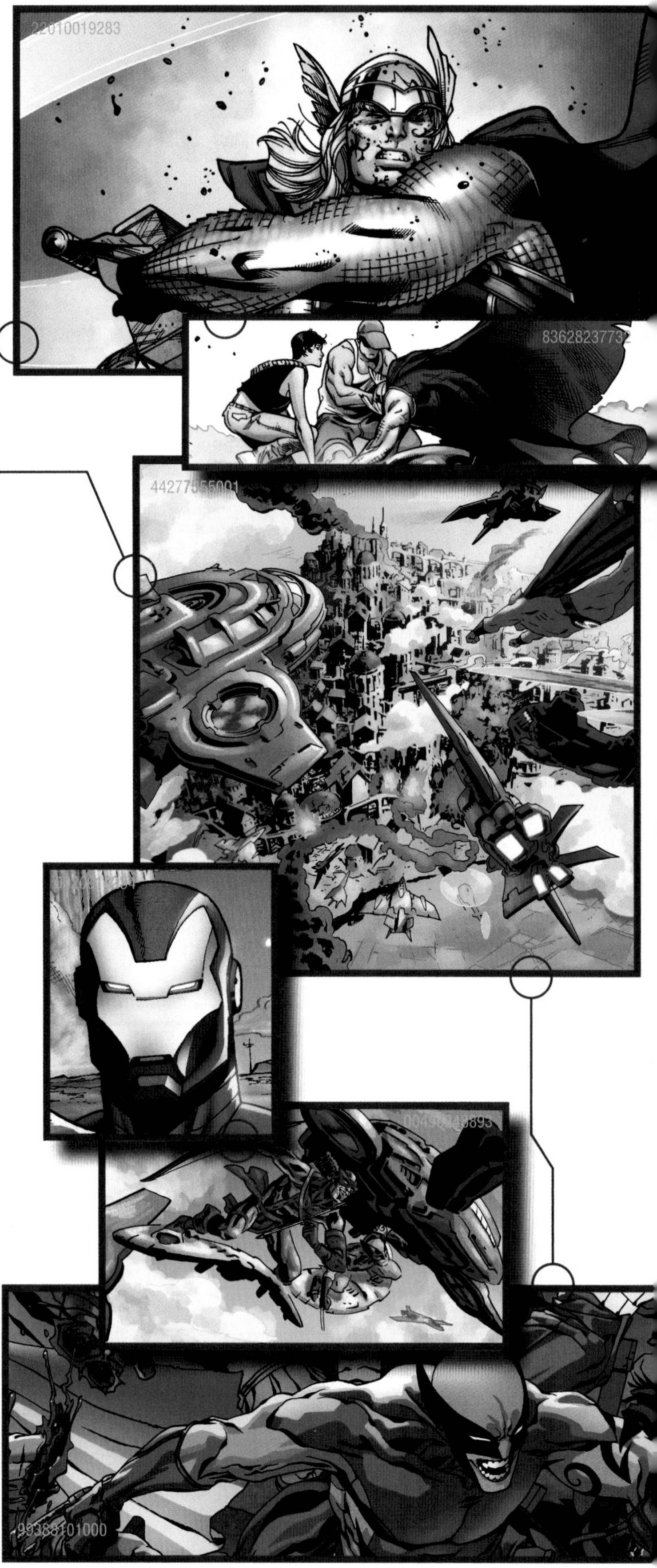

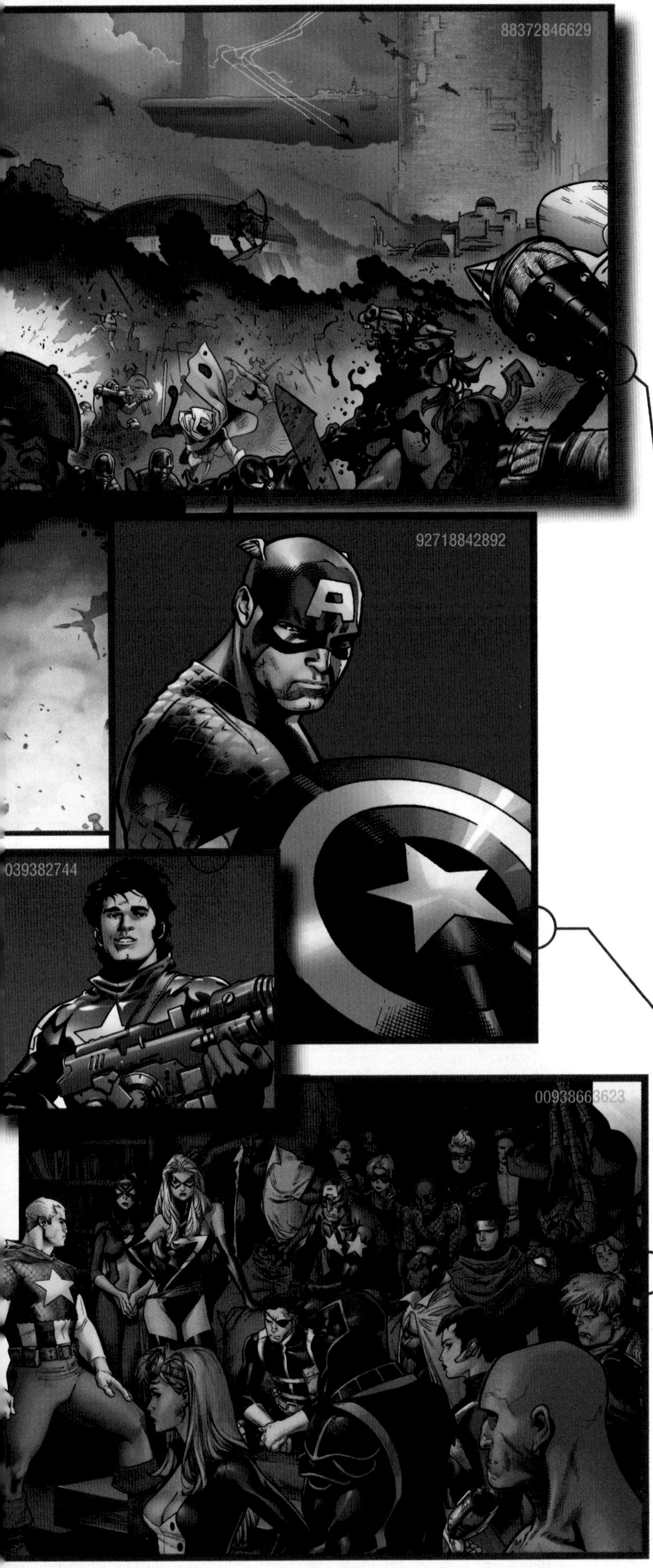
88372846629
92718842892
039382744
00938663623

TRANSMISSION TIME CODE
15:19

MARIA HILL
This is Maria Hill. Both Thor and myself strongly advise against a U.S. military force here on the ground. This entire city will be torn to shreds by even the slightest ground conflict. Do not bring troops into the city. Focus your efforts on the **Helicarrier** and the aerial assault over Asgard itself.

SECRETARY OF DEFENSE RIDELL
We are deploying troops to both Broxton and Asgard. Identify yourself to the first Marines you see. Command is aware of your situation. Send your coordinates and a rescue team will deploy to you.

MARIA HILL
No!!! Do not come for me!! Do not come into the city. **Captain America** and the **Avengers** are now in Asgard. Back them up. Do not come to Broxton! I repeat! Do not come to Broxton.

SECRETARY OF DEFENSE RIDELL
Negative. We are deploying troops into the city. The President asks that you advise the ground troops as needed. Is Thor out of commission? Is Tony Stark alive?

TRANSMISSION TIME CODE
15:27

MARIA HILL
This is Maria Hill. Thor is alive and engaged in battle with the Sentry over the city of Broxton. H.A.M.M.E.R. troops have declared martial law on the streets. I am with **Tony Stark.** He is recovering and suiting up. Mister President, Tony Stark wants your order to go into battle. He is going to go in either way, but he is requesting your order.

SECRETARY OF DEFENSE RIDELL
Tell Mister Stark he has authority and the President's blessing.

MARIA HILL
This is Maria Hill. Iron Man is in the air, I repeat, Iron Man is in the air! But Osborn has called in **reinforcements.** I can't ID them from my rooftop angle, but I strongly advise you put the call out to Scott Summers of the X-Men and Reed Richards of the Fantastic Four. The Avengers need backup. I repeat, the Avengers need backup.

SECRETARY OF DEFENSE RIDELL
Backup and military force are on the way.

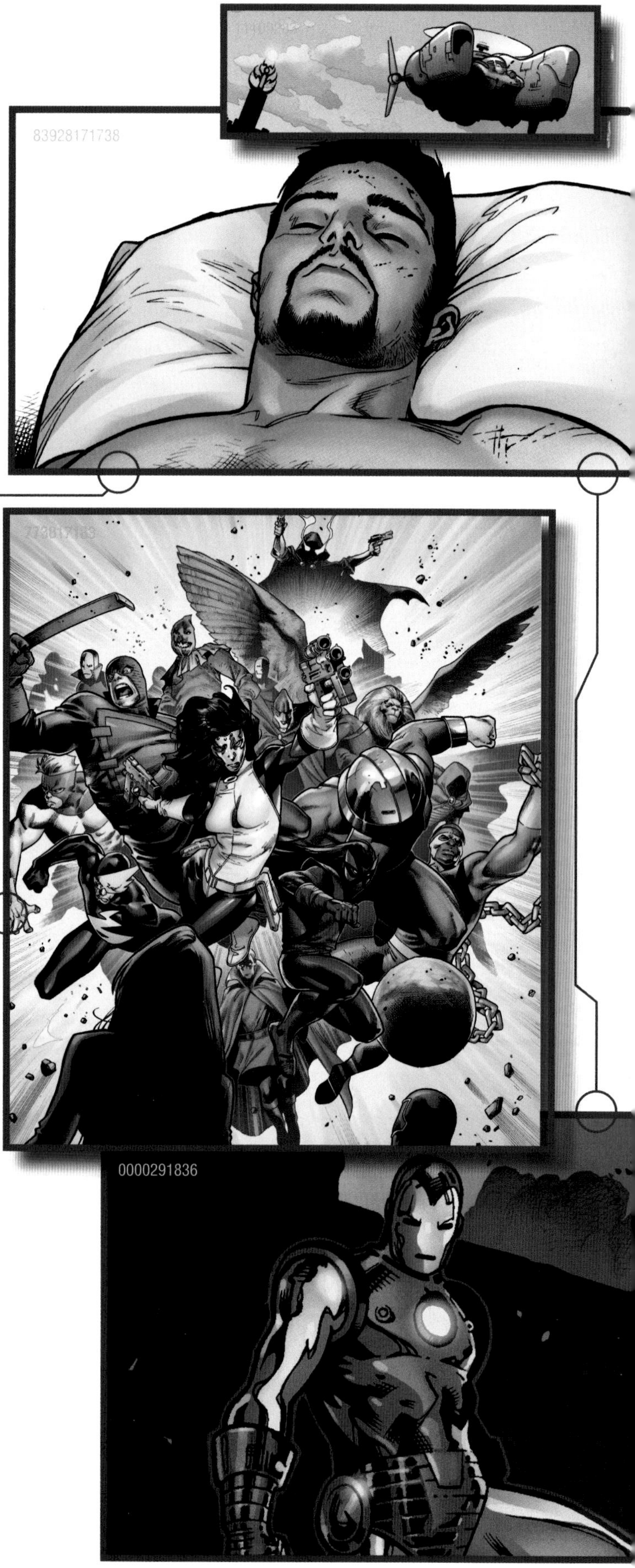
83928171738
0000291836

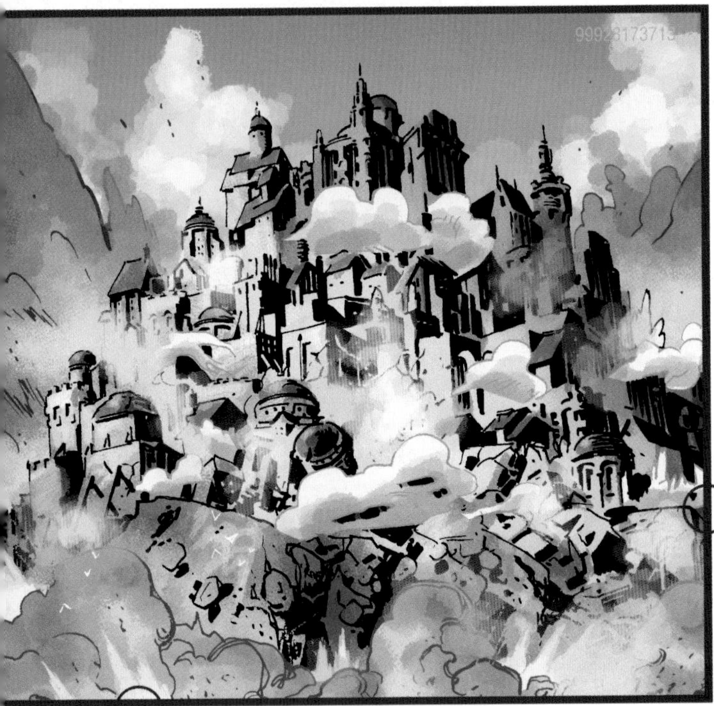

TRANSMISSION TIME CODE
15: 44

MARIA HILL

This is Maria Hill. The Sentry has struck the foundation of Asgard. The entire colony is tipping. If you are hearing me, Asgard is buckling! Its entire city is--is tipping over and--oh Lord! **Asgard is down!** Oh my God! I repeat! Asgard has fallen!! Oh my God! Oh my--

SECRETARY OF DEFENSE RIDELL

We did not copy.

REPEAT TRANSMISSION INTERRUPTED. SERVER DISCONNECTED.
000000441310

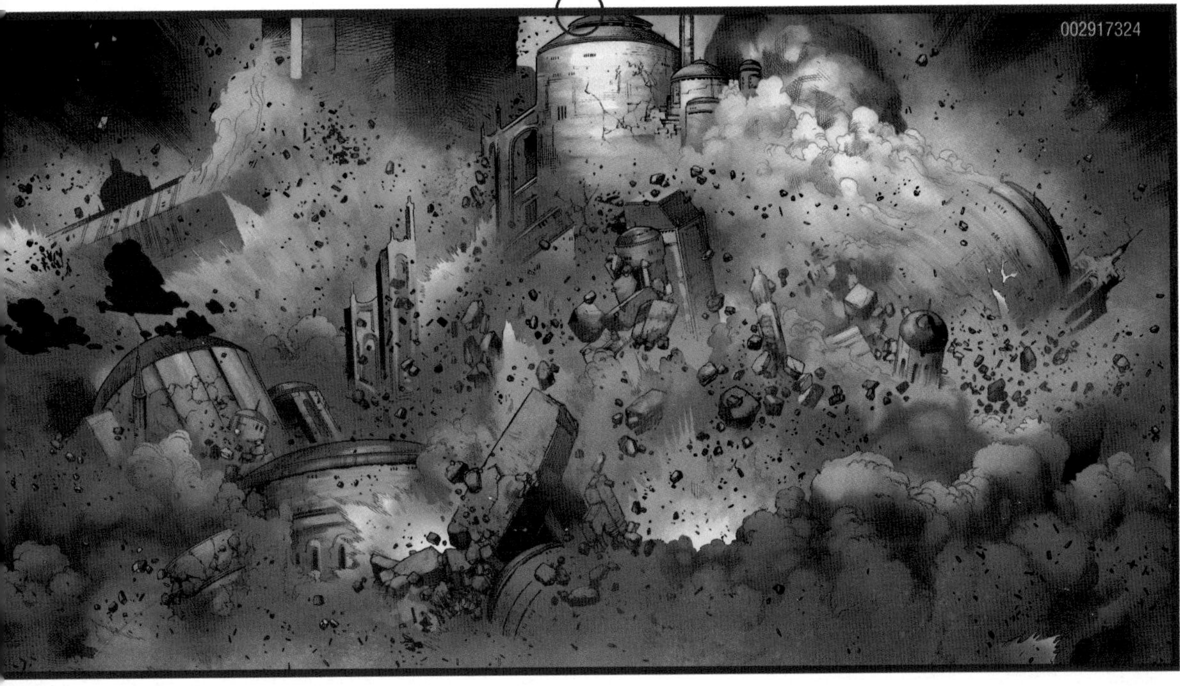
002917324

993784834524-88UUBDHI--CLASSIFIED

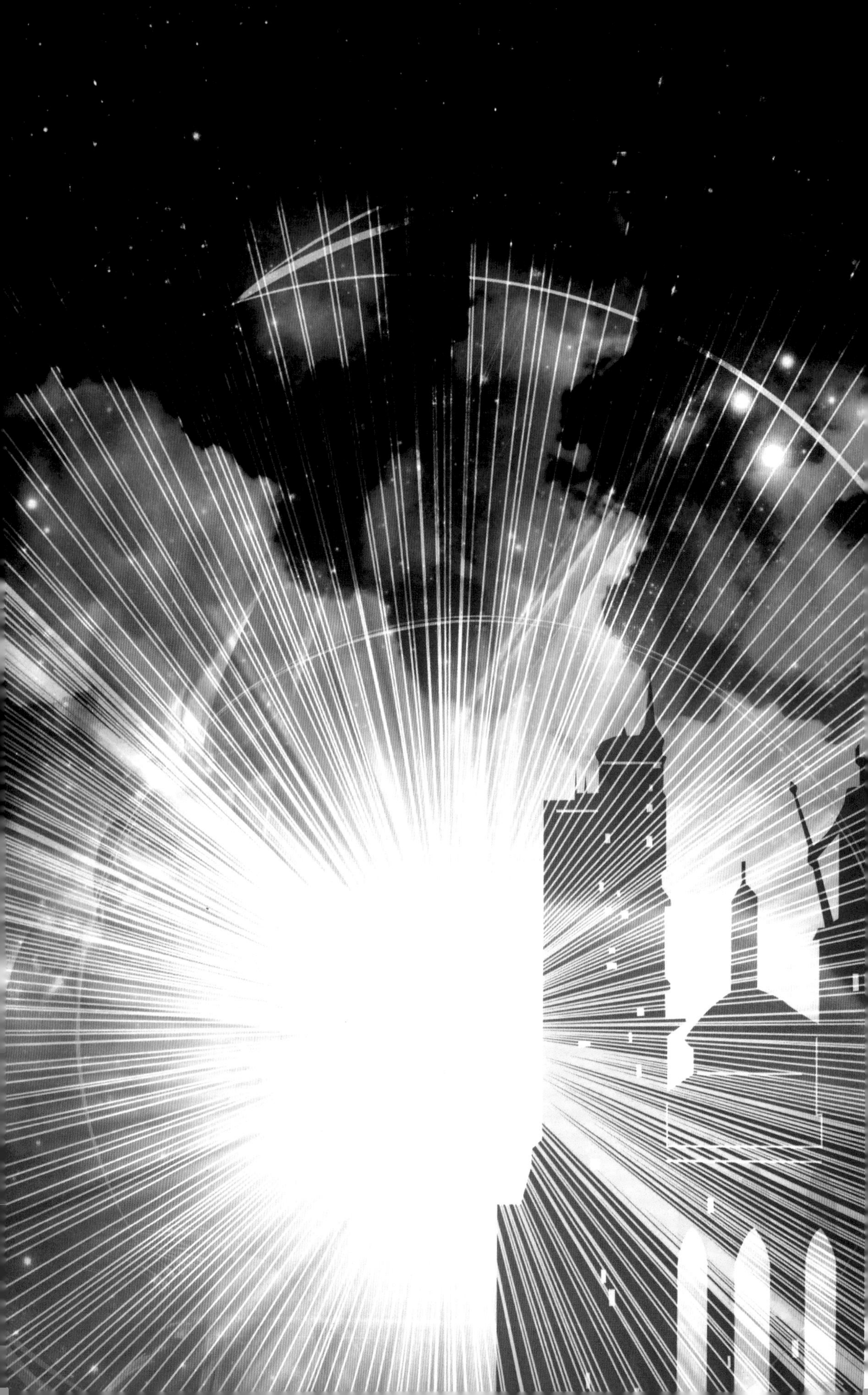

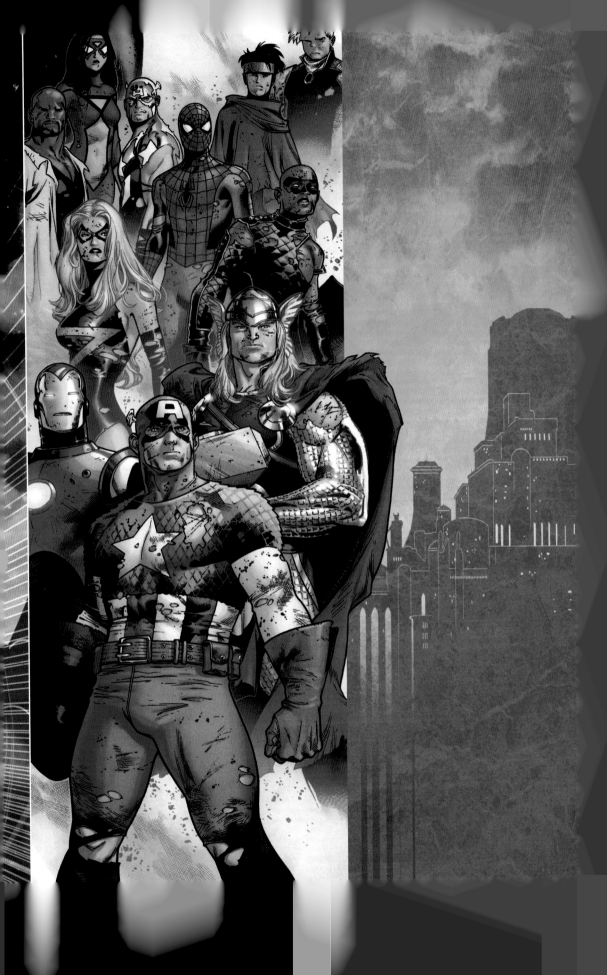

THE SIEGE OF ASGARD-THE FALLEN

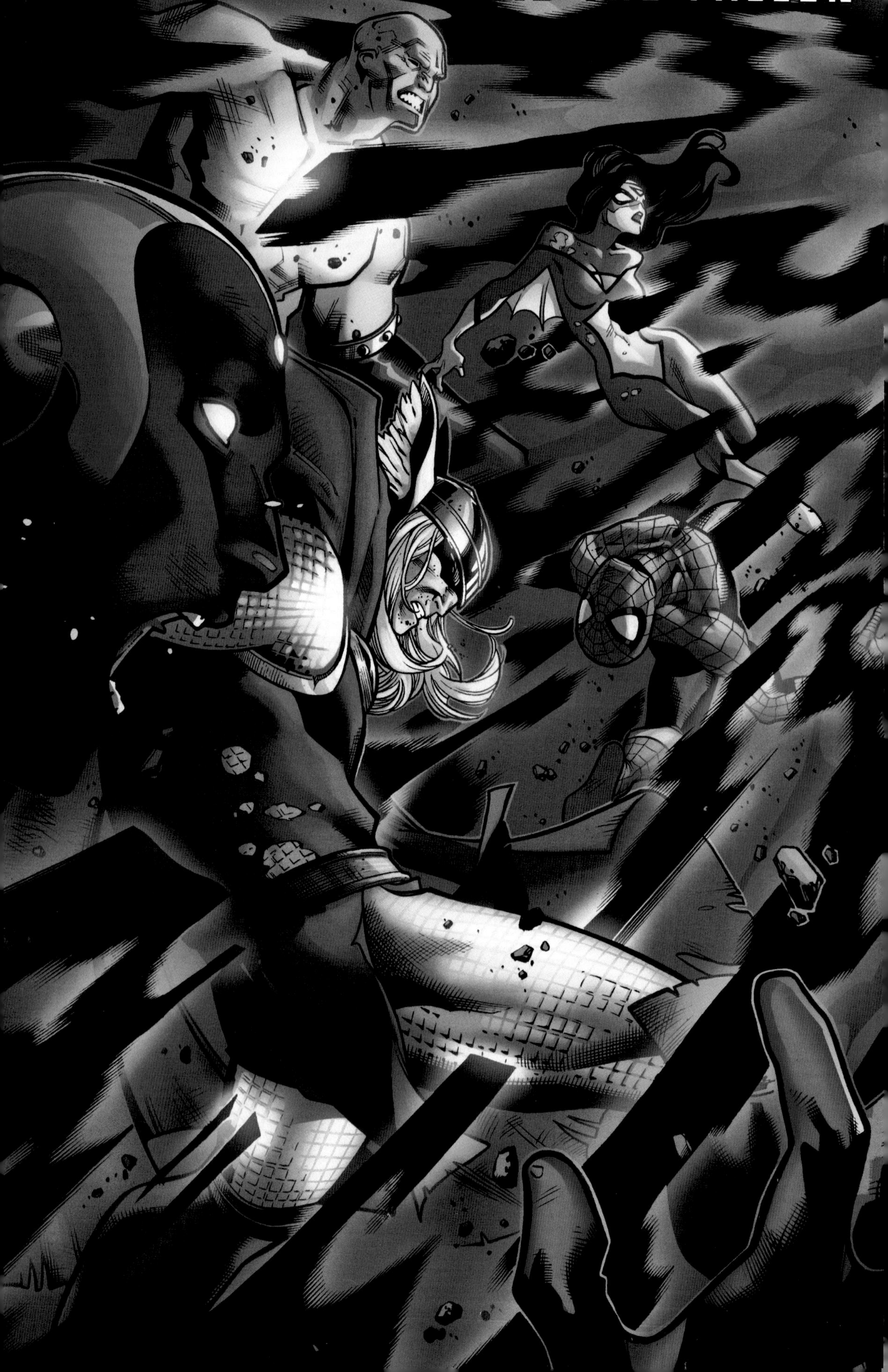

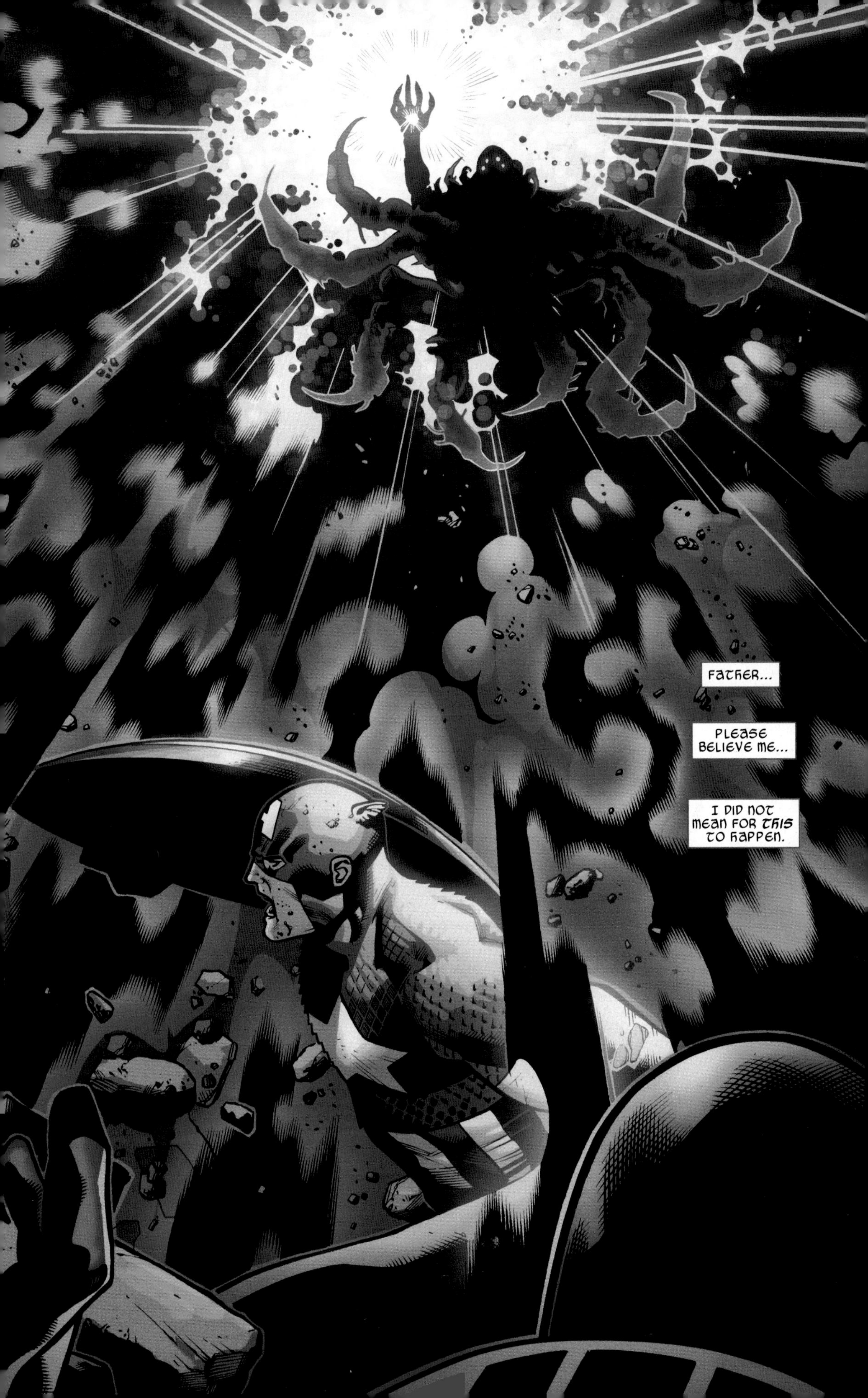

FATHER...
PLEASE BELIEVE ME...
I DID NOT MEAN FOR *THIS* TO HAPPEN.

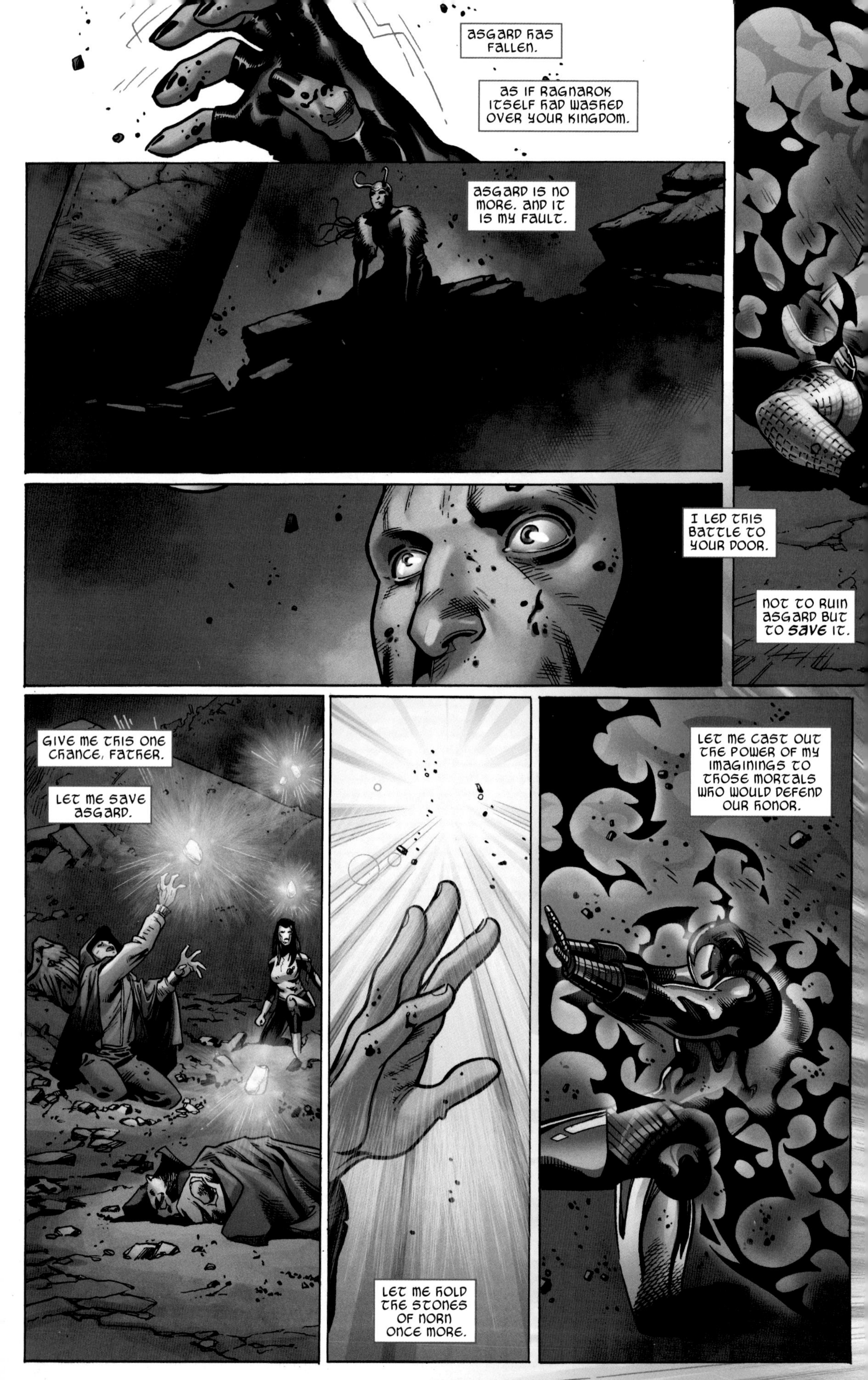
ASGARD HAS FALLEN.
AS IF RAGNAROK ITSELF HAD WASHED OVER YOUR KINGDOM.
ASGARD IS NO MORE. AND IT IS MY FAULT.
I LED THIS BATTLE TO YOUR DOOR.
NOT TO RUIN ASGARD BUT TO SAVE IT.
GIVE ME THIS ONE CHANCE, FATHER.
LET ME SAVE ASGARD.
LET ME HOLD THE STONES OF NORN ONCE MORE.
LET ME CAST OUT THE POWER OF MY IMAGININGS TO THOSE MORTALS WHO WOULD DEFEND OUR HONOR.

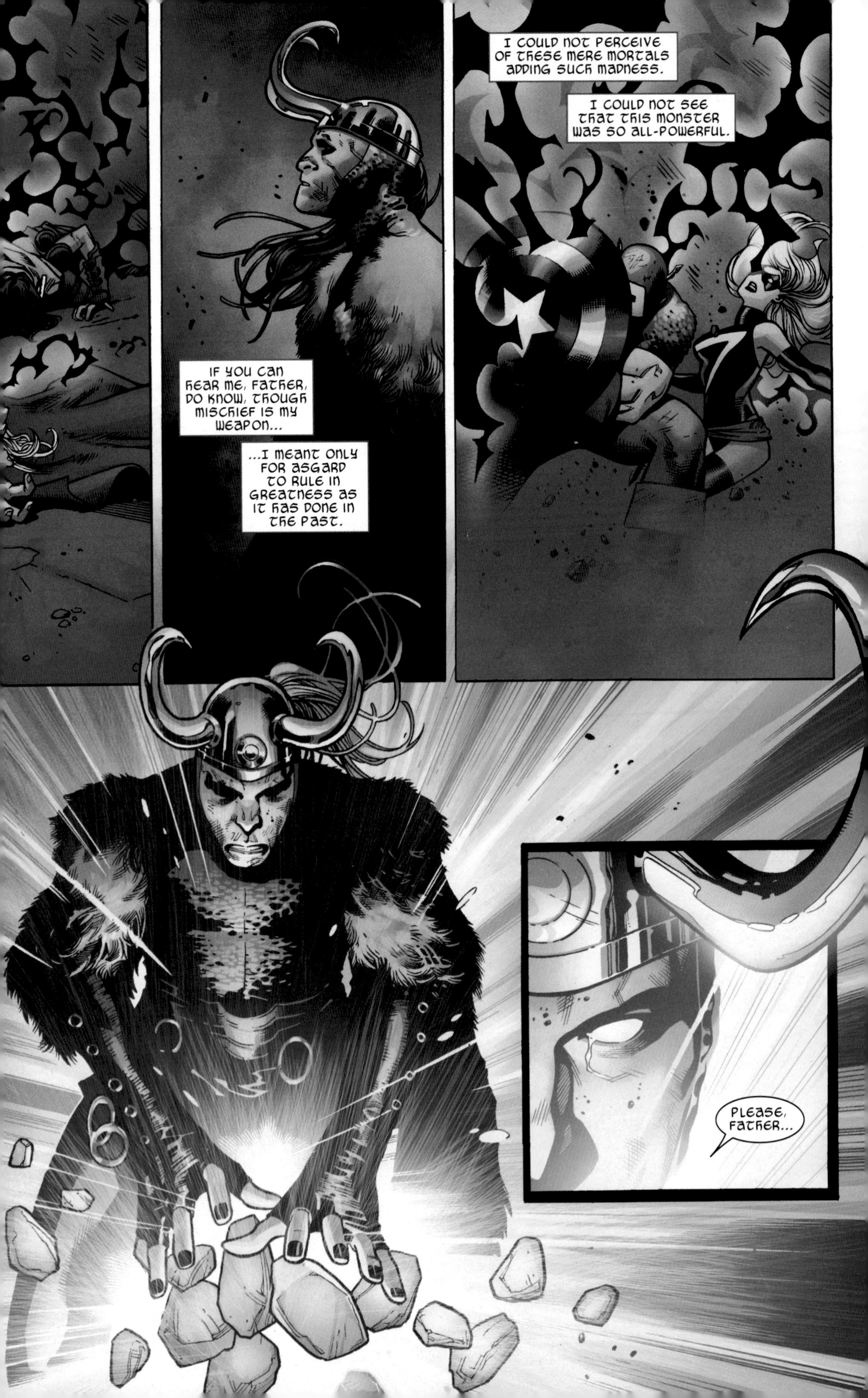
IF YOU CAN HEAR ME, FATHER, DO KNOW, THOUGH MISCHIEF IS MY WEAPON...
...I MEANT ONLY FOR ASGARD TO RULE IN GREATNESS AS IT HAS DONE IN THE PAST.
I COULD NOT PERCEIVE OF THESE MERE MORTALS ADDING SUCH MADNESS.
I COULD NOT SEE THAT THIS MONSTER WAS SO ALL-POWERFUL.
PLEASE, FATHER...

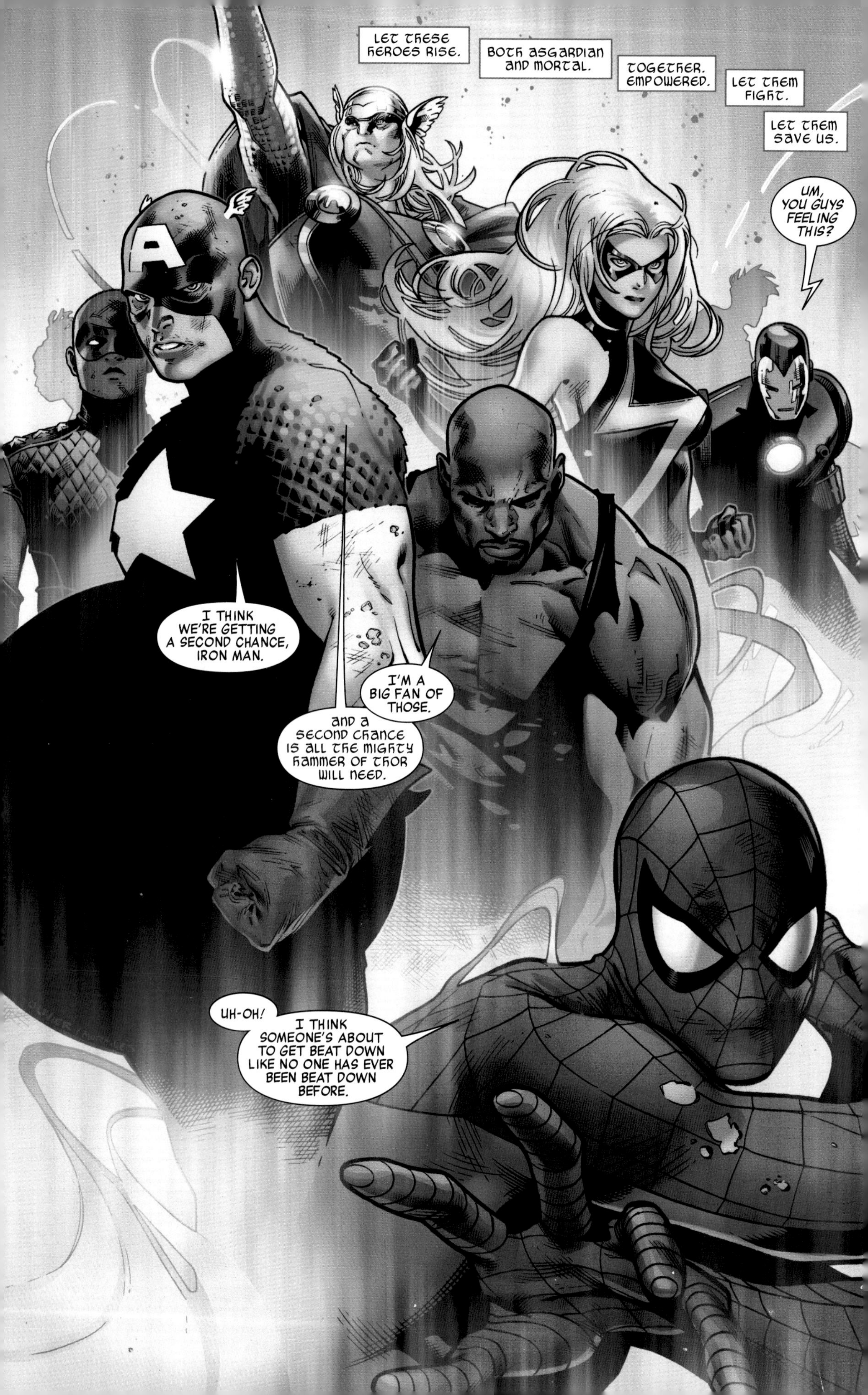
LET THESE HEROES RISE.
BOTH ASGARDIAN AND MORTAL.
TOGETHER. EMPOWERED.
LET THEM FIGHT.
LET THEM SAVE US.
UM, YOU GUYS FEELING THIS?
I THINK WE'RE GETTING A SECOND CHANCE, IRON MAN.
I'M A BIG FAN OF THOSE.
AND A SECOND CHANCE IS ALL THE MIGHTY HAMMER OF THOR WILL NEED.
UH-OH!
I THINK SOMEONE'S ABOUT TO GET BEAT DOWN LIKE NO ONE HAS EVER BEEN BEAT DOWN BEFORE.

LET THEIR AIM BE TRUE.

AAAIIIRRGGH!

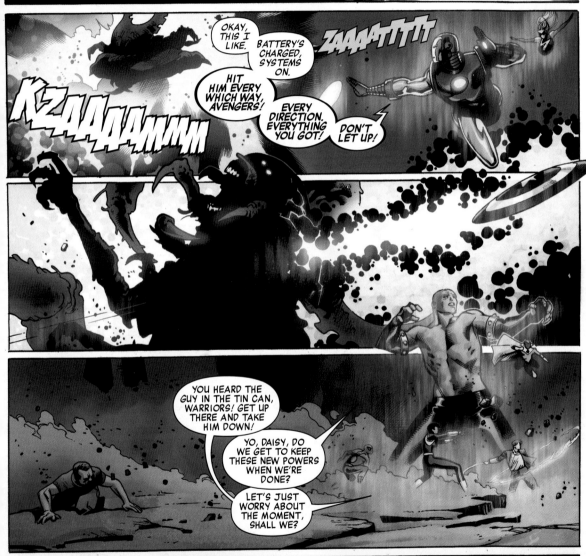

OKAY, THIS I LIKE. BATTERY'S CHARGED, SYSTEMS ON.

ZAAAATTTT!

HIT HIM EVERY WHICH WAY, AVENGERS!

EVERY DIRECTION. EVERYTHING YOU GOT!

DON'T LET UP!

K-ZAAAAMMM

YOU HEARD THE GUY IN THE TIN CAN, WARRIORS! GET UP THERE AND TAKE HIM DOWN!

YO, DAISY, DO WE GET TO KEEP THESE NEW POWERS WHEN WE'RE DONE?

LET'S JUST WORRY ABOUT THE MOMENT, SHALL WE?

WHAT'S GOING ON, MAN?

HOOD?!

I CAN'T BELIEVE LOKI DID THIS. HE TOOK OUR POWER AWAY AND GAVE IT TO THEM!

I CAN'T BELIEVE YOU CAN'T BELIEVE IT.

LISTEN TO ME, PARKER, IT'S TIME WE GO. WE GO NOW.

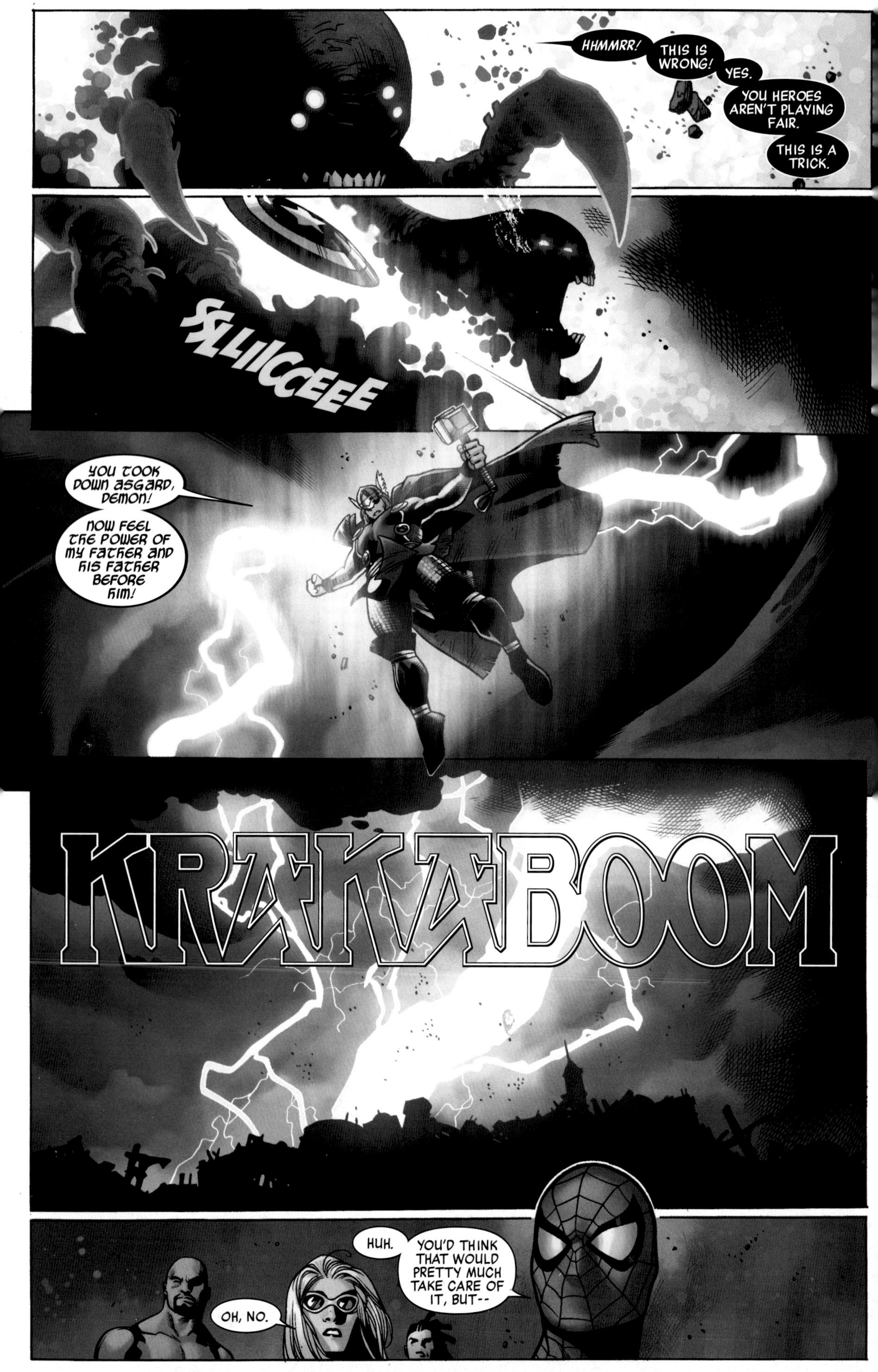
HHMMRR!
THIS IS WRONG!
YES.
YOU HEROES AREN'T PLAYING FAIR.
THIS IS A TRICK.
SSLLIICCEEE
YOU TOOK DOWN ASGARD, DEMON!
NOW FEEL THE POWER OF MY FATHER AND HIS FATHER BEFORE HIM!
KRAKABOOM
HUH.
YOU'D THINK THAT WOULD PRETTY MUCH TAKE CARE OF IT, BUT--
OH, NO.

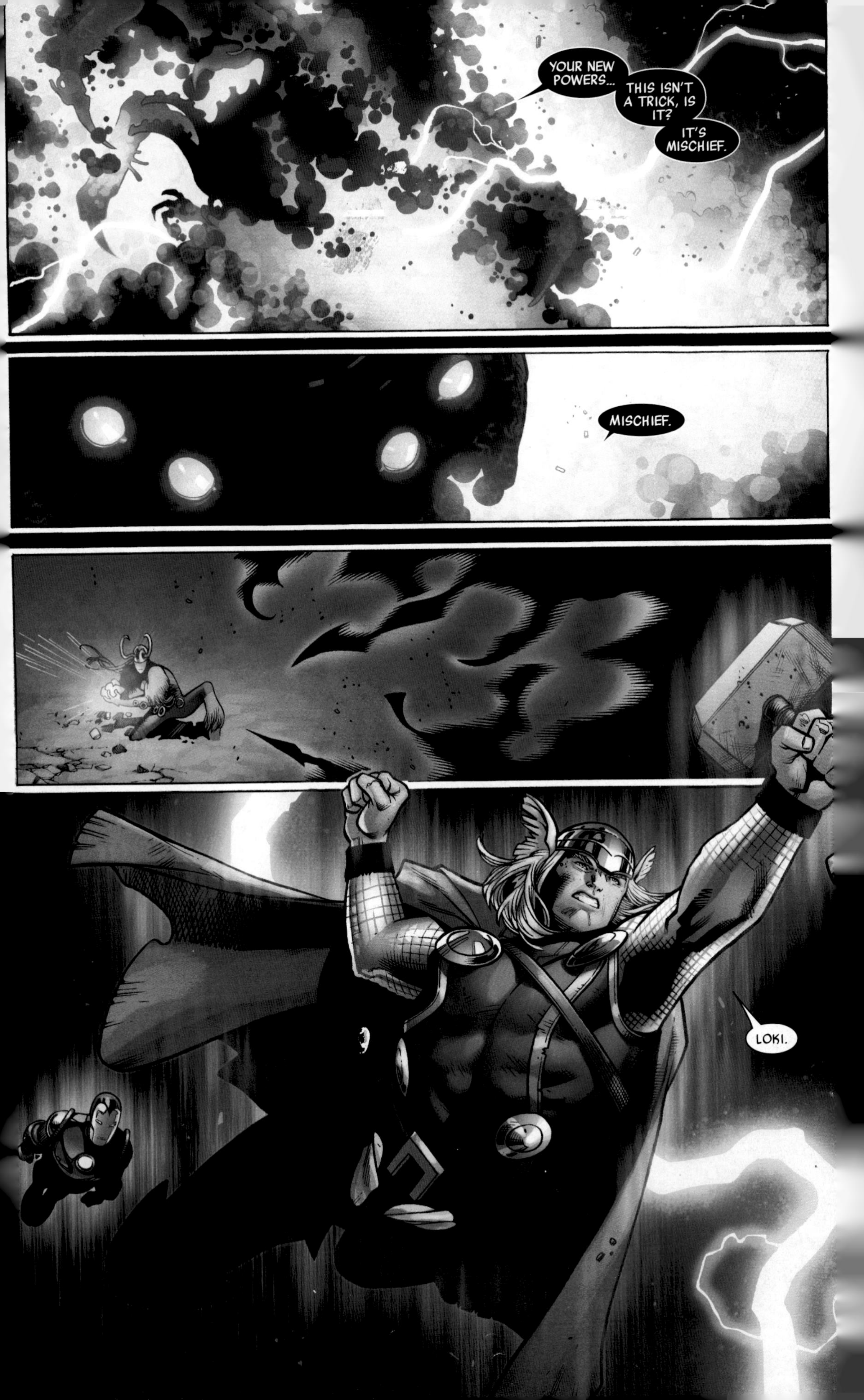
YOUR NEW POWERS...
THIS ISN'T A TRICK, IS IT?
IT'S MISCHIEF.
MISCHIEF.
LOKI.

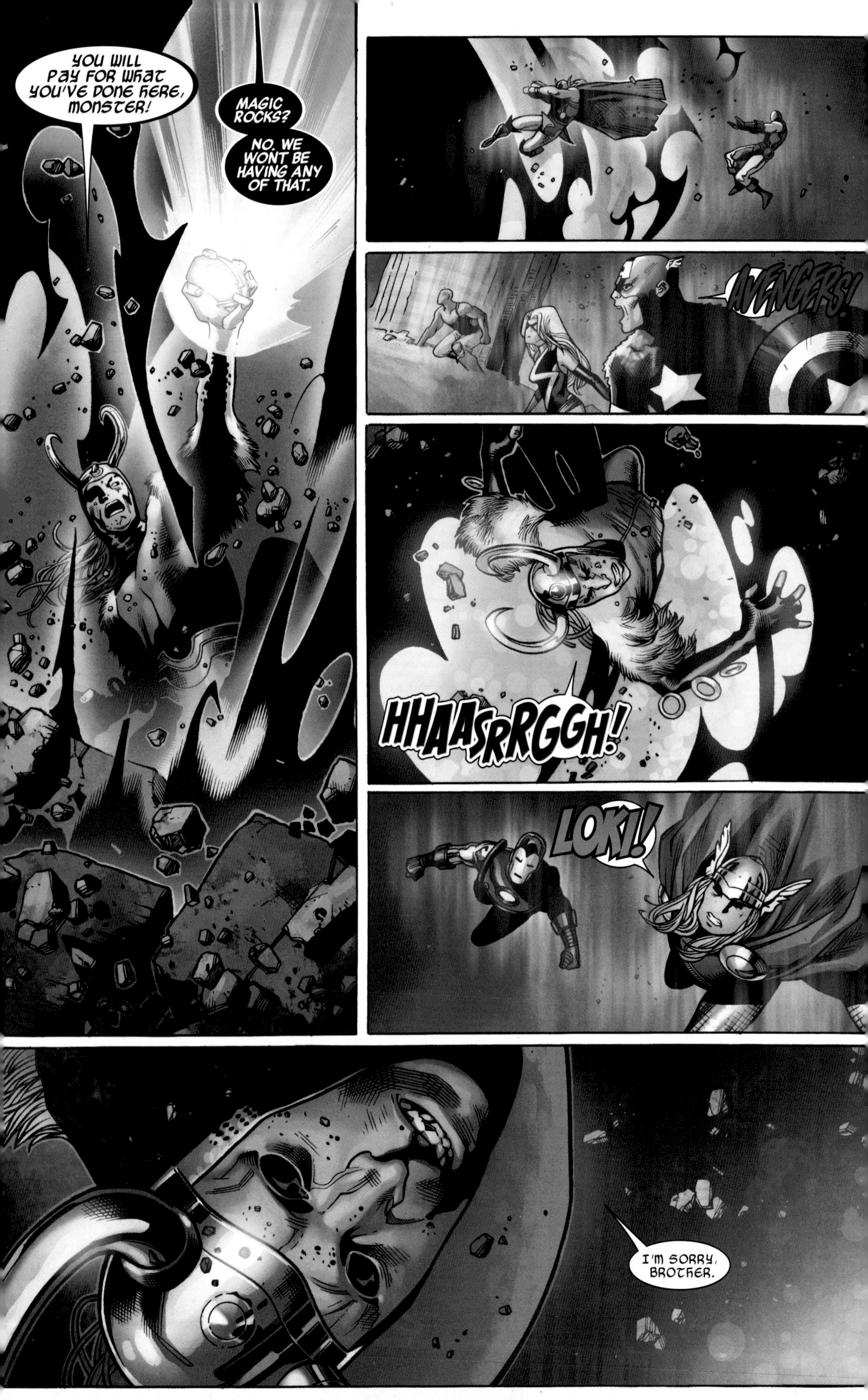
YOU WILL PAY FOR WHAT YOU'VE DONE HERE, MONSTER!
MAGIC ROCKS?
NO. WE WONT BE HAVING ANY OF THAT.
AVENGERS!
HHAASRRGGH!
LOKI!
I'M SORRY, BROTHER.

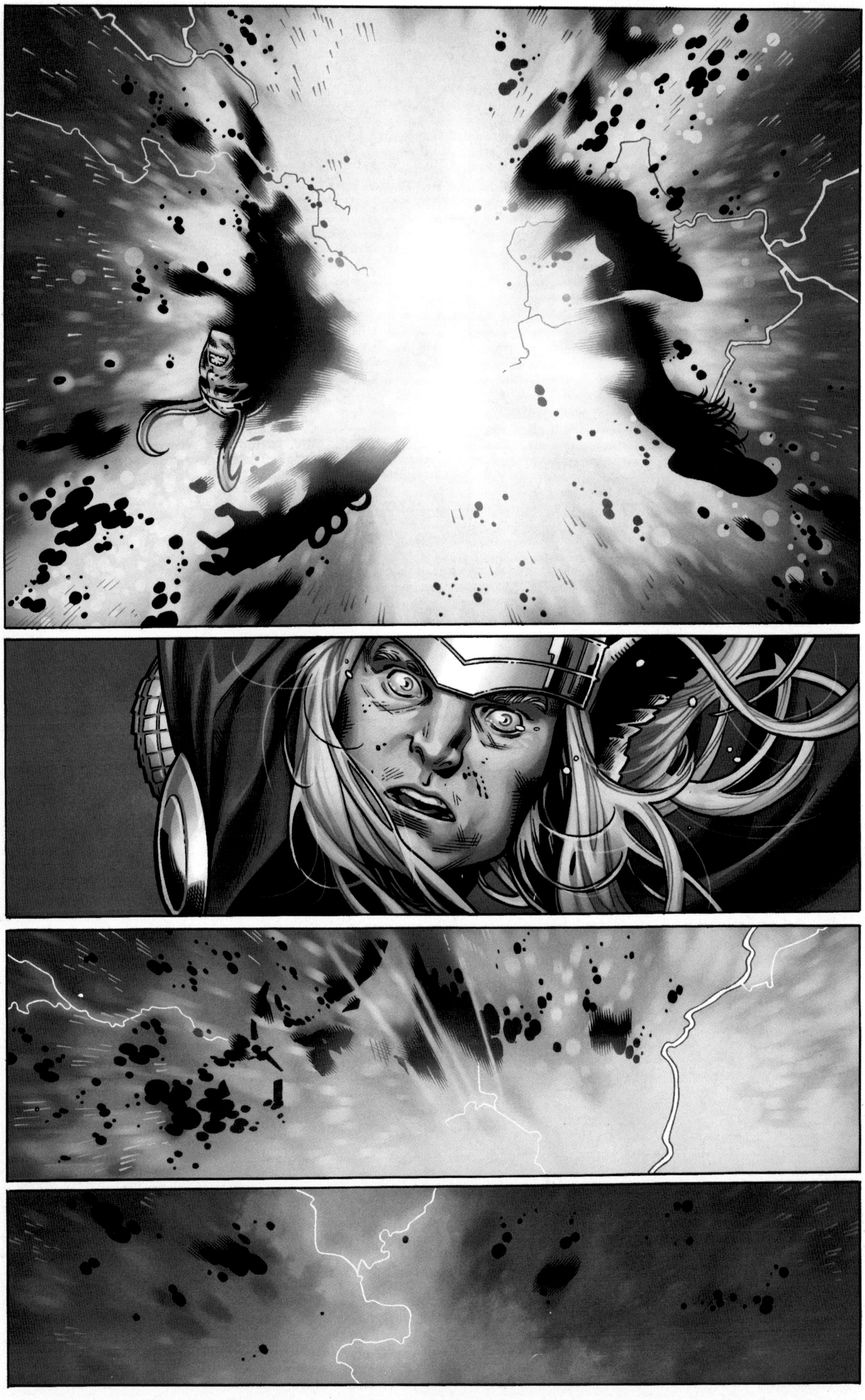

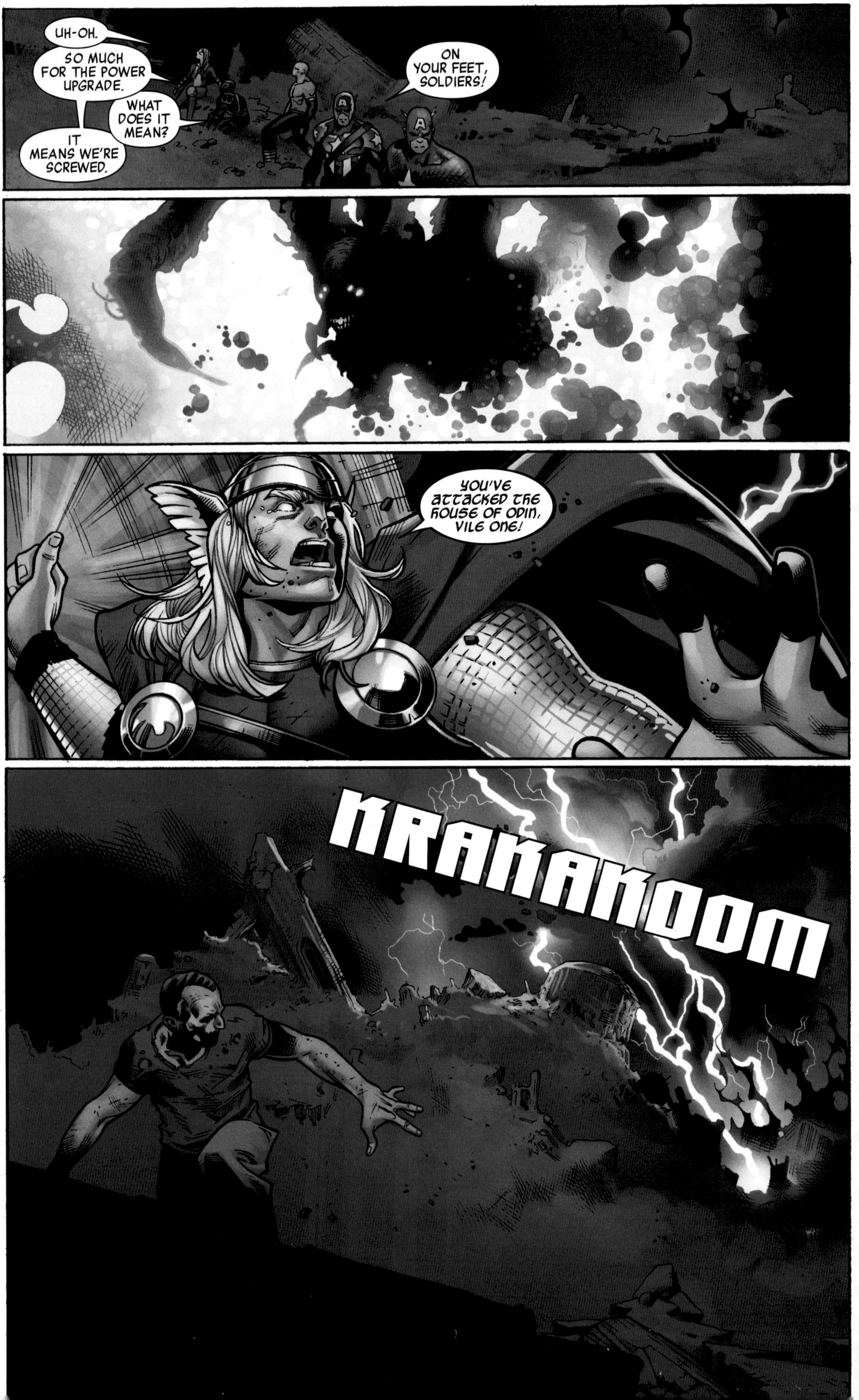
UH-OH.
SO MUCH FOR THE POWER UPGRADE.
WHAT DOES IT MEAN?
IT MEANS WE'RE SCREWED.
ON YOUR FEET, SOLDIERS!
YOU'VE ATTACKED THE HOUSE OF ODIN, VILE ONE!
KRAKAKOOM

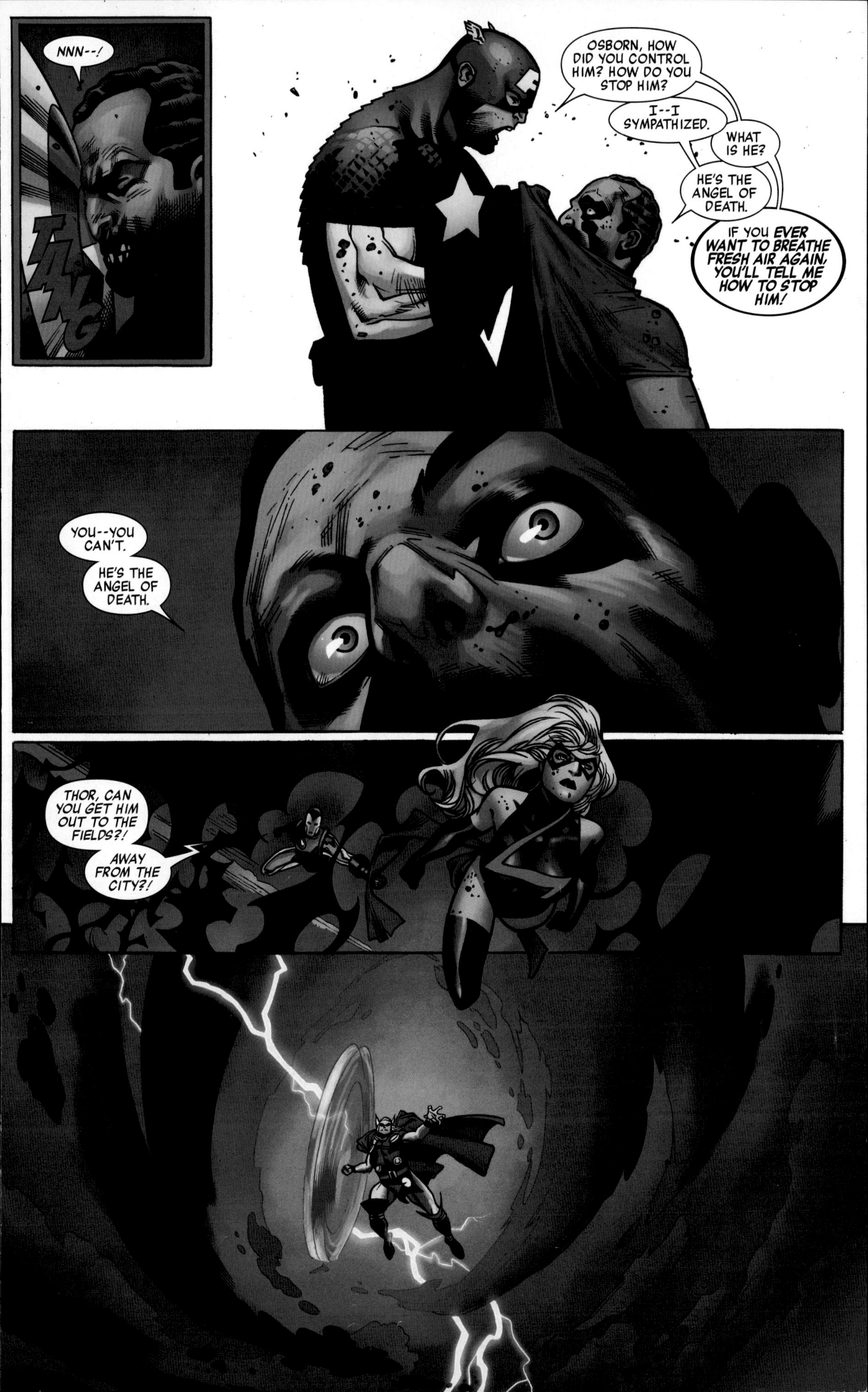
NNN--!
TANG
OSBORN, HOW DID YOU CONTROL HIM? HOW DO YOU STOP HIM?
I--I SYMPATHIZED.
WHAT IS HE?
HE'S THE ANGEL OF DEATH.
IF YOU EVER WANT TO BREATHE FRESH AIR AGAIN, YOU'LL TELL ME HOW TO STOP HIM!
YOU--YOU CAN'T.
HE'S THE ANGEL OF DEATH.
THOR, CAN YOU GET HIM OUT TO THE FIELDS?!
AWAY FROM THE CITY?!

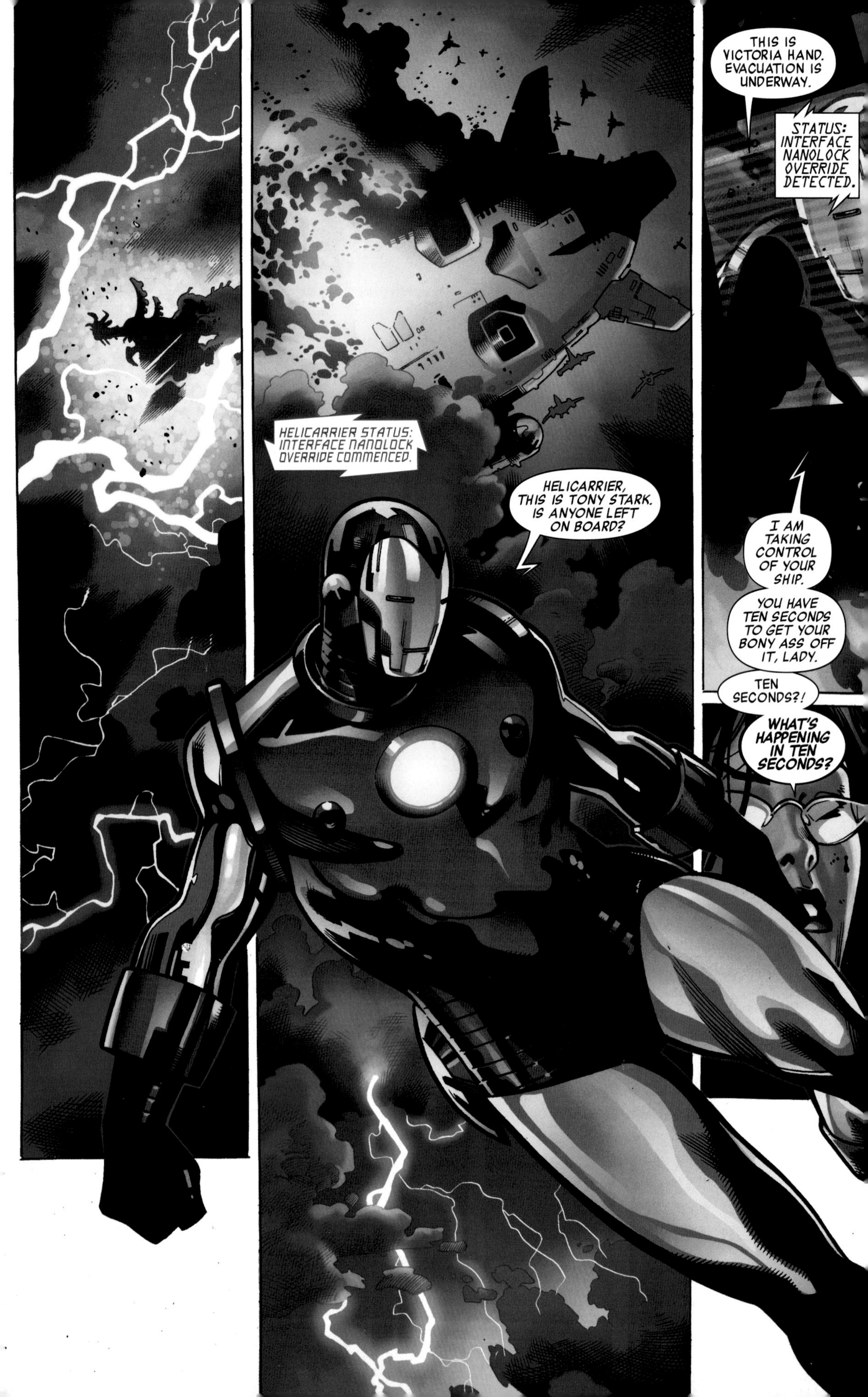
HELICARRIER STATUS: INTERFACE NANOLOCK OVERRIDE COMMENCED.
HELICARRIER, THIS IS TONY STARK. IS ANYONE LEFT ON BOARD?
THIS IS VICTORIA HAND. EVACUATION IS UNDERWAY.
STATUS: INTERFACE NANOLOCK OVERRIDE DETECTED.
I AM TAKING CONTROL OF YOUR SHIP.
YOU HAVE TEN SECONDS TO GET YOUR BONY ASS OFF IT, LADY.
TEN SECONDS?!
WHAT'S HAPPENING IN TEN SECONDS?

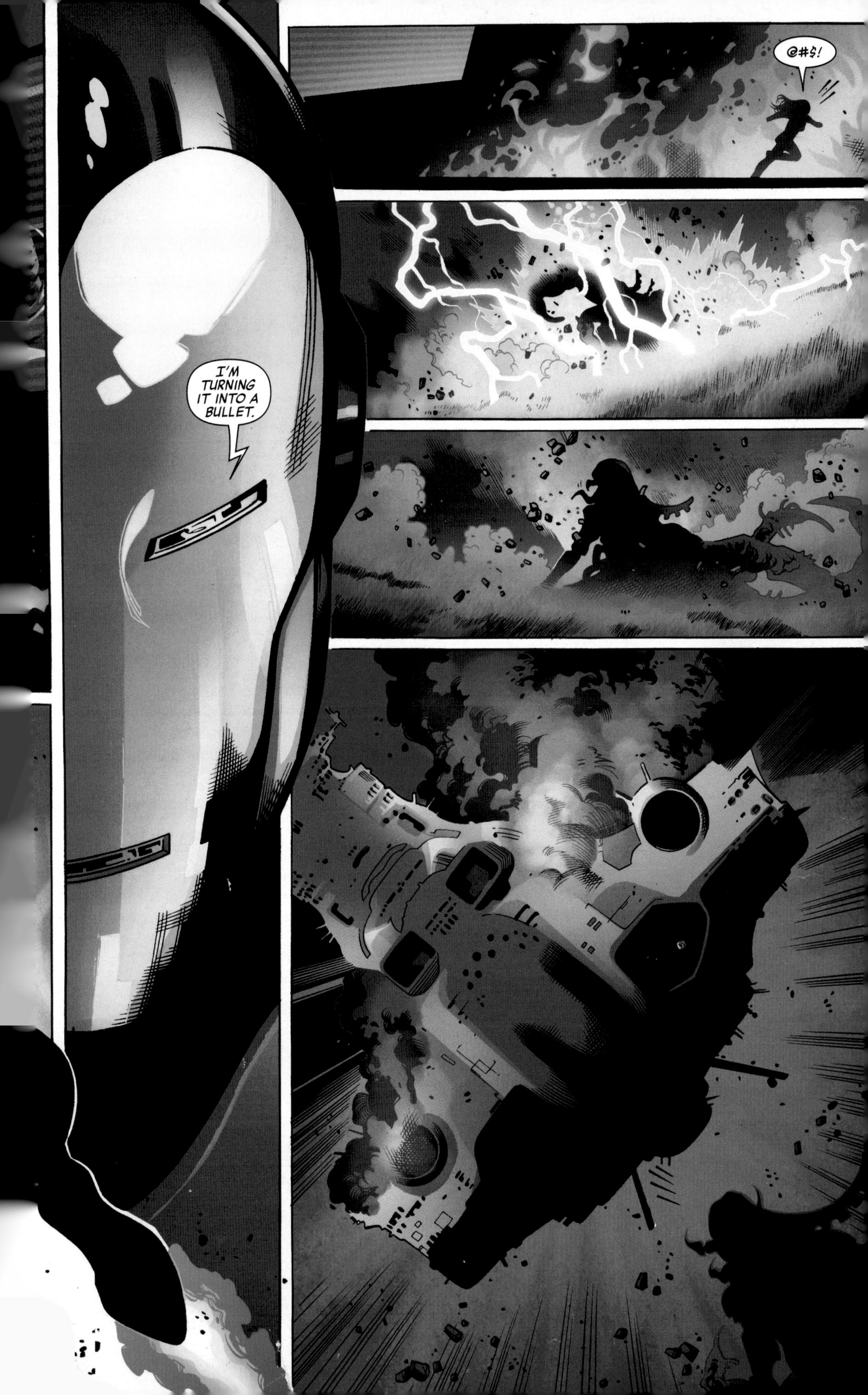
I'M TURNING IT INTO A BULLET.
@#$!

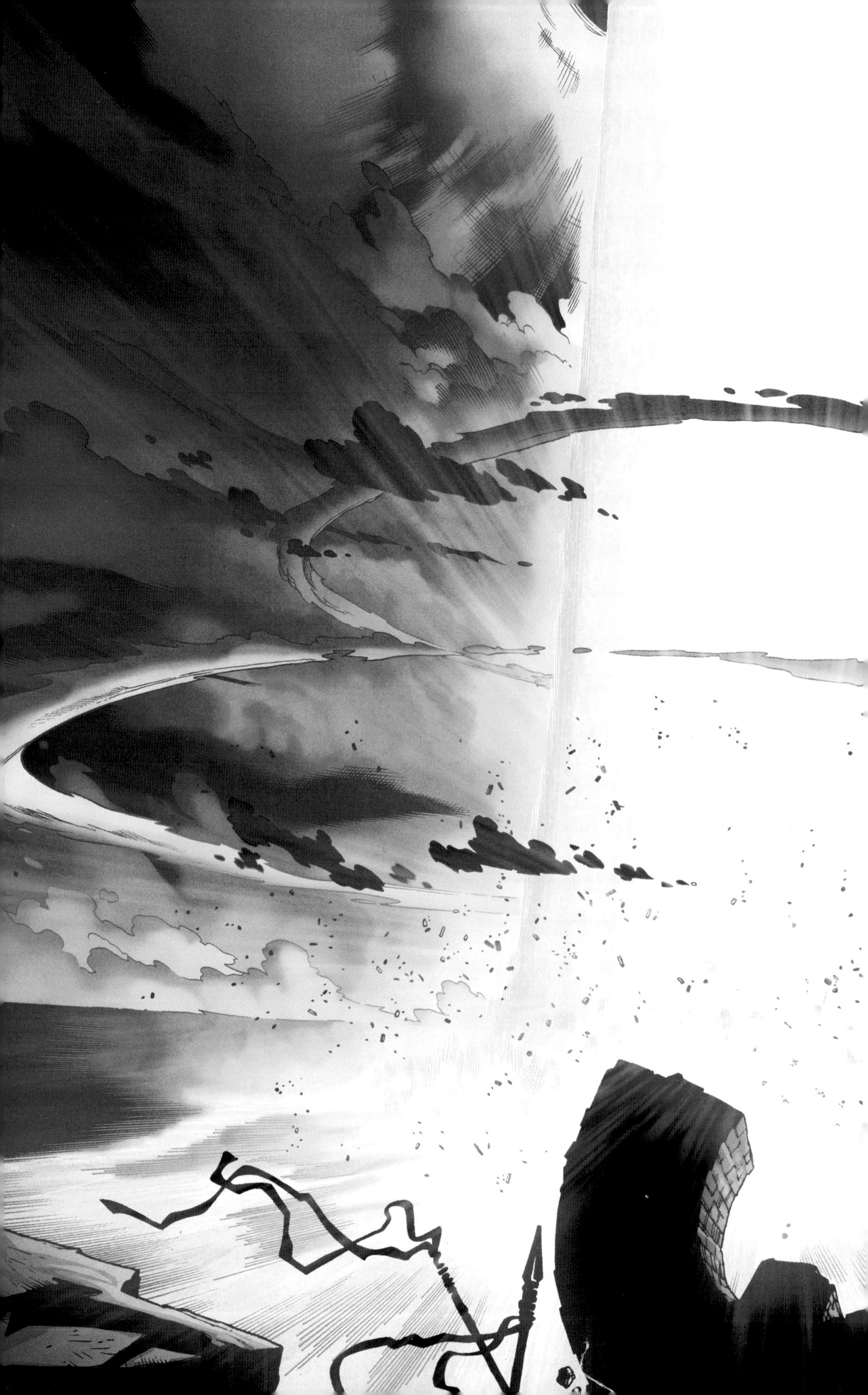

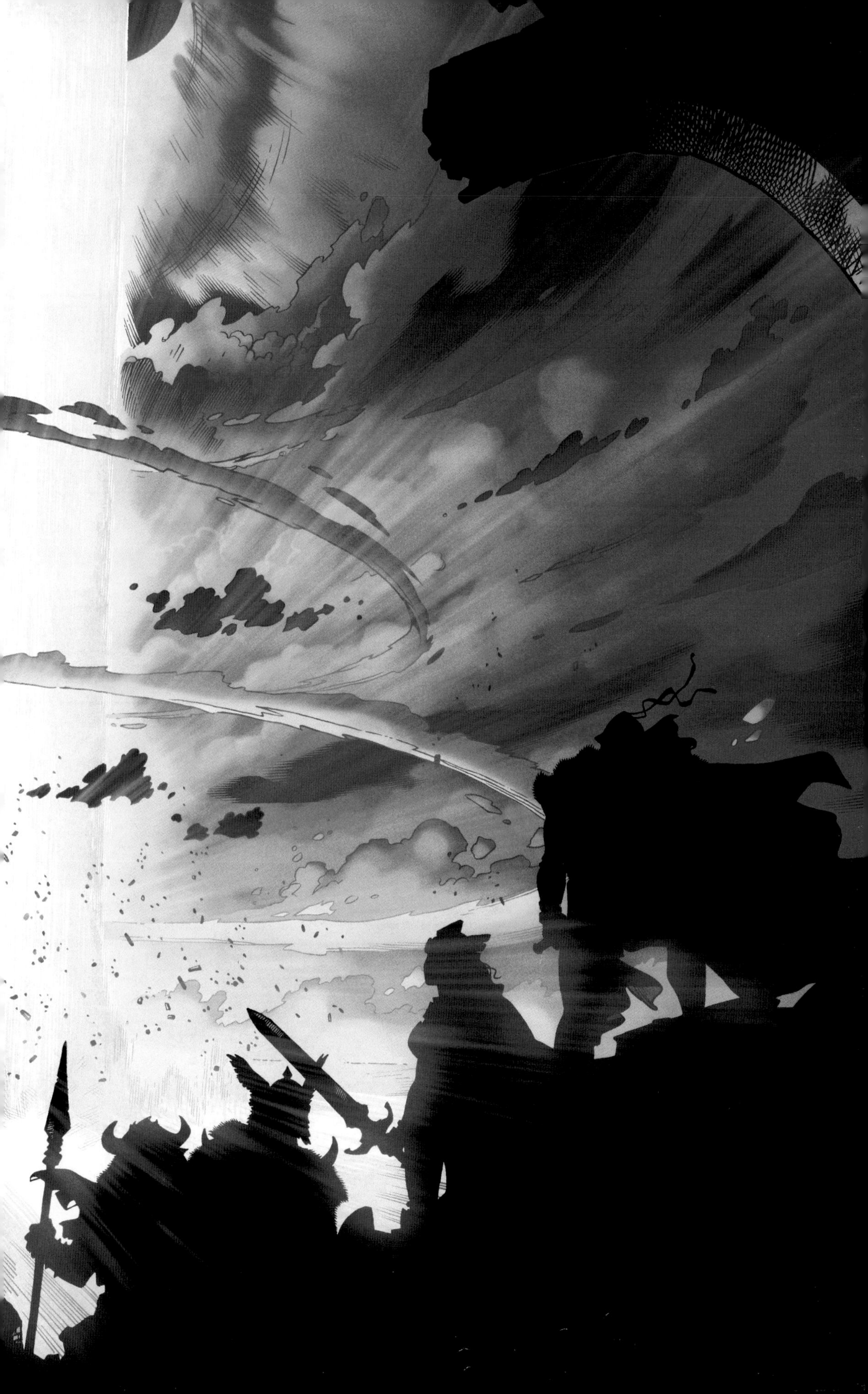

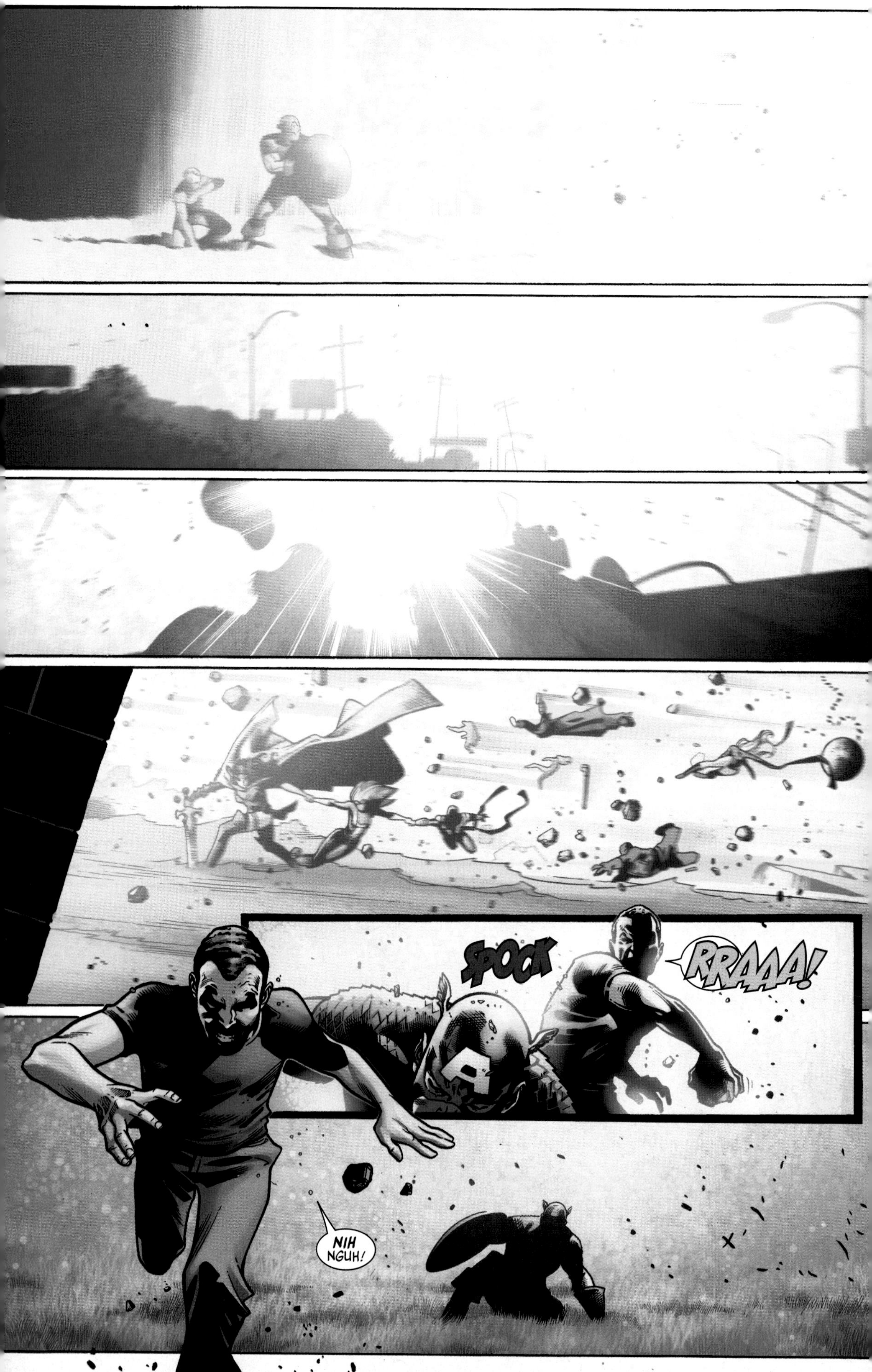
SPOCK
RRAAA!
NIH NGUH!

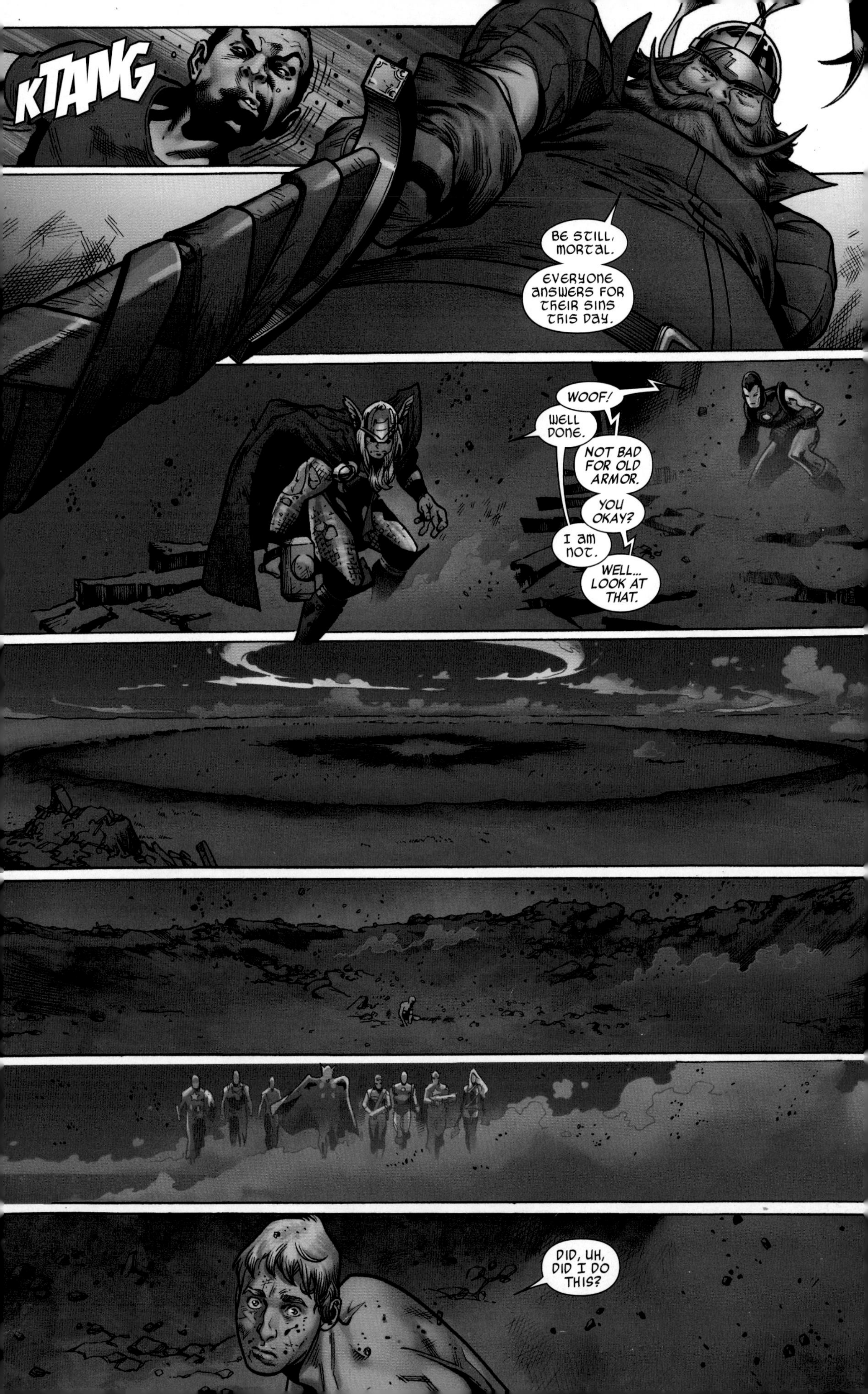
KTANG
BE STILL, MORTAL.
EVERYONE ANSWERS FOR THEIR SINS THIS DAY.
WOOF!
WELL DONE.
NOT BAD FOR OLD ARMOR.
YOU OKAY?
I AM NOT.
WELL... LOOK AT THAT.
DID, UH, DID I DO THIS?

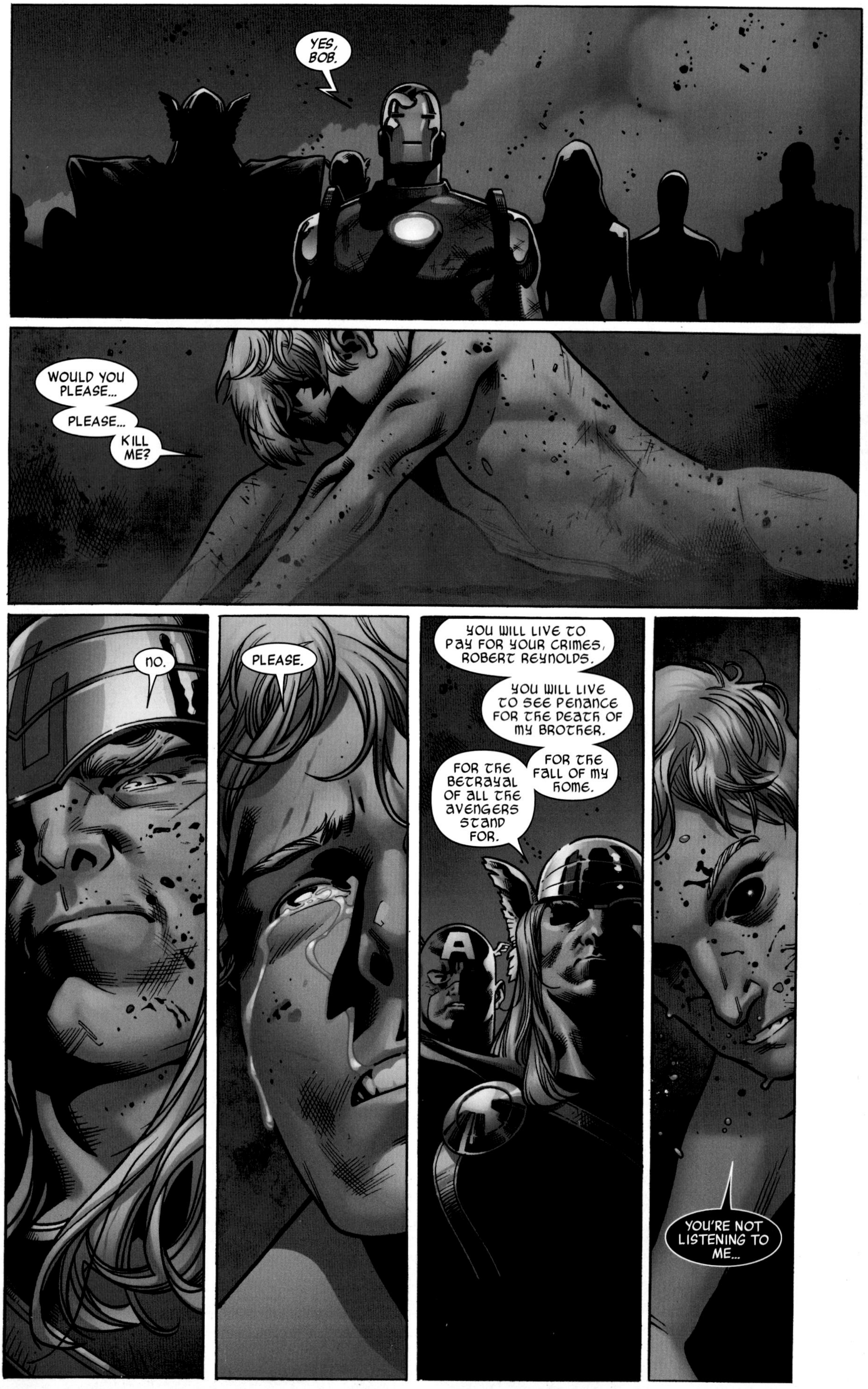
YES, BOB.
WOULD YOU PLEASE...
PLEASE...
KILL ME?
NO.
PLEASE.
YOU WILL LIVE TO PAY FOR YOUR CRIMES, ROBERT REYNOLDS.
YOU WILL LIVE TO SEE PENANCE FOR THE DEATH OF MY BROTHER.
FOR THE FALL OF MY HOME.
FOR THE BETRAYAL OF ALL THE AVENGERS STAND FOR.
YOU'RE NOT LISTENING TO ME...

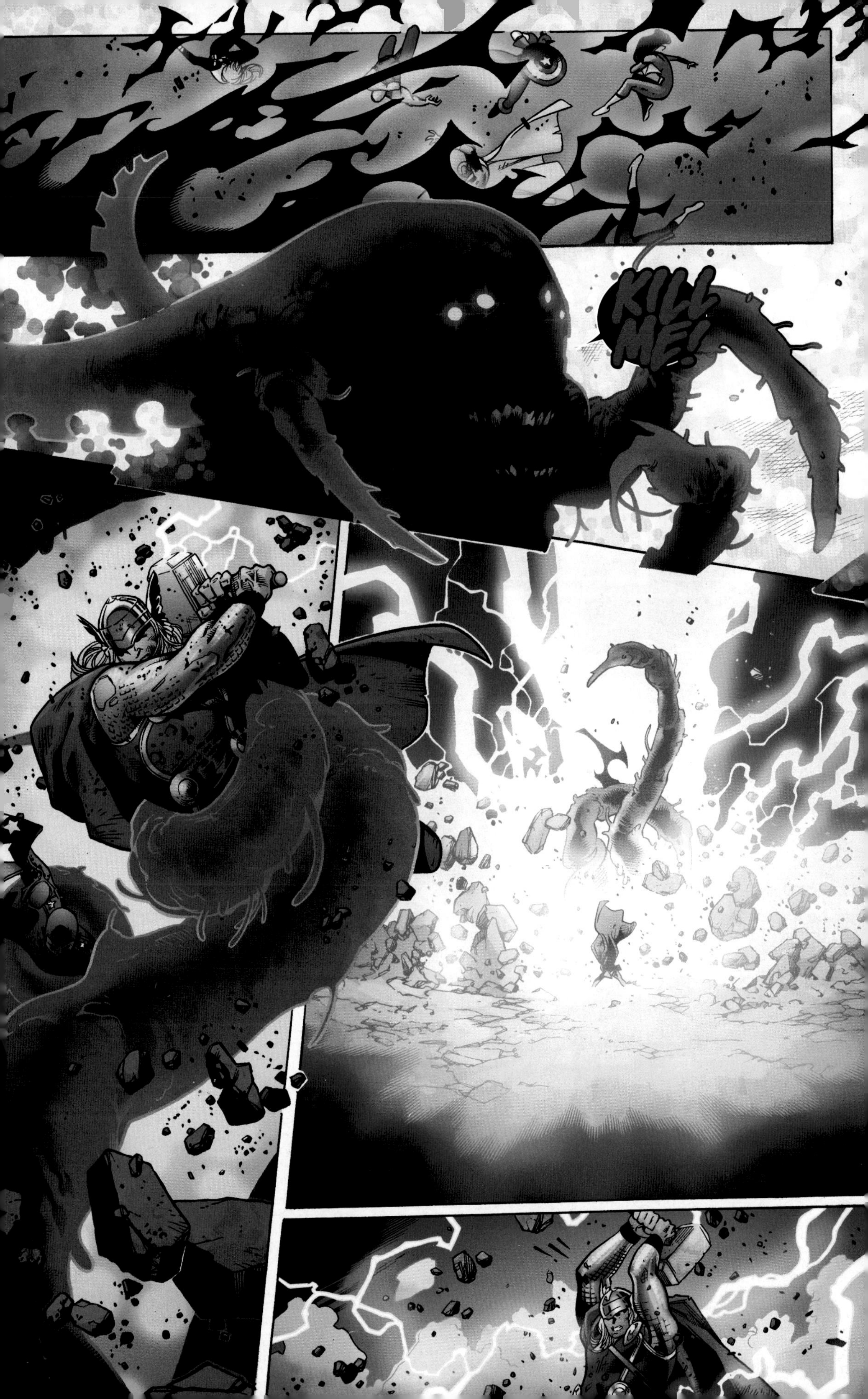
KILL ME!

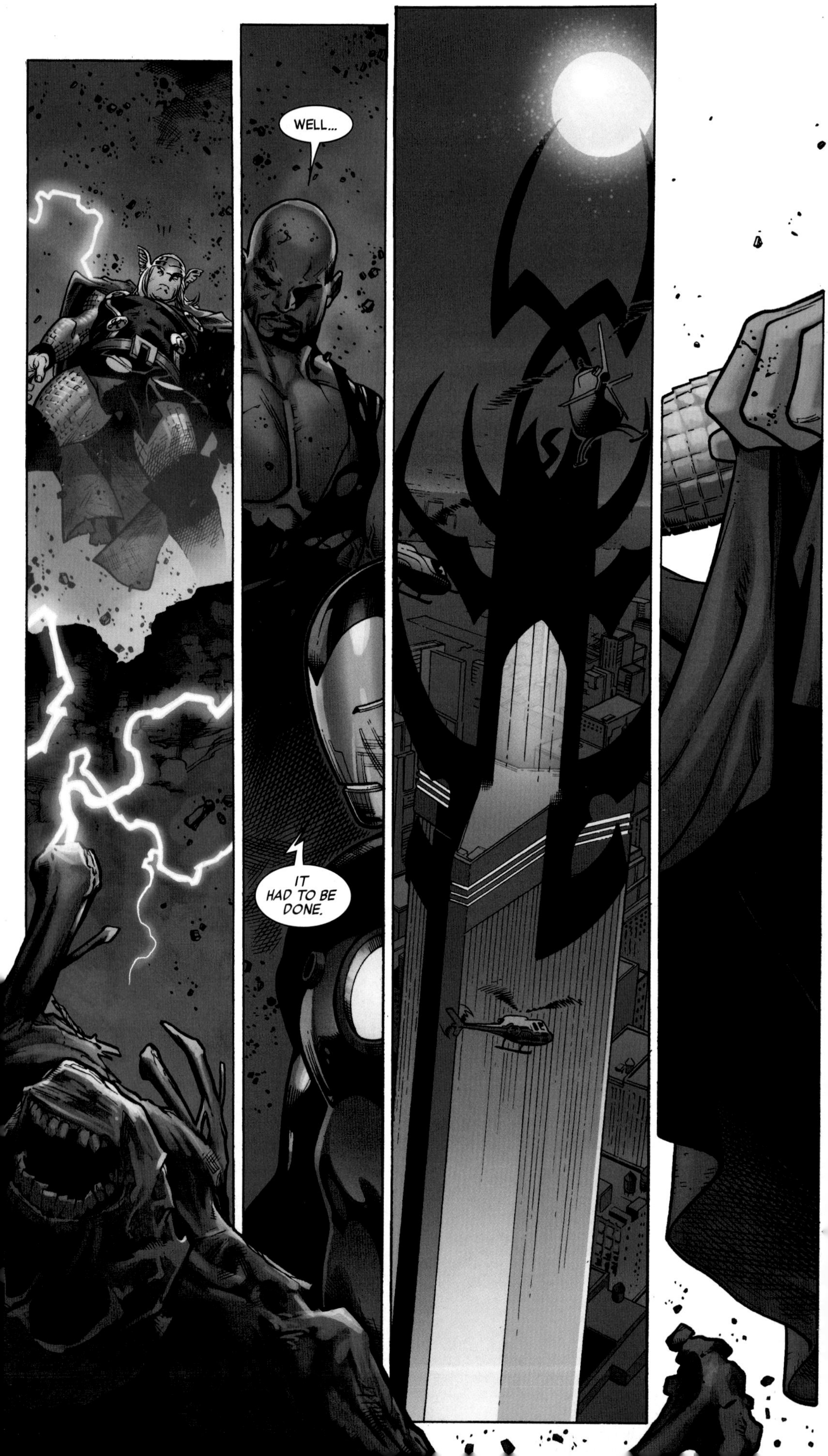
WELL...
IT HAD TO BE DONE.

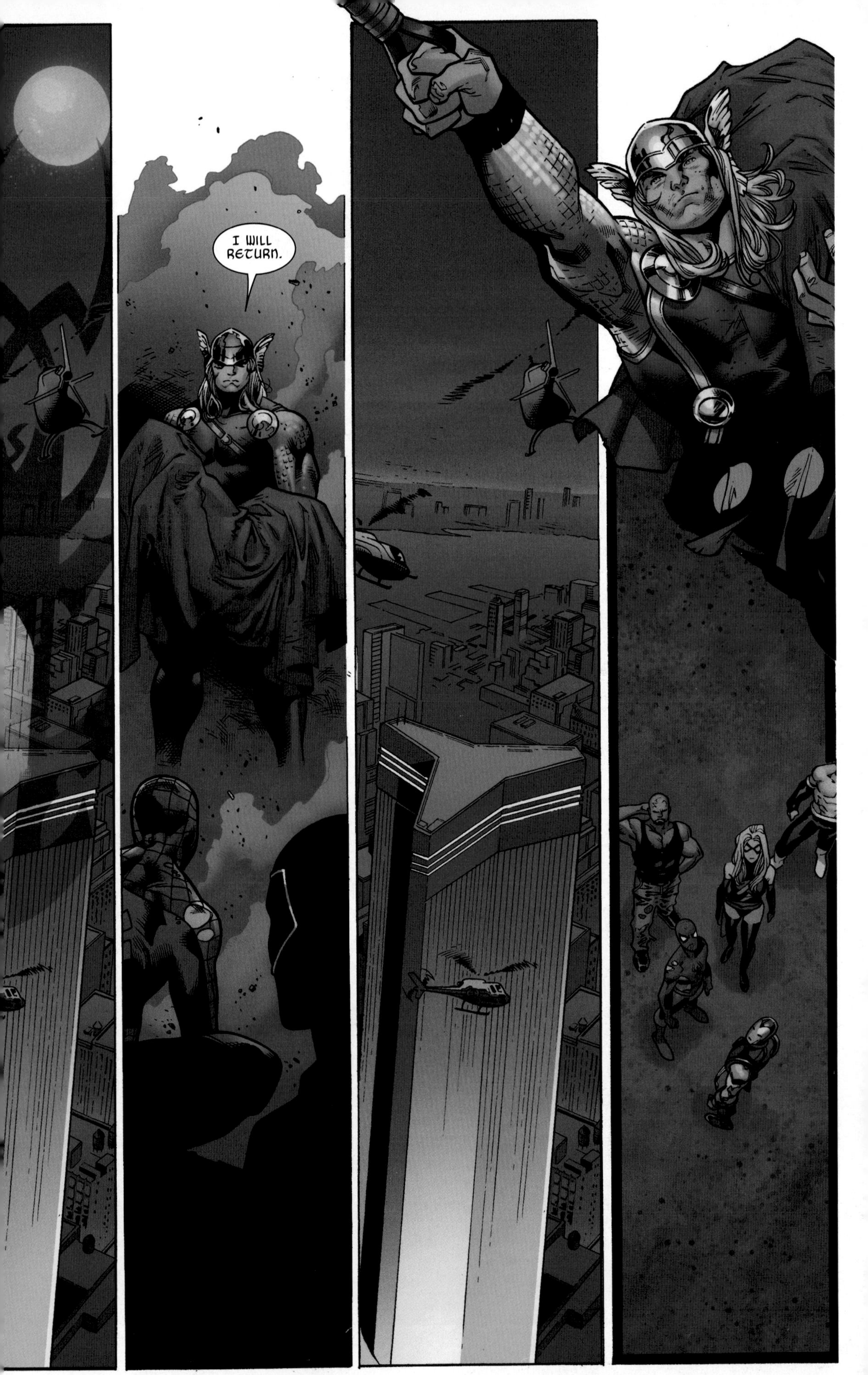
I WILL RETURN.

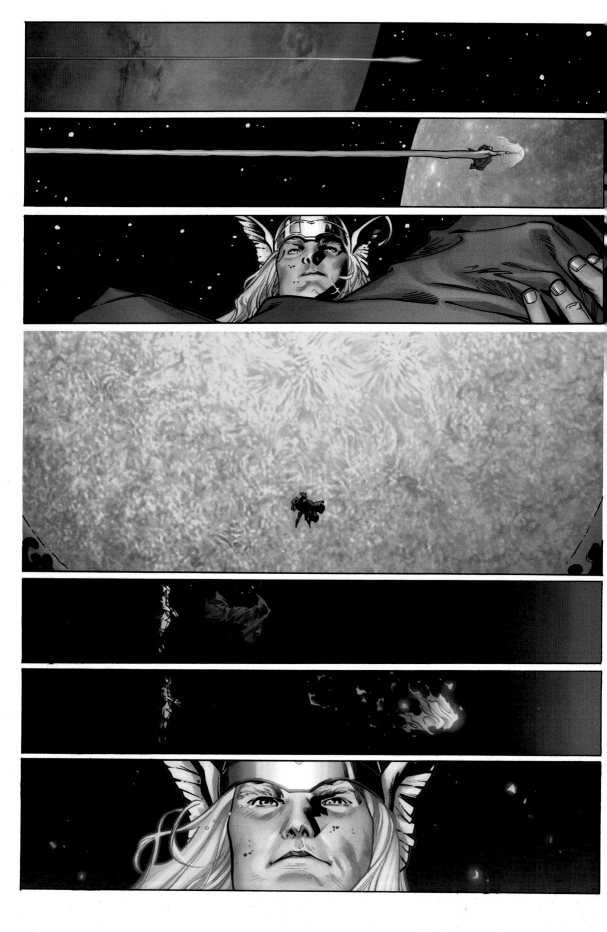

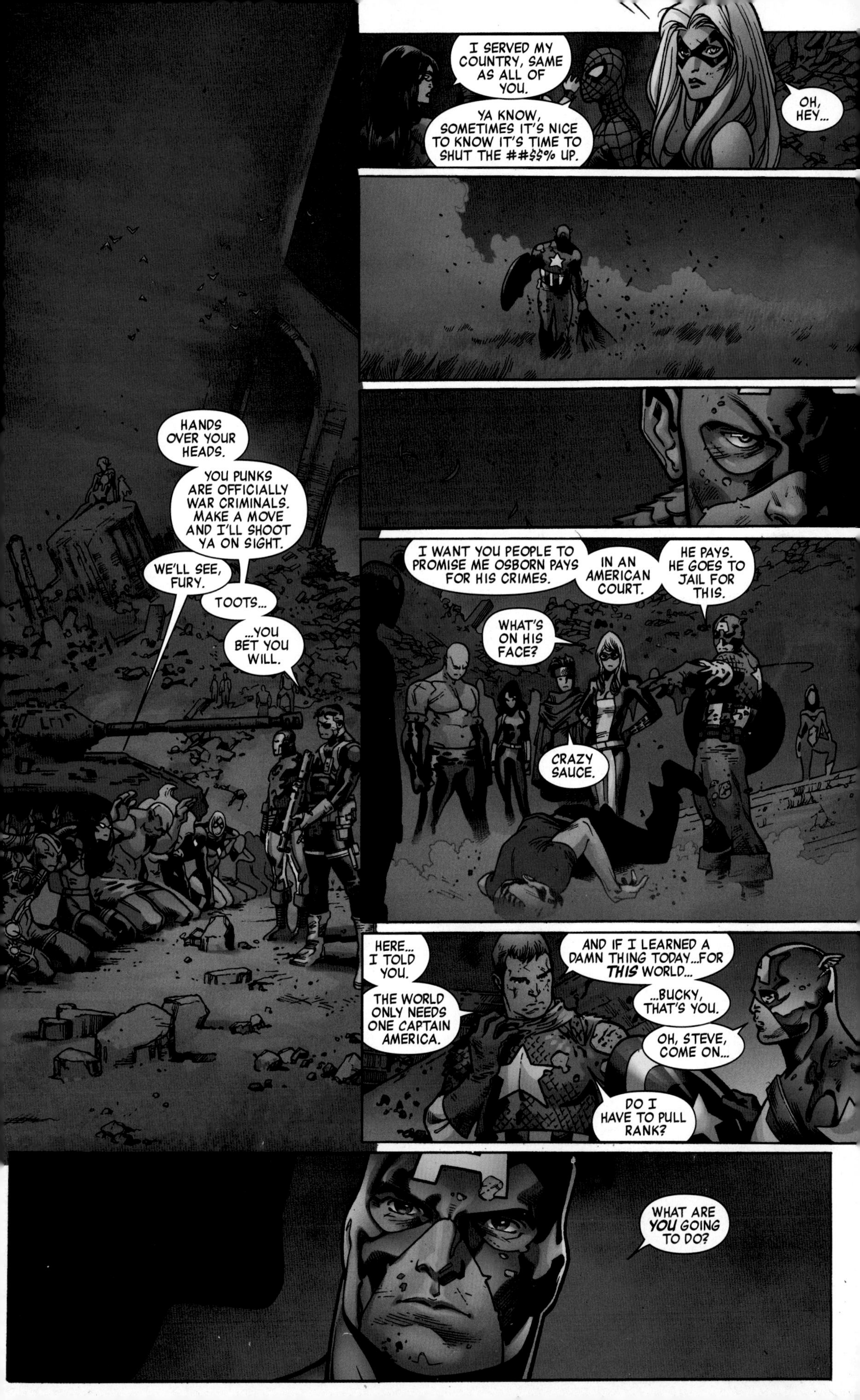
HANDS OVER YOUR HEADS.
YOU PUNKS ARE OFFICIALLY WAR CRIMINALS. MAKE A MOVE AND I'LL SHOOT YA ON SIGHT.
WE'LL SEE, FURY.
TOOTS...
...YOU BET YOU WILL.
I SERVED MY COUNTRY, SAME AS ALL OF YOU.
YA KNOW, SOMETIMES IT'S NICE TO KNOW IT'S TIME TO SHUT THE #$$% UP.
OH, HEY...
I WANT YOU PEOPLE TO PROMISE ME OSBORN PAYS FOR HIS CRIMES.
IN AN AMERICAN COURT.
HE PAYS. HE GOES TO JAIL FOR THIS.
WHAT'S ON HIS FACE?
CRAZY SAUCE.
HERE... I TOLD YOU.
THE WORLD ONLY NEEDS ONE CAPTAIN AMERICA.
AND IF I LEARNED A DAMN THING TODAY...FOR THIS WORLD...
...BUCKY, THAT'S YOU.
OH, STEVE, COME ON...
DO I HAVE TO PULL RANK?
WHAT ARE YOU GOING TO DO?

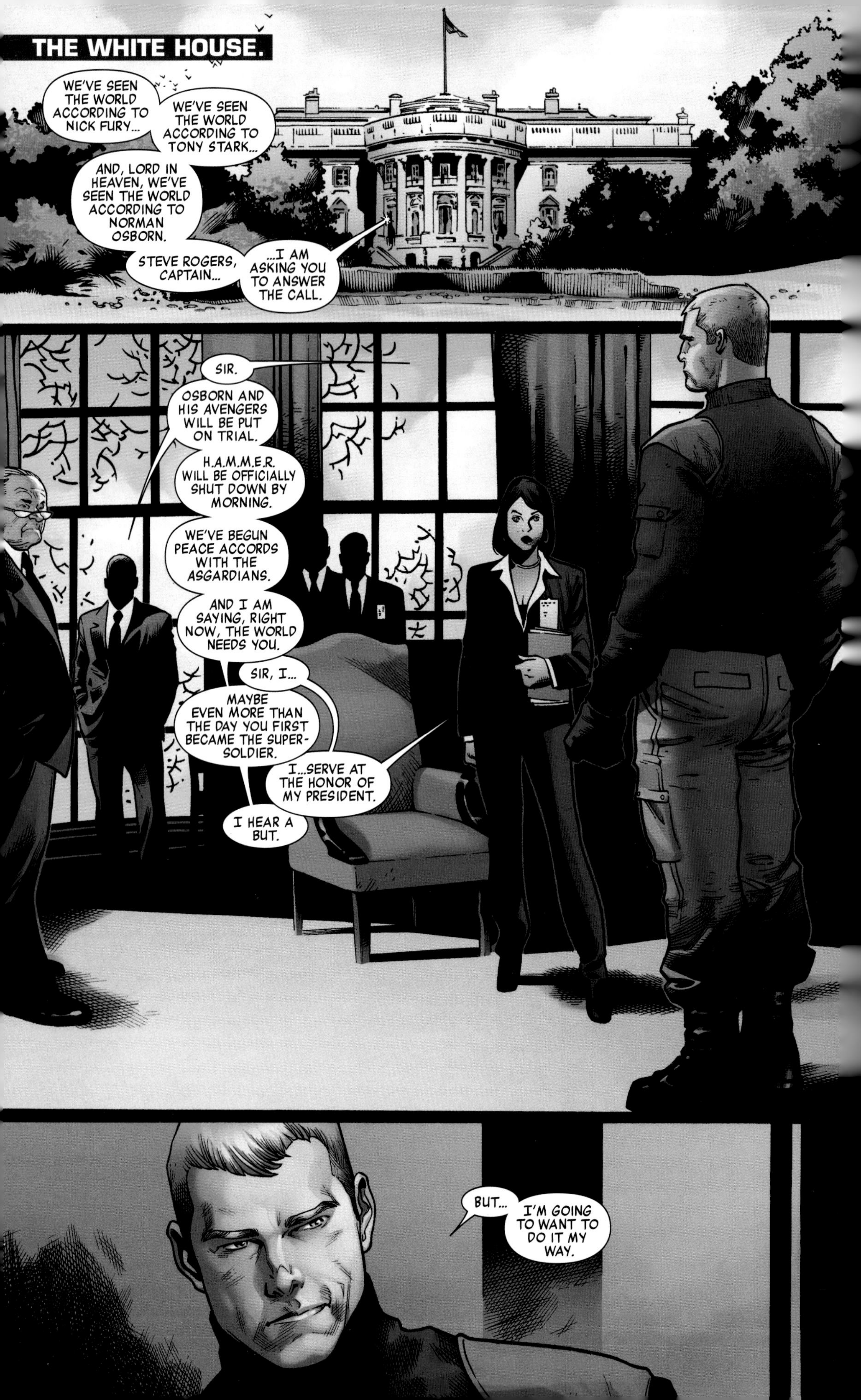
THE WHITE HOUSE.
WE'VE SEEN THE WORLD ACCORDING TO NICK FURY...
WE'VE SEEN THE WORLD ACCORDING TO TONY STARK...
AND, LORD IN HEAVEN, WE'VE SEEN THE WORLD ACCORDING TO NORMAN OSBORN.
STEVE ROGERS, CAPTAIN...
...I AM ASKING YOU TO ANSWER THE CALL.
SIR.
OSBORN AND HIS AVENGERS WILL BE PUT ON TRIAL.
H.A.M.M.E.R. WILL BE OFFICIALLY SHUT DOWN BY MORNING.
WE'VE BEGUN PEACE ACCORDS WITH THE ASGARDIANS.
AND I AM SAYING, RIGHT NOW, THE WORLD NEEDS YOU.
SIR, I...
MAYBE EVEN MORE THAN THE DAY YOU FIRST BECAME THE SUPER-SOLDIER.
I...SERVE AT THE HONOR OF MY PRESIDENT.
I HEAR A BUT.
BUT...
I'M GOING TO WANT TO DO IT MY WAY.

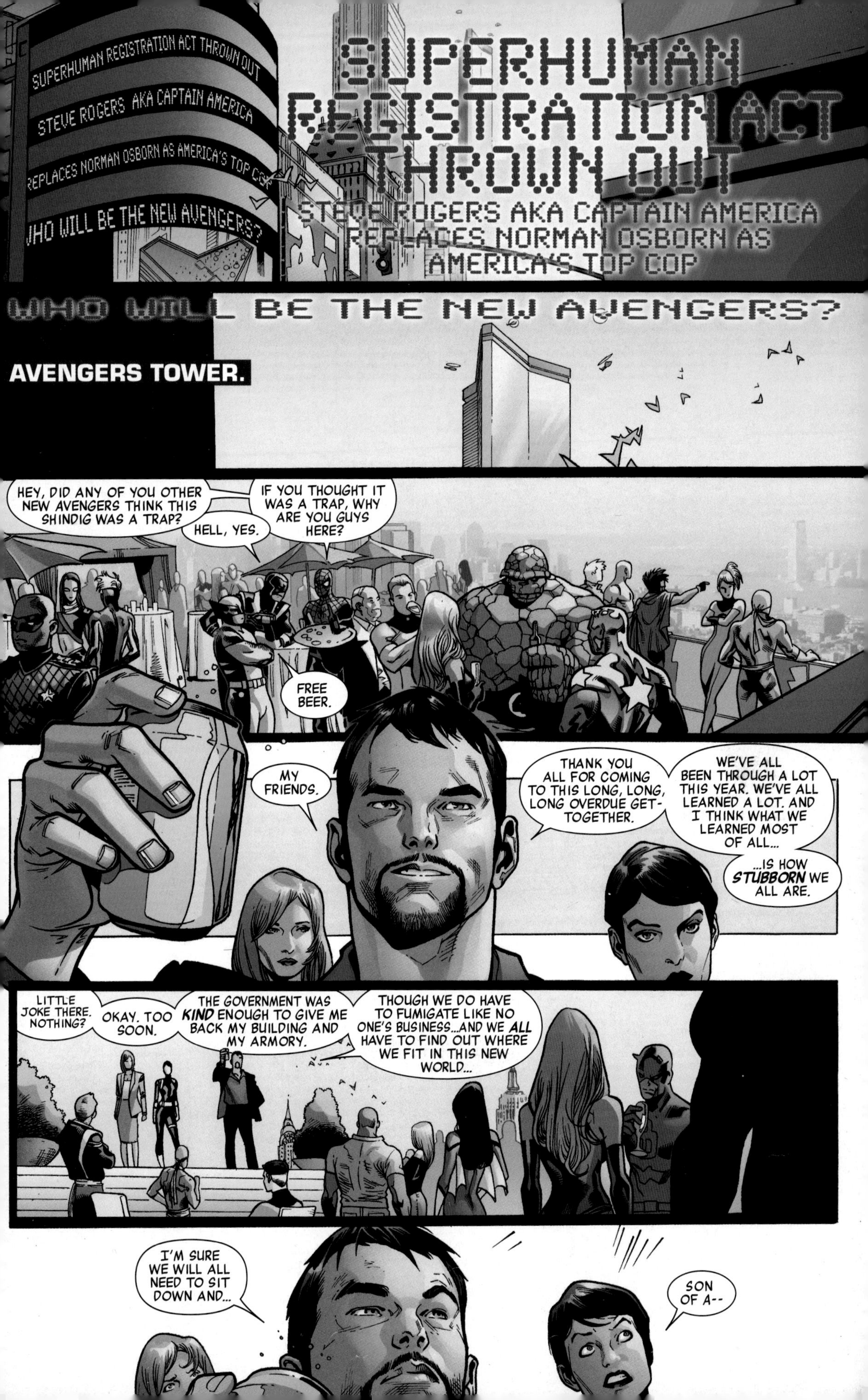
SUPERHUMAN REGISTRATION ACT THROWN OUT
STEVE ROGERS AKA CAPTAIN AMERICA
REPLACES NORMAN OSBORN AS AMERICA'S TOP COP
WHO WILL BE THE NEW AVENGERS?
SUPERHUMAN REGISTRATION ACT THROWN OUT
STEVE ROGERS AKA CAPTAIN AMERICA REPLACES NORMAN OSBORN AS AMERICA'S TOP COP
WHO WILL BE THE NEW AVENGERS?
AVENGERS TOWER.
HEY, DID ANY OF YOU OTHER NEW AVENGERS THINK THIS SHINDIG WAS A TRAP?
HELL, YES.
IF YOU THOUGHT IT WAS A TRAP, WHY ARE YOU GUYS HERE?
FREE BEER.
MY FRIENDS.
THANK YOU ALL FOR COMING TO THIS LONG, LONG, LONG OVERDUE GET-TOGETHER.
WE'VE ALL BEEN THROUGH A LOT THIS YEAR. WE'VE ALL LEARNED A LOT. AND I THINK WHAT WE LEARNED MOST OF ALL...
...IS HOW STÜBBORN WE ALL ARE.
LITTLE JOKE THERE. NOTHING?
OKAY. TOO SOON.
THE GOVERNMENT WAS KIND ENOUGH TO GIVE ME BACK MY BUILDING AND MY ARMORY.
THOUGH WE DO HAVE TO FUMIGATE LIKE NO ONE'S BUSINESS...AND WE ALL HAVE TO FIND OUT WHERE WE FIT IN THIS NEW WORLD...
I'M SURE WE WILL ALL NEED TO SIT DOWN AND...
SON OF A--

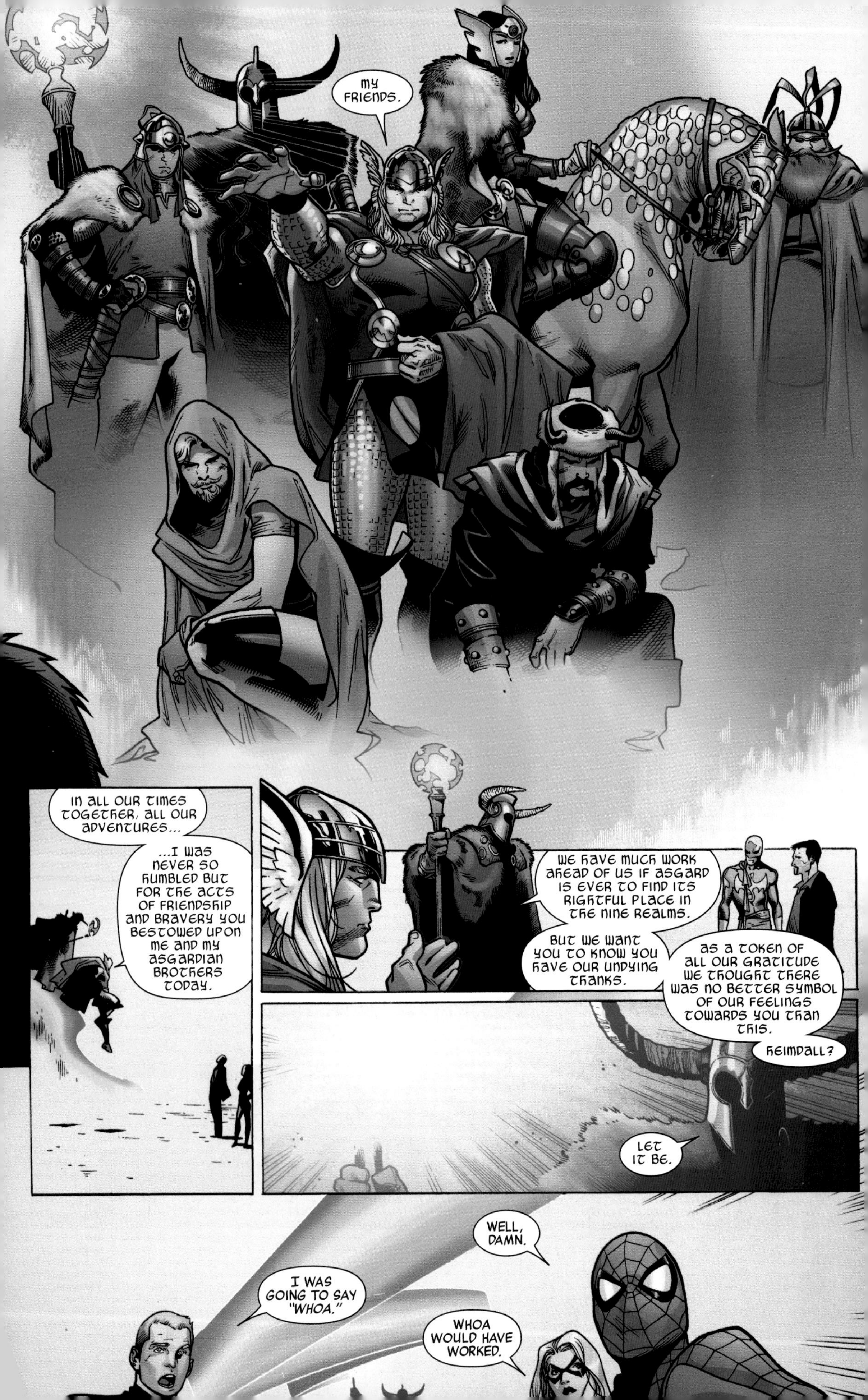
MY FRIENDS.
IN ALL OUR TIMES TOGETHER, ALL OUR ADVENTURES...
...I WAS NEVER SO HUMBLED BUT FOR THE ACTS OF FRIENDSHIP AND BRAVERY YOU BESTOWED UPON ME AND MY ASGARDIAN BROTHERS TODAY.
WE HAVE MUCH WORK AHEAD OF US IF ASGARD IS EVER TO FIND ITS RIGHTFUL PLACE IN THE NINE REALMS.
BUT WE WANT YOU TO KNOW YOU HAVE OUR UNDYING THANKS.
AS A TOKEN OF ALL OUR GRATITUDE WE THOUGHT THERE WAS NO BETTER SYMBOL OF OUR FEELINGS TOWARDS YOU THAN THIS.
HEIMDALL?
LET IT BE.
WELL, DAMN.
I WAS GOING TO SAY "WHOA."
WHOA WOULD HAVE WORKED.

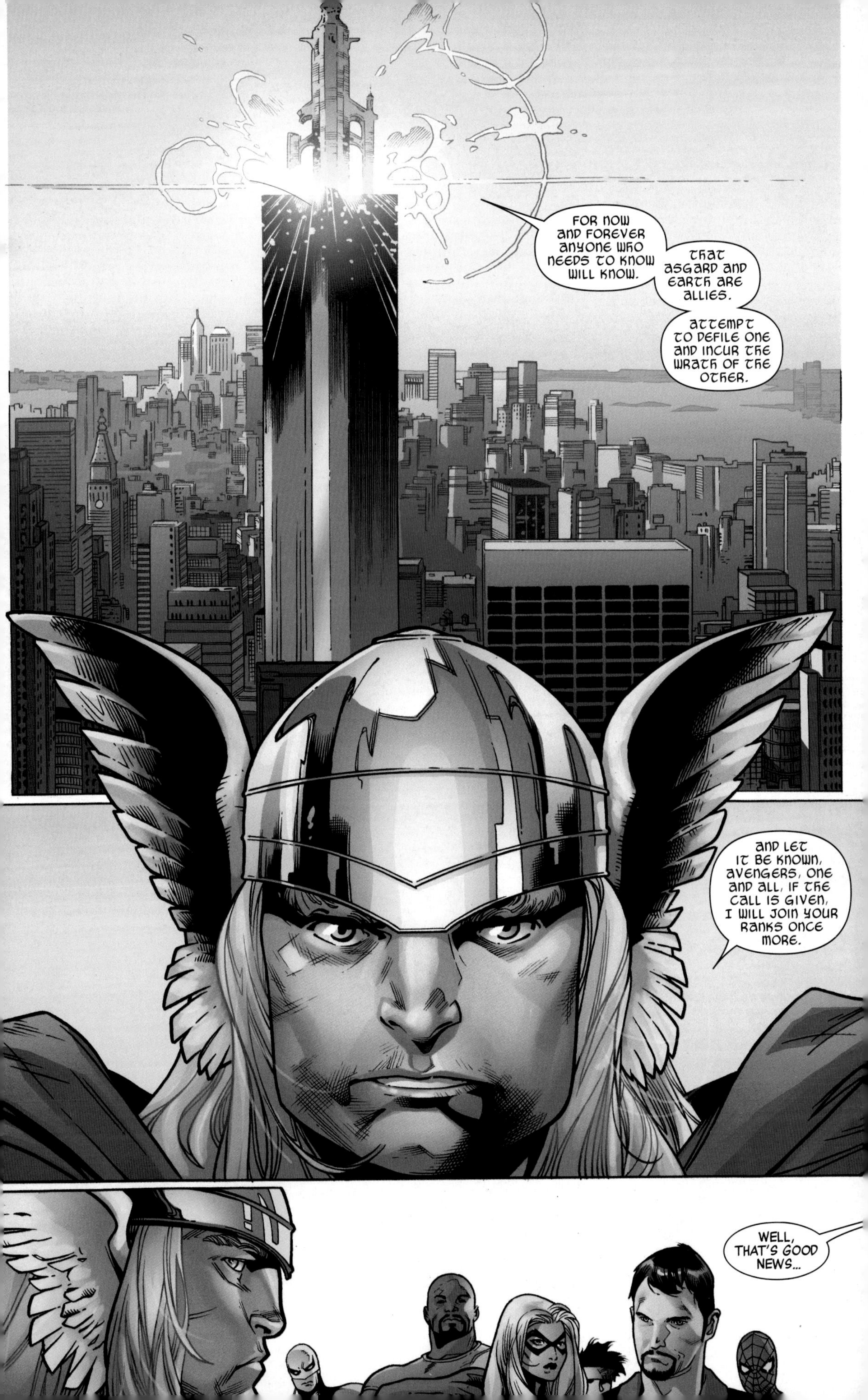
FOR NOW AND FOREVER ANYONE WHO NEEDS TO KNOW WILL KNOW.
THAT ASGARD AND EARTH ARE ALLIES.
ATTEMPT TO DEFILE ONE AND INCUR THE WRATH OF THE OTHER.
AND LET IT BE KNOWN, AVENGERS, ONE AND ALL, IF THE CALL IS GIVEN, I WILL JOIN YOUR RANKS ONCE MORE.
WELL, THAT'S GOOD NEWS...

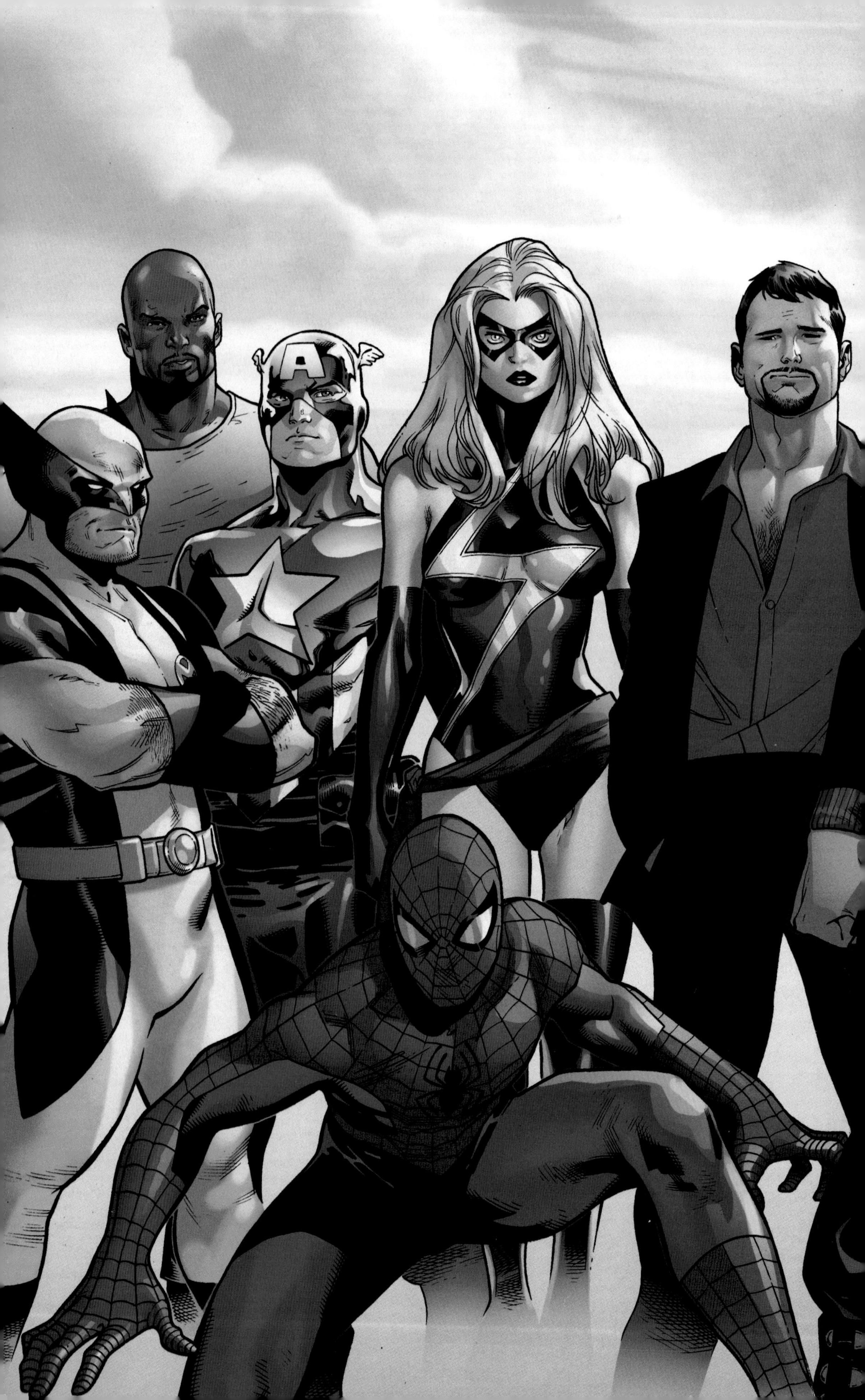

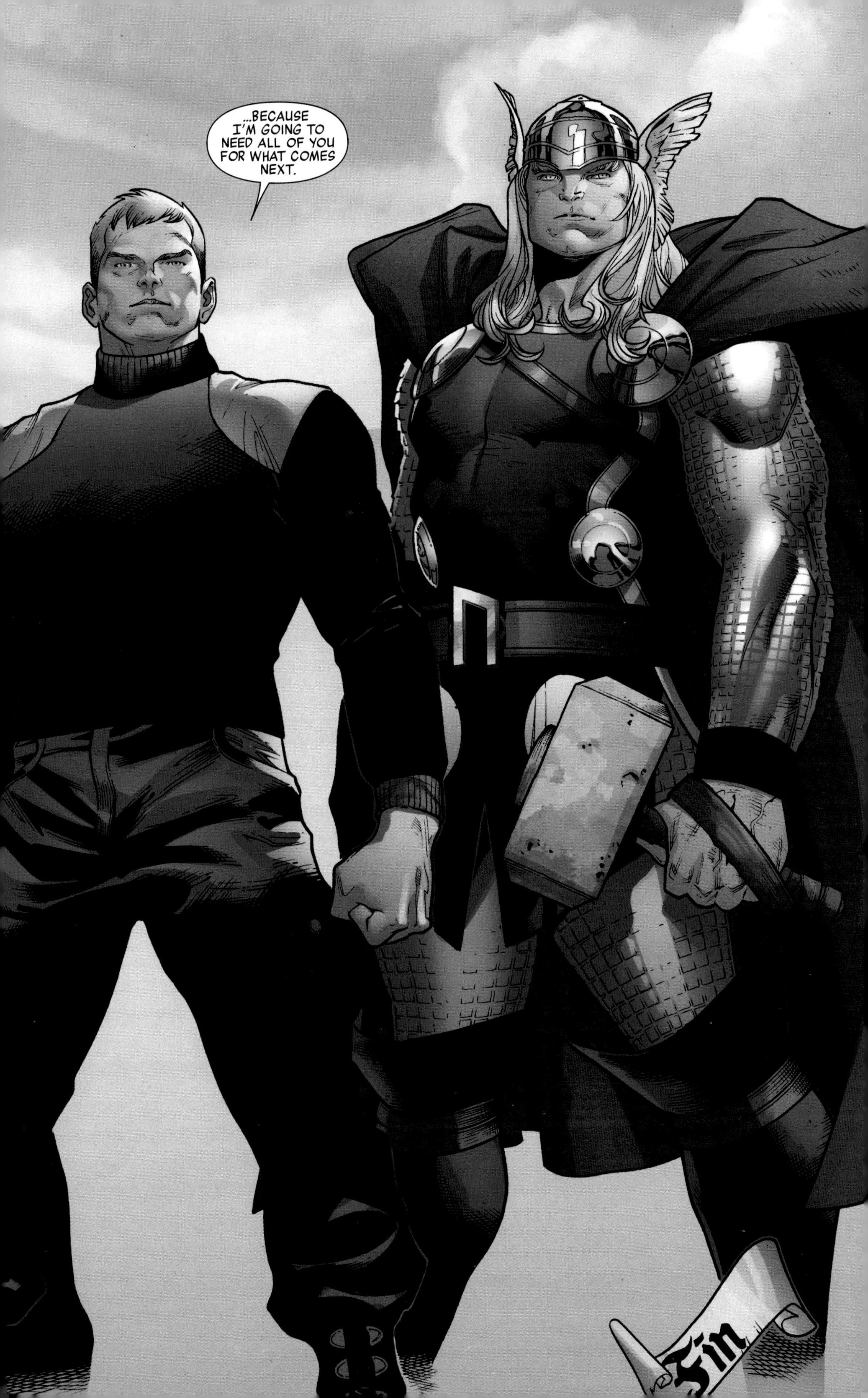
...BECAUSE I'M GOING TO NEED ALL OF YOU FOR WHAT COMES NEXT.
Fin

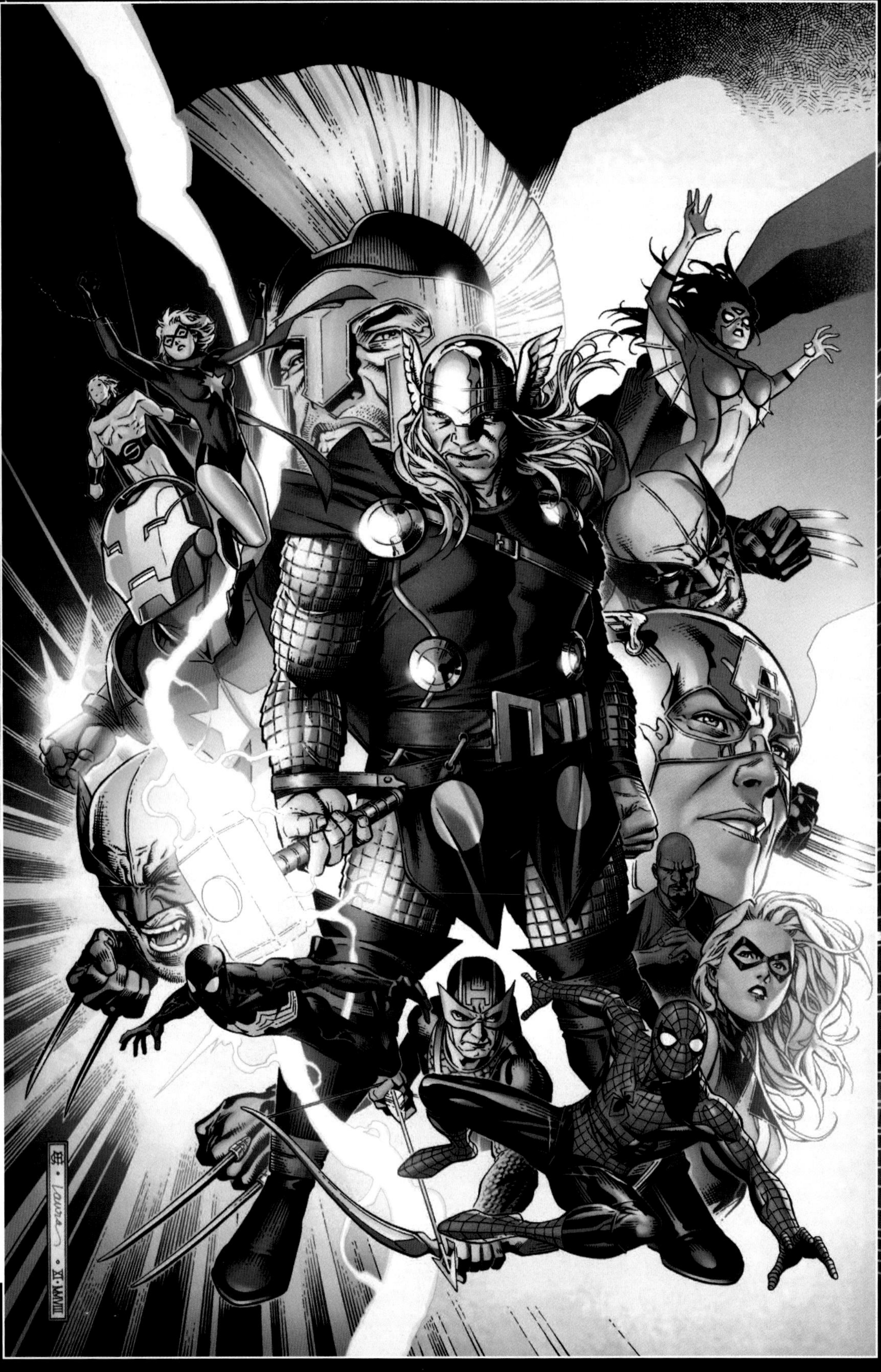

“THE WAY THINGS ARE…”

THIS STORY FROM *FREE COMIC BOOK DAY 2009 NEW AVENGERS* TAKES PLACE BEFORE *SIEGE*

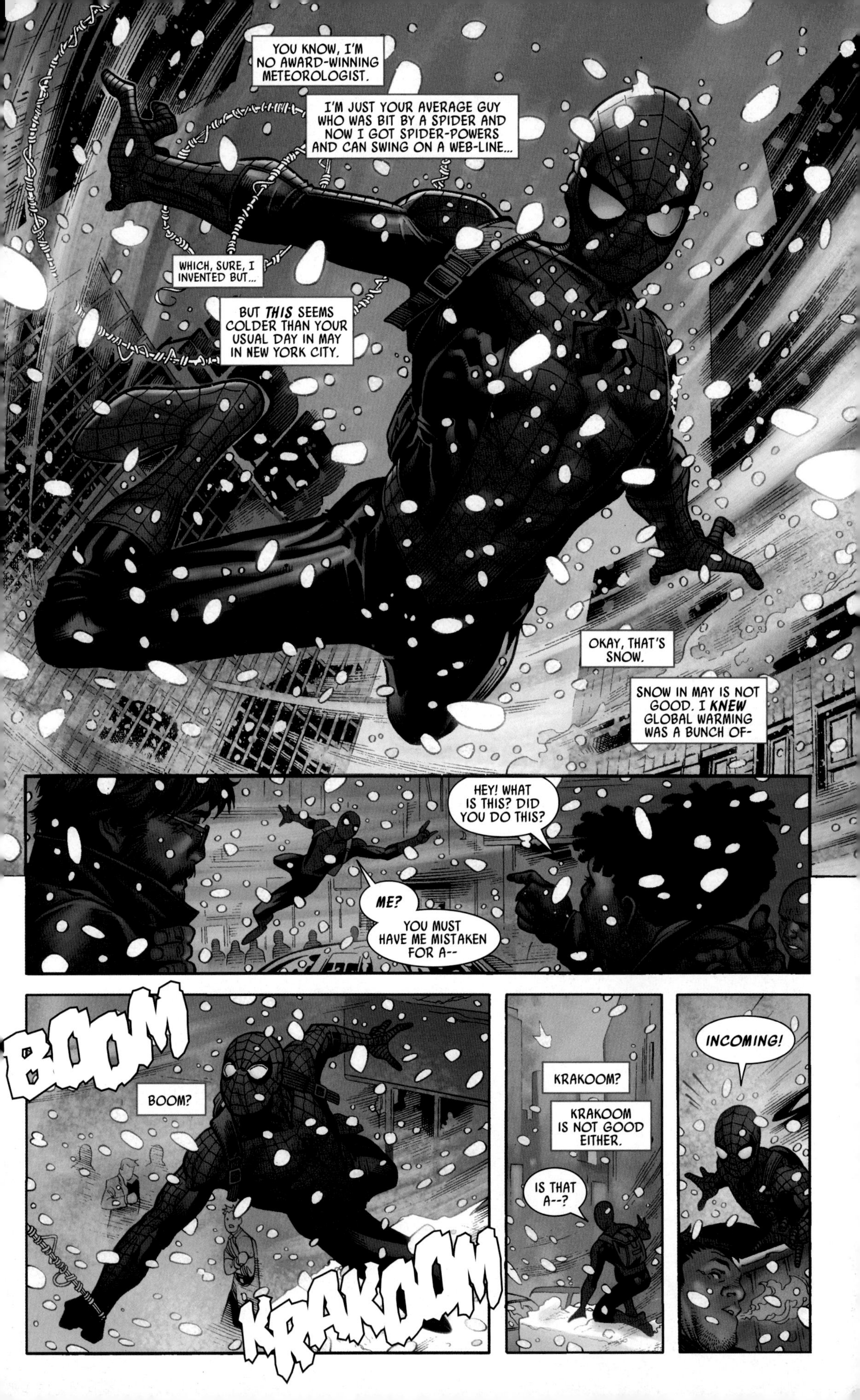
YOU KNOW, I'M NO AWARD-WINNING METEOROLOGIST.
I'M JUST YOUR AVERAGE GUY WHO WAS BIT BY A SPIDER AND NOW I GOT SPIDER-POWERS AND CAN SWING ON A WEB-LINE...
WHICH, SURE, I INVENTED BUT...
BUT *THIS* SEEMS COLDER THAN YOUR USUAL DAY IN MAY IN NEW YORK CITY.
OKAY, THAT'S SNOW.
SNOW IN MAY IS NOT GOOD. I *KNEW* GLOBAL WARMING WAS A BUNCH OF-
HEY! WHAT IS THIS? DID YOU DO THIS?
ME?
YOU MUST HAVE ME MISTAKEN FOR A--
BOOM
BOOM?
KRAKOOM
KRAKOOM?
KRAKOOM IS NOT GOOD EITHER.
IS THAT A--?
INCOMING!

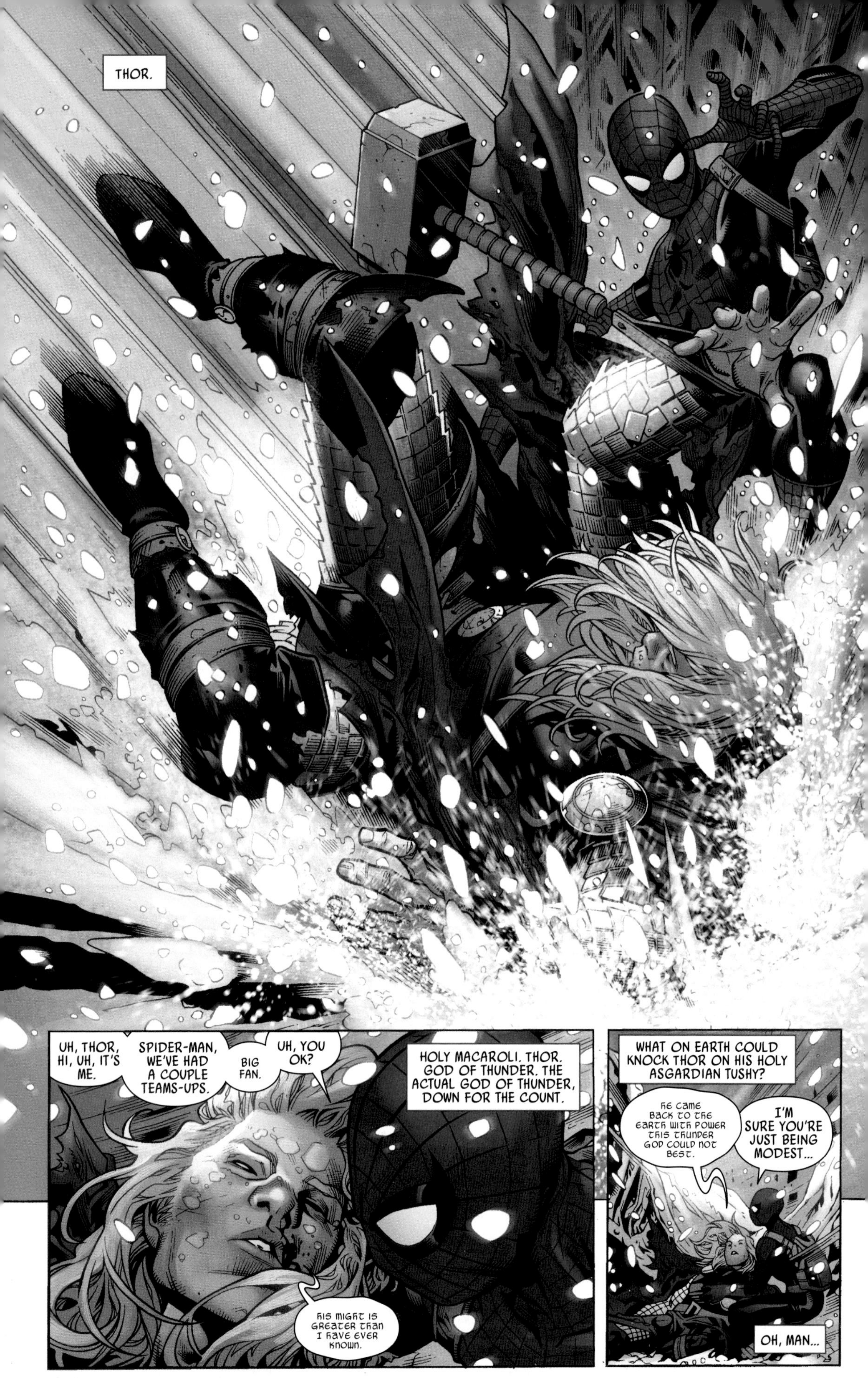
THOR.
UH, THOR, HI, UH, IT'S ME.
SPIDER-MAN, WE'VE HAD A COUPLE TEAMS-UPS.
BIG FAN.
UH, YOU OK?
HOLY MACAROLI. THOR. GOD OF THUNDER. THE ACTUAL GOD OF THUNDER, DOWN FOR THE COUNT.
HIS MIGHT IS GREATER THAN I HAVE EVER KNOWN.
WHAT ON EARTH COULD KNOCK THOR ON HIS HOLY ASGARDIAN TUSHY?
HE CAME BACK TO THE EARTH WITH POWER THIS THUNDER GOD COULD NOT BEST.
I'M SURE YOU'RE JUST BEING MODEST...
OH, MAN...

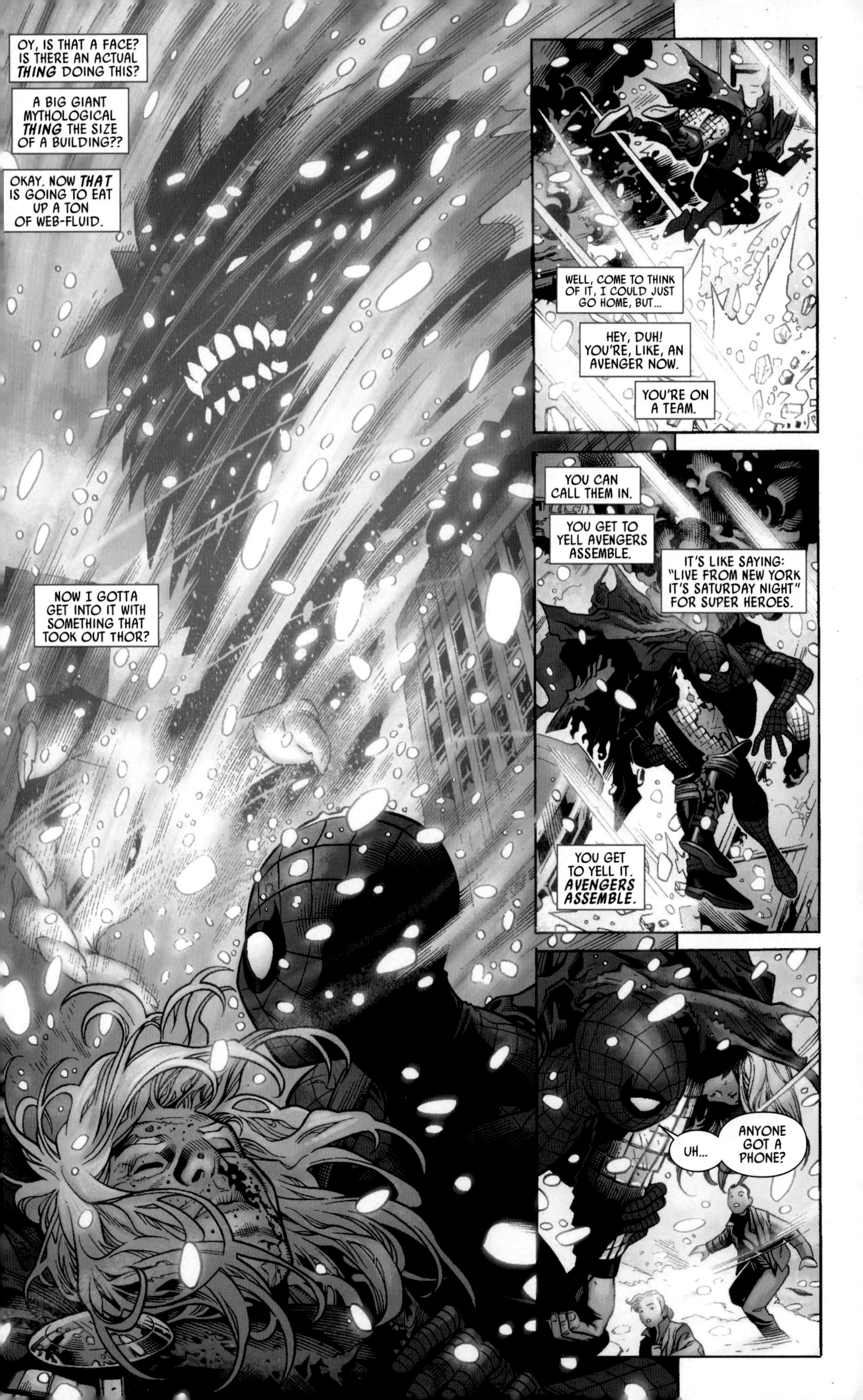
OY, IS THAT A FACE? IS THERE AN ACTUAL THING DOING THIS?
A BIG GIANT MYTHOLOGICAL THING THE SIZE OF A BUILDING??
OKAY. NOW THAT IS GOING TO EAT UP A TON OF WEB-FLUID.
NOW I GOTTA GET INTO IT WITH SOMETHING THAT TOOK OUT THOR?
WELL, COME TO THINK OF IT, I COULD JUST GO HOME, BUT...
HEY, DUH! YOU'RE, LIKE, AN AVENGER NOW.
YOU'RE ON A TEAM.
YOU CAN CALL THEM IN.
YOU GET TO YELL AVENGERS ASSEMBLE.
IT'S LIKE SAYING: "LIVE FROM NEW YORK IT'S SATURDAY NIGHT" FOR SUPER HEROES.
YOU GET TO YELL IT. AVENGERS ASSEMBLE.
UH...
ANYONE GOT A PHONE?

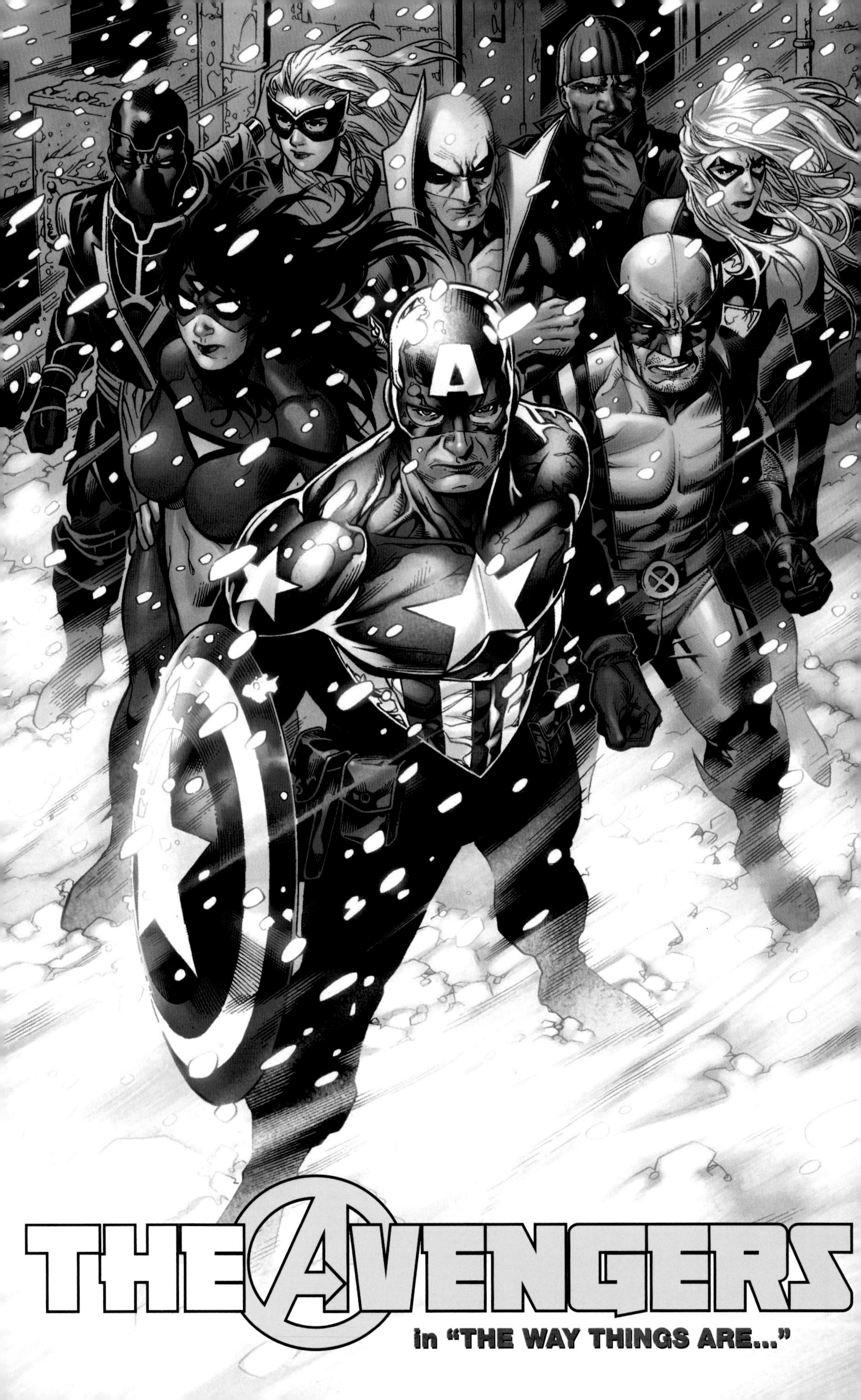
THE AVENGERS
in "THE WAY THINGS ARE..."

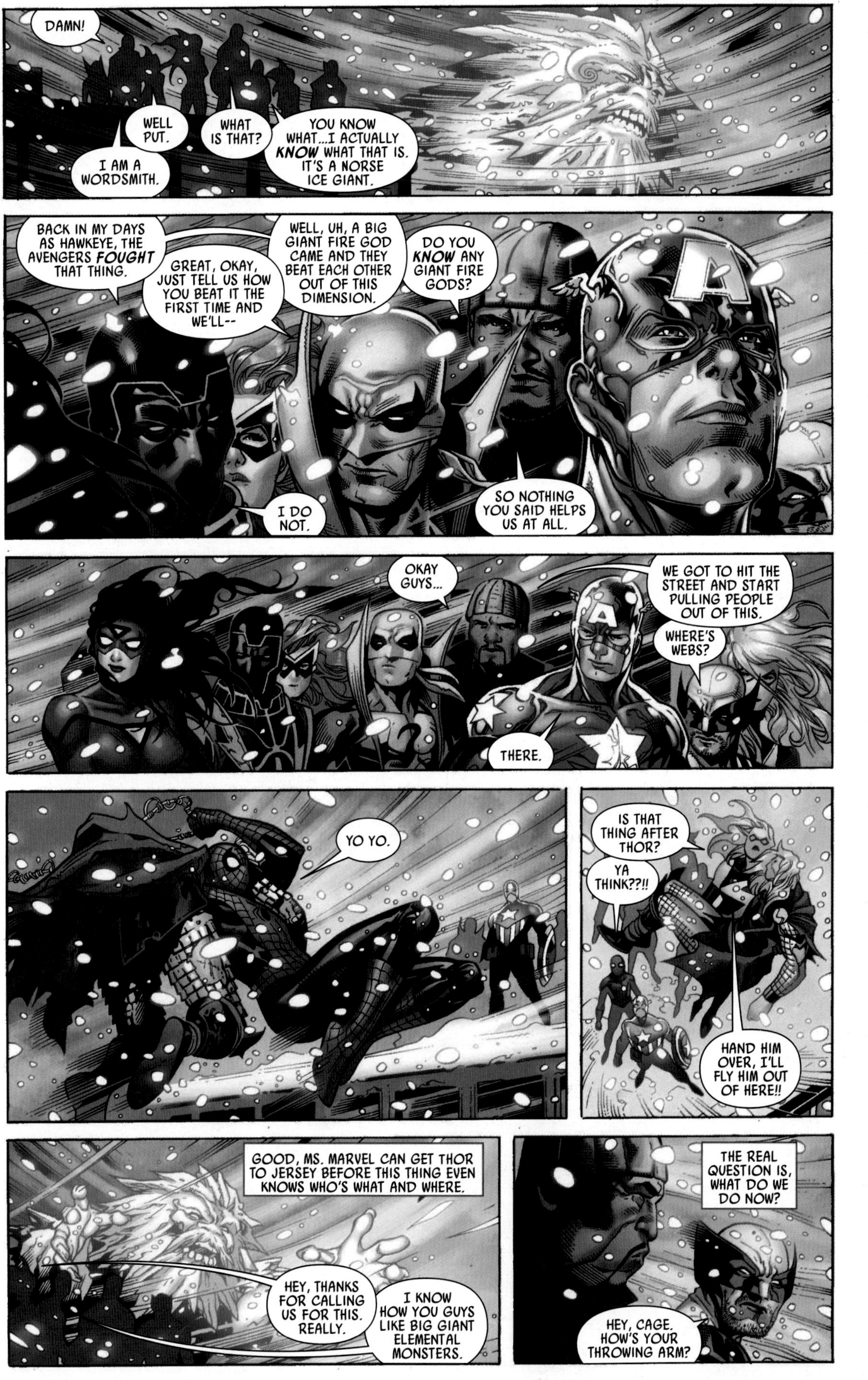
DAMN!
WELL PUT.
I AM A WORDSMITH.
WHAT IS THAT?
YOU KNOW WHAT...I ACTUALLY KNOW WHAT THAT IS. IT'S A NORSE ICE GIANT.
BACK IN MY DAYS AS HAWKEYE, THE AVENGERS FOUGHT THAT THING.
GREAT, OKAY, JUST TELL US HOW YOU BEAT IT THE FIRST TIME AND WE'LL--
WELL, UH, A BIG GIANT FIRE GOD CAME AND THEY BEAT EACH OTHER OUT OF THIS DIMENSION.
DO YOU KNOW ANY GIANT FIRE GODS?
I DO NOT.
SO NOTHING YOU SAID HELPS US AT ALL.
OKAY GUYS...
WE GOT TO HIT THE STREET AND START PULLING PEOPLE OUT OF THIS.
WHERE'S WEBS?
THERE.
YO YO.
IS THAT THING AFTER THOR?
YA THINK??!!
HAND HIM OVER, I'LL FLY HIM OUT OF HERE!!
GOOD, MS. MARVEL CAN GET THOR TO JERSEY BEFORE THIS THING EVEN KNOWS WHO'S WHAT AND WHERE.
HEY, THANKS FOR CALLING US FOR THIS. REALLY.
I KNOW HOW YOU GUYS LIKE BIG GIANT ELEMENTAL MONSTERS.
THE REAL QUESTION IS, WHAT DO WE DO NOW?
HEY, CAGE. HOW'S YOUR THROWING ARM?

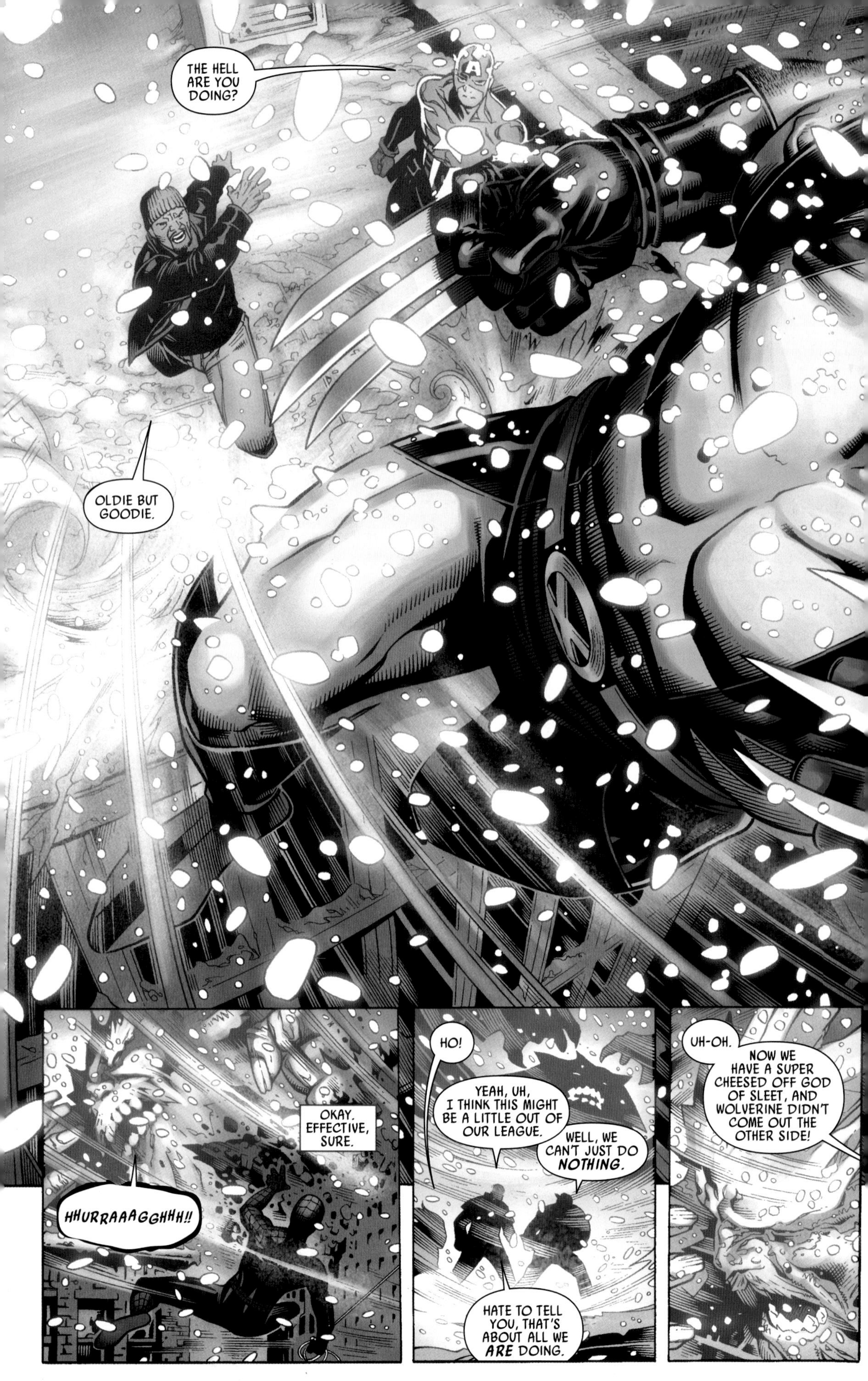
THE HELL ARE YOU DOING?
OLDIE BUT GOODIE.
OKAY. EFFECTIVE, SURE.
HHURRAAAGGHHH!!
HO!
YEAH, UH, I THINK THIS MIGHT BE A LITTLE OUT OF OUR LEAGUE.
WELL, WE CAN'T JUST DO NOTHING.
HATE TO TELL YOU, THAT'S ABOUT ALL WE ARE DOING.
UH-OH.
NOW WE HAVE A SUPER CHEESED OFF GOD OF SLEET, AND WOLVERINE DIDN'T COME OUT THE OTHER SIDE!

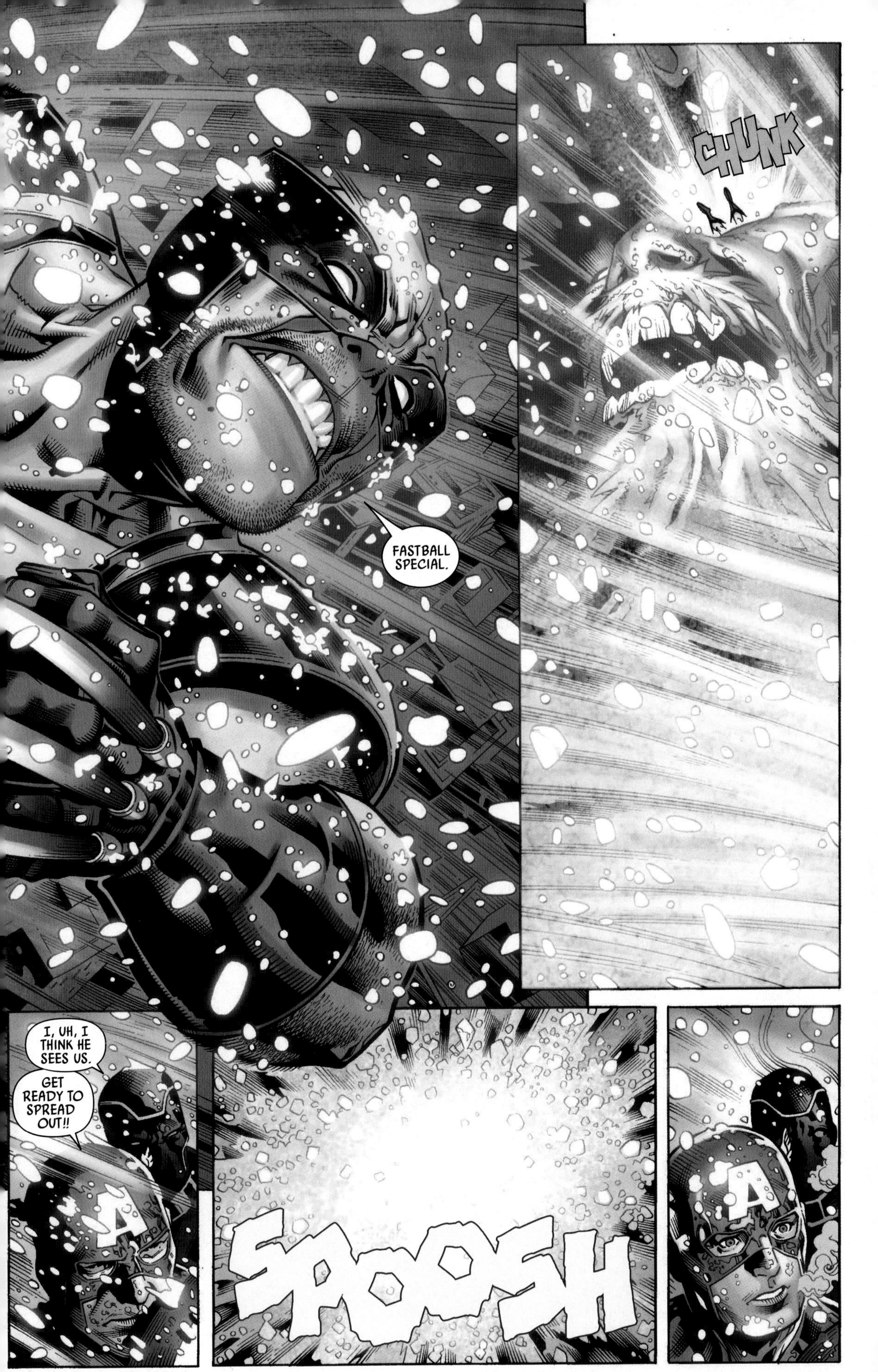
CHUNK
FASTBALL SPECIAL.
I, UH, I THINK HE SEES US.
GET READY TO SPREAD OUT!!
SPOOSH

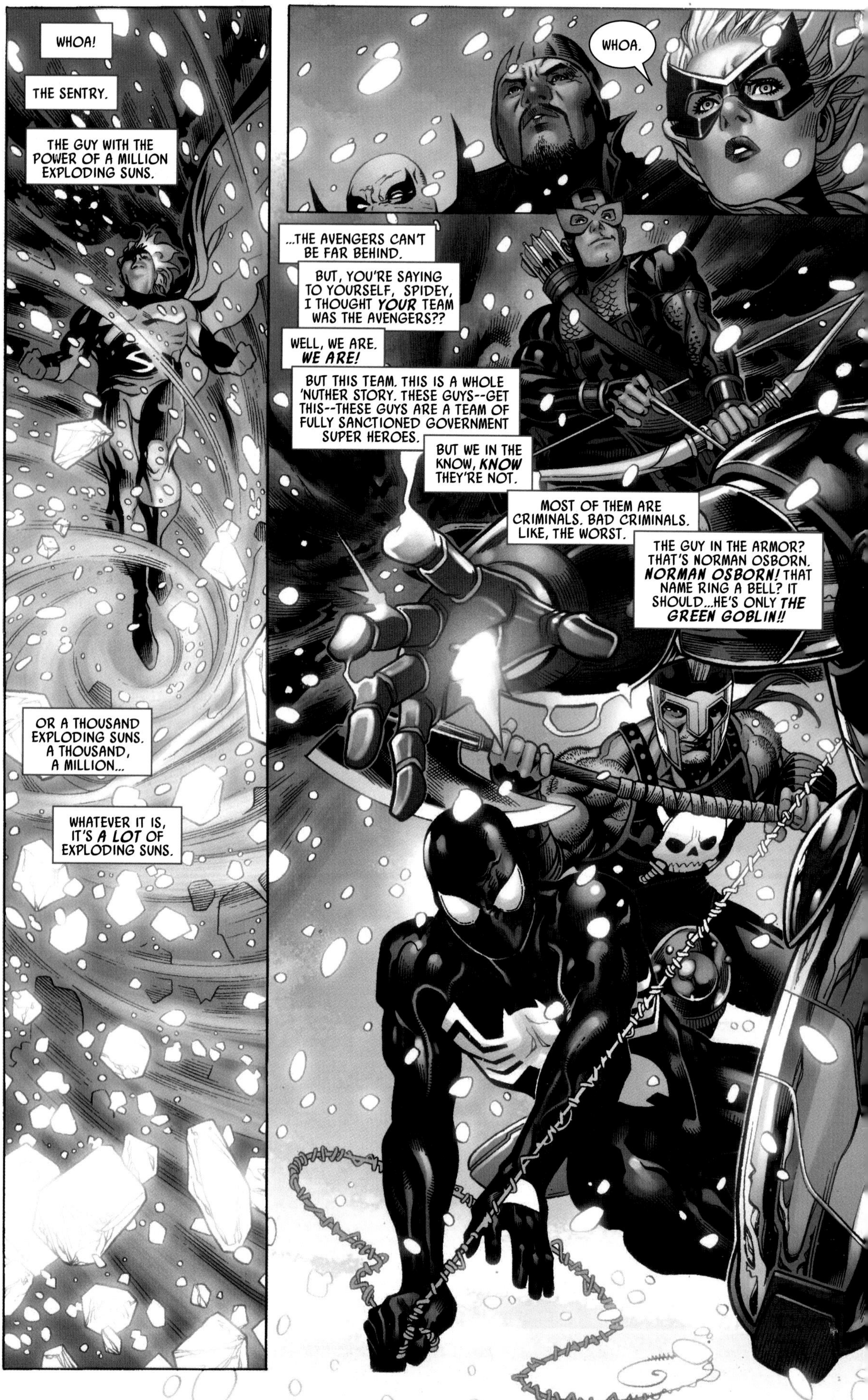
WHOA!
THE SENTRY.
THE GUY WITH THE POWER OF A MILLION EXPLODING SUNS.
OR A THOUSAND EXPLODING SUNS. A THOUSAND, A MILLION...
WHATEVER IT IS, IT'S A LOT OF EXPLODING SUNS.
WHOA.
...THE AVENGERS CAN'T BE FAR BEHIND.
BUT, YOU'RE SAYING TO YOURSELF, SPIDEY, I THOUGHT YOUR TEAM WAS THE AVENGERS??
WELL, WE ARE. WE ARE!
BUT THIS TEAM. THIS IS A WHOLE 'NUTHER STORY. THESE GUYS--GET THIS--THESE GUYS ARE A TEAM OF FULLY SANCTIONED GOVERNMENT SUPER HEROES.
BUT WE IN THE KNOW, KNOW THEY'RE NOT.
MOST OF THEM ARE CRIMINALS. BAD CRIMINALS. LIKE, THE WORST.
THE GUY IN THE ARMOR? THAT'S NORMAN OSBORN. NORMAN OSBORN! THAT NAME RING A BELL? IT SHOULD...HE'S ONLY THE GREEN GOBLIN!!

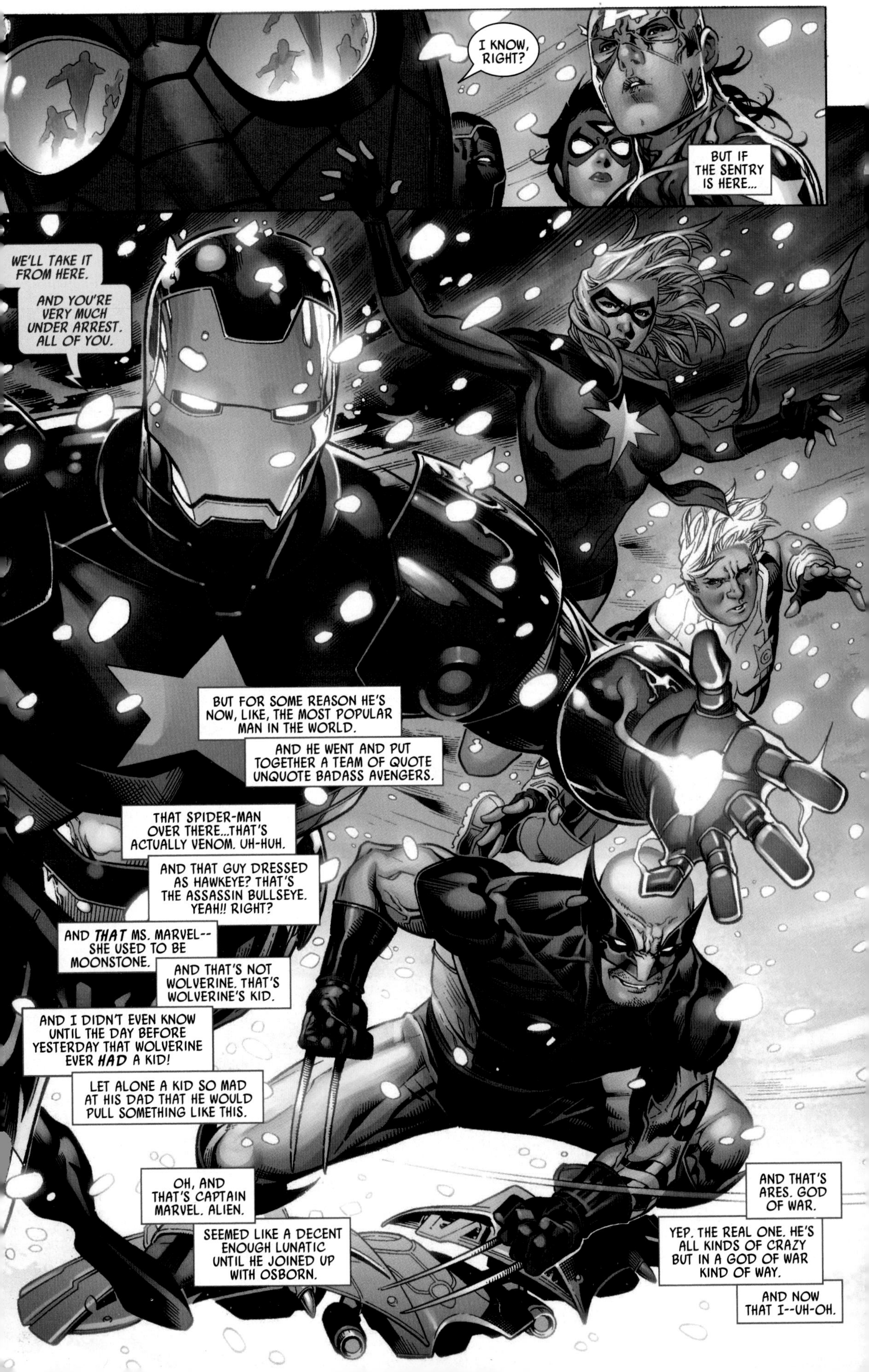
I KNOW, RIGHT?
BUT IF THE SENTRY IS HERE...
WE'LL TAKE IT FROM HERE.
AND YOU'RE VERY MUCH UNDER ARREST. ALL OF YOU.
BUT FOR SOME REASON HE'S NOW, LIKE, THE MOST POPULAR MAN IN THE WORLD.
AND HE WENT AND PUT TOGETHER A TEAM OF QUOTE UNQUOTE BADASS AVENGERS.
THAT SPIDER-MAN OVER THERE...THAT'S ACTUALLY VENOM. UH-HUH.
AND THAT GUY DRESSED AS HAWKEYE? THAT'S THE ASSASSIN BULLSEYE. YEAH!! RIGHT?
AND *THAT* MS. MARVEL-- SHE USED TO BE MOONSTONE.
AND THAT'S NOT WOLVERINE. THAT'S WOLVERINE'S KID.
AND I DIDN'T EVEN KNOW UNTIL THE DAY BEFORE YESTERDAY THAT WOLVERINE EVER *HAD* A KID!
LET ALONE A KID SO MAD AT HIS DAD THAT HE WOULD PULL SOMETHING LIKE THIS.
OH, AND THAT'S CAPTAIN MARVEL. ALIEN.
SEEMED LIKE A DECENT ENOUGH LUNATIC UNTIL HE JOINED UP WITH OSBORN.
AND THAT'S ARES. GOD OF WAR.
YEP. THE REAL ONE. HE'S ALL KINDS OF CRAZY BUT IN A GOD OF WAR KIND OF WAY.
AND NOW THAT I--UH-OH.

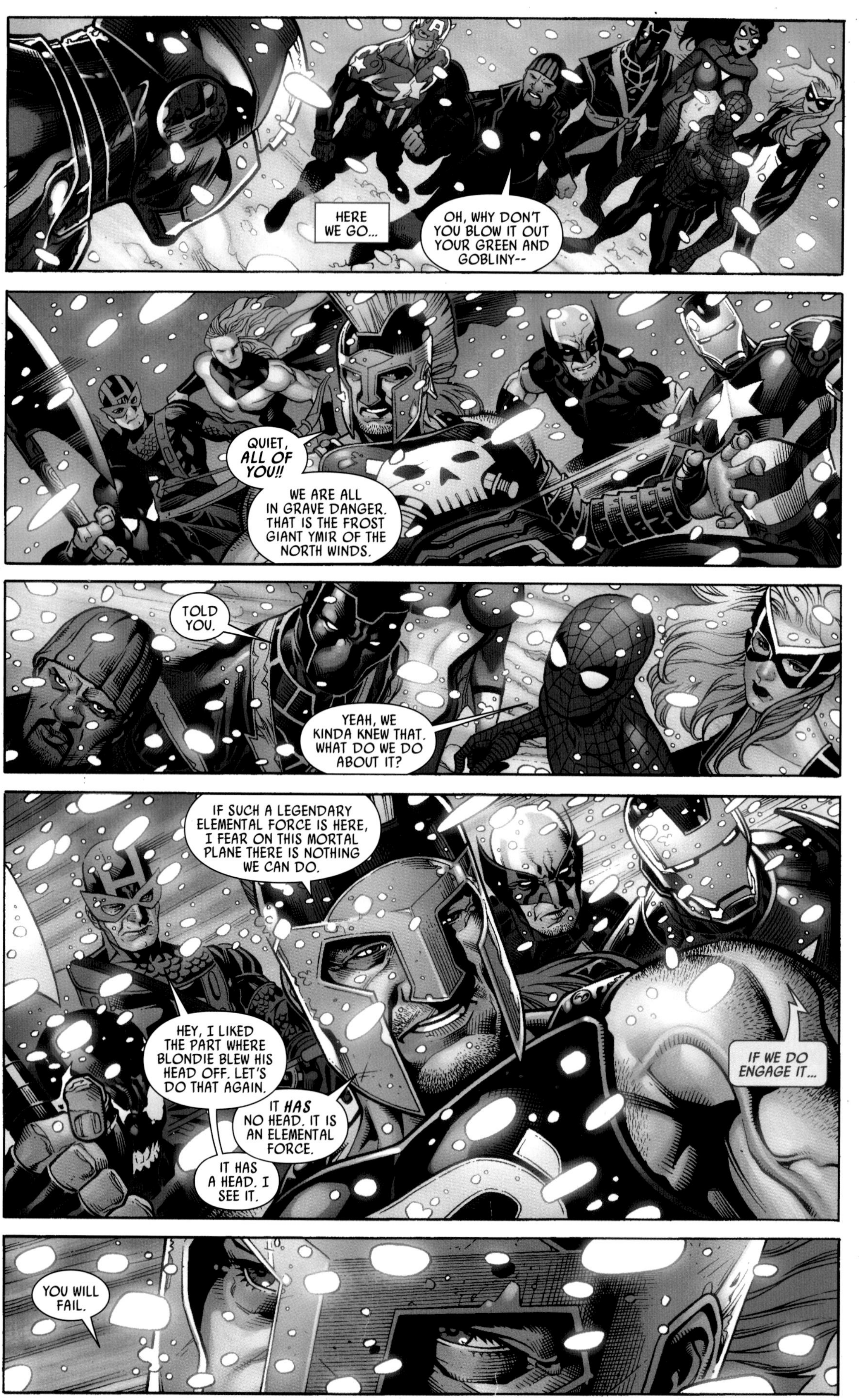
HERE WE GO...
OH, WHY DON'T YOU BLOW IT OUT YOUR GREEN AND GOBLINY--
QUIET, ALL OF YOU!!
WE ARE ALL IN GRAVE DANGER. THAT IS THE FROST GIANT YMIR OF THE NORTH WINDS.
TOLD YOU.
YEAH, WE KINDA KNEW THAT. WHAT DO WE DO ABOUT IT?
IF SUCH A LEGENDARY ELEMENTAL FORCE IS HERE, I FEAR ON THIS MORTAL PLANE THERE IS NOTHING WE CAN DO.
HEY, I LIKED THE PART WHERE BLONDIE BLEW HIS HEAD OFF. LET'S DO THAT AGAIN.
IT HAS NO HEAD. IT IS AN ELEMENTAL FORCE.
IT HAS A HEAD. I SEE IT.
IF WE DO ENGAGE IT...
YOU WILL FAIL.

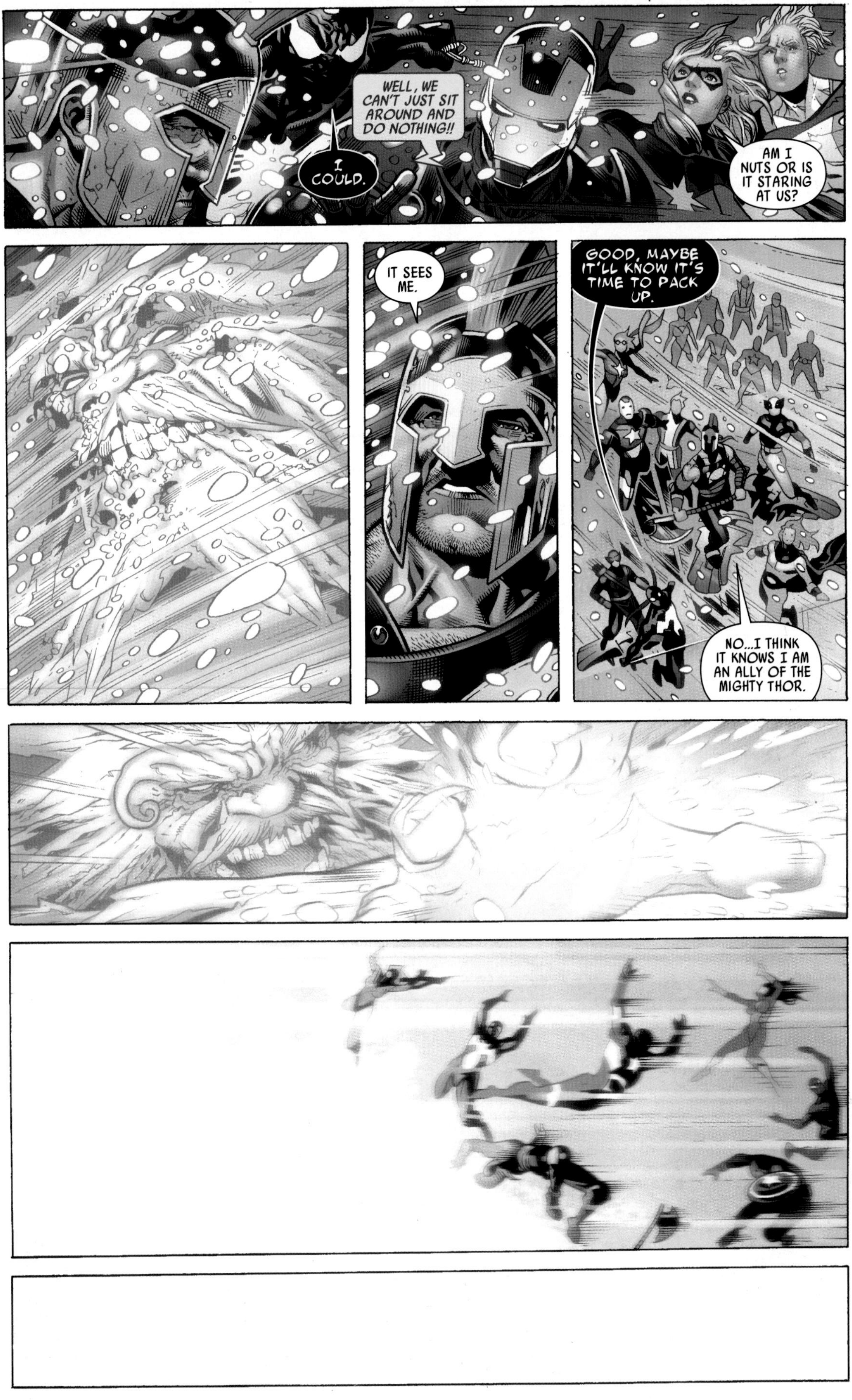
WELL, WE CAN'T JUST SIT AROUND AND DO NOTHING!!
I COULD.
AM I NUTS OR IS IT STARING AT US?
IT SEES ME.
GOOD, MAYBE IT'LL KNOW IT'S TIME TO PACK UP.
NO...I THINK IT KNOWS I AM AN ALLY OF THE MIGHTY THOR.

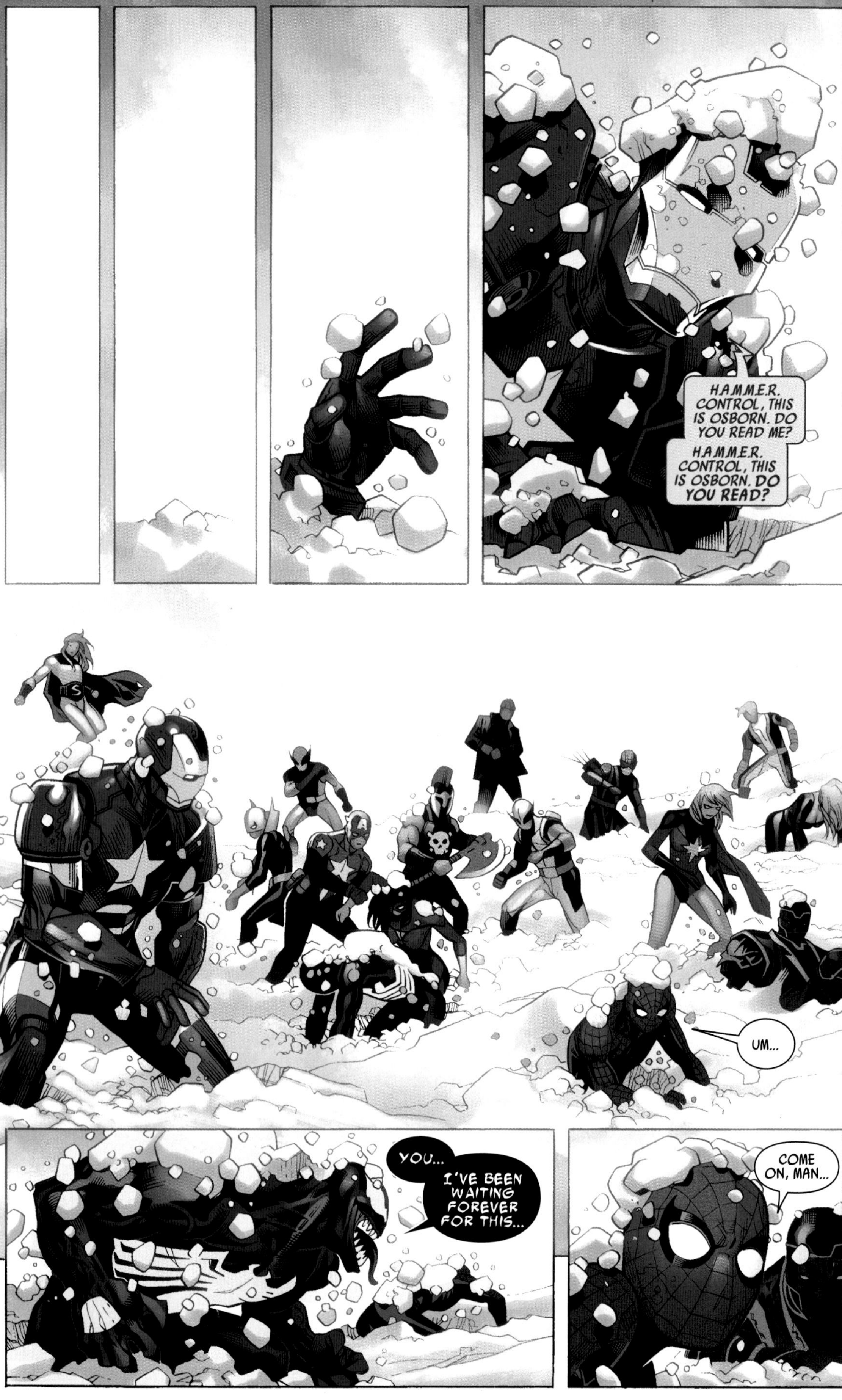
H.A.M.M.E.R. CONTROL, THIS IS OSBORN. DO YOU READ ME?
H.A.M.M.E.R. CONTROL, THIS IS OSBORN. DO YOU READ?
UM...
YOU...
I'VE BEEN WAITING FOREVER FOR THIS...
COME ON, MAN...

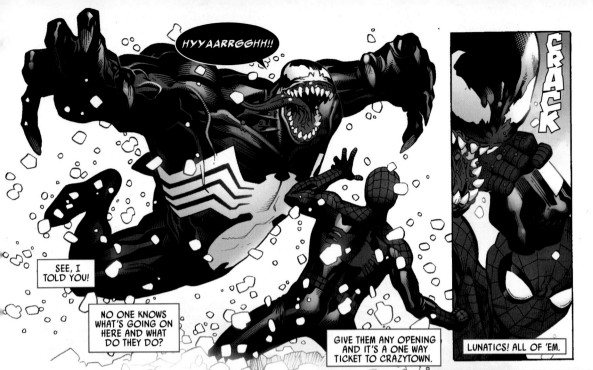

HYYAARRGGHH!!

CRACK

SEE, I TOLD YOU!

NO ONE KNOWS WHAT'S GOING ON HERE AND WHAT DO THEY DO?

GIVE THEM ANY OPENING AND IT'S A ONE WAY TICKET TO CRAZYTOWN.

LUNATICS! ALL OF 'EM.

AND MY GUYS, THEY AIN'T EXACTLY ABOUT TO SIT AND TAKE IT.

WORST AVENGERS SNOWBALL FIGHT EVER.

STOP IT!!

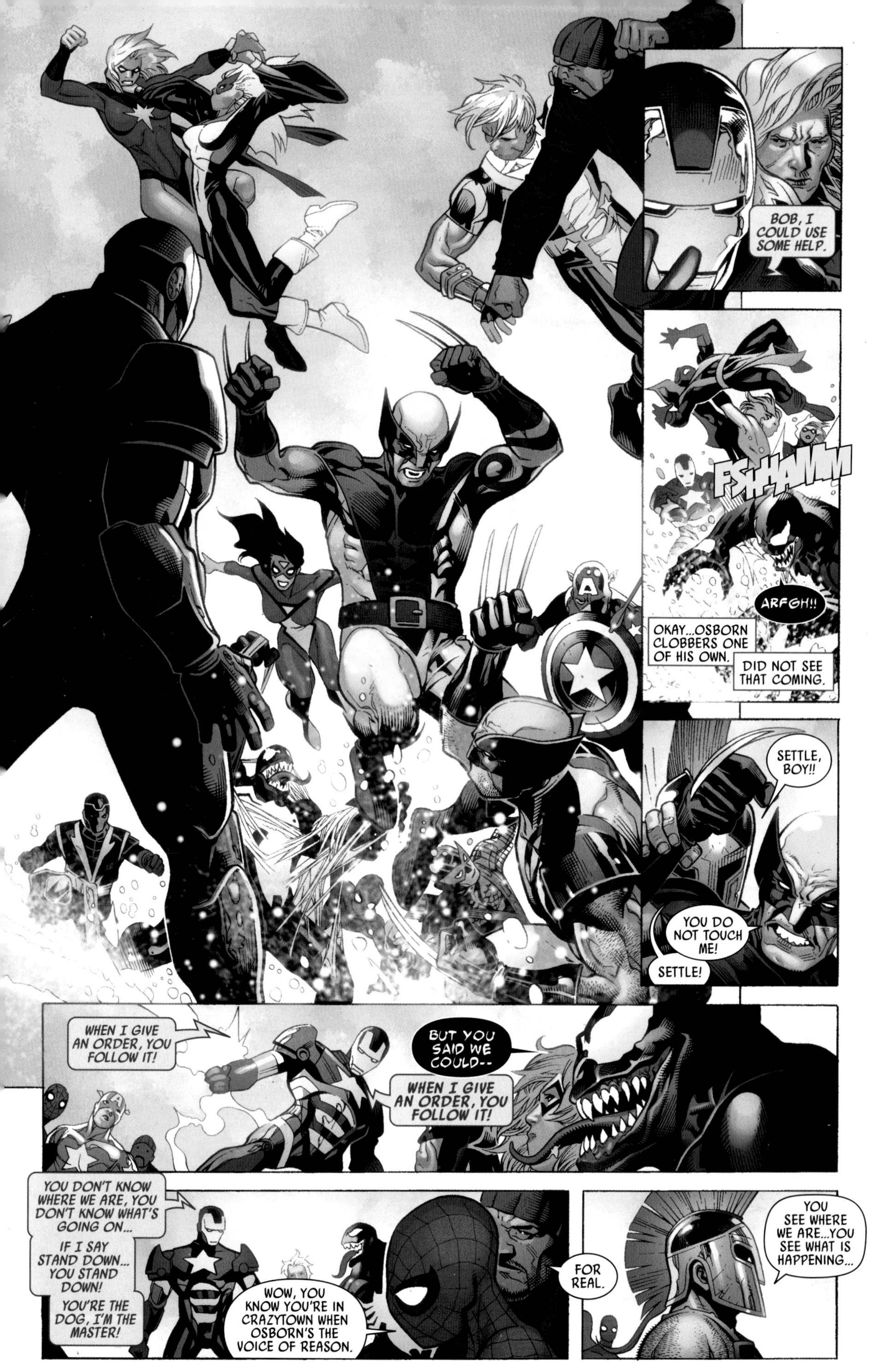
BOB, I COULD USE SOME HELP.
FSHHAMM
ARFGH!!
OKAY...OSBORN CLOBBERS ONE OF HIS OWN.
DID NOT SEE THAT COMING.
SETTLE, BOY!!
YOU DO NOT TOUCH ME!
SETTLE!
WHEN I GIVE AN ORDER, YOU FOLLOW IT!
BUT YOU SAID WE COULD--
WHEN I GIVE AN ORDER, YOU FOLLOW IT!
YOU DON'T KNOW WHERE WE ARE, YOU DON'T KNOW WHAT'S GOING ON...
IF I SAY STAND DOWN... YOU STAND DOWN!
YOU'RE THE DOG, I'M THE MASTER!
WOW, YOU KNOW YOU'RE IN CRAZYTOWN WHEN OSBORN'S THE VOICE OF REASON.
FOR REAL.
YOU SEE WHERE WE ARE...YOU SEE WHAT IS HAPPENING...

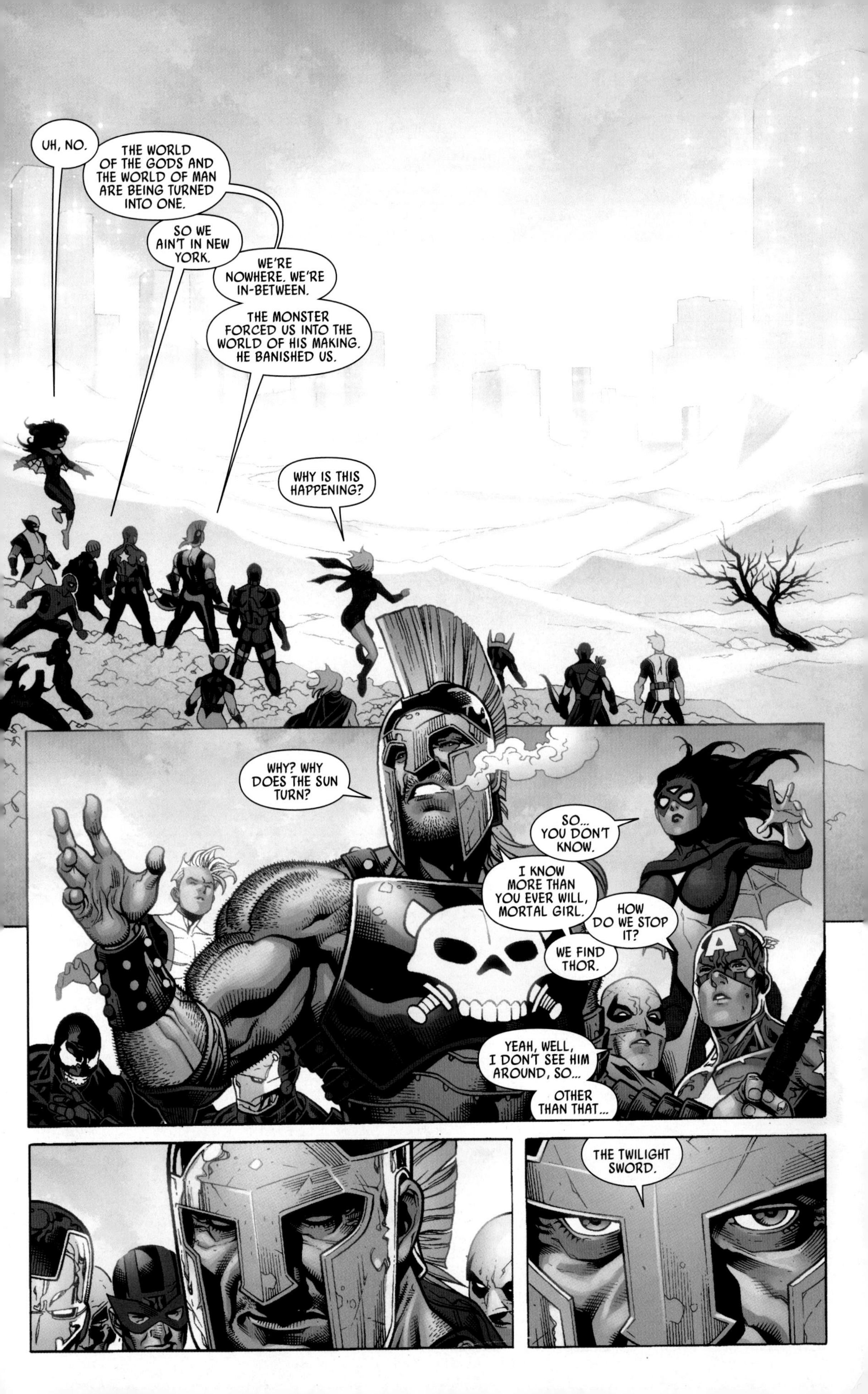
UH, NO.
THE WORLD OF THE GODS AND THE WORLD OF MAN ARE BEING TURNED INTO ONE.
SO WE AIN'T IN NEW YORK.
WE'RE NOWHERE. WE'RE IN-BETWEEN.
THE MONSTER FORCED US INTO THE WORLD OF HIS MAKING. HE BANISHED US.
WHY IS THIS HAPPENING?
WHY? WHY DOES THE SUN TURN?
SO... YOU DON'T KNOW.
I KNOW MORE THAN YOU EVER WILL, MORTAL GIRL.
HOW DO WE STOP IT?
WE FIND THOR.
YEAH, WELL, I DON'T SEE HIM AROUND, SO...
OTHER THAN THAT...
THE TWILIGHT SWORD.

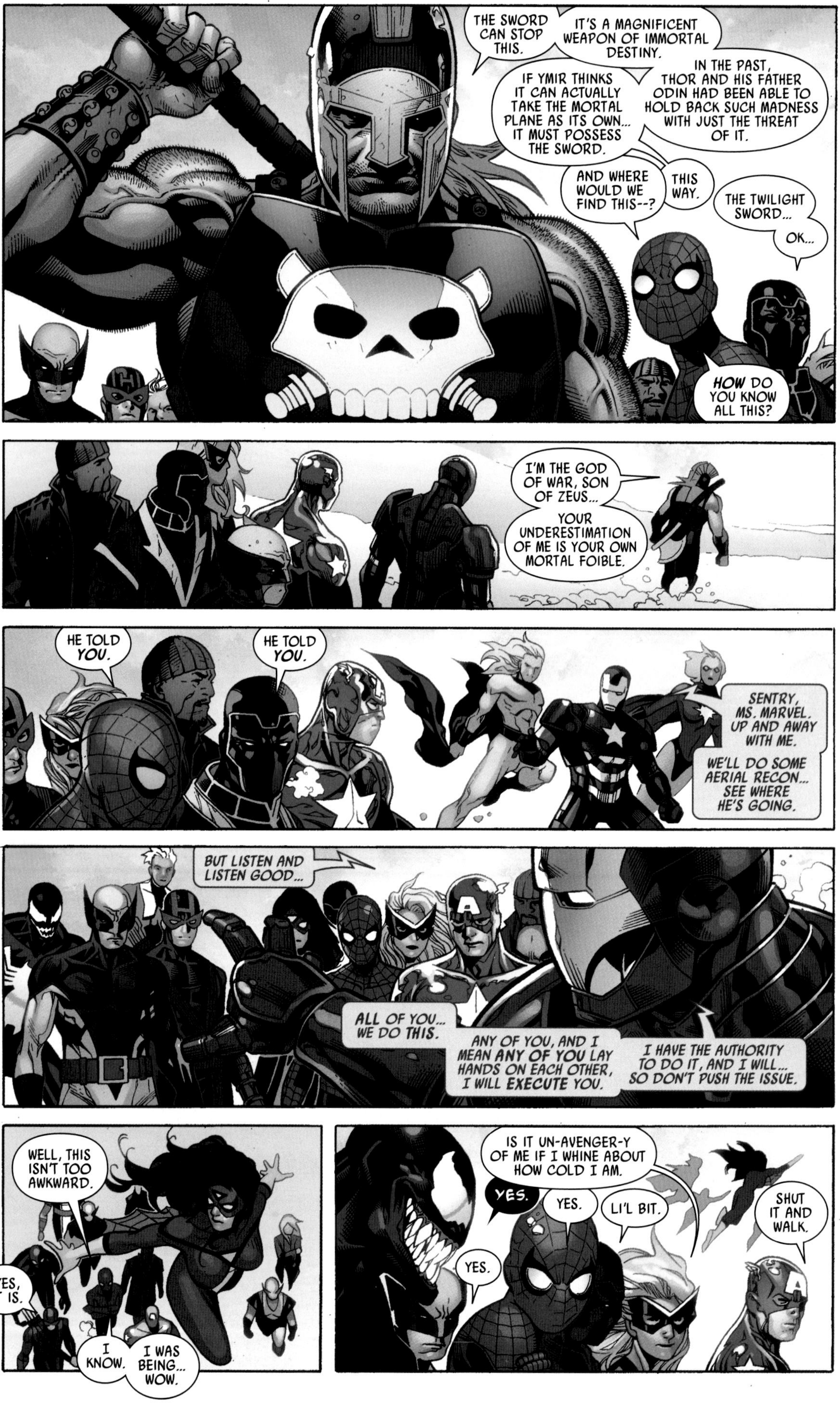
THE SWORD CAN STOP THIS.
IT'S A MAGNIFICENT WEAPON OF IMMORTAL DESTINY.
IN THE PAST, THOR AND HIS FATHER ODIN HAD BEEN ABLE TO HOLD BACK SUCH MADNESS WITH JUST THE THREAT OF IT.
IF YMIR THINKS IT CAN ACTUALLY TAKE THE MORTAL PLANE AS ITS OWN... IT MUST POSSESS THE SWORD.
AND WHERE WOULD WE FIND THIS--?
THIS WAY.
THE TWILIGHT SWORD...
OK...
HOW DO YOU KNOW ALL THIS?
I'M THE GOD OF WAR, SON OF ZEUS...
YOUR UNDERESTIMATION OF ME IS YOUR OWN MORTAL FOIBLE.
HE TOLD YOU.
HE TOLD YOU.
SENTRY, MS. MARVEL. UP AND AWAY WITH ME.
WE'LL DO SOME AERIAL RECON... SEE WHERE HE'S GOING.
BUT LISTEN AND LISTEN GOOD...
ALL OF YOU... WE DO THIS.
ANY OF YOU, AND I MEAN ANY OF YOU LAY HANDS ON EACH OTHER, I WILL EXECUTE YOU.
I HAVE THE AUTHORITY TO DO IT, AND I WILL... SO DON'T PUSH THE ISSUE.
WELL, THIS ISN'T TOO AWKWARD.
YES, IT IS.
I KNOW.
I WAS BEING... WOW.
IS IT UN-AVENGER-Y OF ME IF I WHINE ABOUT HOW COLD I AM.
YES.
YES.
LI'L BIT.
SHUT IT AND WALK.
YES.

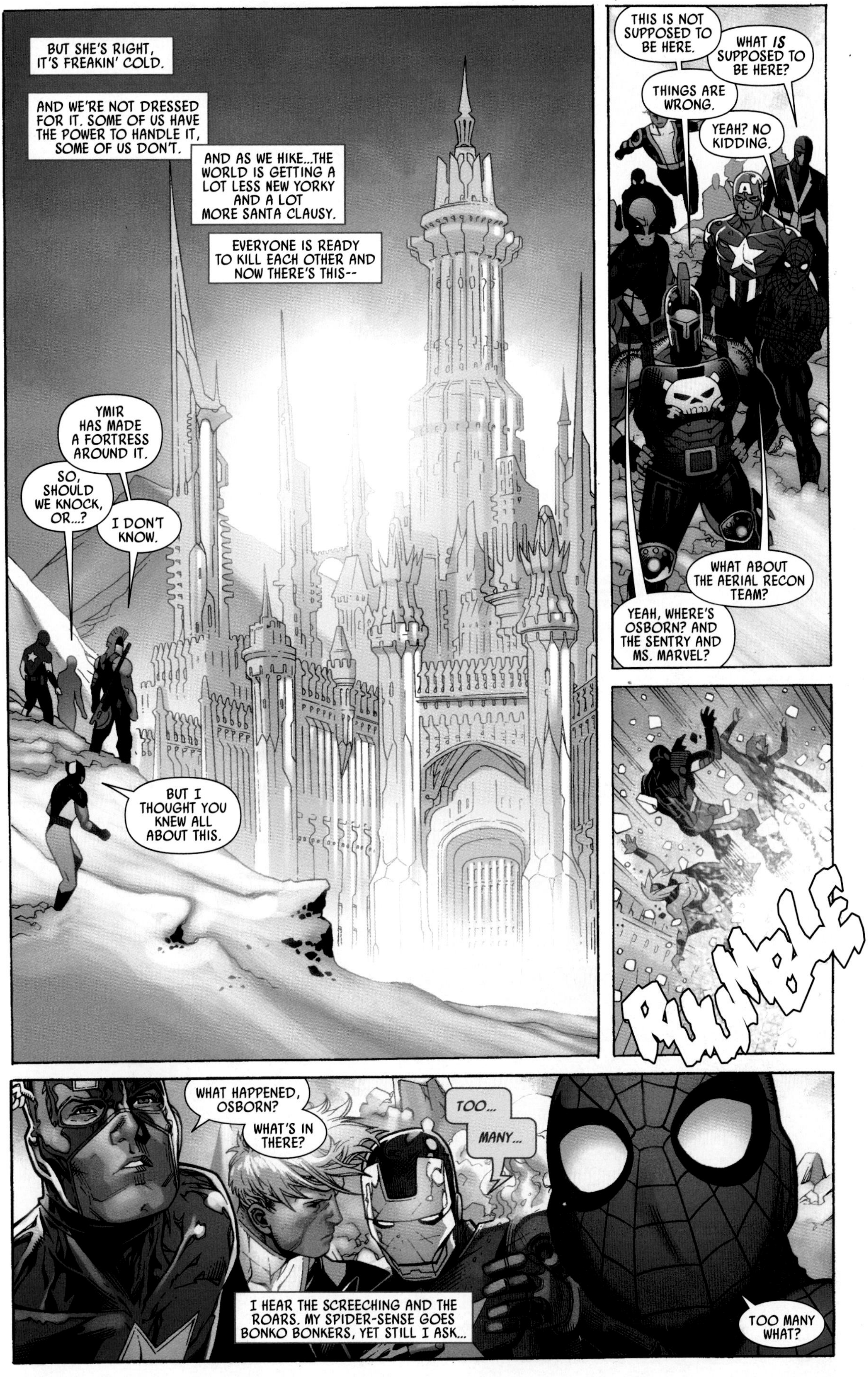
BUT SHE'S RIGHT, IT'S FREAKIN' COLD.
AND WE'RE NOT DRESSED FOR IT. SOME OF US HAVE THE POWER TO HANDLE IT, SOME OF US DON'T.
AND AS WE HIKE...THE WORLD IS GETTING A LOT LESS NEW YORKY AND A LOT MORE SANTA CLAUSY.
EVERYONE IS READY TO KILL EACH OTHER AND NOW THERE'S THIS--
YMIR HAS MADE A FORTRESS AROUND IT.
SO, SHOULD WE KNOCK, OR...?
I DON'T KNOW.
BUT I THOUGHT YOU KNEW ALL ABOUT THIS.
THIS IS NOT SUPPOSED TO BE HERE.
WHAT *IS* SUPPOSED TO BE HERE?
THINGS ARE WRONG.
YEAH? NO KIDDING.
WHAT ABOUT THE AERIAL RECON TEAM?
YEAH, WHERE'S OSBORN? AND THE SENTRY AND MS. MARVEL?
RUMBLE
WHAT HAPPENED, OSBORN?
WHAT'S IN THERE?
TOO...
MANY...
I HEAR THE SCREECHING AND THE ROARS. MY SPIDER-SENSE GOES BONKO BONKERS, YET STILL I ASK...
TOO MANY WHAT?

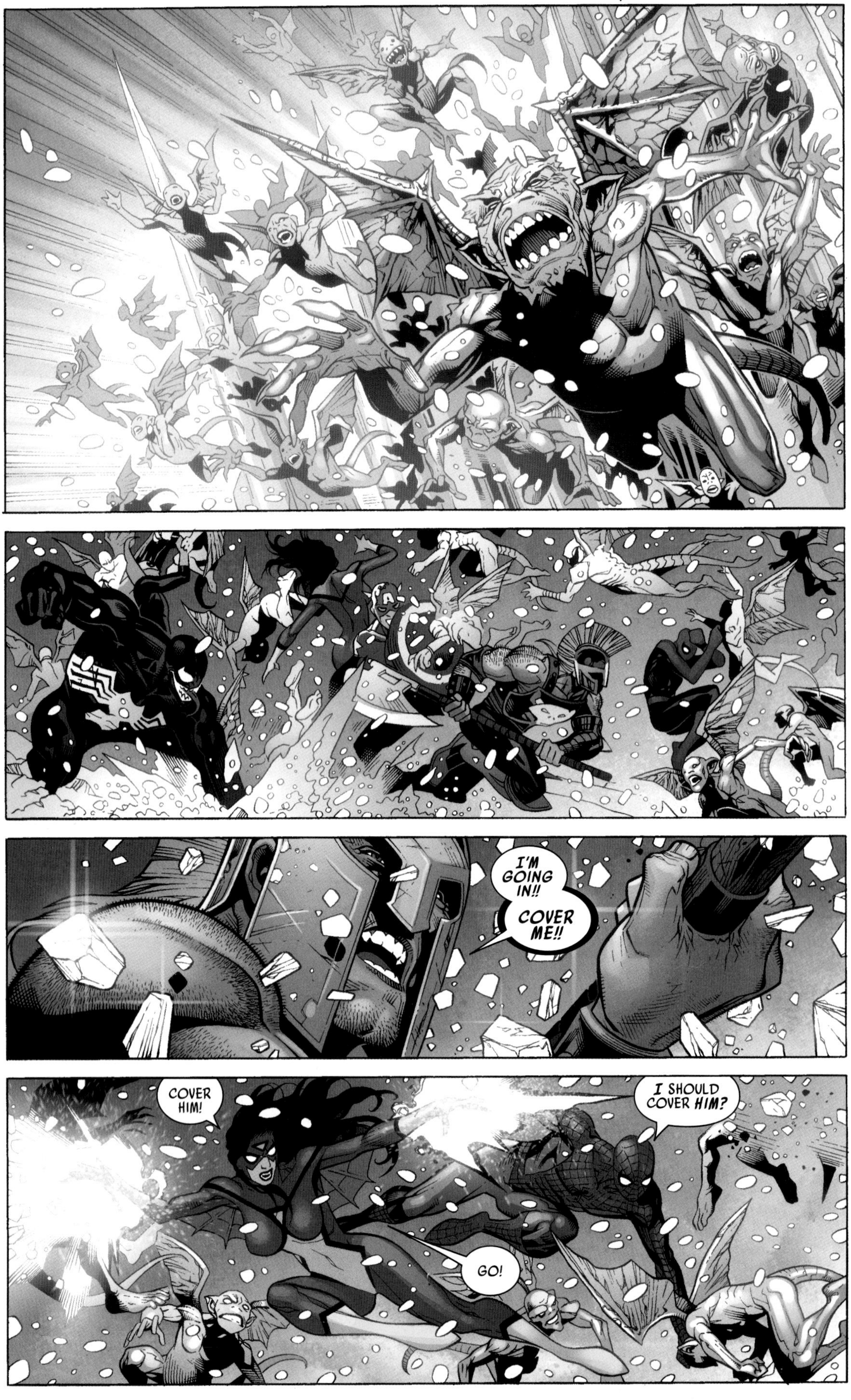
I'M GOING IN!!
COVER ME!!
COVER HIM!
I SHOULD COVER HIM?
GO!

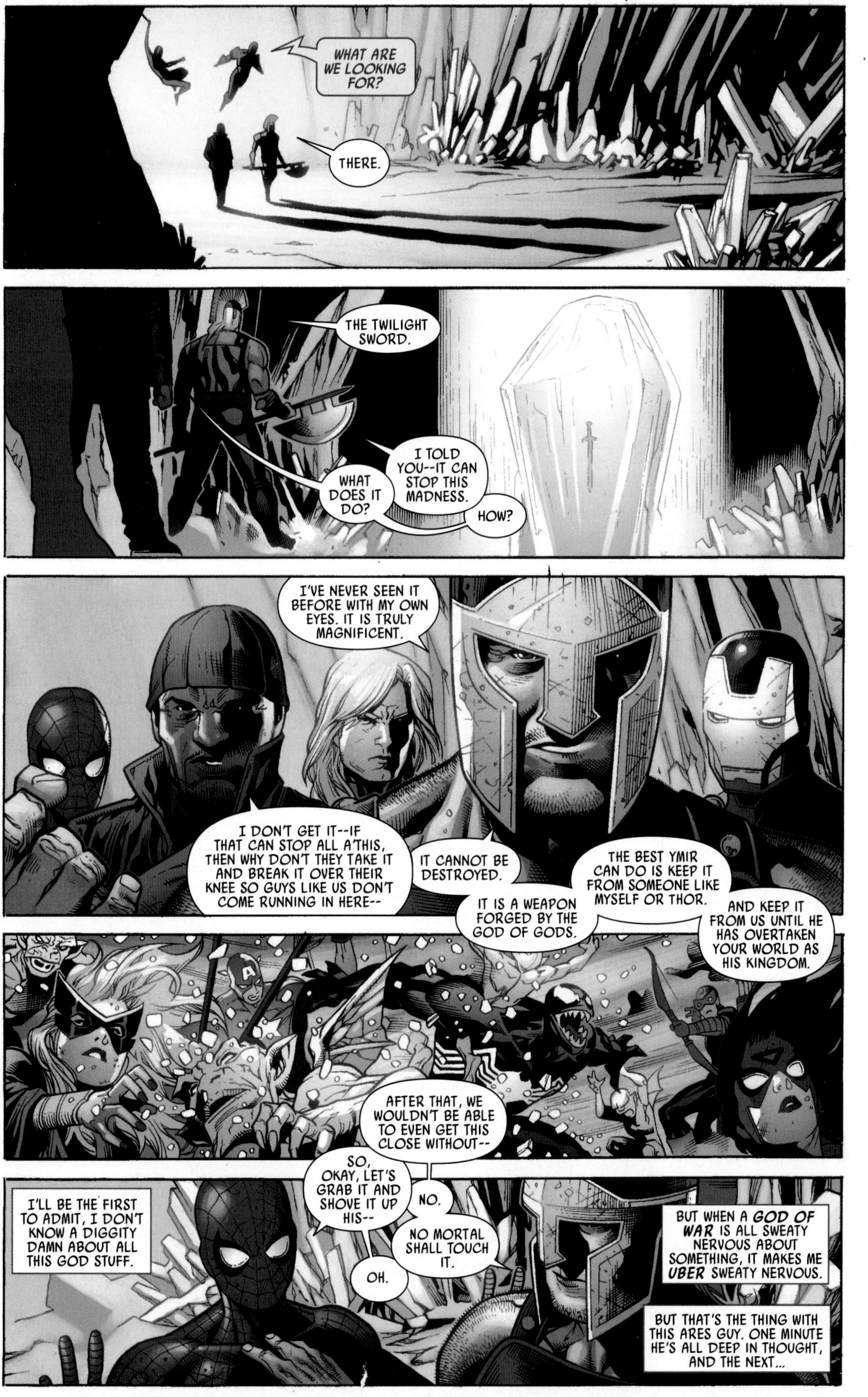
WHAT ARE WE LOOKING FOR?
THERE.
THE TWILIGHT SWORD.
WHAT DOES IT DO?
I TOLD YOU--IT CAN STOP THIS MADNESS.
HOW?
I'VE NEVER SEEN IT BEFORE WITH MY OWN EYES. IT IS TRULY MAGNIFICENT.
I DON'T GET IT--IF THAT CAN STOP ALL A'THIS, THEN WHY DON'T THEY TAKE IT AND BREAK IT OVER THEIR KNEE SO GUYS LIKE US DON'T COME RUNNING IN HERE--
IT CANNOT BE DESTROYED.
IT IS A WEAPON FORGED BY THE GOD OF GODS.
THE BEST YMIR CAN DO IS KEEP IT FROM SOMEONE LIKE MYSELF OR THOR.
AND KEEP IT FROM US UNTIL HE HAS OVERTAKEN YOUR WORLD AS HIS KINGDOM.
AFTER THAT, WE WOULDN'T BE ABLE TO EVEN GET THIS CLOSE WITHOUT--
I'LL BE THE FIRST TO ADMIT, I DON'T KNOW A DIGGITY DAMN ABOUT ALL THIS GOD STUFF.
SO, OKAY, LET'S GRAB IT AND SHOVE IT UP HIS--
NO.
NO MORTAL SHALL TOUCH IT.
OH.
BUT WHEN A GOD OF WAR IS ALL SWEATY NERVOUS ABOUT SOMETHING, IT MAKES ME UBER SWEATY NERVOUS.
BUT THAT'S THE THING WITH THIS ARES GUY. ONE MINUTE HE'S ALL DEEP IN THOUGHT, AND THE NEXT...

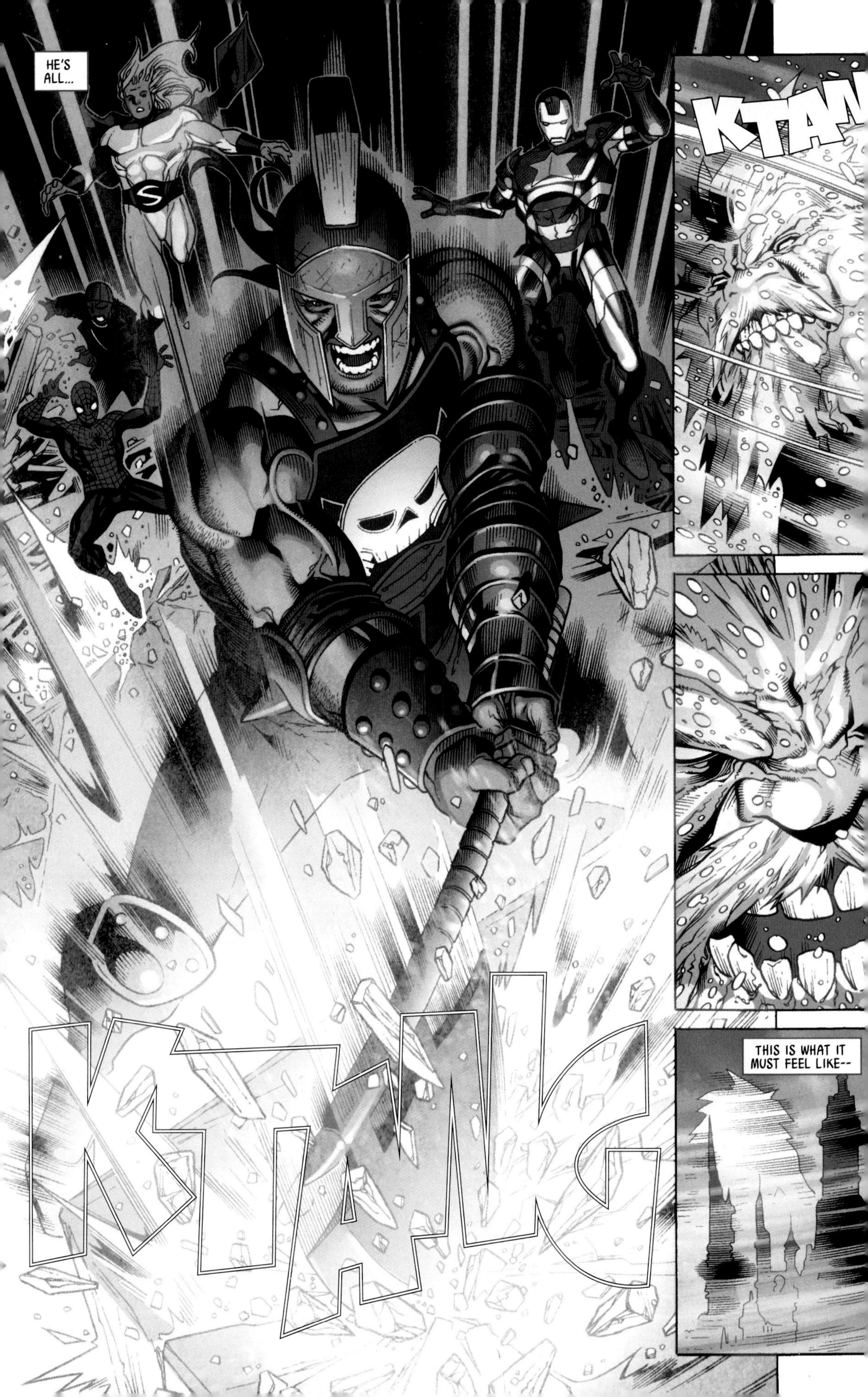
HE'S ALL...
KTANG
KTAN
THIS IS WHAT IT MUST FEEL LIKE--

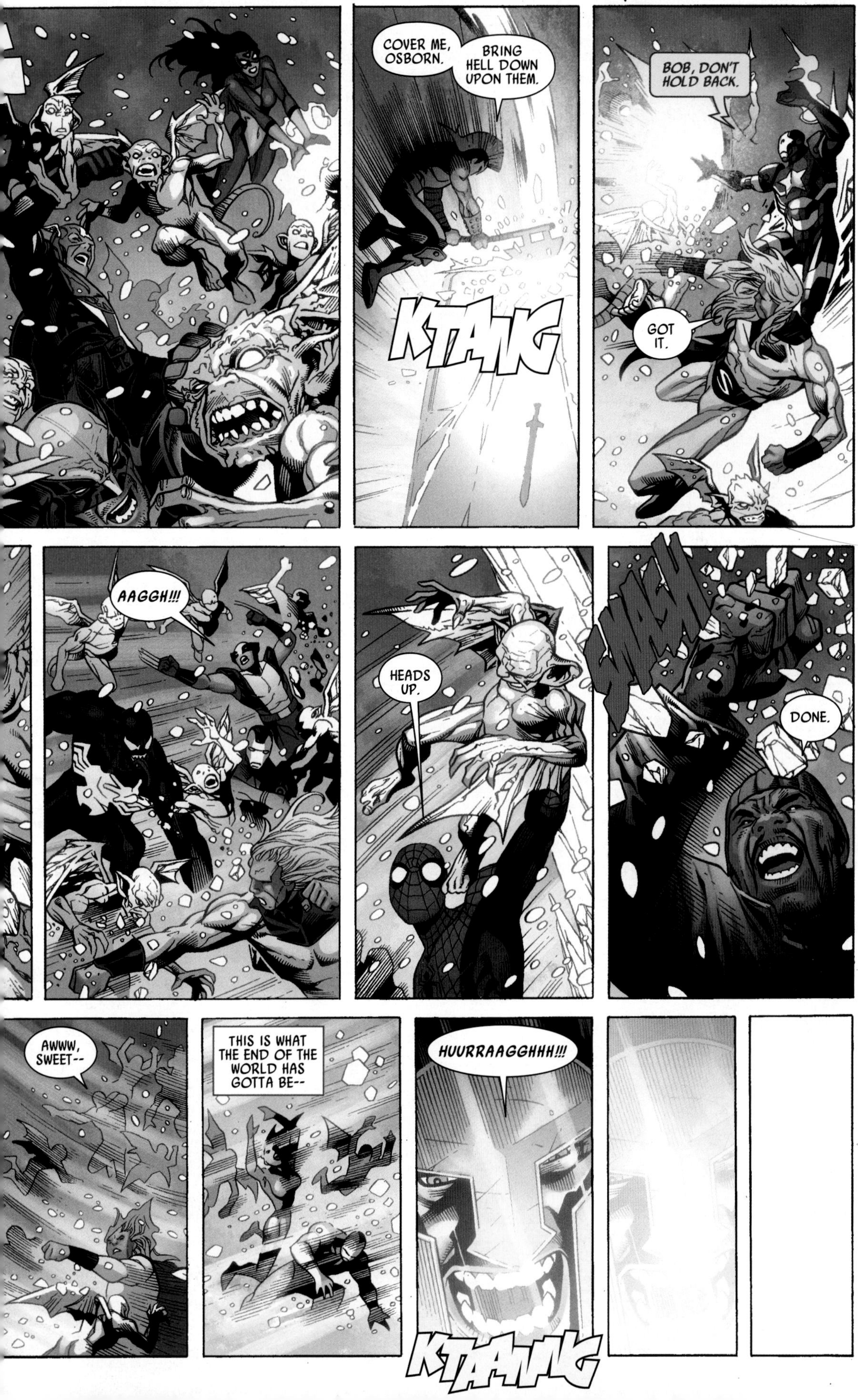
COVER ME, OSBORN.
BRING HELL DOWN UPON THEM.
KTANG
BOB, DON'T HOLD BACK.
GOT IT.
AAGGH!!!
HEADS UP.
DONE.
AWWW, SWEET--
THIS IS WHAT THE END OF THE WORLD HAS GOTTA BE--
HUURRAAGGHHH!!!
KTAANG

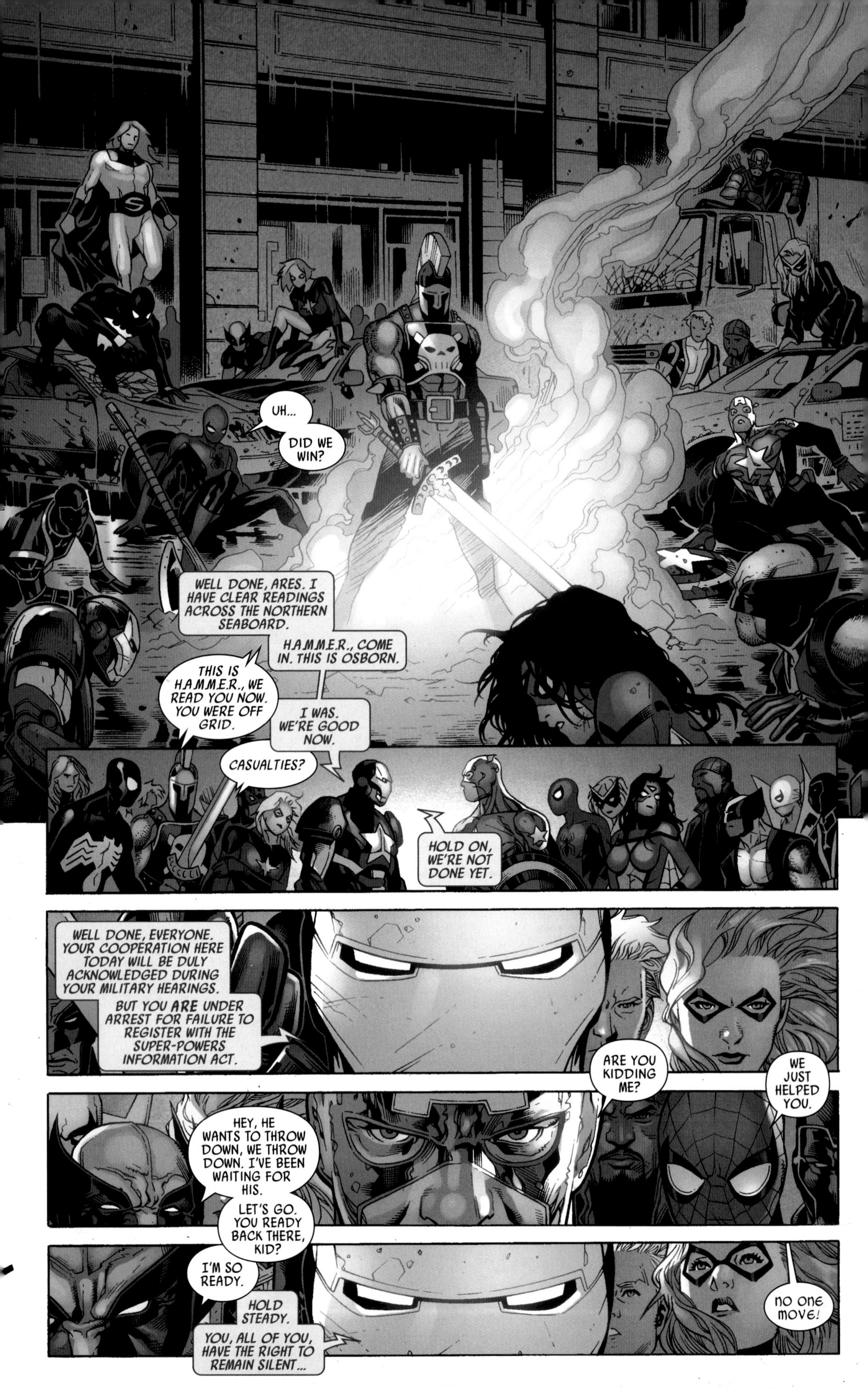
UH...
DID WE WIN?
WELL DONE, ARES. I HAVE CLEAR READINGS ACROSS THE NORTHERN SEABOARD.
H.A.M.M.E.R., COME IN. THIS IS OSBORN.
THIS IS H.A.M.M.E.R., WE READ YOU NOW. YOU WERE OFF GRID.
I WAS. WE'RE GOOD NOW.
CASUALTIES?
HOLD ON, WE'RE NOT DONE YET.
WELL DONE, EVERYONE. YOUR COOPERATION HERE TODAY WILL BE DULY ACKNOWLEDGED DURING YOUR MILITARY HEARINGS.
BUT YOU ARE UNDER ARREST FOR FAILURE TO REGISTER WITH THE SUPER-POWERS INFORMATION ACT.
ARE YOU KIDDING ME?
WE JUST HELPED YOU.
HEY, HE WANTS TO THROW DOWN, WE THROW DOWN. I'VE BEEN WAITING FOR HIS.
LET'S GO. YOU READY BACK THERE, KID?
I'M SO READY.
HOLD STEADY.
YOU, ALL OF YOU, HAVE THE RIGHT TO REMAIN SILENT...
NO ONE MOVE!

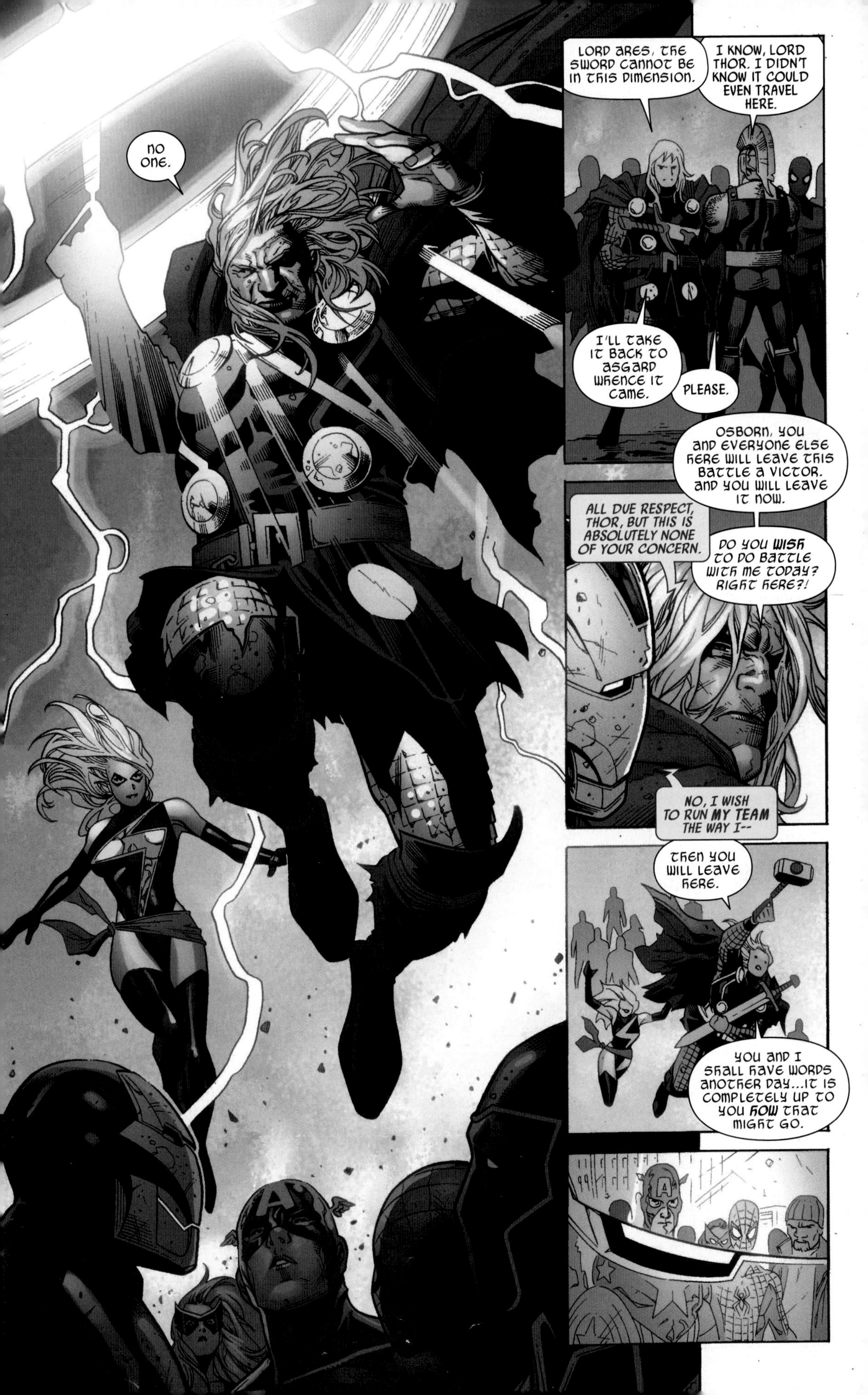
NO ONE.
LORD ARES, THE SWORD CANNOT BE IN THIS DIMENSION.
I KNOW, LORD THOR. I DIDN'T KNOW IT COULD EVEN TRAVEL HERE.
I'LL TAKE IT BACK TO ASGARD WHENCE IT CAME.
PLEASE.
OSBORN, YOU AND EVERYONE ELSE HERE WILL LEAVE THIS BATTLE A VICTOR. AND YOU WILL LEAVE IT NOW.
ALL DUE RESPECT, THOR, BUT THIS IS ABSOLUTELY NONE OF YOUR CONCERN.
DO YOU WISH TO DO BATTLE WITH ME TODAY? RIGHT HERE?!
NO, I WISH TO RUN MY TEAM THE WAY I--
THEN YOU WILL LEAVE HERE.
YOU AND I SHALL HAVE WORDS ANOTHER DAY...IT IS COMPLETELY UP TO YOU HOW THAT MIGHT GO.

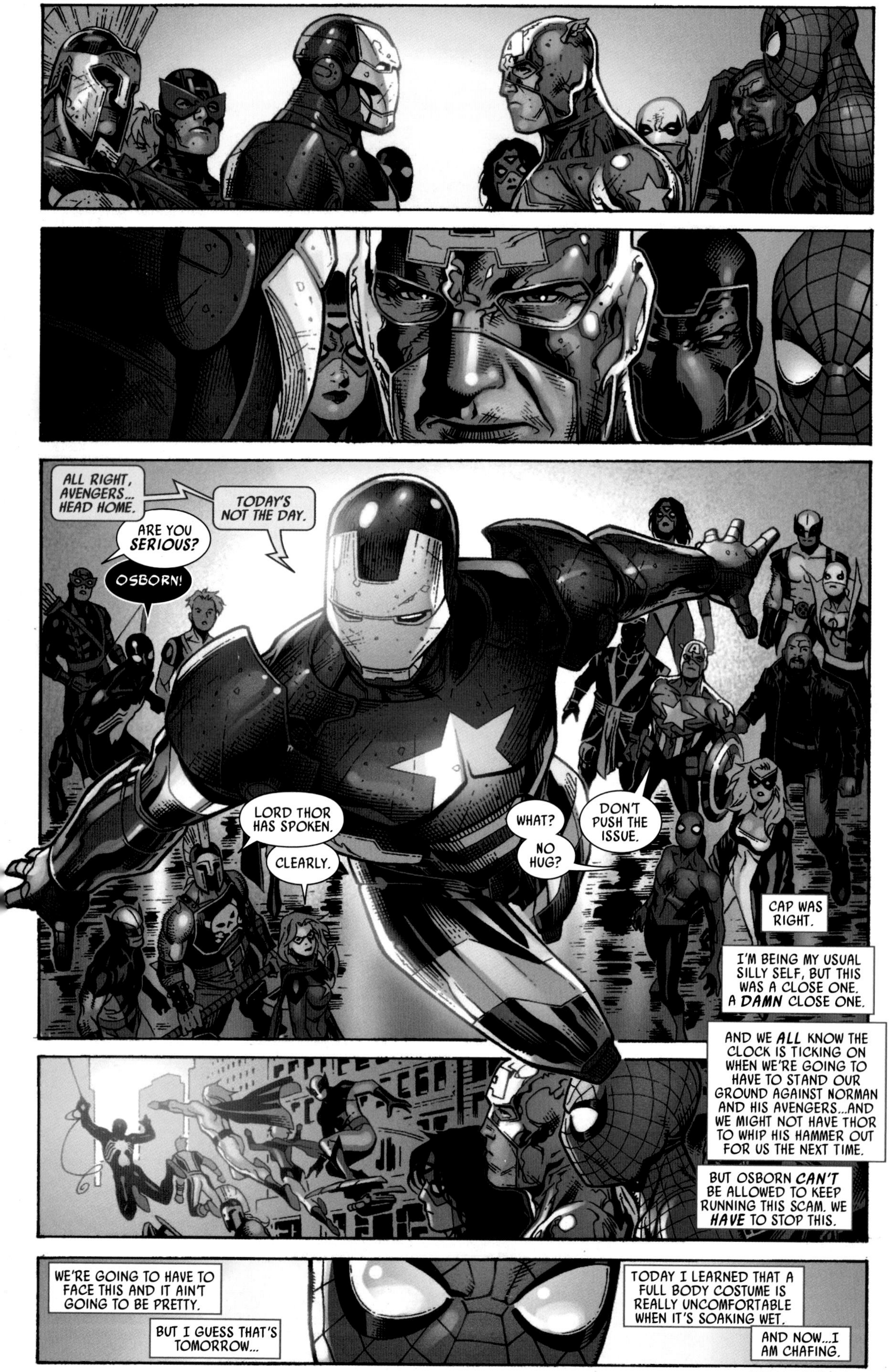
ALL RIGHT, AVENGERS... HEAD HOME.
TODAY'S NOT THE DAY.
ARE YOU SERIOUS?
OSBORN!
LORD THOR HAS SPOKEN.
CLEARLY.
WHAT?
NO HUG?
DON'T PUSH THE ISSUE.
CAP WAS RIGHT.
I'M BEING MY USUAL SILLY SELF, BUT THIS WAS A CLOSE ONE. A DAMN CLOSE ONE.
AND WE ALL KNOW THE CLOCK IS TICKING ON WHEN WE'RE GOING TO HAVE TO STAND OUR GROUND AGAINST NORMAN AND HIS AVENGERS...AND WE MIGHT NOT HAVE THOR TO WHIP HIS HAMMER OUT FOR US THE NEXT TIME.
BUT OSBORN CAN'T BE ALLOWED TO KEEP RUNNING THIS SCAM. WE HAVE TO STOP THIS.
WE'RE GOING TO HAVE TO FACE THIS AND IT AIN'T GOING TO BE PRETTY.
BUT I GUESS THAT'S TOMORROW...
TODAY I LEARNED THAT A FULL BODY COSTUME IS REALLY UNCOMFORTABLE WHEN IT'S SOAKING WET.
AND NOW...I AM CHAFING.

THE END.

SIEGE: THE CABAL VARIANT

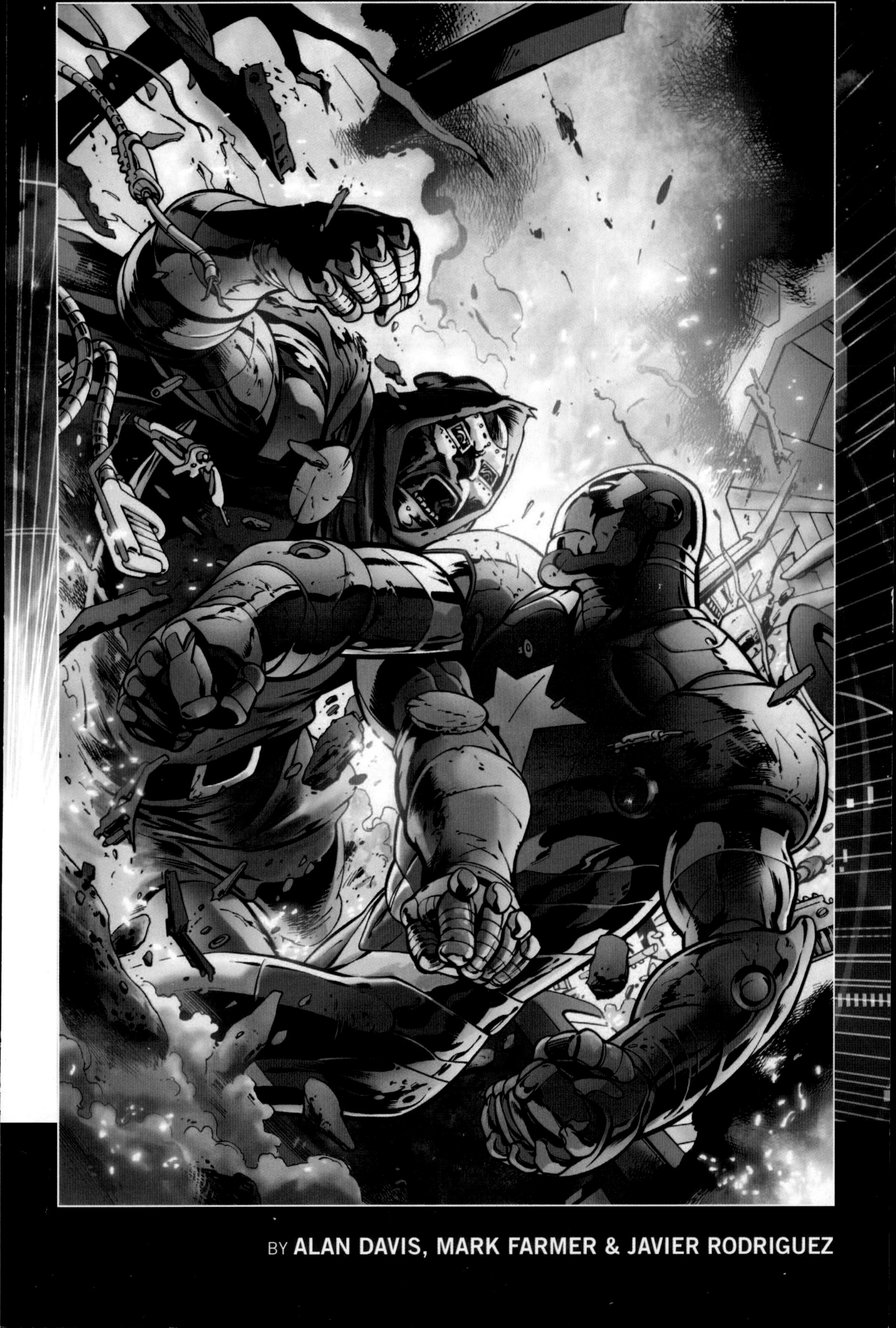

BY **ALAN DAVIS, MARK FARMER & JAVIER RODRIGUEZ**

SIEGE #1 VARIANT

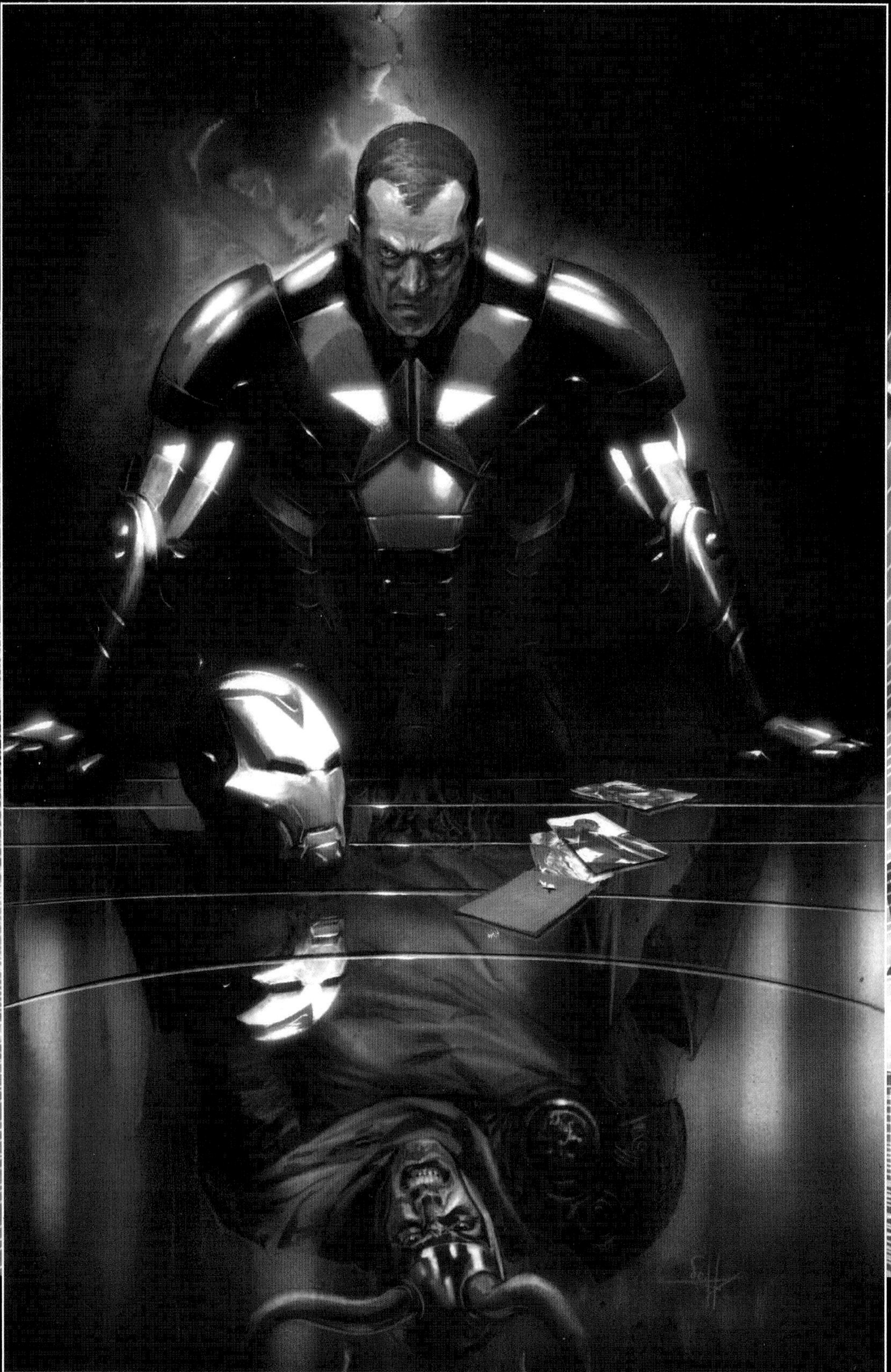

BY **GABRIELE DELL'OTTO**

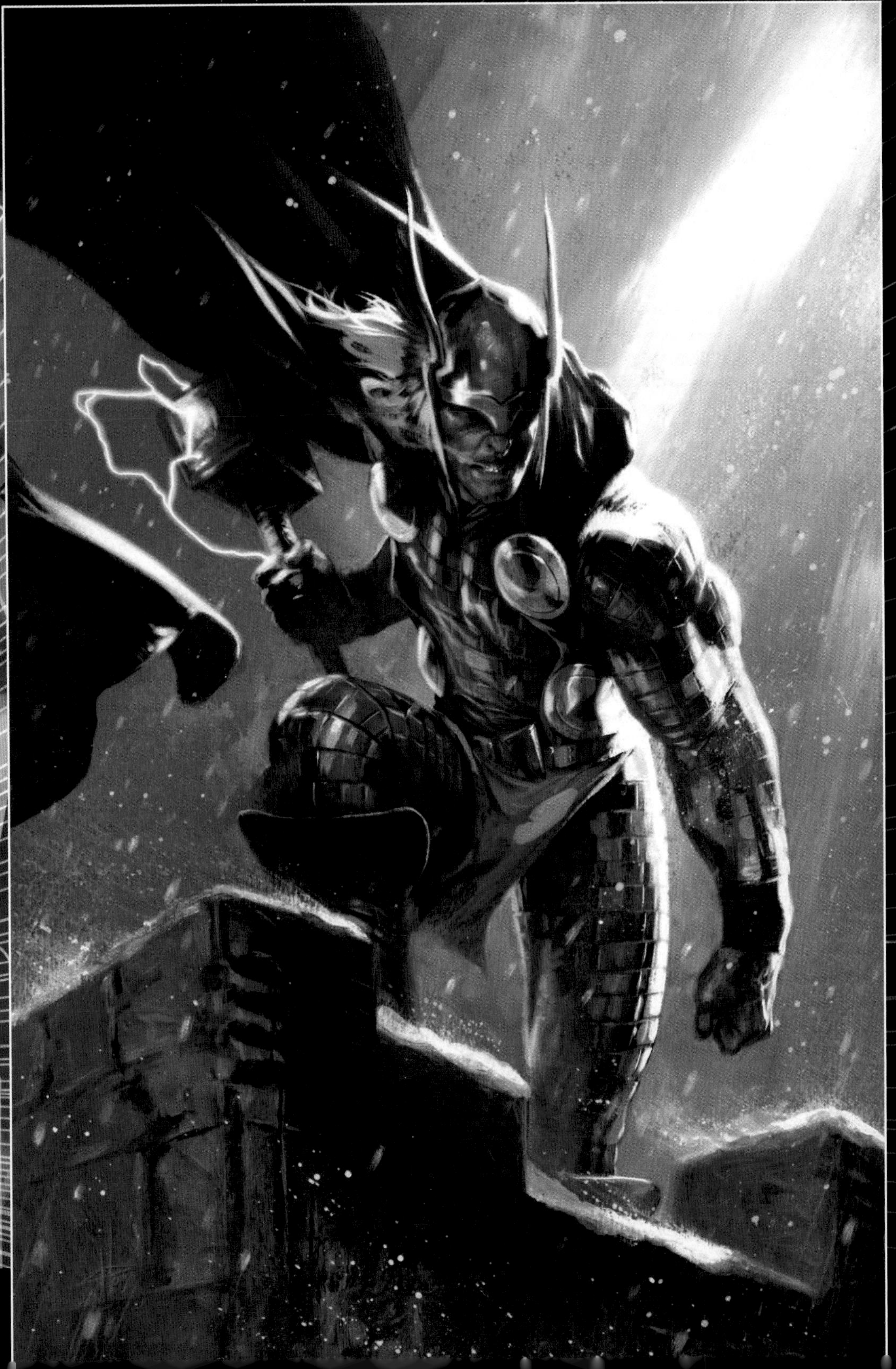

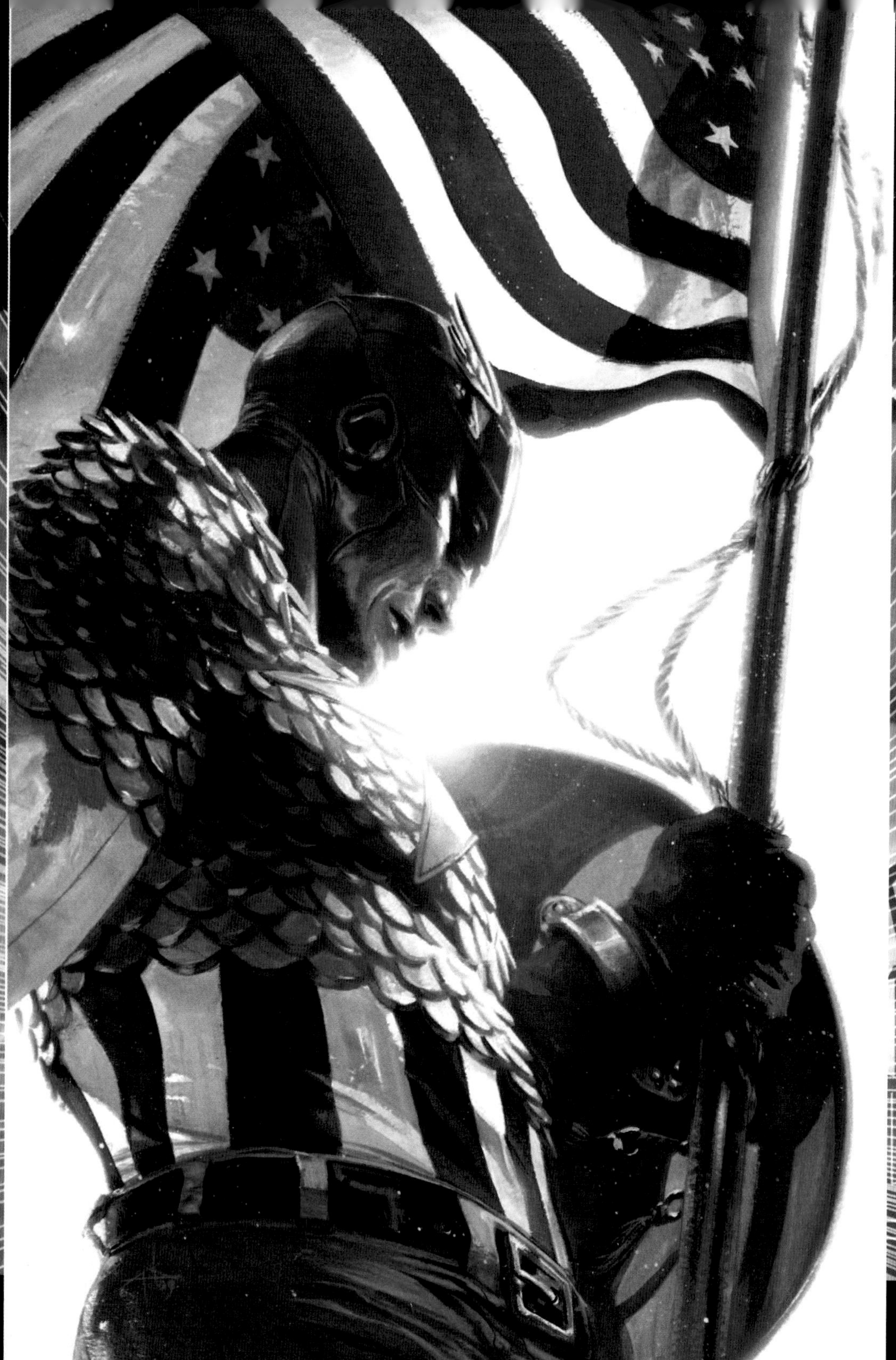

SIEGE #4 VARIANT

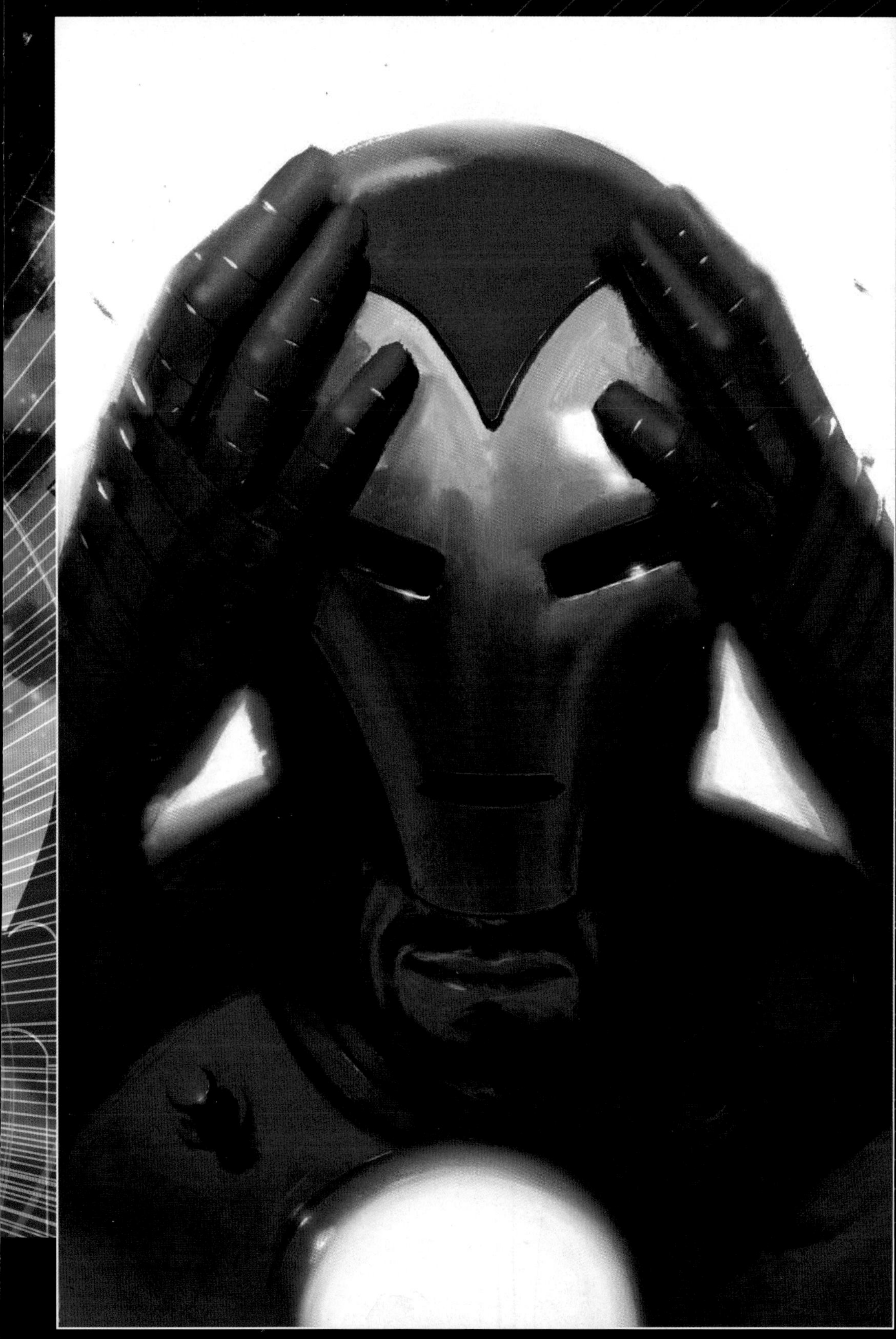

BY **GABRIELE DELL'OTTO**

SIEGE #1–4 COMBINED VARIANTS

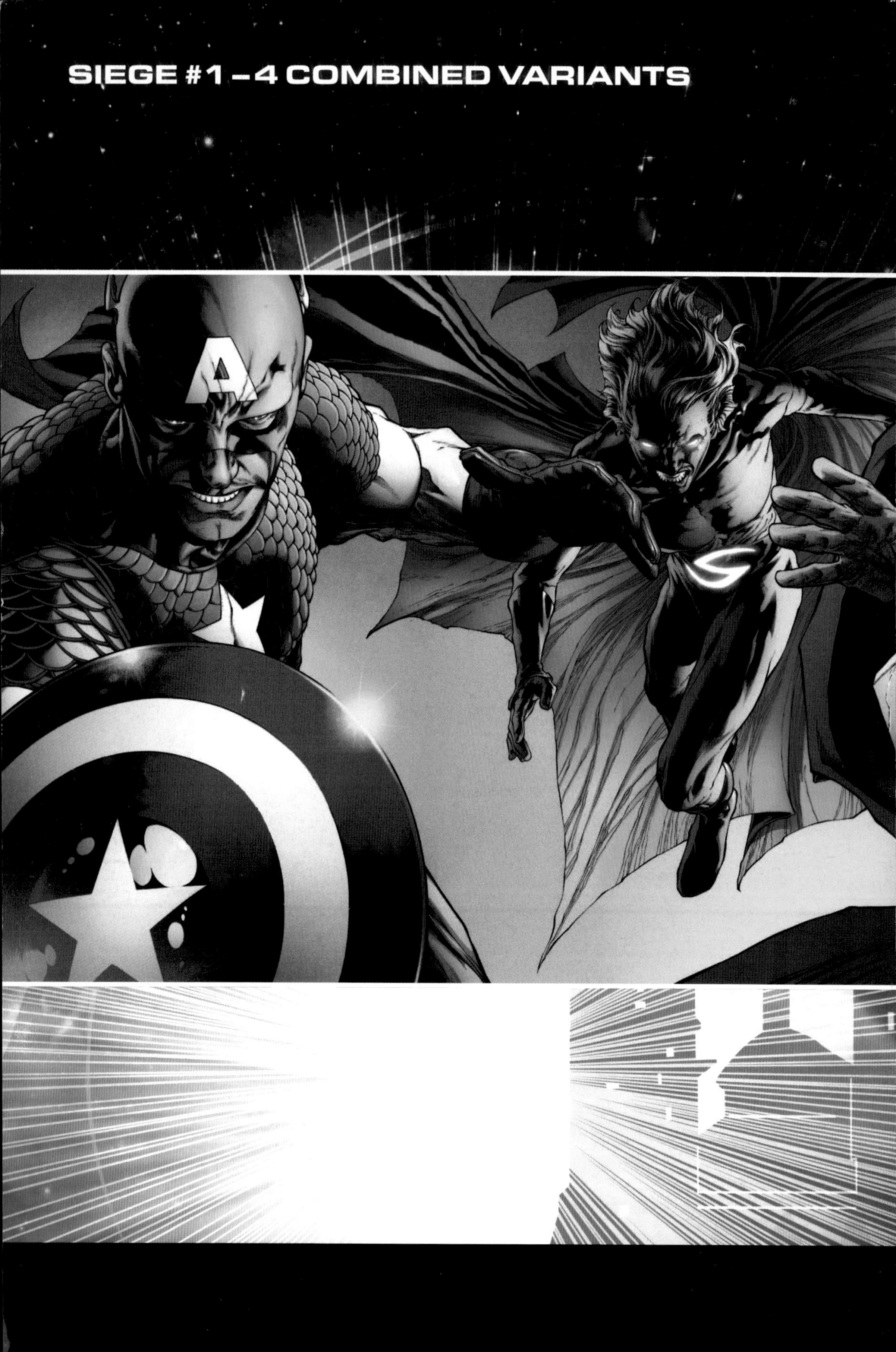

BY JOE QUESADA, DANNY MIKI & RICHARD ISANOVE

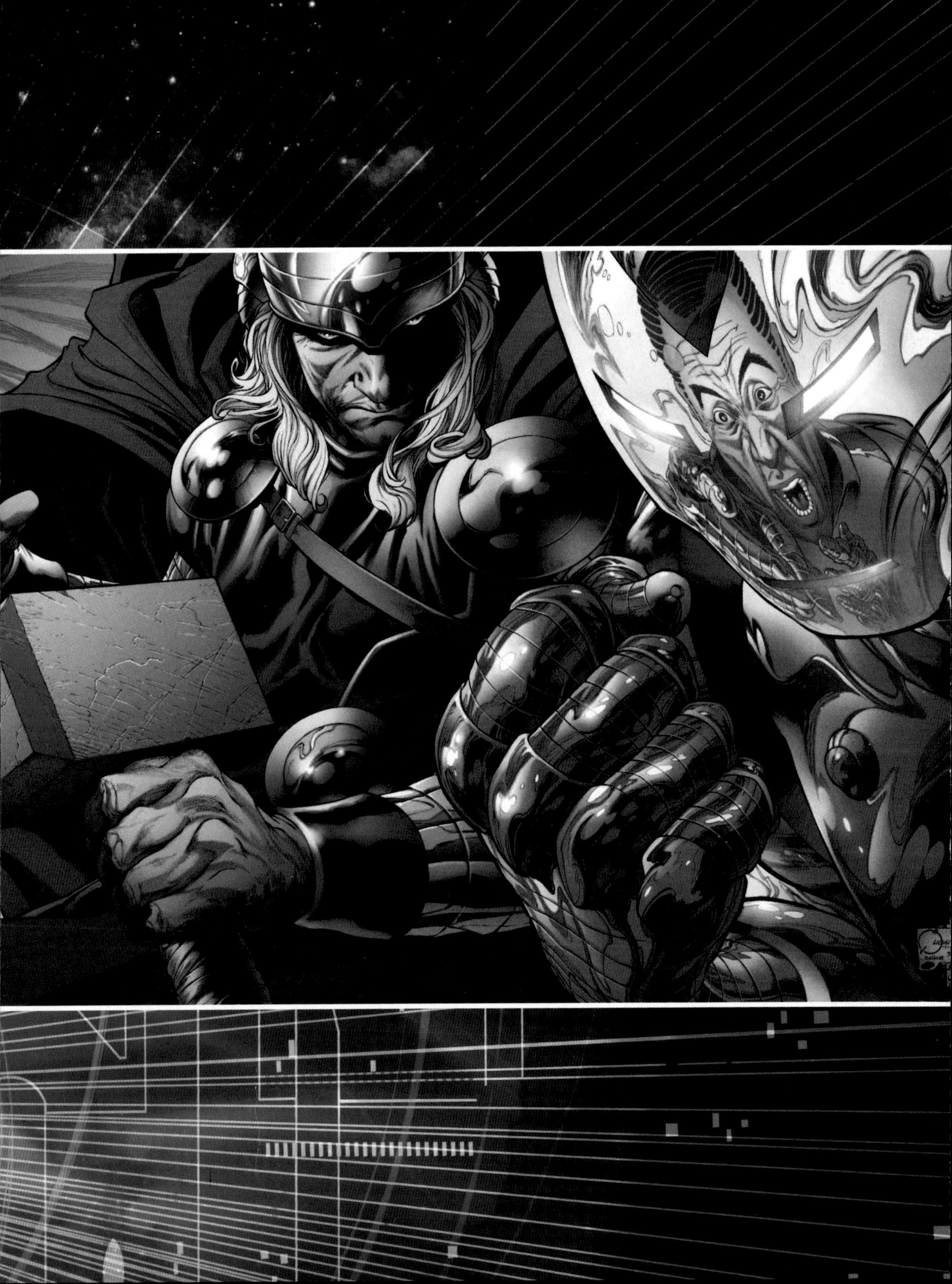

SIEGE #1 – 4 COMBINED SKETCH VARIANTS

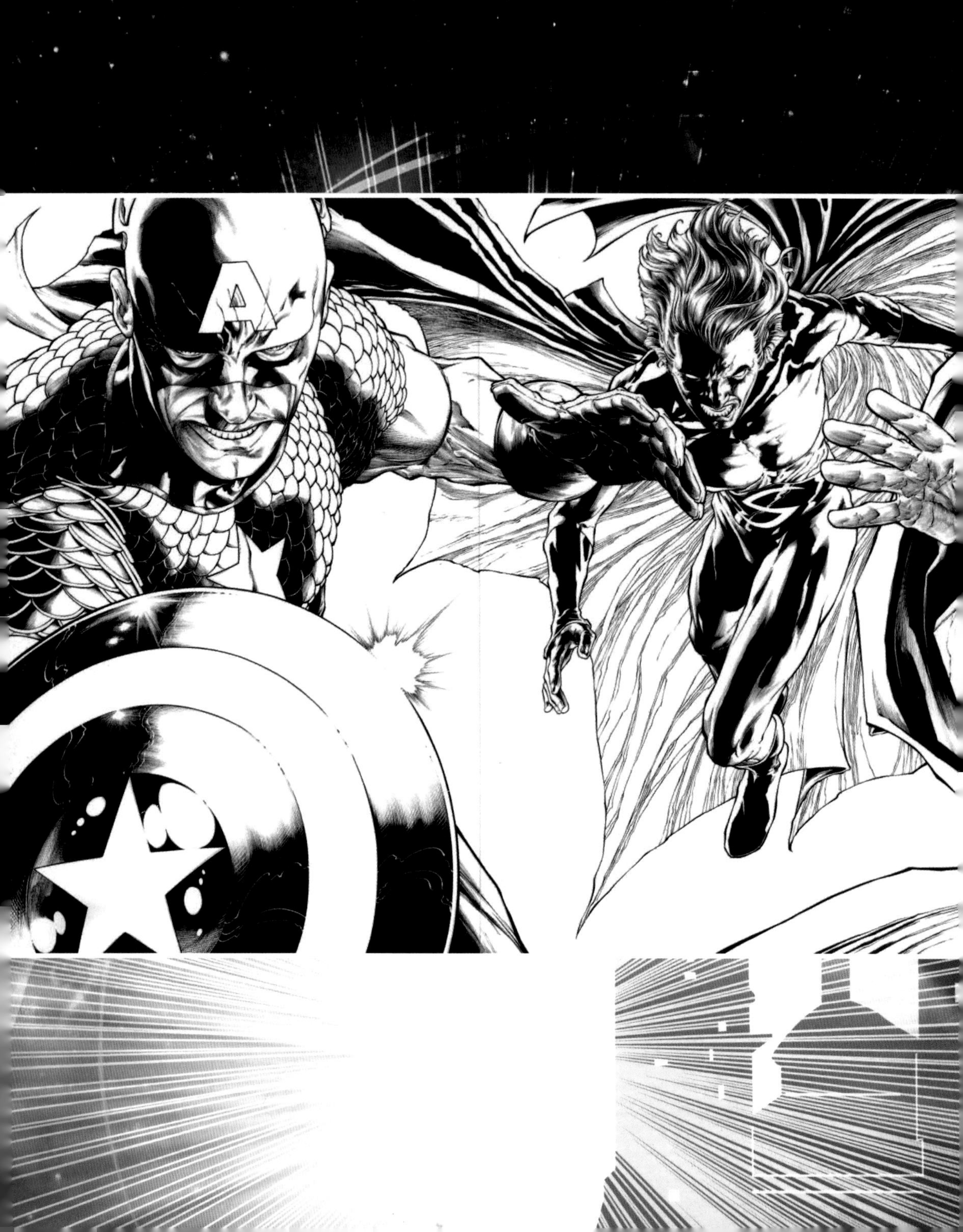

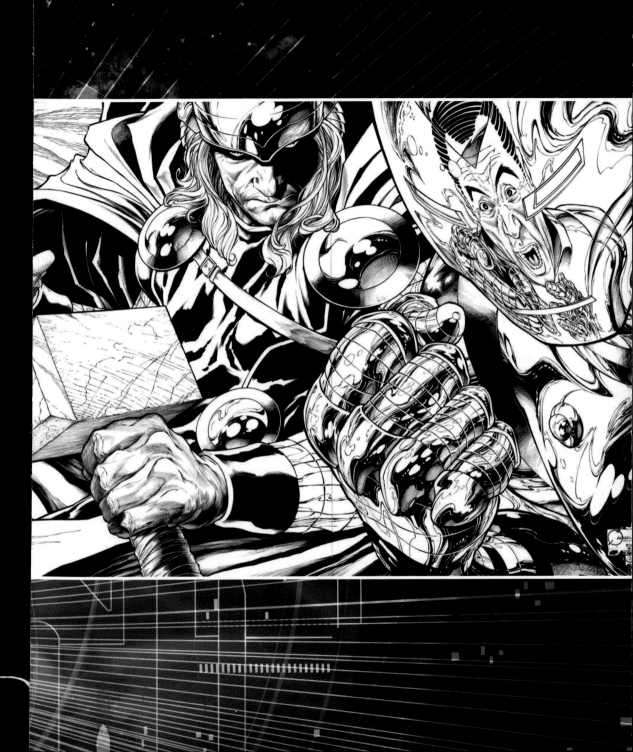

SIEGE #3 DEADPOOL VARIANT

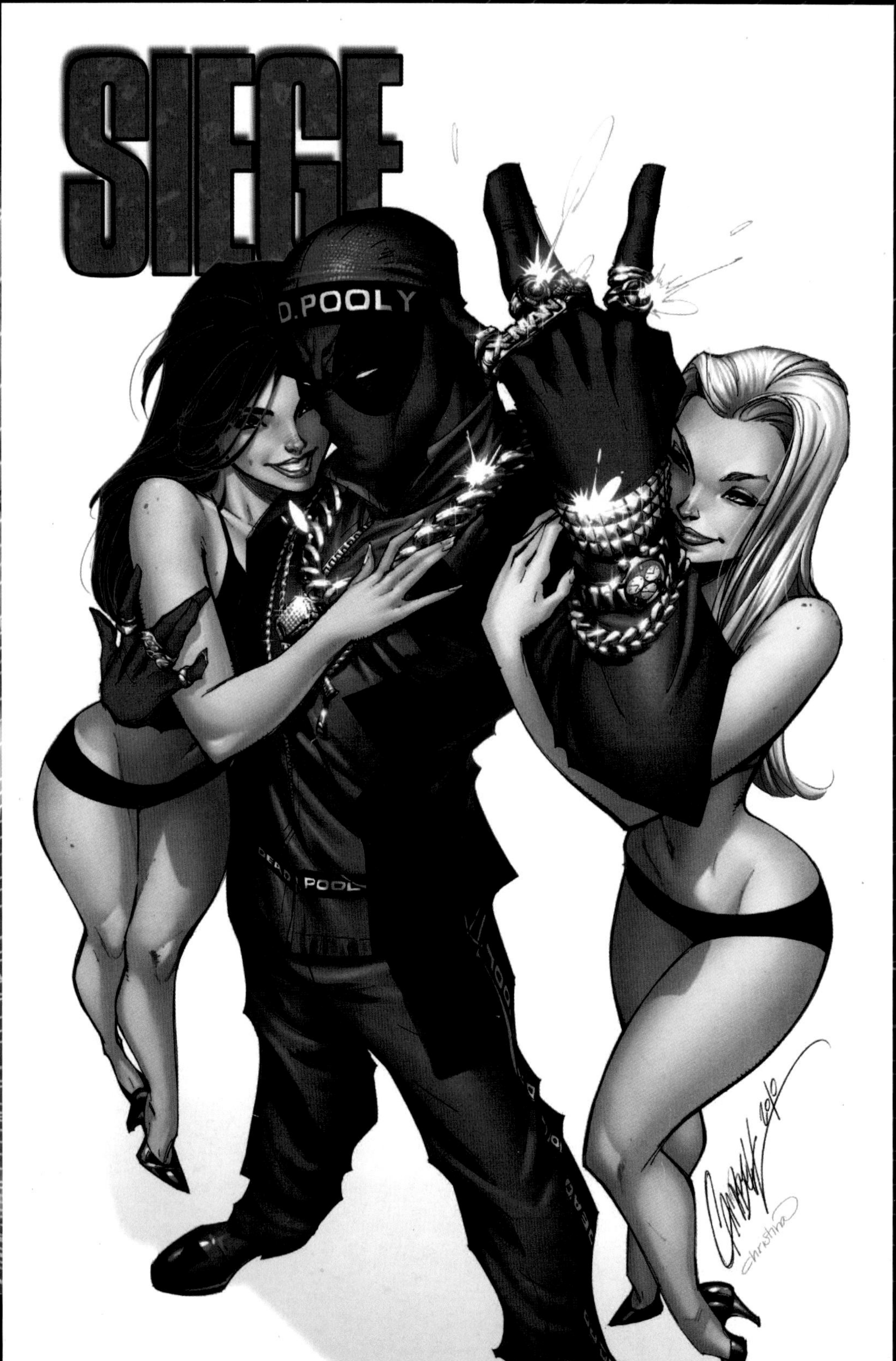
SIEGE
D.POOLY

BY J. SCOTT CAMPBELL & CHRISTINA STRAIN